From Comic Strips to Graphic Novels

From Comic Strips to Graphic Novels

Contributions to the Theory
and History of Graphic Narrative

2nd edition

Edited by
Daniel Stein
Jan-Noël Thon

De Gruyter

The 1st edition of this book was published as vol. 37 of the Narratologia series in 2013.

ISBN 978-3-11-042656-4
e-ISBN (PDF) 978-3-11-042766-0
e-ISBN (EPUB) 978-3-11-042772-1

Library of Congress Cataloging-in-Publication Data
A CIP catalog record for this book has been applied for at the Library of Congress.

Bibliographic information published by the Deutsche Nationalbibliothek
The Deutsche Nationalbibliothek lists this publication in the Deutsche Nationalbibliografie; detailed bibliographic data are available on the Internet at http://dnb.dnb.de.

© 2015 Walter de Gruyter GmbH, Berlin/Boston
Cover Image: Daniel Stein
Printing and binding: Hubert & Co. GmbH & Co. KG, Göttingen
♾ Printed on acid-free paper
Printed in Germany
www.degruyter.com

Table of Contents

DANIEL STEIN AND JAN-NOËL THON
Introduction: From Comic Strips to Graphic Novels..................... 1

PART I
GRAPHIC NARRATIVE AND NARRATOLOGICAL CONCEPTS

SILKE HORSTKOTTE
Zooming In and Out: Panels, Frames, Sequences,
and the Building of Graphic Storyworlds.................................. 27

KARIN KUKKONEN
Space, Time, and Causality in Graphic Narratives:
An Embodied Approach... 49

JAN-NOËL THON
Who's Telling the Tale?
Authors and Narrators in Graphic Narrative................................ 67

KAI MIKKONEN
Subjectivity and Style in Graphic Narratives................................ 101

PART II
GRAPHIC NARRATIVE BEYOND THE 'SINGLE WORK'

NANCY PEDRI
Graphic Memoir: Neither Fact Nor Fiction.................................. 127

DANIEL STEIN
Superhero Comics and the
Authorizing Functions of the Comic Book Paratext...................... 155

GABRIELE RIPPL AND LUKAS ETTER
Intermediality, Transmediality, and Graphic Narrative.................... 191

GREG M. SMITH
Comics in the Intersecting Histories
of the Window, the Frame, and the Panel................................... 219

PART III
GENRE AND FORMAT HISTORIES OF GRAPHIC NARRATIVE

JARED GARDNER
A History of the Narrative Comic Strip......................................241

PASCAL LEFÈVRE
Narration in the Flemish Dual Publication System:
The Crossover Genre of the Humoristic Adventure......................255

CHRISTINA MEYER
Un/Taming the Beast, or Graphic Novels (Re)Considered...............271

HENRY JENKINS
Archival, Ephemeral, and Residual: The Functions of Early
Comics in Art Spiegelman's *In the Shadow of No Towers*....................301

PART IV
GRAPHIC NARRATIVE ACROSS CULTURES

JULIA ROUND
Anglo-American Graphic Narrative..325

JAN BAETENS AND STEVEN SURDIACOURT
European Graphic Narratives:
Toward a Cultural and Mediological History................................347

JAQUELINE BERNDT
Ghostly: 'Asian Graphic Narratives,' *Nonnonba*, and Manga...............363

MONIKA SCHMITZ-EMANS
Graphic Narrative as World Literature.......................................385

Index (Persons)..407

Index (Works)...413

DANIEL STEIN AND JAN-NOËL THON
(Siegen and Tübingen)

Introduction: From Comic Strips to Graphic Novels

Graphic Narratives and Narrative Theory

The story of narratology has been told and retold countless times in the past five decades, so that it seems neither necessary nor desirable to attempt another detailed retelling of the events that have led from the publication of the eighth issue of *Communication* in 1966 and the first works of classical narratology within French structuralism to the current prominence of postclassical 'new narratologies' with widely different epistemological and methodological orientations.[1] In order to situate the present volume within the field of current narratological practice, however, it will still be helpful to introduce what may be considered the three "dominant methodological paradigms of contemporary narratology" (Meister 2009: 340). The first of these paradigms, contextualist narratology, "relates the phenomena encountered in narrative to specific cultural, historical, thematic, and ideological contexts" (Meister 2009: 340). The second paradigm, cognitive narratology, "focuses on the human intellectual and emotional processing of narrative" (Meister 2009: 340). The third paradigm, "transgeneric" and "intermedial approaches" (Meister 2009: 340), includes not only research on the *trans*medial dimensions of narrative, but also a variety of *inter*medial and *intra*medial studies primarily concerned with a single medium or genre other than the literary text, such as poetry, drama, painting, film, computer games, or, indeed, comics.[2] Narratological practices aimed at comics and other forms of graphic narrative evidently belong to the third methodological paradigm identified by Meister, and recent scholarship by comics theorists such as Karin Kukkonen (2011), Kai Mikkonen (2011, 2012), and Martin Schüwer (2008) even suggests that the field of graphic narrative offers a particularly promising 'test case' for the project of a 'transmedial narratology.'[3]

---

1 See e.g., the surveys by Nünning 2003; Fludernik 2005; Meister 2009.
2 On the relations between (intra)mediality, intermediality, and transmediality, see e.g., Wolf 2002; Rajewsky 2010; Thon 2014a.
3 See e.g., Herman 2004, 2009; Ryan 2004, 2005, 2006; Wolf 2005, 2011; Thon 2014c, 2014d for more general discussions of the aims and scope of a transmedial narratology.

While current literary and media studies tend to use 'transmedial narratology' as an umbrella term for a variety of narratological practices concerned with media other than literary texts, a genuinely transmedial narratology should not merely aspire to be a collection of medium-specific narratological models but, rather, should examine a variety of transmedial phenomena across a range of conventionally distinct narrative media.[4] One way or another, though, in order to remain 'media-conscious,' such a transmedial narratology would still have to acknowledge both similarities and differences in the ways in which conventionally distinct media such as literary texts, films, or comics narrate.[5] Moreover, it should be noted that current narratological practice tends to be methodologically inclusive insofar as exploring narrative representations 'beyond the literary text' often goes hand in hand with a particular attention to narrative's cultural and historical contexts as well as a concern for the cognitive processes involved in making narrative meaning.[6]

Likewise, narratology is, of course, not the only possible approach to the study of graphic narrative. Indeed, anyone trying to map the burgeoning field of comics studies will quickly realize that there is no dearth of theories and methods on which scholars may draw.[7] The panoply of available approaches includes various types of formal analysis; both media-conscious and transmediality-oriented research; historical, political, and cultural investigations; economic examinations; philosophical inquiries; as well as semiotic and psycho-semiotic perspectives; not to mention the genre- and format-based work done by many scholars.[8] Yet as Jared Gardner and David Herman write in their introduction to a recent special issue of *SubStance*, we can detect "emerging connections between comics studies and narrative theory" that may eventually converge into a "new, hybridized field of study" (2011b: 3). Gardner and Herman christen this field-to-be 'graphic narrative theory,' and the aim of the present volume is to explore new ways of thinking about the narrativity of comics from this theoretically as well as methodologically refined vantage point.

---

4   See Wolf 2002; Rajewsky 2010; Thon 2014a on 'conventionally distinct media.' See also Ryan 2009, 2014 for a discussion of media's narrative limitations and affordances.
5   See Ryan and Thon 2014 for the notion of a 'media-conscious' narratology. See also Thon 2014c, 2014d for a more detailed version of this argument.
6   See e.g., the contributions in Kindt and Müller 2003; Meister 2005; Olson 2011.
7   For useful surveys, see e.g., the contributions in Heer and Worcester 2009; Eder, Klar and Reichert 2011; Smith and Duncan 2012.
8   To name only a few pertinent studies of a corpus of secondary literature that is much too vast to be referenced in anything resembling its entirety here, see Carrier 2000; Hein, Hüners, and Michaelsen 2002; McLaughlin 2005; Packard 2006; Groensteen 2007, 2013; Schüwer 2008; Ditschke, Kroucheva, and Stein 2009; Duncan and Smith 2009; Chute 2010; Gabilliet 2010; Chaney 2011; Beaty 2012; Gardner 2012; Meskin and Cook 2012; Pustz 2012.

The emergence of graphic narrative theory, Gardner and Herman suggest, is the result of "disciplinary reconfiguration[s]" (2011b: 3) in narratology and in comics studies. These reconfigurations attest to an increasing interest among postclassical narratologists in a broadened textual and medial corpus that includes various types of graphic narrative as well as a growing concern among comics scholars for theoretically and methodologically advanced assessments of the narrative properties and specific medialities of graphic narrative. The present volume is both a reflection of, and a tribute to, this convergence, and it is intended to further the cross-pollination of narratology and comics studies. And just as graphic narrative theory should not only position itself within the field of transmedial narratology but also within the fields of contextualist and cognitive narratology, we would argue that, in order for this cross-pollination to have its full effect, the relation between comics studies and narratology should not be conceptualized as overly exclusive, either.

As Gardner and Herman further note, comics scholarship has too long been hampered by "a defensive relationship to the academy at large" (2011b: 6). This defensiveness, they maintain, has its roots in the generally low cultural esteem of comics and the lack of scholarly interest that has characterized the academic reception of this historically maligned medium roughly until the 1990s.[9] The most effective efforts to overcome this niche status, Gardner and Herman propose, have been characterized by "alliances forged with related [research] fields [such as] autobiography studies, sexuality studies, postcolonial studies, etc." (2011b: 6). But some of these alliances have endorsed a medially unspecific and narratologically questionable literary approach to graphic narrative. This is why Gardner and Herman "believe that of all the alliances forged with related fields in recent years, the most profitable for comics studies will be that of narrative theory, a field increasingly invested in foregrounding and theorizing the differences that medium-specificity (and multimodality) makes to storytelling" (2011b: 6).[10] While current work in narratology offers significant theoretical and methodological reflections, then, it is

---

9 Ecke 2010 speaks of "Comics Studies' Identity Crisis," while Groensteen 2000 asked more than a decade ago: "Why Are Comics Still in Search of Cultural Legitimization?" Cf. also Hatfield: "Academic comics study, not exactly a new but certainly a newly self-conscious field, has been particularly notable for this sort of anxious throat-clearing about how to define its object" (2009: 19). For early, and mostly semiotic and structuralist approaches, see Eco 2004 [1962]; Faust 1971; Harvey 1979, 1994; Abbott 1986. For early German studies, see Fuchs and Reitberger 1971; Hünig 1974; Krafft 1974; an early French example is Rey 1978.

10 Important work in the field of graphic narrative theory beyond Gardner and Herman 2011a includes Ditschke and Anhut 2009; Horstkotte and Pedri 2011; Mikkonen 2011, 2012; as well as many of the essays published in *Image [&] Narrative*, e.g., Lefèvre 2000; Baetens 2003.

worth stressing that the emerging field of comics narratology will also benefit from forging further interdisciplinary alliances of its own.[11]

From Comics to Graphic Novels: Theoretical and Historical Conceptualizations

While we largely agree with Gardner and Herman's assessment of the converging fields of comics studies and narratology as well as with their identification of the challenges facing graphic narrative theory, we want to formulate a series of critical reflections that will foreground the rationale behind, and aims of, the present volume. For one, Gardner and Herman champion 'graphic narrative' in favor of other possible terms, among them the more conventional and more widely embraced 'comics,' without offering much of an explanation for this choice. Of course, rebranding comics as 'graphic narratives' makes particular sense when the focus is on the storytelling mechanisms—and thus: the narrativity—of comics and when the task is to trace the "stylistic specificities of graphic storytelling" as a means of "confront[ing] the verbal bias of foundational work" (Gardner and Herman 2011b: 6) in narratology. But we would argue that existing definitions of 'graphic narrative' tend to be rather fuzzy and geared toward the specific research interests of individual scholars. A few terminological clarifications are therefore in order.

In a U.S.-American context, Hillary Chute and Marianne DeKoven have defined graphic narrative "as narrative work in the medium of comics" (2006: 767) in their introduction to the special issue of *Modern Fiction Studies*, which first brought the term to a wider scholarly audience. Two years later, Chute suggested that "graphic narrative is a book-length work in the medium of comics" (2008: 453) and that the term was able to include nonfictional works in ways that the term 'graphic novel' was not. From a narratological standpoint, however, these definitions seem somewhat problematic. If we can agree that comics prototypically include sequences of panels (unless we are talking about single-panel cartoons) and that they usually combine images with words (unless we are thinking of special cases such as wordless comics), then their narrativity should be

---

11 Jenkins advocates "radically undisciplined" (2012: 6) approaches to the study of comics that poach their shifting tools and vocabulary wherever they appear useful; Hatfield imagines comics as an "antidisciplinary [...] phenomenon, nudging us usefully out of accustomed habits of thought and into productive gray areas where various disciplines [...] overlap and inform one another" (2009: 23). See also Kukkonen and Haberkorn's 2012 proposal for a 'comics studies toolbox.' Suggestions for cross-fertilizations among comics studies and American studies perspectives that seek to foster a mutually beneficial dialogue between these fields of research can be found in Stein, Meyer, and Edlich 2011.

largely self-evident. Moreover, story-length does not qualify as a necessary or sufficient condition for determining a work's narrativity; in fact, one could feasibly argue that even single-panel comics narrate.[12]

Despite these caveats, the terms 'comic' and 'graphic narrative' are frequently used synonymously. Such usage, however, marginalizes salient historical, formal, and cultural differences. Therefore, we propose a historical distinction that locates the beginnings of comics either in the early 1830s, when Rodolphe Töpffer created his *histoiries en estampes*, or in the 1890s and 1900s, when American newspaper cartoonists such as Richard Felton Outcault developed Sunday pages and later daily strips. According to this distinction, artifacts such as ancient cave paintings, the Bayeux tapestry, or stained-glass church windows may be older forms of graphic narrative, but they are historically and culturally distinct from the modern kinds of comics storytelling developed by Töpffer, Outcault, and other artists. Second, we would argue that there is a formal distinction to be made here. When we speak of comics, we generally expect at least some of the following narrative properties, none of which needs to be present in works we would call graphic narratives: sequential storytelling, gutters separating framed panels, direct speech represented in balloons, with additional conventions such as motion lines, thought bubbles, and much more. Third, the term 'comics' is culturally specific as its discursive origins are Anglo-American, and many narrative theories and historical accounts that center on comics also tend to be America-centric. The term 'graphic narrative,' on the contrary, is much more inclusive. Indeed, it is capable of encompassing different forms, formats, genres, and storytelling traditions across cultures and from around the world.[13]

Furthermore, we remain skeptical of approaches that suggest that narrativity does not necessarily represent a constitutive element of comics. Aaron Meskin, for instance, claims that the existence of what he calls "nonnarrative comics" (2007: 372) throws any narrative-based definition into question.[14] This claim, however, rests on a reductive understanding of

---

12 We are also wary of the linguistic lexicon within which Chute and DeKoven and many other comics scholars frame their arguments when they speak of "comics grammar" (Chute 2008: 454) and graphic narrative as an "intricately layered narrative language" (Chute and DeKoven 2006: 767). This is not to say, however, that the authors are not aware of the cross-discursivity and the significance of comics as a hybrid visual-verbal medium (cf. Chute and DeKoven 2006: 768, 769).

13 See e.g., Duncan and Smith 2009; for international and transnational studies, see Berninger, Ecke, and Haberkorn 2010; Denson, Meyer, and Stein 2013.

14 One example in this context is provided by the kind of abstract, or non-representational, comics collected in Molotiu 2009. Then again, recent developments toward an 'unnatural narratology' focus precisely on these kinds of 'non-mimetic' or even 'anti-mimetic' forms of narrative. See the general discussion of 'unnatural narratology' in Alber 2009; Alber et al. 2010; Richardson 2011; as well as Fehrle 2011 for a discussion of 'unnaturalness' in comics.

narrative, which becomes apparent when Meskin argues that a "sequence of juxtaposed pictures" does not *per se* establish a narrative but could be related by being "thematic or character based" (2007: 372). After all, even thematic or character-based connections among image sequences may create simple forms of narrative; following a character from one image to another easily produces the impression of causal or temporal relations that will constitute something akin to a very rudimentary plot, and thus narrative.[15] At the very least, then, Meskin underestimates the reader, whose role in the reception of graphic narratives is especially prominent because she must translate sequential images into a continuous narrative by imaginatively filling in the gutters between panels and by negotiating the complex interaction of pictorial and verbal information on the page.[16] Thus, juxtaposed pictures are always narrativized in the process of reception,[17] and they are routinely accompanied by paratextual and contextual clues that communicate to the reader that she is reading a comic (e.g., the funnies section in the newspaper, the attribution of a work to a creator whose name readers may recognize, the market niche of a particular publisher, etc.).[18]

These and other attempts at defining, or perhaps un-defining, comics and graphic narratives necessitate the further clarification of terms and concepts such as medium, format, and genre, and they call on scholars to specify crucial distinctions among aesthetic, formal, and narratological approaches.[19] Chute, for instance, conceives of comics as a medium determined by its visual-verbal hybridity and its spatial construction of time; she further discriminates among different comics formats, such as comic strips, comic books, and graphic novels, and different genres, such as superhero stories or nonfictional reportage and historical accounts.[20] Finally, she underscores the significance of publication schedules and

---

15 For a more detailed general discussion of narrativity and prototypical features of narratives as a gradable quality, see e.g., Jannidis 2003; Wolf 2003; Ryan 2006: 3–30; Thon 2014b. See also Ryan's distinction between "having narrativity" and "being a narrative" (2006: 11).

16 See e.g., Hatfield 2005; Herman 2010; Kukkonen 2013. The role of the reader in comics and the narrativity of pictorial sequences is also eloquently assessed in Gardner 2010, 2012.

17 For further discussion of the notion of 'narrativization' see e.g., Fludernik 1996; Wolf 2003. See also the discussion of different kinds of relations between panels in e.g., Peeters 1991; McCloud 1993; Saraceni 2003; Packard 2006; Groensteen 2007; Schüwer 2008.

18 Meskin further proposes that comics do not necessarily have to be pictorial, pointing to the possibility of nonpictorial comics that "are blank except for speech balloons and captions" (2007: 374; see also Cook 2011). Here, Meskin downplays the fact that speech balloons and other kinds of text are always also a representation, and not just a presentation.

19 See also Cohn 2005.

20 Cf. Chute 2008: 452–54. On comics as a medium, see also McCloud 1993; Packard 2006; on comics as a popular medium, see Heer and Worcester 2004; Stein, Ditschke, and Kroucheva 2009.

materiality when she mentions "serial forms and contexts from weekly or daily strips to monthly comic books" and refers to "the comics page itself [a]s a material register of seriality" (2008: 453–54). In that sense, the development of graphic narrative has been, and continues to be, intricately tied to the physical media through which individual forms of graphic storytelling have emerged as prominent cultural artifacts and practices in the nineteenth and twentieth centuries.[21]

Francophone, German, and other non-English research traditions have their own vexed terminological controversies. In Germany, the label *Comics* still carries negative connotations as it is mostly associated with earlier academic and non-academic discourses of trivial literature and children's entertainment. Scholars like Schüwer (2008) therefore use the designation *grafische Literatur* (graphic literature), capturing the multimodality (or intermediality) of comics storytelling but implicitly sanctioning a literary approach to comics that seems less desirable than a more general terminological choice such as 'graphic narrative,' which primarily emphasizes their status as a form of multimodal narrative.[22] In the Francophone discourse, *bande dessinée* seems less controversial, but even here, the term is employed to cover works published in French-speaking countries (French, Belgian, French-Canadian, and so forth) but also functions as a generic term to describe any kind of graphic narrative. In that sense, it is similar to the Anglo-American term 'comics': It tends to privilege a specific national and linguistic perspective on an inherently transnational and multilingual form of multimodal narrative.[23]

In the present volume, we retain the historically resonant and culturally specific terms 'comic strip' and 'graphic novel' while also subscribing to the more general notion of 'graphic narrative,' signaling both the aim of developing a comics narratology (or graphic narrative theory) and an awareness of the transcultural and transnational varieties of graphic storytelling from different American comics formats to Francophone *bande dessinée*, Italian *fumetti*, German *Bildergeschichten* or *grafische Literatur*, Asian *manga, manhua,* or *manhwa*, and the whole panoply of globally dispersed types of graphic narratives routinely discussed in the

---

21 On storytelling in comics and graphic narratives as a cultural practice, see also Kelleter and Stein 2009, 2012.
22 On the multimodality of comics, see Herman 2010, who also reviews some of the existing literature on multimodality within linguistics and social semiotics, of which the works by Kress and van Leeuwen 2001; van Leeuwen 2005; Kress 2010 are among the most well-known.
23 See, for instance, Peeters 1991; Groensteen 2007; Miller 2007; Grove 2010; for a study of European comic books, see Beaty 2007; on *bande dessinées* in Quebec, see Hardy-Vallée 2010.

pages of John A. Lent's *International Journal of Comic Art* (1999–).[24] Moreover, we refrain from placing graphic narrative into any set categories of art or entertainment, highbrow or lowbrow, elite culture or popular culture, because we perceive it as a narrative form that can be found across cultural spheres and national borders, performing different narrative functions in a variety of socio-economic contexts.[25] While any attempt to exhaust the breadth of this continuously expanding field would be foolhardy, the contributions to the present volume will examine some of the more salient contexts and their effects on specific *narrative* affordances and limitations, conventions and innovations.

Survey of the Contributions

The volume is divided into four parts that proceed from the examination of fundamental narratological concepts as they apply to different kinds of graphic narrative (Part I) and aspects of the medium that extend beyond the 'single work' (Part II) to format and genre-oriented (Part III) and cross-cultural investigation (Part IV). The chapters collected in these four parts combine (albeit to different degrees and with different goals) an interest in narrative theory and a commitment to historical perspectives that account for the evolution of particular narrative strategies, individual works, genres, formats, and cultural traditions of graphic storytelling. This historically-minded type of graphic narrative theory distinguishes the present volume from previous essay collections and special issues. In making the case for a medium-specific 'comics narratology,' the essays collected here also aim to contribute to the project of bringing narratological theory into conversation with the formal and historical research that has shaped the bulk of comics studies. Thus, we propose that our understanding of what it means (or should mean) to study graphic narrative needs to be broad enough to include narratological reflection focusing on conceptual, theoretical, and methodological questions as well as historically, culturally, and medially specific analyses.

---

24 For transnational perspectives on graphic narratives, see Denson, Meyer, and Stein 2013; on the global spread of manga, see Johnson-Woods 2009; Berndt 2010, 2011, 2012; Berndt and Kümmerling-Meibauer 2013.

25 Some scholars associate comics with discourses of art (which is reflected in terms such as 'comic art,' 'graphic art,' or 'sequential art'), while others conceive of comics as a 'medium.' For different approaches, see Eisner 1985; Abbott 1986; Harvey 1994; McCloud 1993; Sabin 1996; Stein, Ditschke, and Kroucheva 2009. Eisner 1996 uses the phrases "graphic storytelling and visual narrative." In France, comics have been labeled the *9th art* (*neuvième art*) by critics such as Francis Lacassin (1971), while the *locus classicus* of American comics criticism, Gilbert Seldes's *The 7 Lively Arts* (2001 [1924]), discusses them as a popular art.

The chapters in the first part are mainly concerned with how, to what extent, and with which aims in mind fundamental narratological concepts such as story/discourse, storyworld, narrator, or focalization can be applied to different kinds of graphic narrative. Accordingly, Silke Horstkotte's "Zooming In and Out: Panels, Frames, Sequences, and the Building of Graphic Storyworlds" examines the strategies that allow graphic narratives to represent 'graphic storyworlds.' Combining theoretical and terminological reflections on the forms and functions of panels, frames, gutters, and page layouts with detailed analyses of well-known graphic novels such as Alan Moore and Dave Gibbons's *Watchmen*, Neil Gaiman's *Sandman* series, and Charles Burns's *Black Hole*, Horstkotte demonstrates that trying to explain the meaning making processes involved in 'reading' graphic narrative by way of some kind of comics-specific 'grammar' or 'language' tends to be misleading, as it often over-emphasizes the sequentiality of the reading processes. Rather, as Horstkotte argues, "the linear sequence is only one of many possible ways of organizing visual information in comics," and comics scholars would be well advised to take these different dimensions of meaning making into account.

While Horstkotte examines graphic narrative from a neo-formalist perspective that emphasizes the 'discourse' side of the traditional 'story/discourse'-distinction, Karin Kukkonen's "Space, Time, and Causality in Graphic Narratives: An Embodied Approach" turns its attention toward the 'story,' or rather the 'storyworld,' that readers of graphic narrative (re)construct in the process of reading. Taking the kind of 'embodied approach' to cognition that has gained traction in cognitive narratology over the last decade, Kukkonen analyzes the ways in which readers reconstruct the space, time, and causality of the dream-like storyworld(s) represented in Winsor McCay's *Dreams of the Rarebit Fiend* before evaluating the metaphor of transport that is commonly used to describe the process of 'immersive' reading. Against this broader background, Kukkonen examines the role not only of 'embodied simulation' for 'cognitive' as well as 'emotional transport' but also emphasizes that "[t]he actual space of the page turns out to be just as much an arena of embodiment and readerly transportation as the storyspace represented in the panels."

Following Horstkotte's and Kukkonen's discussions of medium-specific strategies such as panels, frames, and gutters and the cognitive processes involved in the reconstruction of a storyworld's space, time, and causality, Jan-Noël Thon's "Who's Telling the Tale? Authors and Narrators in Graphic Narrative" examines contemporary graphic novels from a more traditionally narratological perspective. Arguing that narrators in graphic narratives are best understood as more or less explicitly represented characters, Thon analyzes various prototypical forms of narrators in contemporary graphic novels such as Alan Moore and Kevin O'Neill's *The League of Extraordinary Gentlemen* series, Neil Gaiman's *The Sandman* series, and Craig Thompson's *Habibi*. Furthermore, Thon distinguishes between narratorial representation as (usually fictional) verbal narration that can be attributed to narrating characters, authorial representation as (usually nonfictional) verbal narration that can be attributed to authoring characters, and non-narratorial verbal-pictorial representation that can be attributed either to authoring characters or to what he calls hypothetical author collectives, but usually cannot be attributed to narrators-as-narrating characters.

If Thon's discussion of authors and narrators in graphic narrative addresses one of the two core areas of a post-Genettean 'discourse narratology' embodied in the canonical questions 'Who sees?' (or 'Who perceives?') and 'Who speaks?' (or 'Who narrates?'), Kai Mikkonen's "Subjectivity and Style in Graphic Narratives" covers the other. Emphasizing that "[t]he question of subjectivity in graphic narratives is vast" since it can relate to the subjectivities of (real or hypothetical) authors as well as to (narrating or non-narrating) characters, Mikkonen primarily focuses on particular characters' subjectivities and their graphic representation. After a brief review of the notoriously thorny terminological thicket that surrounds narratological terms such as 'perspective,' 'point of view,' and 'focalization' (the latter of which he distinguishes from 'ocularization' and 'auricularization' *sensu* Jost), Mikkonen uses graphic narratives as different as Marjane Satrapi's *Persepolis*, Fransesco Tullio Altan's *Ada* series, Lewis Trondheim and Matthieu Bonhomme's *Omni-visibilis*, Tommi Musturi's *Walking with Samuel*, and Carlo Collodi's *Pinocchio* to examine the graphic representation of subjectivity as it relates to issues of 'graphic style' and 'mind style.'

The chapters in the second part address various textual, paratextual, and contextual dimensions of graphic narrative beyond the 'single work': nonfictional narrative(s), seriality, intermediality, and transmedia storytelling. Nancy Pedri's "Graphic Memoir: Neither Fact Nor Fiction" examines complex forms of nonfictional representation in 'graphic memoirs' such as Alison Bechdel's *Fun Home*, Art Spiegelman's *Maus*, Marisa Acocella Marchetto's *Cancer Vixen*, and David B.'s *Epileptic*. Building on philosophical theories of fiction as well as on theories of autobiography from literary criticism, Pedri shows that while graphic memoir is no less bound by the 'fidelity constraint' than literary autobiography, more recent works tend to be particularly self-reflexive and employ metafictional strategies in order to deconstruct problematic notions of reliable memory and stable identity. Moreover, Pedri argues that the specific mediality of graphic memoirs may create 'as-if effects' by stressing the mediated nature of both the verbal and the pictorial elements of the representation. According to Pedri, "much can be said to weaken claims that fictionality is inherent to the medium of comics," then, but graphic memoirs still present "complex reading demands born from complementing the fidelity constraint with more general interests in storytelling."

As Daniel Stein argues in "Superhero Comics and the Authorizing Functions of the Comic Book Paratext," the serial publication and reception of superhero comic books has generated genre-shaping authorization conflicts among producers and consumers that find their most consequential expression in the letters pages and fanzines surrounding popular characters. Accordingly, Stein reconstructs the history of paratextually negotiated authorial fictions and author functions in American superhero comics from the 1940s to the 1960s, offering extended close readings of *Batman* letter columns and fanzines as well as suggesting that the diversification and increasing narrative complexity of the *Batman* storyworld can be traced back to the authorizing powers of such comic book paratexts. Long-running popular series, Stein proposes, demand mechanisms through which their inherent drive toward proliferation and their tendency toward narrative sprawl are managed, and paratextual negotiations have historically been a particularly effective means of serial complexity management.

While the contributions by Pedri and Stein are, each in their own way, concerned with specific textual, paratextual, and contextual manifestations of graphic narrative, Gabriele Rippl and Lukas Etter's "Intermediality, Transmediality, and Graphic Narrative" is the first contribution in the present volume to explicitly transgress not only the boundaries of individual works but also the boundaries of comics as a medium. Referring to a variety of different examples from Alan Moore and David Lloyd's *V for Vendetta* to Alison Bechdel's *Are You My Mother?*, Rippl and Etter not only distinguish between word specific combinations, alternating combinations, montage, parallel combinations, and picture specific combinations as five prototypical forms of word-image combinations that define the mediality of graphic narrative through what can be described as media combinations on a fairly basic level. They also use the concepts of 'intermediality' and 'transmediality' to illuminate graphic narrative's position within the broader media landscape and assess the promises of a comics narratology specifically dedicated to graphic narrative within the more encompassing field of transmedial narratology.

The final chapter in the second part of the volume, Greg M. Smith's "Comics in the Intersecting Histories of the Window, the Frame, and the Panel," is likewise concerned with the interrelation between media, in particular comics and film. Noting that "both audiovisual and graphic narrative have engaged in considerable interaction," Smith traces the 'traveling concepts' of windows, frames, and panels throughout the precursors of contemporary multimodal storytelling. After a *tour de force* that leads him from Renaissance painting to the camera obscura, from photography to early cinema, and from early cinema to computer games, Smith arrives at a discussion of the panel's many forms and functions in graphic narrative. As he suggests, "[a]lthough comics images themselves are static, their component lines capture a kind of movement, with the artist's hand movement across the panels guiding how the reader's eye traverses the page." Despite certain similarities between comics and film (as well as other potentially narrative media such as computer games), then, a historically informed perspective illuminates the differences between these media, as well, allowing us to better understand the ways in which windows, frames, and panels are used in graphic narrative.

The third part of the present volume introduces some of the most important formats of graphic narrative from both a historical and a narratological perspective: comic strips, albums, and graphic novels. It begins with Jared Gardner's "A History of the Narrative Comic Strip," which traces the narrative development of the American newspaper comic strip from its inception to the present day. Gardner focuses especially on changes from single-panel cartoons to sequentially structured newspaper comic strips, which quickly led to ongoing serial narratives with extended plotlines and recurring characters, and the development of new styles and genres. Ingrained in Gardner's argument is the idea that the narrative properties of the American comic strip are the result of a long historical process during which cartoonists have developed and refined their narrative apparatus as they have been creating ever new stories within increasingly detailed serial storyworlds. The daily need for new material and the cartoonists' creative solutions to the endless demand for commercially attractive forms of serial storytelling thus contributed to the creation of new formats of graphic narrative and new ways of verbal-pictorial storytelling. While Gardner does not engage in any extended transmedial analysis *per se*, he maintains that the narrative evolution of the comic strip in the United States has been driven by various forms of media competition and by the existence of a larger, and evolving, media ecology, including film, radio, comic books, and television.

Gardner's analysis of the American comic strip, its narrative evolution, and its embeddedness in specific production contexts is followed by Pascal Lefèvre's historical reconstruction of the narrative peculiarities stemming from the Flemish dual publication system, "Narration in the Flemish Dual Publication System: The Crossover Genre of the Humoristic Adventure." This system is in some ways similar to the American system of publishing daily strips and Sunday pages, but it is also quite different because it produces daily strips with the specific purpose of a later release as an album. Lefèvre argues that the two intersecting publication formats in Flanders have shaped their own "aesthetic system with a set of norms that offer[ed] a bounded set of alternatives to the individual creators of comics." As his detailed analysis of *Suske en Wiske* strips from the 1950s and 1960s shows, the Flemish dual publication system did not just determine the length of individual stories, the number of panels available to the artists, and the overwhelming linearity of plot constructions, but it also facilitated the emergence of a new crossover genre, the humoristic adventure story.

The European format of the comic album has often been perceived as a precursor to, or relative of, the American graphic novel format. In "Un/Taming the Beast, or Graphic Novels (Re)Considered," Christina Meyer zooms in on the terminological controversies surrounding the 'graphic novel' label. Focusing on what she calls the narrativity of comics and its impact on, and self-reflexive realization in, the creator-driven American series *The Unwritten* by Mike Carey and Peter Gross, Meyer examines 'patterns of narrative' and 'generic promptings' ranging from intertextual references to paratextual cues that continually challenge the postmodern reader by pointing back to the rich history of the comics medium and the American comics industry. Contemporary series such as *The Unwritten*, Meyer argues, display a strong awareness of their own role and position within the genre histories and storytelling modes of, as well as public debates about, American comics, and they develop and display their very own understanding of what a graphic novel might be and which narrative tools it may deploy to tell stories.

Henry Jenkins's "Archival, Ephemeral, and Residual: The Functions of Early Comics in Art Spiegelman's *In the Shadow of No Towers*" connects Gardner's focus on the American comic strip with Meyer's treatment of the graphic novel format. Singling out Spiegelman's critically acclaimed and purposely fragmentary response to 9/11, Jenkins investigates "the ways old icons transmit old values into the present, representing the locus of conflicting claims and bids on legacy and tradition (archive), offering vehicles for expressing autobiographical and collective memories (ephemera), and embodying old ideologies which still exert a claim on our current thinking (the residual)." Jenkins's analysis serves as a reminder that narrative and history are inseparably intertwined: that graphic novels frequently graft historical meanings onto objects (or 'stuff') and, in turn, derive some of their narrative meaning from them. In light of the resulting interrelations, any adequately informed and culturally sensitive analysis of such narratives will be well advised to combine narratological approaches with a historical, material, and media-sensitive perspective on meaning making processes.

The contributions in the fourth and final part of this volume trace the breadth of graphic narratives across cultures by reflecting on historically influential traditions of graphic storytelling. All of the chapters in this part display an awareness of the fact that any simplistic assumptions of distinctive national lineages of graphic storytelling are not only becoming increasingly problematic in the age of multinational corporations and the global dispersal of narratives but have always been grossly reductive. Accordingly, in "Anglo-American Graphic Narrative," Julia Round discusses the most influential transatlantic narrative convergences in recent superhero comic books that have largely evolved from the so-called British invasion of the American comics industry by prominent writers like Alan Moore, Grant Morrison, Neil Gaiman, and Warren Ellis since the 1980s. These convergences, Round explains, were prepared by the parallel histories of American and British comics, including censorship campaigns in both countries, and they derive much of their innovative potential from metafictional and postmodern engagements with the possibilities and limits of comics storytelling: experiments with narrative voices, alterities, and different modes of audience address, as well as self-reflexive interrogations of comics' most basic narrative strategies.

If Round traces the narratological implications of the recent transatlantic reformulation of the comic book superhero, Jan Baetens and Steven Surdiacourt examine the *longue durée* of European graphic narratives. As their chapter title "European Graphic Narratives: Toward a Cultural and Mediological History" indicates, they pursue a cultural approach that opens up narratological questions to "historical contexts and the social stakes of storytelling," and they propose a connected mediological perspective that ties changes in the production and reception of graphic narratives to various kinds of media transformations. Baetens and Surdiacourt stress "the correlation between the evolution of visual storytelling and a wide range of technological and communicational innovations" such as nineteenth-century engraving and printed magazine publication as well as twentieth-century strip serialization, album production, and web-based stories. Their reading of European graphic narratives from Rodolphe Töpffer and Wilhelm Busch to Hergé and the

L'Association publishing cooperative challenges traditional approaches to graphic narrative theory, treating these works not "as isolated and independent genres or media, but as parts of continually reconfigured media networks or dynamic cultural series."

In the wide world of contemporary graphic narrative, manga easily outsell any other type of comics. Today's manga include Japanese and other Asian productions as well as European and American stylistic and narrative adaptations. As Jaqueline Berndt argues in "Ghostly: 'Asian Graphic Narratives,' *Nonnonba*, and Manga," conventional views of Asian graphic narratives tend to falsely homogenize an inherently diverse field of cultural production and imagine manga as a representative of the cultural Other to European and/or American comics. In her close reading of Mizuki Shigeru's *Nonnonba*, Berndt reveals narrative structures and storytelling devices that have irritated Western commentators unfamiliar with their indebtedness to Japanese folklore and rhetorical principles such as *ki-sho-ten-ketsu* that diverge from the more familiar Western tripartite dramatic structure and shape the narrative progression of Mizuki Shigeru's manga. Focusing on narrative ambiguities such as indeterminate frames and fields of vision as well as innovative mixtures of fantastic and realist elements, Berndt discusses 'manga's ghostliness' as a condition that haunts both Western projections of Asian Otherness in the context of orientalism and a mode of resisting "evaluative criteria based on modern notions of authorship, work, and aesthetic sophistication."

The volume concludes with Monika Schmitz-Emans's "Graphic Narrative as World Literature." Complicating structuralist and semiotic approaches that implicitly or explicitly associate graphic narrative with verbal storytelling, and critically questioning the tendency of visual analyses to conceive of images as universally understandable, Schmitz-Emans documents the discursive maneuvers through which different forms of graphic narrative have been identified as examples of world literature and through which the graphic novel has been offered as a new paradigm of the latter. Schmitz-Emans then categorizes different genres of such a potential graphic world literature vis-à-vis already established literary genres. She ends her chapter by relating today's graphic narratives to Goethe's notion of *Weltliteratur*, arguing that the transgressions of cultural borders and the cross-adaptations of narrative styles, subject matters, and publication formats do not only induce new genres and modes of graphic storytelling but also reflect back on "one's own cultural and literary heritages," which increasingly "appear as renewed and open to innovative interpretation and continuation."

Conclusion

In further enriching the interdisciplinary and cross-disciplinary dialogue that has shaped recent studies of graphic narrative, the chapters collected in the following pages will provide a theoretically and methodologically refined basis for future investigations of comics and other forms of graphic narrative in the context of a dedicated comics narratology. When positioning itself vis-à-vis ongoing debates in postclassical and transmedial narratology as well as in comics and media studies, such a comics narratology will need to pay attention to the specific mediality as well as to the various intermedial and transmedial frames of reference that define graphic narratives. But it will also have to take seriously the diverse cultural and historical contexts in which graphic narratives have been, and continue to be, created and read, and to whose further diversification they inevitably contribute, as well. Against this background, we believe that the present volume constitutes an important step toward refining existing theories of graphic narrative by emphasizing not only theoretical and methodological questions extensively discussed within the narratological tradition, but also the historical breath as well as the transcultural and transnational diversity of narrative representations as they are realized in the conventionally distinct medium of comics.

Last but not least, we would like to express our gratitude to Wolf Schmid and the other editors of the Narratologia series for their steadfast belief in the project through its various stages of realization; to our contributors for their captivating work, their dedication to the volume's aims, and the collegial spirit in which they engaged with our editorial concerns; to the two anonymous reviewers of the manuscript for their astute comments and constructive criticism; to Manuela Gerlof at De Gruyter for the outstanding support along the way; and to Martin Gerecht for his assistance with formatting and standardizing the book's layout.

Works Cited

Abbott, Lawrence L. (1986). "Comic Art: Characteristics and Potentialities of a Narrative Art Medium." *Journal of Popular Culture* 19: 155–76. Print.

Alber, Jan (2009). "Impossible Storyworlds—and What to Do With Them." *Storyworlds: A Journal of Narrative Studies* 1: 79–96. Print.

Alber Jan, Stefan Iversen, Henrik S. Nielsen, and Brian Richardson (2010). "Unnatural Narratives, Unnatural Narratology: Beyond Mimetic Models." *Narrative* 18.2: 113–36. Print.

Baetens, Jan (2003). "Comic Strips and Constrained Writing." *Image [&] Narrative* 4.1: n.p. Web.
Beaty, Bart (2007). *Unpopular Culture: Transforming the European Comic Book in the 1990s*. Toronto: U of Toronto P. Print.
— (2012). *Comics versus Art*. Toronto: U of Toronto P. Print.
Berndt, Jaqueline (ed.) (2010). *Comics Worlds and the World of Comics: Towards Scholarship on a Global Scale*. Kyoto: imrc. Print.
— (ed.) (2011). *Intercultural Crossovers, Transcultural Flows: Manga/Comics*. Kyoto: imrc. Print.
— (ed.) (2012). *Manhwa, Manga, Manhua: East Asian Comics Studies*. Leipzig: Leipzig UP. Print.
Berndt, Jaqueline, and Bettina Kümmerling-Meibauer (eds.) (2013). *Manga's Cultural Crossroads*. New York: Routledge. Print.
Berninger, Mark, Jochen Ecke, and Gideon Haberkorn (eds.) (2010). *Comics as a Nexus of Cultures: Essays on the Interplay of Media, Disciplines and International Perspectives*. Jefferson: McFarland. Print.
Carrier, David (2000). *The Aesthetics of Comics*. University Park: Pennsylvania State UP. Print.
Chaney, Michael A. (ed.) (2011). *Graphic Subjects: Critical Essays on Autobiography and Graphic Novels*. Madison: U of Wisconsin P. Print.
Chute, Hillary (2008). "Comics as Literature? Reading Graphic Narrative." *PMLA* 123.2: 452–65. Print.
— (2010). *Graphic Women: Life Narrative and Contemporary Comics*. New York: Columbia UP. Print.
Chute, Hillary, and Marianne DeKoven (2006). "Introduction: Graphic Narrative." Hillary Chute and Marianne DeKoven (eds.). *Graphic Narrative*. Special issue of *Modern Fiction Studies* 52.4: 767–82. Print.
Cohn, Neil (2005). "Un-Defining 'Comics': Separating the Cultural from the Structural in Comics." *International Journal of Comic Art* 7.2: 236–48. Print.
Cook, Roy T. (2011). "Do Comics Require Pictures? Or Why *Batman* #663 Is a Comic." *Journal of Aesthetics and Art Criticism* 69.3: 285–96. Print.
Denson, Shane, Christina Meyer, and Daniel Stein (eds.) (2013). *Transnational Perspectives on Graphic Narratives: Comics at the Crossroads*. London: Bloomsbury. Print.
Ditschke, Stephan, and Anjin Anhut (2009). "Menschliches, Übermenschliches: Zur narrativen Struktur von Superheldencomics." Stephan Ditschke, Katerina Kroucheva, and Daniel Stein (eds.). *Comics: Zur Geschichte und Theorie eines populärkulturellen Mediums*. Bielefeld: transcript. 131–78. Print.

Ditschke, Stephan, Katerina Kroucheva, and Daniel Stein (eds.). *Comics: Zur Geschichte und Theorie eines populärkulturellen Mediums*. Bielefeld: transcript. Print.
Duncan, Randy, and Matthew J. Smith (2009). *The Power of Comics: History, Form and Culture*. London: Continuum. Print.
Ecke, Jochen (2010). "Comics Studies' Identity Crisis: A Meta-Critical Survey." Tim Lanzendörfer and Matthias Köhler (eds.). *Beyond Moore, Miller, Maus: Literary Approaches to Contemporary Comics*. Special issue of *ZAA: Zeitschrift für Anglistik und Amerikanistik* 59.1: 71–84. Print.
Eco, Umberto (2004 [1962]). "The Myth of Superman." Jeet Heer and Kent Worcester (eds.). *Arguing Comics: Literary Masters on a Popular Medium*. Jackson: UP of Mississippi. 146–64. Print.
Eder, Barbara, Elisabeth Klar, and Ramón Reichert (eds.) (2011). *Theorien des Comics: Ein Reader*. Bielefeld: transcript. Print.
Eisner, Will (1985). *Comics and Sequential Art*. Tamarac: Poorhouse. Print.
— (1996). *Graphic Storytelling and Visual Narrative*. Tamarac: Poorhouse. Print.
Faust, Wolfgang (1971). "Comics and How to Read Them." *Journal of Popular Culture* 5.1: 194–202. Print.
Fehrle, Johannes (2011). "Unnatural Worlds and Unnatural Narration in Comics?" Jan Alber and Rüdiger Heinze (eds.). *Unnatural Narratives— Unnatural Narratology*. Berlin: De Gruyter. 210–45. Print.
Fludernik, Monika (1996). *Towards a "Natural" Narratology*. London: Routledge. Print.
— (2005). "Histories of Narratology (II): From Structuralism to the Present." James Phelan and Peter J. Rabinowitz (eds). *A Companion to Narrative Theory*. Malden: Blackwell. 36–59. Print.
Fuchs, Wolfgang J., and Reinhold C. Reitberger (1971). *Comics: Anatomie eines Massenmediums*. München: Moos. Print.
Gabilliet, Jean-Paul (2010). *Of Comics and Men: A Cultural History of American Comic Books*. Trans. Bart Beaty and Nick Nguyen. Jackson: UP of Mississippi. Print.
Gardner, Jared (2010). "Same Difference: Graphic Alterity in the Work of Gene Luen Yang, Adrian Tomine, and Derek Kirk Kim." Frederick L. Aldama (ed.). *Multicultural Comics: From* Zap *to* Blue Beetle. Austin: U of Texas P. 132–47. Print.
— (2012). *Projections: Comics and the History of Twenty-First-Century Storytelling*. Stanford: Stanford UP. Print.
Gardner, Jared, and David Herman (eds.) (2011a). *Graphic Narratives and Narrative Theory*. Special issue of *SubStance* 40.1. Print.

— (2011b). "Graphic Narratives and Narrative Theory: Introduction." Jared Gardner and David Herman (eds.). *Graphic Narratives and Narrative Theory*. Special issue of *SubStance* 40.1: 3-13. Print.
Groensteen, Thierry (2000). "Why Are Comics Still in Search of Legitimization?" Anne Magnussen and Hans-Christian Christiansen (eds.). *Comics & Culture: Analytical and Theoretical Approaches to Comics*. Copenhagen: Museum Tusculanum P. 29–41. Print.
— (2007). *The System of Comics*. Trans. Bart Beaty and Nick Nguyen. Jackson: UP of Mississippi. Print.
— (2013). *Comics and Narration*. Trans. Ann Miller. Jackson: UP of Mississippi. Print.
Grove, Laurence (2010). *Comics in French: The Bande Dessinée in Context*. New York: Berghahn. Print.
Hardy, Valée, Michel (2010). "The Carrefour of Practice: Québec BD in Transition." Mark Berninger, Jochen Ecke, and Gideon Haberkorn (eds.). *Comics as a Nexus of Cultures: Essays on the Interplay of Media, Disciplines and International Perspectives*. Jefferson: McFarland. 85–98. Print.
Harvey, Robert C. (1979). "The Aesthetics of the Comic Strip." *Journal of Popular Culture* 12.4: 640–52. Print.
— (1994). *The Art of the Funnies: An Aesthetic History*. Jackson: UP of Mississippi. Print.
Hatfield, Charles (2005). *Alternative Comics: An Emerging Literature*. Jackson: UP of Mississippi. Print.
— (2009). "Defining Comics in the Classroom; or, The Pros and Cons of Unfixability." Stephen E. Tabachnick (ed.). *Teaching the Graphic Novel*. New York: MLA. 19–27. Print.
Heer, Jeet, and Kent Worcester (eds.) (2004). *Arguing Comics: Literary Masters on a Popular Medium*. Jackson: UP of Mississippi. Print.
— (2009). *A Comics Studies Reader*. Jackson: UP of Mississippi. Print.
Hein, Michael, Michael Hüners, and Torsten Michaelsen (eds.) (2002). *Ästhetik des Comic*. Berlin: Schmidt. Print.
Herman, David (2004). "Toward a Transmedial Narratology." Marie-Laure Ryan (ed.). *Narrative across Media: The Languages of Storytelling*. Lincoln: U of Nebraska P. 47–75. Print.
— (2009). *Basic Elements of Narrative*. Chichester: Wiley-Blackwell. Print.
— (2010). "Word-Image/Utterance-Gesture: Case Studies in Multimodal Storytelling." Ruth Page (ed.). *New Perspectives on Narrative and Multimodality*. New York: Routledge. 78–98. Print.
Horstkotte, Silke, and Nanci Pedri (2011). "Focalization in Graphic Narrative." *Narrative* 19.3: 330–57. Print.

Hünig, Wolfgang K. (1974). *Strukturen des Comic Strip: Ansätze zu einer textlinguistisch-semiotischen Analyse narrativer Comics*. Hildesheim: Olms. Print.

Jannidis, Fotis (2003). "Narratology and the Narrative." Tom Kindt and Hans-Harald Müller (eds.). *What Is Narratology? Questions and Answers Regarding the Status of a Theory*. Berlin: De Gruyter. 35–54. Print.

Jenkins, Henry (2012). "Introduction: Should We Discipline the Reading of Comics?" Matthew J. Smith and Randy Duncan (eds.). *Critical Approaches to Comics: Theories and Methods*. New York: Routledge. 1–14. Print.

Johnson-Woods, Toni (ed.) (2009). *Manga: An Anthology of Global and Cultural Perspectives*. London: Continuum. Print.

Kelleter, Frank, and Daniel Stein (2009). "*Great, Mad, New*: Populärkultur, serielle Ästhetik und der frühe amerikanische Zeitungscomic." Stephan Ditschke, Katerina Kroucheva, and Daniel Stein (eds.). *Comics: Zur Geschichte und Theorie eines populärkulturellen Mediums*. Bielefeld: transcript. 81–117. Print.

— (2012). "Autorisierungspraktiken seriellen Erzählens: Zur Gattungsentwicklung von Superheldencomics." Frank Kelleter (ed.). *Populäre Serialität: Narration—Evolution—Distinktion. Zum seriellen Erzählen seit dem 19. Jahrhundert*. Bielefeld: transcript. 259–90. Print.

Kindt, Tom, and Hans-Harald Müller (eds.) (2003). *What Is Narratology? Questions and Answers Regarding the Status of a Theory*. Berlin: De Gruyter. Print.

Krafft, Ulrich (1978). *Comics Lesen: Untersuchungen zur Textualität von Comics*. Stuttgart: Klett-Cotta. Print.

Kress, Gunther (2010). *Multimodality: A Social Semiotics Approach to Contemporary Communication*. Abingdon: Routledge. Print.

Kress, Gunther, and Theo van Leeuwen (2001). *Multimodal Discourse: The Modes and Media of Contemporary Communication*. London: Arnold. Print.

Kukkonen, Karin (2011). "Comics as a Test Case for Transmedial Narratology." Jared Gardner and David Herman (eds.). *Graphic Narratives and Narrative Theory*. Special issue of *SubStance* 40.1: 34–52. Print.

— (2013). *Contemporary Comics Storytelling*. Lincoln: U of Nebraska P. Print.

Kukkonen, Karin, and Gideon Haberkorn (2010). "Workshop 1: Toward a Toolbox of Comics Studies." Mark Berninger, Jochen Ecke, and Gideon Haberkorn (eds.). *Comics as a Nexus of Cultures: Essays on the Interplay of Media, Disciplines and International Perspectives*. Jefferson: McFarland. 237–44. Print.

Lacassin, Francis (1971). *Pour un neuvième art: La bande dessinée*. Paris: Édition des Paris. Print.
Lefèvre, Pascal (2000). "Narration in Comics." *Image [&] Narrative* 1.1: n.p. Web.
McCloud, Scott (1993). *Understanding Comics: The Invisible Art*. Northampton: Kitchen Sink. Print.
McLaughlin, Jeff (ed.) (2005). *Comics as Philosophy*. Jackson: UP of Mississippi. Print.
Meister, J. Christoph (ed.) (2005). *Narratology beyond Literary Criticism: Mediality—Disciplinarity*. Berlin: De Gruyter. Print.
— (2009). "Narratology." Peter Hühn, John Pier, Wolf Schmid, and Jörg Schönert (eds.). *Handbook of Narratology*. Berlin: De Gruyter. 329–49. Print.
Meskin, Aaron (2007). "Defining Comics?" *Journal of Aesthetics and Art Criticism* 65.4: 369–79. Print.
Meskin, Aaron, and Roy T. Cook (eds.) (2012). *The Art of Comics: A Philosophical Approach*. Malden: Wiley-Blackwell. Print.
Mikkonen, Kai (2011). "Graphic Narratives as a Challenge to Transmedial Narratology: The Question of Focalization." Daniel Stein, Christina Meyer, and Micha Edlich (eds.). *American Comic Books and Graphic Novels*. Special issue of *Amerikastudien/American Studies* 56.4: 637–52. Print.
— (2012). "Focalization in Comics: From the Specificities of the Medium to Conceptual Reformulation." *Scandinavian Journal of Comic Art* 1: 65–95. Print.
Miller, Ann (2007). *Reading Bande Dessinée: Critical Approaches to French-Language Comic Strip*. Chicago: Intellect. Print.
Molotiu, Andrei (ed.) (2009). *Abstract Comics: The Anthology*. Seattle: Fantagraphics. Print.
Nünning, Ansgar (2003). "Narratology or Narratologies? Taking Stock of Recent Developments, Critique and Modest Proposals for Future Usage of the Term." Tom Kindt and Hans-Harald Müller (eds.). *What Is Narratology? Questions and Answers Regarding the Status of a Theory*. Berlin: De Gruyter. 239–75. Print.
Olson, Greta (ed.) (2011). *Current Trends in Narratology*. Berlin: De Gruyter. Print.
Packard, Stephan (2006). *Anatomie des Comics: Psychosemiotische Medienanalyse*. Göttingen: Wallstein. Print.
Peeters, Benoît (1991). *Case, planche, récit: Comment lire une bande dessinée*. Paris: Casterman. Print.
Pustz, Matthew (ed.) (2012). *Comic Books and American Cultural History: An Anthology*. London: Continuum. Print.

Rajewsky, Irina O. (2010). "Border Talks: The Problematic Status of Media Borders in the Current Debate about Intermediality." Lars Elleström (ed.). *Media Borders, Multimodality and Intermediality*. Basingstoke: Palgrave Macmillan. 51–68. Print.

Rey, Alain (1978). *Les Spectres de la Bande: Essai sur la B.D.* Paris: Les éditions de Minuit. Print.

Richardson, Brian (2011). "What is Unnatural Narrative Theory?" Jan Alber and Rüdiger Heinze (eds.). *Unnatural Narratives—Unnatural Narratology*. Berlin: De Gruyter. 23–40. Print.

Ryan, Marie-Laure (2004). "Introduction." Marie-Laure Ryan (ed.). *Narrative across Media: The Languages of Storytelling*. Lincoln: U of Nebraska P. 1–40. Print.

— (2005). "On the Theoretical Foundations of Transmedial Narratology." J. Christoph Meister (ed.). *Narratology beyond Literary Criticism: Mediality—Disciplinarity*. Berlin: De Gruyter. 1–23. Print.

— (2006). *Avatars of Story*. Minneapolis: U of Minnesota P. Print.

— (2009). "Narration in Various Media." Peter Hühn, John Pier, Wolf Schmid, and Jörg Schönert (eds.). *Handbook of Narratology*. Berlin: De Gruyter. 263–81. Print.

— (2014). "Story/Worlds/Media: Tuning the Instruments of a Media-Conscious Narratology." Marie-Laure Ryan and Jan-Noël Thon (eds.). *Storyworlds across Media: Toward a Media-Conscious Narratology*. Lincoln: U of Nebraska P. 25–49. Print.

Ryan, Marie-Laure, and Jan-Noël Thon (2014). "Introduction: Storyworlds across Media." Marie-Laure Ryan and Jan-Noël Thon (eds.). *Storyworlds across Media: Toward a Media-Conscious Narratology*. Lincoln: U of Nebraska P. 1–21. Print.

Sabin, Roger (1996). *Comics, Comix & Graphic Novels: A History of Comic Art*. London: Phaidon. Print.

Saraceni, Mario (2003). *The Language of Comics*. London: Routledge. Print.

Schüwer, Martin (2008). *Wie Comics erzählen: Grundriss einer intermedialen Erzähltheorie der grafischen Literatur*. Trier: Wissenschaftlicher Verlag Trier. Print.

Seldes, Gilbert V. (2001 [1924]). *The 7 Lively Arts: The Classic Appraisal of the Popular Arts (Comic Strips, Movies, Musical Comedy, Vaudeville, Radio, Popular Music, Dance)*. Introd. Michael Kammen. New York: Dover. Print.

Smith, Matthew J., and Randy Duncan (eds.) (2012). *Critical Approaches to Comics: Theories and Methods*. New York: Routledge. Print.

Stein, Daniel, Stephan Ditschke, and Katerina Kroucheva (2009). "Birth of a Notion: Comics als populärkulturelles Medium." Stephan Ditschke, Katerina Kroucheva, and Daniel Stein (eds.). *Comics:*

Zur Geschichte und Theorie eines populärkulturellen Mediums. Bielefeld: transcript. 7–27. Print.

Stein, Daniel, Christina Meyer, and Micha Edlich (eds.) (2011). *American Comic Books and Graphic Novels*. Special issue of *Amerikastudien/American Studies* 56.4. Print.

Thon, Jan-Noël (2014a). "Mediality." Marie-Laure Ryan, Lori Emerson, and Benjamin J. Robertson (eds.). *Johns Hopkins Guide to Digital Media*. Baltimore: Johns Hopkins UP. 334–37. Print.

— (2014b). "Narrativity." Marie-Laure Ryan, Lori Emerson, and Benjamin J. Robertson (eds.). *Johns Hopkins Guide to Digital Media*. Baltimore: Johns Hopkins UP. 351–55. Print.

— (2014c). "Subjectivity across Media: On Transmedial Strategies of Subjective Representation in Contemporary Feature Films, Graphic Novels, and Computer Games." Marie-Laure Ryan and Jan-Noël Thon (eds.). *Storyworlds across Media: Toward a Media-Conscious Narratology*. Lincoln: U of Nebraska P. 67–102. Print.

— (2014d). "Toward a Transmedial Narratology: On Narrators in Contemporary Graphic Novels, Feature Films, and Computer Games." Jan Alber and Per Krogh Hansen (eds.). *Beyond Classical Narration: Transmedial and Unnatural Challenges*. Berlin: De Gruyter. 25–56. Print.

Van Leeuwen, Theo (2005). *Introducing Social Semiotics*. Abingdon: Routledge. Print.

Wolf, Werner (2002). "Intermediality Revisited: Reflections on Word and Music Relations in the Context of a General Typology of Intermediality." Suzanne M. Lodato, Suzanne Aspden, and Walter Bernhart (eds.). *Word and Music Studies: Essays in Honor of Steven Paul Scher on Cultural Identity and the Musical Stage*. Amsterdam: Rodopi. 13–34. Print.

— (2003). "Narrative and Narrativity: A Narratological Reconceptualization and Its Applicability to the Visual Arts." *Word & Image* 19.3: 180–97. Print.

— (2005). "Metalepsis as a Transgeneric and Transmedial Phenomenon: A Case Study of the Possibilities of 'Exporting' Narratological Concepts." J. Christoph Meister (ed.). *Narratology beyond Literary Criticism: Mediality–Disciplinarity*. Berlin: De Gruyter. 83–107. Print.

— (2011). "Narratology and Media(lity): The Transmedial Expansion of a Literary Discipline and Possible Consequences." Greta Olson (ed.). *Current Trends in Narratology*. Berlin: De Gruyter. 145–80. Print.

PART I

GRAPHIC NARRATIVE AND NARRATOLOGICAL CONCEPTS

SILKE HORSTKOTTE
(Leipzig)

Zooming In and Out: Panels, Frames, Sequences, and the Building of Graphic Storyworlds

Narrative Beginnings

Comics—defined by Scott McCloud as "juxtaposed pictorial and other images in deliberate sequence, intended to convey information and/or to produce an aesthetic response in the viewer" (1993: 9)—are often considered to be one of the most recent narrative media. On the other hand, theorists anxious to respond to cultural criticism have sometimes been at pains to rehabilitate sequential storytelling as an "ancient form of art" (Eisner 2008: xi), pointing to predecessors from the Bayeux tapestry to William Hogarth's print series. There are arguments for as well as against both positions. Telling a story through a series of discrete images accompanied by textual elements is an old and efficient method of addressing, instructing, and entertaining the illiterate or semi-literate. However, there is a vast gulf separating these early examples of pictorial storytelling from the highly sophisticated graphic novels by authors such as Art Spiegelman, Neil Gaiman, or Alan Moore that have emerged from the broader tradition of comics since the mid-1980s. Moreover, graphic novels owe as much to the tradition and conventions of the literary novel and to the narrative strategies of film as to the comic strip. The present chapter concerns itself with these latter, more complexly structured graphic narratives. In introducing readers of this volume to the narrative operations particular to comics and graphic novels, I will begin by comparing how two of the earliest comics to use ambitious narrative techniques and structures—Alan Moore's *Watchmen* (1986–1987) and *Preludes & Nocturnes* (1988–1989), the first volume in Neil Gaiman's ongoing *Sandman* series—go about constructing complex narrative worlds with the medium-specific tools and techniques of comics.

Both books had originally been serialized by DC Comics. They introduce readers into the narrative world by means of a splash page, a full-page panel (the basic narrative unit of comics) that is a conventional starting point for comics narration.[1] Like the establishing shot in a movie, such an introductory splash page serves to set the tone of the ensuing narrative, and it introduces key symbols, scenes, and/or characters. In *Watchmen*, the opening page shows part of a yellow smiley button in a sea of red liquid in an extreme close-up view. The second page, based on a grid pattern, then zooms out of this close-up in a series of successive panels revealing that the red liquid is a pool of blood on a sidewalk that is being flushed into the gutter by a clean-up man with a spray nozzle, while another male character with a cardboard sign stating "The end is nigh" walks through the clean-up operation (see figure 1).

Thus, the first page introduces both the graphic novel's theme of extreme violence and its clash with incongruent elements, here the smiley button, later the very existence of a band of costumed superheroes. More than that, however, it also establishes a narrative point of origin that is both elevated, suggesting omniscience, and curiously limited. For the six panels through which the narrative zooms out are all seen from an extremely elevated, 'eye-of-God' vantage point, which is finally, in a wider panel across the bottom of the second page, revealed to be slightly above a balding man who looks down on the blood puddle from a broken window on a high floor of a skyscraper while saying, "Hmm. That's quite a drop." Thus, the elevated spectator, although possessing a privileged vantage point on reality, is far from omniscient. This tension between the suggestions of omniscience inherent in an extremely elevated perspectival point, on the one hand, and the curiously limited knowledge and trivial commentary of the spectator who seems to embody that perspective, on the other, has important consequences for the reader's ability to gain orientation in the storyworld. For readers cannot draw any specific inferences about the events preceding this narrative beginning from what they encounter on the page. The zooming-out operation of the first pages is therefore symptomatic of a narrative strategy that only appears to be objective while constantly withholding or disguising crucial information from its readers. For instance, it will be a while before careful readers will be able to conclude that the character walking through the pool of blood is the mysterious Rorschach, whose journal is quoted in the non-diegetic text boxes accompanying the diegetic representation of the second page.

Another graphic narrative with a cult following, a different way into the storyworld: The first chapter, "Sleep of the Just," of Neil Gaiman's *The Sandman: Preludes & Nocturnes* opens with a crayon-style drawing of a dark head with white, glowing eyes that seems to be emerging from a sea of grass in an eerie underwater world. Two columns to the sides of this

---

1 On the comic book splash page, cf. Eisner 2008: 64.

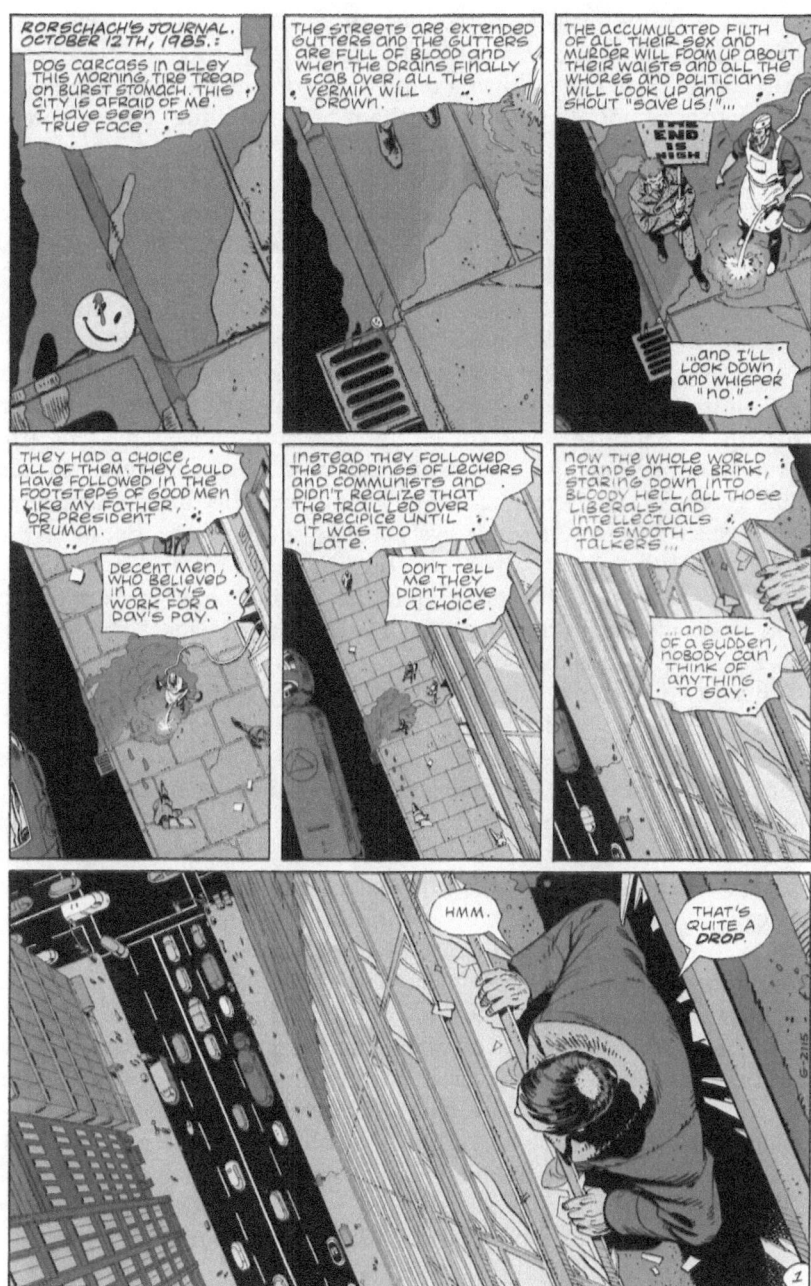

Figure 1: Alan Moore and Dave Gibbons, *Watchmen* (2005).
© DC Comics. All rights reserved.

image show photorealistic depictions of flowers, a book page, a cat statuette, a chunk of rock crystal, an hourglass, and other objects arranged as if in a showcase. The following recto page contains the beginning of the narrative proper, and it constitutes a sharp break with the stillness and still life aesthetics of the verso page (see figure 2). Like the second page of *Watchmen*, it appears to be arranged in a grid pattern combining panels that span the width of the page with sequences of narrower panels. However, the succession of perspectival angles on this page is much jumpier than the zooming out that smoothes the way into the *Watchmen* storyworld. The top panel establishes the locale in a large country mansion and sets a gothic tone by focusing on the looming bird of prey statues by the sides of the gate. A speech bubble reads, "Wake up, sir. We're *here*." The panel below introduces the character being addressed thusly: an elderly gentleman in a top hat being driven up in an automobile, emerging from the car and approaching the doorway hesitantly, drops of sweat forming on his forehead. A narrow close-up view shows his hand grasping the door knocker and then a man's eye peeking out the door. Below, a wide panel represents the two characters on both sides of the door from a slightly elevated, bird's eye view, while the bottom panel mirrors the top one in all details except that the speech balloon now reads, "The master is in his study, sir. Please follow me."

These two narrative beginnings will serve as my starting point for discussing how storyworlds are built in comics and graphic novels, and for critically engaging with some of the topics and concepts that have been proposed for studying comics as a narrative medium, especially concerning the basic elements of comics narration: panels, frames, and gutters.[2] In their different ways, both sequences highlight the importance of narrative beginnings for setting the mood and tone of a storyworld, and they can be used to show the complexity that multimodality, or the simultaneous communication on verbal and visual tracks, introduces to the building of such a narrative world in graphic narrative.[3] While *Preludes & Nocturnes* uses non-diegetic text sparingly in its initial pages, in *Watchmen* the visual zooming out is accompanied by and commented upon in a series of journal entries that, even though they echo motives and elements from the visual track, do not refer to it directly. Thus, the first text box speaks of a "Dog carcass in alley this morning, tire tread on burst stomach," taking up the theme of death and blood in the streets while shifting the locale from a wide main street to a dark alleyway and contrasting the killed man on the sidewalk with a dog run over by a car.

---

2   On comics as a medium, see Ditschke, Kroucheva, and Stein 2009; see esp. the contribution by Hoppeler, Etter, and Rippl 2009.
3   See Kress and van Leeuwen 2001.

Figure 2: Neil Gaiman, *The Sandman: Preludes & Nocturnes* (2010).
© DC Comics. All rights reserved.

The unique way in which graphic narrative creates narrative coherence forms a distinct path, but it also draws on established narrative patterns adapted from other media. In particular, classic Hollywood film is an important reference point for comics narration. In *Watchmen*, for instance, techniques for establishing plot and character, as well as the positioning of the murder sequence in the narrative, have been adapted from film. The opening with a murder mystery relates *Watchmen*'s narrative beginning to 1950s *noir* film, and it is in this context that the contrast between the visual and the verbal track has to be read. Non-diegetic voice-over narration is a standard feature of *noir*, and it is often employed to create an unreliable narration.[4] Similarly, even though graphic narrative is not photorealistic, the choice of panel size and perspectival angle may be described productively by using the terminology of film studies, as Hans-Christian Christiansen (2000) has shown: close-ups, panoramic shots, and birds' eye views, as well as specific ways of composing shots in a sequence by means of editing and montage have established meanings and functions in film narrative which graphic narrative here productively adapts. This should not surprise us since it is, according to Marshall McLuhan, a rule of media history that "[the] content of a movie is a novel or a play or an opera" (1964: 31). That is, new media routinely develop their narrative vocabulary and syntax by adapting and expanding the narrative capacity of an older medium; although comics and film first developed their narrative propensities around the same time, more recent graphic novels have added to the medium's narrative complexity by building upon filmic devices.

However, film shots and camera angles as well as film editing are constricted by technology, while hand-drawn comics are much more variable in style and composition. Panel size, shape, and placement, drawing style, coloring, and the use of frames, as well as the use or lack of narrative text boxes, their size, shape, color, and position in- or outside panels are just some of the elements that contribute toward the unique ways in which a graphic narrative draws its readers into the storyworld. Because of the multiplicity of factors at play, the style of each graphic narrative is much more variable and distinctive than is the case in other narrative media. Every reading of graphic narrative has to calibrate these formal aspects, or *syuzhet*, with the story, or *fabula*, evoked in a graphic narrative,[5] and there is no universal grammar for this decoding as there is in verbal narrative in a natural language, or in the established narrative format of the Hollywood movie. Because of the infinite variety of graphic

---

4 See Kozloff 1988; Ferenz 2005.
5 In the sense of Tomashevsky 1965. See also Chatman 1978; Meister 2003.

styles, each graphic narrative evokes not only a storyline but a complete narrative universe with a highly distinctive feel. As Pascal Lefèvre argues, "a graphic style creates the fictive world, giving a certain perspective on the diegesis" (2011: 16). The strongly stylized, hand-drawn quality of much cartooning serves to highlight the discursive qualities of the narrative representation, rather than emphasizing a story-level similarity to the actual world. Of all media that developed in technical modernity, graphic narrative alone has not effaced the line, thereby indexing its embodied creation.[6] While the viewer of a movie, particularly of mainstream Hollywood film, is able to imagine the filmic diegesis as an addition or supplementation of the real,[7] the foregrounding of different drawing styles in graphic narrative and the endless variety of ways in which panels can speak to each other require a new comics literacy that engages much more closely with individual choices in style and patterning.

Beyond Gaps and Gutters

Despite these infinite choices, one of the most repeated dogmas of comics studies is the understanding of comics as a linear or "sequential art" with a "grammar" composed of panels and frames separated by gaps and gutters.[8] By "dividing the picture into several distinct frames," the argument goes, graphic narrative "uses the eye of the spectator moving from panel to panel to keep narrative time running. The reader (for the eye movement amounts to an act of reading) constructs a story" (Ryan 2004: 141; see also Ewert 2000). According to this school of thought, comics narrative is structured by means of grids and gutters, that is, it breaks the narrative flow down into discrete panels, and it opens up a space between the panels that offers a way in for readerly engagement and imagination.[9]

Yet while *Watchmen* uses a continuous zooming-out technique that opens up an almost seamless path through the panels that are all seen from a high-angle perspective, the visual sequence in *Preludes & Nocturnes* is much jumpier, alternating between close-ups and long 'shots' and using only one high-angle panel, which thus gains a special emphasis.[10] Remarkably, although the recto page in *Preludes & Nocturnes* appears at first to be constructed on a grid pattern, a closer look reveals the page to

---

6   Cf. Gardner 2011: 56.
7   Cf. Grodal 1997: 29.
8   Prominent representatives are Eisner 2008; McCloud 1993.
9   See Berlatsky 2009.
10 The reference to 'shots' is, of course, metaphorical here.

be based on a continuous background image that shows the old gentleman approaching as he would be seen by someone peeking out from the house, with the top and bottom of the picture overlaid by the other panels on the page. This embedding or overlaying of panels within and above a more continuous background, which reoccurs on many of the pages in *Preludes & Nocturnes*, contributes to the distinctive style of the *Sandman* series, and it is charged with meaning and with atmosphere. It can indicate the simultaneity of geographically distant events and experiences, as on the fourth page of *Preludes & Nocturnes*, where the very different dreams of Ellie Marsten, Daniel Bustamonte, Stefan Wasserman, and Unity Kincaid are framed within the menacing gates of Wych Cross (see figure 3). However, this framing also implicates the other characters within the grandiose plans and actions of Roderick Burgess, Wych Cross's "master," which will have very serious if entirely unforeseen consequences for all of them.

As the *Sandman* example indicates, then, gaps are not necessarily just empty spaces. Instead, the space between panels is here shown to be continuous. Panels are embedded within other panels, indicating the continuity of the storyworld or actually of the plural worlds in *The Sandman*, as the main theme of the series is the interaction between waking and dreaming states and the role of supernatural characters, especially the eponymous Sandman, who mediate between them. A continuity between various characters' experience in *Preludes & Nocturnes* is often also expressed through the distinctive color coding of the background against which panels on a page are set: the background to the scenes in Burgess's castle is dominantly black, suitably so for the rituals of black magic in the course of which Burgess captures Dream, while a light background embeds the dreams of different characters within a continuous range of experientiality later in the first chapter.[11] Switches in background color or frame within the same page, on the other hand, are frequently used to indicate a sudden change of atmosphere or a shift in the ontological order (reality vs. dreamworld).

Even in graphic narratives that follow a more formal grid pattern, the linear understanding implied by the term 'sequentiality' may be too reductive and the emphasis on gaps and gutters misleading. After all, readerly engagement with the storyworld is bound to focus not on the space between panels but on what is inside the panels as well as on the ways in which panels speak to each other. A responsible comics hermeneutics would do well to move away from the linguistic-structuralist idea that comics narrative has a "grammar" (Eisner 2008: 2) and

---

11   On experientiality as a defining characteristic of narrative, see Fludernik 1996.

Figure 3: Neil Gaiman, *The Sandman: Preludes & Nocturnes* (2010).
© DC Comics. All rights reserved.

that this grammar entails a linear reading. As film semiotician Christian Metz (1974) has shown, the images in a visual narrative do not function as signs in a manner comparable to words in a sentence.[12] The image in a visual narrative may be understood more productively as a full statement whose relation to preceding and following statements is much "less embedded in paradigmatic networks of meaning" (Metz 1974: 26) than that of words in a sentence. An understanding of comics in terms of signs as it is proposed, for instance, by Ole Frahm (2010), is reductive.

In fact, the linear sequence is only one of many possible ways of organizing visual information in comics. Since narrative directionality in comics is not dictated by technology, as it is in film, graphic artists may, and increasingly do, choose other ways of presenting a course of action than that of grids and sequences—either exclusively or intermittently. For instance, the third page of *The Sandman* combines no less than six distinct scenes of varying size and detail within one overall frame (see figure 4). The top half of the page is enclosed within a highly detailed gilded frame decorated with the skull of a goat at the top, other demonic heads on the sides, and runes running around the bottom. While the enclosure within an overall frame highlights the temporal and spatial unity of the individual scenes, the frame's details create a sinister mood and prepare the reader emotionally for the evolving plot, in which the evil character Roderick Burgess, an occultist contemporary and competitor of the historical Aleister Crowley, captures Dream, the mythical entity governing people's dreams, with the aid of a grimoire acquired from the museum curator Dr. Hathaway. The third page chronicles Hathaway's arrival at Burgess's house and the handing over of the grimoire in three sets of scenes. First, there are the two large scenes at the top and bottom, each covering close to half a page. The top half, which seems to grow out of the gilded frame that here blends into a curtain rod from which a heavy chintz curtain hangs, shows Hathaway standing in Burgess's library at some distance from the seated Burgess, while the servant Compton hovers in the doorway. Behind both protagonists, the library interior is depicted in some detail; however, in the middle of the scene between the two characters, pale yellow rays appear to emanate from a light blue oval crossed by yellow dashes. The incongruity of this element within the library setting (it does not appear to be a window) renders it difficult, if not impossible, to comprehend within a realistic reference frame. The bottom half of the page shows Burgess and Hathaway at a slightly later point in time: Burgess has just been handed the Magdalene grimoire. The perspectival orientation

---

12 On pictures as 'signs close to perception' ('wahrnehmungsnahe Zeichen'), see also Sachs-Hombach 2003.

Figure 4: Neil Gaiman, *The Sandman: Preludes & Nocturnes* (2010).
© DC Comics. All rights reserved.

of this scene seems to have turned by 180 degrees in relation to the top half, as the position of the two characters is now inverted. But Burgess is not illuminated from the front, as he would have to be if the blue oval were a window, and the yellow rays a source of light, leaving readers to wonder about the mysterious nature of these pictorial elements.

A second, superimposed set of scenes consists of three round frames, one in the top-left corner of the page and two in the middle, each showing one or both protagonists in greater detail. The top-left panel, superimposed over the head of the servant Compton in the larger scene, shows a close-up view of Burgess's face at a moment in time preceding the larger scene (Burgess greets Hathaway, before offering him a seat). The two round panels in the middle indicate the transition between the two larger scenes. In the left one, Hathaway still holds the grimoire; in the right one, we see the grimoire being handed over. Superimposed on the point where the two round frames meet—adding a third layer—is a narrow rectangular panel showing an extreme close-up view of Burgess's eye, as already seen in the top-left frame, and indicating his reaction to the words, uttered by Hathaway, that "he"—Hathaway's son Edmund—"is dead."

While a linear reading of these elements is, in principle, possible—as the scenes follow a left-to-right, top-to-bottom path—such a reading does not do justice to the architecture of the page, which calls for a simultaneous reading that takes into account the size and positioning of the separate elements within the page layout, their layering one on top of the other, and the resulting foregrounding of Burgess's eye and the words "he's dead" in the center of the page. As this example shows, it is often neither possible nor desirable to "secure control of the reader's attention and dictate the sequence in which the reader will follow the narrative" (Eisner 2008: 40). In any case, this assumption is based on a dated and overly strict conception of reading as linear and directed. As Sabine Gross (1994) has convincingly argued, the flexibility of eye movement in reading even a verbal text is not at all dissimilar from the roaming eye of the spectator of a picture or painting. Moreover, reading a text in any medium is always a dynamic hermeneutic process that combines bottom-up and top-down interpretive schemata.[13] The idea of linear reading therefore has to be discarded as myth. Graphic narrative in particular, with its infinite possibilities of arranging frames, panels, and individual scenes within frames and panels (including, but by no means limited to, arrangement in a sequence), should provide ample illustration for the necessity to employ a more dynamic and multileveled conception of reading that takes into

---

13 Cf. Gross 1994: 10, 12ff.

account the manifold schemata, assumptions, inferences, and hypotheses that readers rely on to impute narrative meanings to a sequence of images.[14]

Furthermore, the third page of *Preludes & Nocturnes* suggests that the interplay between elevated cut-out and background has to be considered in the context of the entire page frame and in relation to the mysterious source of light. Indeed, the "language" (Eisner 2008: 44) of the panel border is an important way in which comics and graphic novels often encode the ontology of that which is seen, i.e., action that is 'real' within the storyworld as opposed to subjective dreams, memories, and so forth, as well as the epistemology of its perception. Moreover, frames serve an important emotional function. By setting the mood of a panel, the frame directs the reader's affective and empathetic engagement with the scene and with the character whose experience it encodes. In many graphic novels, discordant or missing frames (i.e., the incongruent appearance of unframed panels in a dominantly framed context) are used to self-consciously mark flashbacks, dreams, hallucinations, or other forms of subjective representation from the perspective of one of the characters.[15]

In Charles Burns's *Black Hole* (2005), straight-edged frames indicate a realistic narration, while wavy-lined frames signal the representation of a character's subjective perception, of dreams, memories, and hallucinations. At times, straight and curvy framing combine around long, narrow panels that indicate the split between a character's social reality (bottom) and his or her fantasies (top) (see figure 5). This is an important distinction to make since the narrative is set in a weird storyworld in which a sexually transmitted "bug" is causing bizarre holes and disfigurations, distorting the physique of its protagonists, while characters are constantly slipping in and out of consciousness and frequently comment on the seeming irreality of their lives and world. Moreover, the narrative frequently jumps back and forth in time, so that readers have to negotiate a complex way through temporal layers and through the interlocking planes of objective and subjective narration. Indeed, one reviewer suggested that the entire narrative may be "imaginary" (Raney 2005: n.p.), stemming from the protagonist Keith's fainting episode early in the novel.

---

14 See Lefèvre 2000.
15 See Horstkotte and Pedri 2011; Thon 2014.

Figure 5: Charles Burns, *Black Hole* (2005). © Charles Burns. All rights reserved.

Like *Preludes & Nocturnes*, then, *Black Hole* projects a storyworld that is self-consciously preoccupied with what is and is not real. Because of its manifold prolepses and analepses and the inclusion of dream and fantasy sequences whose meaning often only becomes clear much later in the narrative, a linear understanding of sequentiality that sees a single panel mainly in a syntagmatic relationship with the previous and subsequent panel but does not account for the ways in which panels speak to each other across pages and entire chapters would be too reductive.

Braiding, Repetition, and the Memorable Panel

More productive than the doctrine of sequentiality is Thierry Groensteen's (2007) theory of braiding, which argues that graphic narrative puts every panel in a potential, if not actual, relation with every other. The relations between individual panels can be of an iconic as well as a rhetorical nature, and this results in a semantic overdetermination of graphic narrative: a single panel only acquires meaning in a sequence, but it is always part of multiple sequences of varying length, from the triad of preceding, current, and following panel through the "hyperframe" of an entire page and up to systems of panel proliferation such as the "multiframe" and the "multistage multiframe" (Groensteen 2007: 30–31; see also Hatfield 2005), which are increasingly inclusive. For instance, the recurrent use of metaphor and metonymy may connect panels across pages.[16] In *Black Hole*, the frequent appearance of snake imagery connects the different characters' working-through of their condition in one continuous collective imaginary of which the they themselves are, however, unaware.

The panel, then, has to be simultaneously read on at least three levels. According to Philippe Marion (1993), the panel is an expressive element traversed by two contradictory dimensions—the story (*fonction-récit*), which makes the spectator glide over the image, and the picture (*fonction-tableau*), which strives to focus the viewer's attention by isolating the image from the story. Thus, every panel addresses the reader on two complementary, sometimes contradictory levels, to which we must add a third function that refers the panel to the narrative structure in its entirety, thereby increasing the likelihood of a roaming, non-linear reading pattern. This is brought to particular attention in the case of "memorable" (Mikkonen 2010: 82) panels or series of panels—panels that are incongruent in form, style, or content with their syntagmatic surroundings or panels that are repeated in different contexts.

"Summer vacation," one of the chapters in *Black Hole* (which was originally published serially), ends with a death fantasy of one of the focal characters, Chris, who has been camping in the lepers' colony of those disfigured by the "bug"—an AIDS metaphor—for months. In this dream sequence, marked by the wavy frame lines as well as by Chris's running commentary in inserted text boxes, she wades into the waters of a lake through shards of broken glass, discarded skins (another symptom of the "bug"), and surreal snake parts. Finally, Chris imagines herself "floating on my back and I'm not scared anymore … There's nothing left to be scared of. I'm floating" (see figure 6).

---

16 Metaphor and metonymy in graphic narratives are further discussed in Kukkonen 2008.

Figure 6: Charles Burns, *Black Hole* (2005). © Charles Burns. All rights reserved.

In a graphic novel where many scenes refer forward and backward to each other, panels are frequently repeated with a difference, and episodes that were introduced through flash-forwards or flashbacks get retold from different points of view in the first narrative, the bottom two panels in this sequence stand out because they are repeated at the very end of the text, closing the book. These two scenes, separated by dozens of pages, cannot be understood apart from each other and from the minute differences between them. As indicated by the frame lines, the two panels first occur in a fantasy sequence, whereas the second scene is real, thereby opening up the possibility of a real, as opposed to an imagined, suicide. However, Chris ends up *not* killing herself, and the change of attitude toward her life is also apparent in the fact that she now *opens* her eyes, whereas she had moved to *close* them in her suicide fantasy. Even though the repetition with a difference thus signals an important change in Chris's evaluation of herself, her life, and the disease that has made her an outsider, the close visual echoes between the two sequences also highlight that this is just one of two possible endings and therefore not a necessary outcome: with no cure on the horizon, suicide remains an option.

Repetition also plays a key role in *Watchmen*, where Blake's murder—the central mystery of the novel—is narrated no less than three times in nearly identical sequences.[17] It occurs for the first time on the pages immediately following the narrative beginning that I outlined earlier in this chapter. As becomes clear quickly, however, the narrative of Blake's murder on these two pages is not depicted from the privileged narrative vantage point of an omniscient narrator but constitutes a visualization of two police detectives' interpretation of the murder scene. The narrative switches back and forth between two series of panels that are differentiated by their distinctive coloring and that stem from two different ontological orders. While the green, brown, and yellow panels showing the detectives at work refer to real events and characters in the storyworld, the alternating, monochromatically red panels indicate what *may* have happened if the detectives' suspicion that "the occupant was *home*," that "he would have put up *some* kind fight, I'm certain," and that "you'd have to be *thrown*" is right (see figure 7). Not only are the two series of panels based on distinct modes of enunciation and refer to the ontologically separate domains of the 'is' and the 'may have,' then, they also each combine in unique ways with the second, verbal track of the narrative, which reports the two detectives' dialogue in the form of direct speech in text bubbles and boxes (while the ironic combination with the commentary from Rorschach's journal on the previous page has dropped away).

The dynamic interaction between the visual and verbal has to be studied in the context of the entire graphic novel since it is only here that panels gain their full meaning. Although the sequence is almost identical each time it occurs, the variation in context—i.e., the alternating panels of the first narrative—and the reference of all three occurrences to each other as well as the minute variations of the series and their various combinations with different verbal tracks call for a more layered account than a linear understanding of sequentiality is able to provide. Where the first narration of the murder sequence placed it in the context of the police investigation of the putative murder scene, its repetition in the second chapter of *Watchmen* contextualizes it within the narrative of Blake's funeral as it is commented on by the mysterious character Rorschach, whose diary notes also opened the first chapter. This second repetition, like the first, is cast in a hypothetical mode, as it is doubtful, at this point in the narrative, whether Rorschach was a witness to the murder, whether he is the murderer, or whether the red sequence is, once again, the effect of hypothesizing. The alternating panels, too, tell not

---

17 See also Horstkotte and Pedri 2011.

what is, but constitute themselves as a subjective representation of Rorschach's memories of events in the 1940s. This embedding of one subjective representation within another may also account for the lower degree of tension between the coloring of the two alternating sequences.

Figure 7: Alan Moore and Dave Gibbons, *Watchmen* (2005).
© DC Comics. All rights reserved.

It is not until the third repetition of the red sequence that the identity of the murderer is revealed. This time, no questions arise as to the truth status of the panels, as they are accompanied by the spoken confession of Blake's murderer, Veidt. This revelatory function of the third repetition is illustrated when the sixth panel shows Veidt as he lifts Blake up above his head and is about to throw him out of the window. A final change is introduced into the sequence when the following panel, which shows

Blake going through the window, is reduced in size and moved to a less semantically charged position than the central one it had held in the previous sequences. This change refers readers back once more to the subjectivity of the focal character, in this case Veidt and his cynical disregard for the value of human life. The repetition of this sequence calls for a simultaneous reading of each individual sequence on not only two, but at least three and sometimes even four levels: (1) Individually, each panel deserves close and careful attention, as minute details and changes in content, color, and perspectival angle open up different interpretive possibilities. (2) Each panel is part of a sequence, narrating a self-contained series of events, unified by stylistic choices. In the case of the repeated murder sequence, the dominant unifying factor is the red color, which serves to establish mood and tone (red is the color of blood and violence in *Watchmen*). (3) Each sequence, moreover, has to be read in the larger context of a narrative and has to be interpreted with reference to its narratorial origin and its perspectivation. This is particularly pertinent for the murder sequence, both since the ontological and epistemological status of the first two repetitions remains underdetermined, and because the alternating arrangement with the panels of a first narrative causes readers to repeat the questioning of the red sequence with every shift forward and backward. However, similar interpretive operations, although less foregrounded, occur in all graphic narrative. (4) The three repetitions as well as their embedding speak to each other across chapters through a process of braiding, thereby necessitating a successive gathering of information while highlighting the preliminary status of all previous narrative information. While not all panels or sequences are as complexly embraided as the red murder sequence, the reevaluation of intradiegetic narratives or of subjective representations is actually a common operation in graphic novels, and the fourth level should therefore at least be considered, even if it remains optional.

To conclude, then, the position, color, shape, and framing of a panel are just some of the factors that contribute to its meaning, which it always acquires on several levels simultaneously, as the image within a panel has to be related to sequences of varying length and to other architectural units such as the page or the multi-page. It is this capacity to communicate on several levels simultaneously that has enabled the evolving segment of comics known as graphic novels to construct complex narratives that, while taking up impulses from literary and filmic storytelling, are less bound to linear restrictions. At the same time, graphic narrative's multi-layered communication constantly challenges readers' interpretive choices, and it therefore requires a sophisticated hermeneutics that remains an ongoing task for comics studies.

Works Cited

Berlatsky, Eric (2009). "Lost in the Gutter: Within and Between Frames in Narrative and Narrative Theory." *Narrative* 17.2: 162–87. Print.
Burns, Charles (2005). *Black Hole*. New York: Pantheon. Print.
Chatman, Seymour (1978). *Story and Discourse: Narrative Structure in Fiction and Film*. Ithaca: Cornell UP. Print.
Christiansen, Hans-Christian (2000). "Comics and Film: A Narrative Perspective." Anne Magnusson and Hans-Christian Christiansen (eds.). *Comics & Culture: Analytical and Theoretical Approaches to Comics*. Copenhagen: Museum Tusculanum P. 107–21. Print.
Ditschke, Stephan, Katerina Kroucheva, and Daniel Stein (eds.) (2009). *Comics: Zur Geschichte und Theorie eines populärkulturellen Mediums*. Bielefeld: transcript. Print.
Eisner, Will (2008). *Comics and Sequential Art: Principles and Practices from the Legendary Cartoonist*. New York: Norton. Print.
Ewert, Jeanne (2000). "Reading Visual Narrative: Art Spiegelman's *Maus*." *Narrative* 8.1: 87–103. Print.
Ferenz, Volker (2005). "Fight Clubs, American Psychos and Mementos: The Scope of Unreliable Narration in Film." *New Review of Film and Television Studies* 3.2: 133–59. Print.
Fludernik, Monika (1996). *Towards a "Natural" Narratology*. London: Routledge. Print.
Frahm, Ole (2010). *Die Sprache des Comics*. Hamburg: Philo Fine Arts.
Gaiman, Neil (2010). *The Sandman: Preludes & Nocturnes*. Vol. 1. Art by Sam Kieth, Mike Dringenberg, and Malcolm Jones III. Colors by Daniel Vozzo. Lettered by Todd Klein. Covers by Dave McKean. Originally published in single magazine form as *The Sandman* #1–8, 1988–1989. New York: DC Comics. Print.
Gardner, Jared (2011). "Storylines." Jared Gardner and David Herman (eds.). *Graphic Narratives and Narrative Theory*. Special issue of *SubStance* 40.1: 53–69. Print.
Grodal, Torben (1997). *Moving Pictures: A New Theory of Film Genres, Feelings, and Cognition*. Oxford: Clarendon. Print.
Groensteen, Thierry (2007). *The System of Comics*. Trans. Bart Beaty and Nick Nguyen. Jackson: UP of Mississippi. Print.
Gross, Sabine (1994). *Lese-Zeichen: Kognition, Medium und Materialität im Leseprozeß*. Darmstadt: Wissenschaftliche Buchgesellschaft. Print.
Hatfield, Charles (2005). *Alternative Comics: An Emerging Literature*. Jackson: UP of Mississippi. Print.

Hoppeler, Stephanie, Lukas Etter, and Gabriele Rippl (2009). "Intermedialität in Comics: Neil Gaimans *The Sandman.*" Stephan Ditschke, Katerina Kroucheva, and Daniel Stein (eds.). *Comics: Zur Geschichte und Theorie eines populärkulturellen Mediums.* Bielefeld: transcript. 53–79. Print.

Horstkotte, Silke, and Nancy Pedri (2011). "Focalization in Graphic Narrative." *Narrative* 19.3: 330–57. Print.

Kozloff, Sarah (1988). *Invisible Storytellers: Voice-Over Narration in American Fiction Film.* Berkeley: U of California P. Print.

Kress, Gunther, and Theo van Leeuwen (2001). *Multimodal Discourse: The Modes and Media of Contemporary Communication.* London: Arnold. Print.

Kukkonen, Karin (2008). "Beyond Language: Metaphor and Metonymy in Comics Storytelling." *English Language Notes* 46.2: 90–98. Print.

Lefèvre, Pascal (2000). "Narration in Comics." *Image & Narrative* 1.1: n.p. Web.

— (2011). "Some Medium-Specific Qualities of Graphic Sequences." Jared Gardner and David Herman (eds.). *Graphic Narratives and Narrative Theory.* Special issue of *SubStance* 40.1: 14–33. Print.

Marion, Philippe (1993). *Traces en cases.* Louvain-la-Neuve: Academia. Print.

McCloud, Scott (1993). *Understanding Comics: The Invisible Art.* New York: Harper Collins. Print.

McLuhan, Marshall (1964). *Understanding Media: The Extensions of Man.* New York: Signet. Print.

Meister, J. Christoph (2003). *Computing Action: A Narratological Approach.* Berlin: De Gruyter. Print.

Metz, Christian (1974). *Film Language: A Semiotics of the Cinema.* Oxford: Oxford UP. Print.

Mikkonen, Kai (2010). "Remediation and the Sense of Time in Graphic Narratives." Joyce Goggin and Dan Hassler-Forest (eds.). *The Rise and Reason of Comics and Graphic Literature: Critical Essays on the Form.* Jefferson: McFarland. 74–86. Print.

Moore, Alan (2005). *Watchmen.* Illustrated and lettered by Dave Gibbons. Colors by John Higgins. Originally published in single magazine form as *Watchmen* #1–12, 1986–1987. New York: DC Comics. Print.

Raney, Vanessa (2005). "Review of Charles Burns' 'Black Hole.'" *ImageTexT: Interdisciplinary Comics Studies* 2.1: n.p. Web.

Ryan, Marie-Laure (ed.) (2004). *Narrative across Media: The Languages of Storytelling.* Lincoln: U of Nebraska P. Print.

Sachs-Hombach, Klaus (2003). *Das Bild als kommunikatives Medium: Elemente einer allgemeinen Bildwissenschaft.* Köln: von Halem. Print.

Thon, Jan-Noël (2014). "Subjectivity across Media: On Transmedial Strategies of Subjective Representation in Contemporary Feature Films, Graphic Novels, and Computer Games." Marie-Laure Ryan and Jan-Noël Thon (eds.). *Storyworlds across Media: Toward a Media-Conscious Narratology*. Lincoln: U of Nebraska P. 67–102. Print.

Tomashevsky, Boris (1965). "Thematics." Lee T. Lemon and Marion J. Reis (eds.). *Russian Formalist Criticism: Four Essays*. Lincoln: U of Nebraska P. 61–95. Print.

KARIN KUKKONEN
(Turku)

Space, Time, and Causality in Graphic Narratives: An Embodied Approach[1]

Sometimes faster than a speeding bullet, sometimes slow like an elephant descending a staircase, comics present us with bodies moving through time and space. An embodied approach considers how the ways in which these bodies relate to and interact with each other and the world around them shape readers' perception of time, space, and causality in graphic narratives. To some extent, the embodied approach inverts the Kantian perspective that time and space structure human experience, which underlies much of the narratological understanding of these parameters,[2] and proposes that they arise as a consequence of readers' experience. This article will treat the time, space, and causality of the storyworlds of graphic narratives not as objective, external parameters but as emergent properties, related to the immediate physical resonances of drawn bodies, the texture of the emotional and social interaction of characters, and the gestalts of their composition on the page. Outlining an analytical perspective on these embodied features, I will then trace how they configure the storyworld's conceptual shape in graphic narratives.

The Great Svengali

Anything is possible in the dreamworlds that arise from Winsor McCay's experiments in the comics form. In one installment from *Dreams of the Rarebit Fiend* (16 Aug. 1905; see figure 1), the hypnotist Svengali moves a dreamer's body, defying gravity against the background of blank panels. While the name Svengali evokes the manipulating hypnotist of George Du

---

[1] Acknowledgements: This article emerges from my work in the Balzan Interdisciplinary Seminar "Literature as an Object of Knowledge" at St John's College (University of Oxford). I would like to thank Marco Caracciolo, Rikke Platz Cortsen, Sabine Müller, Emily Troscianko, and the editors of this volume for their kind and thoughtful comments on earlier drafts of this article.
[2] See Ryan 2012 for an overview.

Figure 1: Winsor McCay, *Dreams of the Rarebit Fiend* (16 Aug. 1905).

Maurier's highly popular novel *Trilby* (1894), the blank panels and the physical unnaturalness of the events on the comics page deny the standard reference points of space in narrative: there is no setting and, at first glance, no real-world experience against which we can model what we see on the page.[3] This throws the importance of the embodied dimension of reading time, space, and causality in comics into sharp relief because we can get a sense of time, space, and causality of the storyworld without the standard reference points of detailed setting and realism.

It all starts rather harmlessly, as the dreamer and Svengali look at each other in the first panel and then align their bodies to face each other in the second. In the third, Svengali makes his move: he leans forward and extends a hand toward the hapless dreamer. Svengali enters the personal space of the dreamer, who lurches backwards to avoid him. According to an embodied, enactive account of cognition, movements such as these "are the starting point from which our body *maps* the space that surrounds us, and it is due to their goal-directedness that space acquires form for us" (Rizzolatti and Sinigaglia 2008: 67, original emphasis). As Svengali approaches the dreamer, the dreamer protects himself by moving backwards and by raising his arms to protect his body. These movements respectively expand and diminish the personal space around the two characters, giving it shape. Their encounter becomes what Giacomo Rizzolatti and Corrado Sinigaglia term a dynamic system of relations.[4] Even if the characters do not actually touch, their interaction has all the intensity of a physical duel.

To a large extent, our perception is constituted by the way we (can) appropriate the space around us. "*Perceiving is an activity of exploring the environment drawing on an understanding of the ways in which one's movements affects one's sensory relation to things*" (Noë 2008: 663, original emphasis).[5] On this account, perception is not exclusively visual but involves the entire body. If we take Svengali and the dreamer as stand-ins for human experience once more, we see that their movements and their perception of the space around them are closely correlated. Perception is "a kind of skillful bodily activity," as Alva Noë (2004: 2) puts it, not a detached contemplation of the world or an achievement just of eye and brain. Considering the bodily activites of characters, readers can get a sense of how they perceive the storyworld around them, without having to read about their mental states in thought bubbles and without having to see the storyworld from their point of view. For the discussion of focalization and narration in visual

---

3   See again Ryan 2012 for a categorization of the uses of space in narrative.
4   Cf. Rizzolatti and Sinigaglia 2008: 77.
5   See O'Regan and Noë 2001; Noë 2004 for overviews of the sensorimotor account of perception.

media like comics and film, the embodied approach obviously holds great potential.[6]

As the perceived interaction potentials are realized, causality comes into play. Observers of the interaction can easily infer that Svengali's arm movement causes and controls the dreamer's movement once the hypnosis is successful. In a series of now famous experiments, Albert Michotte (1963)[7] demonstrated that our perception of causality depends on the so-called launching effect: one object moves until it reaches another object; then the second object begins to move. There are two distinct objects, but we perceive the spatio-temporal unity of one continuous motion, and our causal perception makes us see a single motion transferred, causally, from one object to the other, even if they do not actually collide. The investigations of Michotte and his followers suggest that our intuitive perception of causality allows us to relate the movement of the hypnotist's arm to that of the dreamer's body. A single motion seems to be transferred from one body to another because of the spatio-temporal unity of the movement, and we thereby perceive a causal relationship being established.

The facility with which I just related Michotte's moving dots to the bodies on the page (which in fact do not move) should give us pause. Even though this is a still image, the hypnotist's arm seems to exert forces of push and pull, and the dreamer's body seems to respond to them. All this happens, in Shaun Gallagher's memorable phrase, "*before we know it*" (2005: 2, original emphasis). This understanding is part of our 'body schema,' that is, the way in which our body shapes our perceptual field, integrates sensory information about our body moving through an environment and intracorporal information about our posture and movement.[8] The body schema gives us an immediate sense of being in space (and time), different from the body image, which is our reflected understanding of our body. What Gallagher calls the 'body schema' seems also to be at stake in the 'image schemata' identified particularly in visual art.[9] Image schemata, like 'balance,' relate to our immediate bodily experience of the world. When we see a perpendicular composition in an image, with clear horizontal and vertical lines of composition, this relates to our bodily experience of being perpendicular (thanks to gravity), and we literally experience the composition as 'balanced.' Viewers' bodily experience seems to relate directly to the depicted figures and their composition. Similarly, when the hypnosis takes effect in McCay's comic,

---

6 See Thomson-Jones 2012.
7 See also Wagemans, van Lier, and Scholl 2006.
8 Cf. Gallagher 2005: 38–39.
9 See Johnson 2007.

the dreamer's body follows the guidance of the hypnotist. It appears to have no muscle movement of its own but seems to follow Svengali's kinesic impetus. From their own physical experience of the forces of push and pull, readers understand that the gestures of the hypnotist control and direct the body of the dreamer.[10] Through the relay of their own embodied experience, readers understand the two-dimensional characters on paper as having bodies like theirs and as moving around in the space of the storyworld.

Interactions between bodies, compositional lines, and the implied movements of characters are closely entwined in comics. In the penultimate panel, Svengali loses control over the dreamer. His arm movement and the impetus of the dreamer's body disconnect, as Svengali raises his arm and the dreamer plunges headlong downwards. Svengali's body plays out the drama here: by contrast with the seventh and eighth panels, Svengali's gaze does not match the direction of his arm movement. The arm movement indicates the direction in which the gaze should have been going; the gaze diverted to the dreamer's body indicates that something has gone utterly wrong. This disjuncture also manifests itself on the level of composition. In the seventh and eighth panels, the dominant compositional lines of the bodies of the hypnotist and the dreamer match up. In the ninth panel, the hypnotist's body describes an upward diagonal whereas the dreamer describes a downward diagonal. Compositional lines, which can be related to Mark Johnson's 'image schemata,' are often rendered in bodies of characters and create an immediate bodily understanding of their (conceptual) relation to each other or to objects in the storyspace.[11] Again, in the ninth panel, causality goes back to the relation between the two bodies: the connection between the hynotist's arm and the dreamer's body has been cut, the compositional lines are at odds, and the hypnotist loses control.

Various research programs, from the work on 'mirror neurons' in our brains that fire in imitation when we perceive an action[12] to the investigation in 'motor resonance' that reading about (explicit and implicit) motion seems to elicit,[13] suggest that it is likely that readers of comics, too, experience bodily echoes of the motions and actions they observe. As The Great Svengali lurches toward the dreamer in the third panel, we experience the dreamer being literally 'taken aback,' and it is perhaps our own impulse which suggests a backwards movement when

---

10 Simply reading these motion verbs here might already give you a bodily sense of their effects, accoding to Glenberg and Kaschak 2002.
11 See especially Arnheim 2009 [1982].
12 See Gallese et al. 1996.
13 See Zwaan and Taylor 2006.

we look at the drawn figure. Just from the drawn individual images of Svengali's movements in the fifth, sixth, and seventh panel, we get a sense of how smooth and controlled they are. To some extent, readers run an 'embodied simulation' of the characters' bodies.[14]

Where does such an embodied account leave time, space, and causality in graphic narrative? Embodiment grounds time and space in terms of our perception, experience, and exploration of them, which are all closely interconnected. Space in comics unfolds on two levels, that of the storyspace represented in the panels and that of the arrangement of panels on the face of the page. Both spaces gain shape for readers through the action potentials of characters and the compositional lines in the mise-en-page, that is, the page layout. We relate our bodies in space, perceive the space around us in terms of available interaction potentials, and run embodied simulations of what we see on the page. Since our experience of space is best understood as an activity, it "plays out in time" (Noë 2006: 32) as well.

The measure of time in comics is notoriously difficult to pin down: sometimes a repetition of the same image in two panels indicates length, sometimes an elongated panel does, sometimes depending on the time it takes us to read the text in the speech bubble or to take in all the detail in a crowded panel. All these examples are taken from Scott McCloud, who states that "in the world of comics, time and space are one and the same" (1994: 100). However, as McCloud rolls out the measuring tape of time over the face of the page, matching the one on the other, he has to contend with Lessing's problem that while the image extends in space but is only a moment in time, the words (as visualized in speech bubbles) extend in both time and space. Thierry Groensteen (1999) tries to solve this problem by focusing on the spatial extension and the visual features of comics. He coins the term "système spatio-topique" (Groensteen 1999: 31) to refer to the actual and symbolic spatial extension and relations on the page, which for him take precedence over time. Order, time, and rhythm are supplied by the reader and by the order and duration in which the panels are read.[15]

On the embodied account of cognition, not only the order and duration of panel sequences, but also the individual panel itself can be considered as unfolding in both space and time.[16] Even if the panel image indicates only a single moment, the readers' engagements with the interaction potentials that the bodies imply make it unfold in time (this could be an embodied paraphrase of Lessing's notion of the 'pregnant

---

14   See Gallese 2011 on embodied simulation and fictional narratives.
15   Cf. Groensteen 1999: 43, 49, 64, 157–58.
16   See also Schüwer 2008.

moment'[17]). What we perceive, such as the push and the pull of the hypnotist's arm, remains "virtual," as Noë (2004: 215) puts it—it is not fully actualized but holds interaction potentials. The imprecise measures of time I introduced before indeed all point toward perceptual activities with these panels: long spaces for the eye to roam in, many words to read, and several interactions to consider. An objective measure this is not, but then an embodied account sees our experience of time and space as inherently subjective and tied to our bodily experience of the environment.

What Transports!

In a sense, the dreamer's body on the page acts as a proxy for readers' bodies. The hypnotist's movements manipulate readers' bodies as well as the dreamer's, and just as The Great Svengali transports the dreamer across the page, so too do the bodies on the comics pages transport readers. It is now time to complicate this account a bit. There is a distinction to be made between the bodies in the storyworld and the bodies on the page, and the verb "to transport" means more than just moving a body in space and time. First recorded in 1658, "being transported" also carries an emotional sense, that is, experiencing transports of joy, rage, or rapture, according to the *Oxford English Dictionary*. The bodies on the page therefore "transport" readers in three different ways: (1) they evoke readers' embodied simulations of being in the storyworld; (2) they make them experience the emotional involvements of the characters; (3) they guide them across the face of the page. On each of these levels, time, space, and causality enforce each other through the bodies on the page.

Transport into the Storyworld

Both the cognitive psychology of reading and cognitive narratology, mutually informed, have used the 'transport'-metaphor to refer to readers' understanding of storyworlds, one of the key concepts of transmedial narratology.[18] Richard Gerrig (1993) suggests that readers are 'transported' into storyworlds, Marie-Laure Ryan (2001) holds that we relocate our attention into fictional worlds when we are immersed, and David Herman

---

17 Cf. Lessing 2003 [1766]: 23.
18 See Herman 2009 and Ryan 2014.

(2002) suggests similarly that we realign our deictic center when we read. 'Deictic center' is a term from linguistics, denoting our sense of the here and now. For me, the here and now is my office chair and the piece of paper, as I write the first draft of this sentence. When I look at the comic, the here and now becomes the undefined location in which the dreamer and Svengali encounter each other. As I realign my deictic center, I relocate my attention into the storyworld and begin to process incoming information in terms of how it relates to other elements in the storyworld. Arguably, the mirror neurons which are firing when I consider the bodies of the dreamer and Svengali, or the motor resonance I experience, are connected to the perceptual and motorsensory processes underlying the interaction potentials which shape the storyworld, and thereby the characters' bodies on the page reinforce the sense of being transported.

Running an embodied simulation, however, does not mean that we mentally place our bodies completely into a different environment and that we create a continuous, high-definition mental image of this storyworld. Rather, it seems that we switch between the bodily echoes of different characters such as the dreamer and Svengali as the storyworld gains shape. As on a see-saw, we feel the hypnotist's lurch in the second panel and the dreamer's defense against it. We feel Svengali's smooth, controlled directions and the slack body of the dreamer kept afloat by their impetus. Even though the embodied response to these bodies involves a substantial degree of perspective-taking, by means of which readers develop a dense causal web of interactions, this probably does not lead to a mental representation of the storyworld that is continuous between panels.

In his discussion of closure, Scott McCloud states that "comics panels fracture both time and space, offering a jagged staccato rhythm of unconnected moments—but closure allows us to connect these moments and mentally construct a continuous, unified reality" (1994: 67). Through the capacity for closure, our minds fill in the events between panels, even to the extent of including other sensory modalities such as smell or touch. While it may be the case that we tend to construct a continuity of consciousness,[19] it seems unlikely that readers construct a high-definition, continuous mental representation of what happens between the panels. Anecdotally, we know that 'mistakes' between panels, such as swords changing hands, characters disappearing from the frame, or pieces of furniture being rearranged, are rarely noticed by comics readers. As research on 'change blindness'[20] suggests, human minds are rather poor at

---

19 See Dennett 1993.
20 See Rensink, O'Regan, and Clark 1997; Simons and Rensink 2005.

spotting changes in the visual world because our perception relies not just on our eyes but also on our bodies and motorsensory systems. Work in this area seems to suggest that if changes are to be noticed quickly, they need to be highlighted through verbal cues, through the attention of figures within the image or through indicators of motion. Speech bubbles, the deictic gazes of characters (like Svengali's in the ninth panel), and their moving bodies are such sources of attention in reading comics. On this account, comics readers would attend to causally relevant detail connecting the bodies, but not construct continuous, high-definition renditions of the storyworld between panels.[21] To counter McCloud's famous example of the axe murder between panels, readers probably do not "[hold] the axe," and they may well not "choose the spot" (1994: 68) unless it is shown in a panel image. While further research needs to be done on the specificity of embodied simulations, and thereby the degree of actual 'transportation,' the mind's difficulties with retaining and comparing visual information suggests that readers should be acquitted from McCloud's indictment for now.

Emotional Transport

These interactions between bodies in the storyworld are not mindless. The dreamer and Svengali are not billiard balls with faces and hats but characters to which we attribute (among other features) intentions and emotions.[22] Looking at the second, third, and forth panels, the dreamer's discourse in the speech bubble gives us much relevant information: he feels "funny" in the second panel, he is scared, angry and surprised in the third panel, and "fine," serene, and relaxed in the forth panel. This linguistic information serves to specify the embodied information readers get from the dreamer's bodily postures and facial expressions. It points to two functions that have been ascribed to emotions in psychology: they help us appraise a situation, and they confer a particular action readiness.[23] The dreamer's queasiness in the second panel is an appraisal of his situation; he does not know whether the hypnotist will not be dangerous for him. Hypnotism always involves a quantum of disbelief as to whether it is actually possible or not, and the dreamer's queasiness reflects this. It also outlines an action potential to him, in this instance, not to advance any further. In the next panel, his anger and surprise coincide with his

---

21 See Walsh 2006 for a similar argument.
22 See Eder 2010 for an overview of the kinds of features (cognitive, cultural, and generic) which contribute to characterization.
23 See Oatley, Keltner, and Jenkins 2006, esp. ch. 4 and ch. 7.

withdrawal. What Antonio Damasio (2006) calls 'somatic markers,' our bodily emotional responses, form part of our decision-making experience. As our facial expressions communicate emotions, they serve to inform others of our sense of the situation and our potential responses. The social cause and effect of behaviour is facilitated and communicated through emotions in the faces, bodies, and minds of the characters. The appraisal and action readiness that come with emotions and their somatic markers shape the social fabric of the storyworld.

Readers can gain a sense of these emotional processes through several sets of clues in comics: the words in the speech bubbles, the facial expressions of the characters, and their bodily postures. To a certain extent, readers empathize with the characters' emotions through simulation, which includes the appraisal and outline of potential responses. This embodied simulation can be understood as facilitated by the bodily echoes of mirror neurons and our body schemata. In other words, we do not only get a bodily echo of the movements of characters through time and space in the storyworld, but also of their emotional movement in the social fabric.[24] The intentional and emotional causality that runs through human interactions, prompting us to ascribe intentions to others (through what is known as 'theory of mind')[25] and leading us to connect emotions, intentions, and actions, gives rise to our perception of social causality. This, in turn, contributes to the meaningful enchainment of events in a story, as E. M. Forster's minimal example of plot suggests: "The king died and then the queen died of grief" (1949: 82).

Transport across the Page

The bodies of Svengali and the dreamer do not only move around in the space of the storyworld, which is represented in the individual panels. They also move on the surface of the page. Readers arguably take in an entire comics page before devoting their attention to the individual panels, and the dynamics between the entire layout of a page and the individual panels are a much-discussed issue in comics studies.[26] On the left-hand column of panels, readers see at one glance how the body of the dreamer is more and more destabilized through the compositional lines. As follows from the discussion of image schemata in the first section, we recognize balanced or unbalanced compositions in images immediately because we

---

[24] See Gallese, Eagle, and Migone 2007 for an overview of research on these issues and their interconnectedness.
[25] See Goldman 2006 for a simulation-based take on theory of mind.
[26] See Peeters 1998 or Groensteen 1999.

respond to them with our own bodily sense of being in balance, that is, responding evenly to gravity. After the stable, perpendicular composition of the first panel, in the third panel, the dreamer leans back and gets slightly destabilized. In the fifth panel, he leans forward again at a yet steeper angle. The see-saw movement continues in the seventh and ninth panel in escalating scope until the body of the dreamer seems completely reversed in direction. That is to say, he describes a 180-degree flip between these two panels. Like a whirligig, the body of the dreamer swerves away from the ideal perpendicular line until he topples for good. This basic pattern, placed in the prominent left-hand column of the panels, communicates to readers at one glance the gist of the page and its basic causality: through the hypnotist, the dreamer's world is more and more destabilized until it is finally shaken out of kilter.

There is another pattern discernible on the *Dreams of the Rarebit Fiend* page. It is laid out in a regular pattern of two by five panels. The dreamer's body describes an approximate circle across the fifth to the eighth panels as they are arranged on the page. Svengali's control of the dreamer's body seems to have no discernible beginning and ending, like the circle in which the dreamer's body seems to move. If these four panels were laid out differently, however, we would notice that neither the dreamer's body nor the hypnotist's movements describe a circle. In fact, the hypnotist moves in a sideways sweep to align the dreamer's body in front of him between panels four and five, and then from right to left, moving the dreamer's body in a 180-degree flip from lying on his belly in panel five to lying on his back in panel six. Lying on his belly and lying on his back are two likely positions the dreamer will take in his sleep. McCay presents a double scheme of embodiment here: the dreamer's actual bodily movement in bed, referred to in the 180-degree flip, and the dreamer's bodily experience as he dreams, in the endless circle free from gravity. Both schemes of embodiment rely on the patterns which the bodies configure on the face of the page. The ways in which the panel layout arranges bodies prompts readers to perceive movement between panels and thereby engages the body schemata of readers, thus contributing to the embodied reading experience in comics. The actual space of the page turns out to be just as much an arena of embodiment and readerly transportation as the storyspace represented in the panels.

Situated in a Hall of Mirror Neurons

Through his use of space, time, and causality in *Dreams of the Rarebit Fiend*, Winsor McCay creates what Lawrence Barsalou (2003, 2008) calls 'situated conceptualization.' According to Barsalou, we process concepts not as abstract, detached conglomerates of features but as "agent-dependent instruction manuals" (2008: 244) to run an embodied simulation. These embodied simulations are tied to the context of particular situations, which include objects and agents involved; actions and bodily states; motivations, emotions, and cognitive operations; and, often, settings.[27] In Barsalou's model, thinking about concepts like 'dog,' 'truth,' or 'chair' (Barsalou's examples) means placing ourselves in a situation with them. Through the embodied simulations he evokes in *Dreams of the Rarebit Fiend*, McCay places readers in the situation of the dreamer, as he loses control of his body to the hypnotist, experiences the double embodiment, and finally wakes up when the swerve of destabilization goes too far. Reading the comic in terms of a situated conceptualization brings the individual elements of my analysis together: embodiment and composition contribute here to create an embodied simulation of dreaming in which time, space, and causality are shaped in a particular pattern. Dreaming can be experienced as a loss of control, here in the push and pull of the hypnotist, as a floating feeling, here in the freedom from gravity for the dreamer, and as a seemingly endless circle, here in the arrangement of the four panels. McCay's presentation of a double scheme of movement, circle and tossing, renders the double bodily presence of the dreamer in bed and in the experience of the dream.

During the dream, in the circle of the fifth to ninth panel, the bodily experience of floating free from gravity is foregrounded over the 180-degree flip of the body itself, which is much more difficult to discern on the comics page. In the final panel, however, this foregrounding is reversed. As the action leaves the storyworld of the dream and takes us back into the real world, the circle is broken and the actual physical movement of the 180-degree flip comes to the fore again. This change in foregrounding in the double scheme of embodiment coincides with other events. The detailed setting of the last panel and the disappearance of the hypnotist establish the new, realist storyworld over the previous dream storyworld. The fall out of bed, or rather, the dreamer's impact on the floor, changes the state of consciousness of the protagonist, revealing the previous to have been a dream. Time and space, the deictic parameters of the world in which we just found ourselves, are abruptly discontinued, and

---

27 Cf. Barsalou 2008: 245.

a new set of deictic parameters asserts itself. The dreamer is jolted from one storyworld to another, or rather, the framework within which he moves changes abruptly. This abrupt transition simulates for readers the experience of waking up. With the coincidence of the switch from experienced to actual embodiment, the change of setting, the return of gravity, and the awakening of the dreamer, the situated conceptualization of dreaming is brought to its most obvious conclusion—the dreamer wakes up.

Perhaps no other comics author has worked on dreams and sleeping as much as Winsor McCay. In his series *Dreams of the Rarebit Fiend* (1904–1905), he chronicles the bad dreams that digesting a Welsh rarebit can give you, and in *Little Nemo in Slumberland* (1905–1914), he follows the gorgeous and colorful dreams of a little boy. Both series feature the basic traits that I have identified here: the effortless sequences of characters' movements, seemingly unaffected by gravity; the patterns of order and disorder, balance and imbalance; and the characteristic jolt at the end of the comic that takes us back into the real world. McCay proliferates variations of these basic traits in his various series, as he explores different embodied renditions of the situated conceptualization of dreaming.

The notion of situated conceptualization provides a feedback loop between immediate embodied experience and more abstract conceptual reflections. In both respects, cognition is grounded in the body and gives rise to particular patterns of time, space, and causality through which the storyworld is experienced. Along this feedback loop, we can trace analytically how details of characters' bodies and their composition on the page contribute to the shape of the storyworld and to the larger conceptual point the author might want to make.

While McCay's rendition of a situated conceptualization of dreaming addresses a rather straightforward, everyday concept, other comics present more specific and abstract concepts. Consider Warren Ellis and J. H. Williams III's situated conceptualization of "supermodernism" in *Desolation Jones* (see figure 2). Jones explains the concept of supermodernism to his assistant Robina in his discourse in the speech bubbles. Through the constellation of time, space, and causality on the page, however, readers are given an embodied experience of the concept as well. Supermodernism is the architectural equivalent of what Zygmunt Bauman (2005) calls 'liquid society': a world in which nothing is stable anymore—no social structures, no lasting work relationships, and no permanent homes.

Figure 2: Warren Ellis and J. H. Williams III, *Desolation Jones: Made in England* (2008). ™ and © Warren Ellis and J. H. Williams III. Used with permission of DC Comics. All rights reserved.

In the world of supermodernism, we are continuously on the move, and the page from *Desolation Jones* represents just such a constellation of time, space, and causality. The dominant line, in red in the original comic, moves readers through the page. It is a sideline on the road, a reflection in Jones's glasses and a route on the map in the middle of the page, each referring to the trajectory of their trip across town. The line also describes the reading path throughout the page and ties the individual panels together in a smooth and clear movement. Jones's deictic gazes, an important indicator for readers as to what to look at, direct our attention along the path of the line as well. Each of these elements evokes a sense of flow and movement. The page, with its sophisticated use of embodied cues and situated conceptualization, brings readers into what we could playfully term a 'hall of mirror neurons,' where they experience the transience of supermodernism in their bodies as they read this page.

Conclusions

With my final outline of how the experience of supermodernism emerges out of the particular ways in which the embodied elements of the page shape the time, space, and causality of the storyworld, I have arrived at what Ryan calls the "thematization of space" (2012: n.p.) As Ryan puts it, "[t]he lived experience of space offers a particularly rich source of thematization" (2012: n.p.). An embodied account of comics proposes that this experience of space is not a given (that can be violated in unnatural or metafictional narratives), but emerges from each reading in the explorative and embodied perception of the page and forms meaningful patterns of situated conceptualization both in realist and non-realist storyworlds. It stretches through all levels of storyworld construction and is not tied to thematic aspects only.

A phenomenological perspective on time and space in comics like Martin Schüwer's (2008) posits similarly that the parameters of the storyworld emerge from our perception of it, and there are many points of contact between Schüwer's approach and mine. However, whereas Schüwer distinguishes (analytically) between *Bewegungsbild* (images of linear, sequential motion), *Zeitbild* (more distancing, contemplative conceptual images), and other categories, my embodied account stresses that each of the aspects of embodiment works as a layer running through every panel: interaction potentials, somatic markers, composition, and situated conceptualization. An embodied analysis of comics like McCay's *Dreams of the Rarebit Fiend* can draw on cognitive sciences' detailed vocabulary for each of these layers and highlight the connections between them.

Embodiment on the basis of our body schema, namely, our preconscious capacities of proprioception, posture, and movement, which I have discussed in this chapter, is only one of the multiple aspects which the body can take.[28] McCay's comic isolates this aspect, and I consider it most central for the way in which readers perceive time, space, and causality in comics. However, other aspects of bodies can become salient, for example, in relation to setting and geometrical perspective in space (on which Schüwer has much to say) or in relation to social and cultural bodies and chronotopes.[29] This chapter has offered a basic outline of the scope and possible applications of an embodied perspective on comics that opens up a new dimension of mimesis to be explored through motor resonance, embodied simulation, and situated conceptualization.

Works Cited

Arnheim, Rudolf (2009 [1982]). *The Power of the Center: A Study of Composition in the Visual Arts*. Berkeley: U of California P. Print.

Barsalou, Lawrence W. (2003). "Situated Simulation and the Human Conceptual System." *Language and Cognitive Processes* 18.5–6: 513–62. Print.

— (2008). "Situating Concepts." Philipp Robbins and Murat Ayede (eds.). *Cambridge Handbook of Situated Cognition*. Cambridge: Cambridge UP. 236–63. Print.

Bauman, Zygmunt (2005). *Liquid Life*. Cambridge: Polity Press. Print.

Cortsen, Rikke P. (2011). "Multiple Living, One World? On the Chronotope in Alan Moore and Gene Ha's *Top 10*." *Studies in Comics* 2.1: 135–46. Print.

Damasio, Antonio (2006). *Descartes' Error: Emotion, Reason, and the Human Brain*. London: Vintage. Print.

Dennett, Daniel (1993). *Consciousness Explained*. London: Penguin. Print.

Eder, Jens (2010). "Understanding Characters." *Projections* 4.1: 16–40. Print.

Ellis, Warren (2008). *Desolation Jones 1: Made in England*. Art by J. H. Williams III. New York: DC Wildstorm. Print.

Forster, E. M. (1949). *Aspects of the Novel*. London: E. Arnold. Print.

Gallagher, Shaun (2005). *How the Body Shapes the Mind*. Oxford: Oxford UP. Print.

---

28 Cf. also Johnson 2007: 274–78.
29 See Cortsen 2011 for an example of this approach.

Gallese, Vittorio (2011). "Embodied Simulation Theory: Imagination and Narrative." *Neuropsychoanalysis* 13.2: 196–200. Print.
Gallese, Vittorio, Morris N. Eagle, and Paolo Migone (2007). "Intentional Attunement: Mirror Neurons and the Neural Underpinnings of Interpersonal Relations." *Journal of the American Psychoanalytic Association* 55: 131–78. Print.
Gallese, Vittorio, Luciano Fadiga, Leonardo Fogassi, and Giacomo Rizzolatti (1996). "Action Recognition in the Premotor Cortex." *Brain* 119: 593–609. Print.
Gerrig, Richard (1993). *Experiencing Narrative Worlds: On the Psychological Activities of Reading*. New Haven: Yale UP. Print.
Glenberg, Arthur M., and Michael B. Kaschak (2002). "Grounding Language in Action." *Psychonomic Bulletin and Review* 9.3: 558–65. Print.
Goldman, Alvin (2006). *Simulating Minds: The Philosophy, Psychology, and Neuroscience of Mindreading*. Oxford: Oxford UP. Print.
Groensteen, Thierry (1999). *Système de la bande dessinée*. Paris: PU de France. Print.
Herman, David (2002). *Story Logic: Problems and Possibilities of Narrative*. Lincoln: U of Nebraska P. Print.
— (2009). *Basic Elements of Narrative*. Chichester: Wiley-Blackwell. Print.
Johnson, Mark (2007). *The Meaning of the Body: Aesthetics of Human Understanding*. Chicago: U of Chicago P. Print.
Lessing, Gotthold E. (2003 [1766]). *Laokoon oder über die Grenzen der Malerei und Poesie*. Stuttgart: Reclam. Print.
McCay, Winsor (2002). *Early Works*. Miamisburg: Checkers. Print.
McCloud, Scott (1994). *Understanding Comics: The Invisible Art*. New York: Harper Perennial. Print.
Michotte, Albert (1963). *The Perception of Causality*. London: Methuen. Print.
Noë, Alva (2004). *Action in Perception*. Cambridge: MIT Press. Print.
— (2006). "Experience of the World in Time." *Analysis* 66.1: 26–32. Print.
— (2008). "Precis of *Action in Perception*." *Philosophy and Phenomenological Research* LXXVI.3: 660–65. Print.
Oatley, Keith, Dacher Keltner, and Jennifer M. Jenkins (2006). *Understanding Emotions*. 2nd edition. Malden: Blackwell. Print.
O'Regan, J. Kevin, and Alva Noë (2001). "A Sensorimotor Account of Vision and Visual Consciousness." *Behavioral and Brain Sciences* 24: 939–73. Print.
Peeters, Benoît (1998). *Case, planche, récit: Lire la bande dessinée*. Paris: Casterman. Print.

Rensink, Robert A., J. Kevin O'Regan, and James J. Clark (1997). "To See or Not to See: The Need for Attention to Perceive Changes in Scenes." *Psychological Science* 8.5: 368–73. Print.
Rizzolatti, Giacomo, and Corrado Sinigaglia (2008). *Mirrors in the Brain: How Our Minds Share Actions, Emotions and Experience.* Oxford: Oxford UP. Print.
Ryan, Marie-Laure (2001). *Narrative as Virtual Reality: Immersion and Interactivity in Literature and Electronic Media.* Baltimore: Johns Hopkins UP. Print.
— (2012). "Space." Peter Hühn, J. Christoph Meister, John Pier, and Wolf Schmid (eds.). *living handbook of narratology.* Hamburg: Hamburg UP. N.p. Web.
— (2014). "Story/Worlds/Media: Tuning the Instruments of a Media-Conscious Narratology." Marie-Laure Ryan and Jan-Noël Thon (eds.). *Storyworlds across Media: Toward a Media-Conscious Narratology.* Lincoln: U of Nebraska P. 25–49. Print.
Schüwer, Martin (2008). *Wie Comics erzählen: Grundriss einer intermedialen Erzähltheorie der grafischen Literatur.* Trier: Wissenschaftlicher Verlag Trier. Print.
Simons, Daniel J., and Robert A. Rensink (2005). "Change Blindness: Past, Present, and Future." *Trends in Cognitive Science* 9.1: 16–20. Print.
Thomson-Jones, Katherine J. (2012). "Narration in Motion." *British Journal of Aesthetics* 52.1: 31–43. Print.
"Transport n." (2012). *Oxford English Dictionary.* N.p. Web.
Wagemans, Johan, Rob van Lier, and Brian J. Scholl (2006). "Introduction to Michotte's Heritage in Cognition and Perception Research." *Acta Psychologica* 123: 1–19. Print.
Walsh, Richard (2006). "Narrative Imagination across Media." Hillary Chute and Marianne DeKoven (eds.). *Graphic Narrative.* Special issue of *Modern Fiction Studies* 52.4: 855–68. Print.
Zwaan, Rolf A., and Lawrence J. Taylor (2006). "Seeing, Acting, Understanding: Motor Resonance in Language Comprehension." *Journal of Experimental Psychology: General* 135.1: 1–11. Print.

JAN-NOËL THON
(Tübingen)

Who's Telling the Tale?
Authors and Narrators in Graphic Narrative

Comics tell stories. Not just some comics, either, but most if not all of them—from the *histoires en estampes* of Rodolphe Töpffer and the newspaper strips of Winsor McCay to their more recent incarnations in the form of graphic novels or webcomics. Indeed, one might be tempted to use *graphic narrative* as a synonym for *comics*, with non-narrative comics—if there is such a thing—being confined to the outskirts of what we would consider prototypical forms of the medium.[1] Strangely enough, however, a medium-specific comics narratology still appears fairly underdeveloped when compared to literary and film narratology, even though there has been an increasing interest in the intersection of comics studies and narrative theory in the past decade or so.[2]

Located within a larger project on transmedial narratology, the present chapter aims to contribute to such a comics narratology by examining 'who's telling the tale' in graphic narrative.[3] I will begin by giving a brief survey of the concept of the narrator as it has been developed in literary narratology and film narratology, followed by analyses of what can be considered prototypical uses of narrators in contemporary graphic novels. Finally, I will examine 'who's telling the tale' in cases where (elements of) the narrative representation cannot be attributed to a more or less explicitly represented narrator, arguing that we attribute such elements to hypothetical authors or author collectives, instead.

---

1 I use the term medium as referring to conventionally distinct media *sensu* Rajewsky 2010, emphasizing what Ryan calls "a cultural point of view" (2006: 23). While comics are clearly a medium in this sense, graphic narrative could arguably be conceptualized in this way, too.
2 See the introduction to this volume for further remarks on the aims and scope as well as on the general state of comics narratology as a specialized field of comics studies. For some further discussion of the project of transmedial narratology, see Thon 2014b, 2014c.
3 In fact, I will mainly focus on graphic novels, even though what should or should not be called a graphic novel continues to be a matter of debate. One way or another, it seems evident that the narrative strategies realized in prototypical graphic novels can, at least in principle, also be found in other forms of graphic narrative. On what I would consider 'contemporary graphic novels,' see also e.g., Gravett 2005; Weiner 2010.

The Concept of the Narrator[4]

In literary narratology, the concept of the narrator is strongly connected to the idea that narrative texts should be treated not merely as communication, but as 'communicated communication,'[5] not merely as representation, but as represented representation. Or, as Wolf Schmid remarks, "a narrative work does [not] just narrate, but represents an act of narration" (2010: 33, my typo correction). However, even when we focus exclusively on literary texts, it soon becomes clear that the modes in which acts of narration—and, therefore, narrators—are represented differ widely. As the works of Gérard Genette and others have established by now, literary narrators may not only be located on various diegetic levels and may be more or less strongly involved in the stories they tell (allowing us to distinguish between extradiegetic and intradiegetic as well as between heterodiegetic and homodiegetic narrators),[6] but they may also represent themselves explicitly or implicitly through their narration (allowing us to describe narrators as more or less overt or covert).[7]

But what *is* a narrator? What do we mean when we say that a narrator 'tells the tale' of a literary text or a graphic narrative? Considering the spatial limitations inherent in the present chapter's form and its focus on narrators in graphic narrative, I cannot discuss the development of the concept of the narrator in literary narratology in too much detail here. But I would like to at least briefly examine two major lines of 'post-Genettean' arguments regarding the concept of the narrator. On the one hand, narratologists such as Richard Walsh emphasize the (self-)representation of a narrating character who is clearly distinct from the author as a necessary condition for speaking of a narrator.[8] On the other hand, narratologists such as Richard Aczel propose an understanding of the term 'narrator' as referring to a bundle of occasionally rather basic narratorial functions ranging from the selection, organization, and (re)presentation of elements of the storyworld to evaluative comments and self-characterizations of a narrating character.[9]

Walsh's position boils down to understanding the concept of the narrator as exclusively referring to (narrating) characters: "There is nothing about the internal logic of fictional representation that demands a qualitative distinction between narrators and characters. Such narrators,

---

4 Thon 2014c discusses much of the following from a transmedial perspective.
5 See Janik 1973.
6 Cf. e.g., Genette 1980: 212–62, 1988: 79–129; Schmid 2010: 57–78, 175–215.
7 Cf. e.g., Chatman 1978: 198–262; Schmid 2010: 57–78.
8 See Walsh 1997, 2007, 2010.
9 See Aczel 1998.

being represented, *are* characters" (1997: 498, original emphasis). While Walsh's insistence that we ascribe the verbal narration in literary narrative texts either to a narrating character or to the author seems plausible at first glance,[10] he may be overstating his case when he claims that extradiegetic heterodiegetic narrators "cannot be represented without thereby being rendered homodiegetic or intradiegetic" and that, therefore, these 'non-represented' narrators "are in no way distinguishable from the author" (1997: 510–11). Walsh certainly has a point regarding the somewhat problematic in-between status of the 'extradiegetic level,' but extradiegetic narrators can, at least in literary narrative texts, *by definition* be represented through their own narration without necessarily being homodiegetic or becoming intradiegetic narrators.

The core question raised here, then, seems to be what we mean when we say that narrators are (and have to be) more or less explicitly 'represented' by a narrative representation, literary or otherwise: what are the 'cues' that allow us to assume the presence of a narrator to whom we can ascribe the (verbal) narration? Despite being increasingly contested by Walsh and others, the common view that (fictional) verbal narration in literary texts "always provides symptoms, no matter how weak they may be" (Schmid 2010: 64), that allow the reader to construct a (fictional) speaker as distinct from the author may remain defensible with regard to literary narrative texts.[11] When transferred to graphic narrative, however, such a view becomes even less plausible, since the former is not limited to verbal narration and, hence, does not as easily or self-evidently activate the cognitive schema underlying what Ansgar Nünning has described as the 'mimesis of narration'[12]—i.e., the impression that (fictional) verbal narration is, indeed, the representation of an act of representation.

Aczel therefore argues for a clear distinction between the concepts of 'voice' and 'narrator': "A text either has a narrator or it hasn't, but voice is a relative category: it can be more or less strongly detectable. If narrative voice is the (effective) *means* of identifying a narrator function as such, the two must necessarily be held as discrete" (1998: 490, original emphasis).

---

10 "The narrator is always either a character who narrates or the author. There is no intermediate position. The author of a fiction can adopt one of two strategies: to narrate a representation or to represent a narration" (Walsh 1997: 505). However, see the work of Lanser 1981 for a discussion of how readers may often actually ascribe the narration in literary narrative texts to both a narrating character and the author. Lanser's elegant discussion of the both/and logic of attributing authorial and narratorial voices is also taken up in Branigan's (1992) influential work on film narration.
11 For critical voices, see also e.g., Lanser 1981; Banfield 1983; Kania 2005; as well as the concise survey and critical discussion in Köppe and Stühring 2011.
12 See Nünning 2001 as well as Bareis 2006. See also Schüwer 2008, who takes a position similar to my own on narratorial representation in graphic narrative.

However, if one follows Walsh's argument that authors can choose to either "narrate a representation or represent a narration" (1997: 505), it remains questionable whether "style necessarily evokes a subjective center" (Aczel 1998: 472) different from the author. As Aczel (1998: 492) remarks himself:

> The issue here is at least partly terminological. If one chooses to restrict the term "narrator" to an identifiable teller persona, then there ostensibly are narratorless narratives. This does not, however, address the problem of to whom one attributes functions of (nonpersonified) selection, organization, and comment. I prefer to see the "narrator" as an umbrella term for a cluster of possible functions, of which some are necessary (the selection, organization, and presentation of narrative elements) and others optional (such as self-personification as teller, comment, and direct reader/narratee address).

Though the 'narratorial functions' Aczel identifies are evidently important for graphic narrative, as well, the proposal to use the term 'narrator' as an umbrella term for a bundle of 'narratorial functions' seems unsatisfactory both from a conceptual and from a terminological perspective, as it prevents a clear distinction between the (obligatory) presence of (the results or traces of) processes of selection, organization, and presentation of storyworlds elements, on the one hand, and the (facultative) presence of a (verbally realized) narratorial voice that is distinct from that of the author, on the other. Perhaps not surprisingly, then, I propose to follow Walsh, Fotis Jannidis, and others in *generally* treating narrators as constructs "organized in the form of characters" (Jannidis 2006: 159; my translation from the German: "in figuraler Gestalt organisiert") while at the same time acknowledging that these 'narrating characters' do *not* always have to be fully realized.[13] Accordingly, readers of graphic narratives and literary texts alike can construct a 'narrating character' even if there are only very few, conflicting, or problematic cues given by the narration. One of the very basic cues that is nearly always necessary, however,—and that literary narratologists, for obvious reasons, tend to take for granted—seems to be the presence of verbal narration that we can ascribe to a 'speaker.'

On a fairly general level, then, it might be helpful to distinguish between, first, *narratorial representation* as referring to the kind of verbal narration attributable to a more or less explicitly represented (usually fictional) narrator-as-narrating-character that is distinct from the author, second, *authorial representation* as referring to the kind of verbal narration attributable not to such a narrator but rather to an authoring character that functions 'as narrator,' and, third, *non-narratorial representation* as referring, for example, to the kind of verbal-pictorial representation in panels or sequences of panels, which is evidently also the result of a

---

13 For a survey of current research on characters, see Eder, Jannidis, and Schneider 2010.

process of creation but whose 'source' is usually not—or at least not explicitly—represented and whose multimodal configuration prevents us from attributing it to a 'speaker' as readily as is the case with exclusively verbal forms of narration. The distinction between narratorial and authorial representation as two modes of verbal representation may occasionally be difficult to draw, and extradiegetic heterodiegetic narrators can be so 'covert' that their respective 'voices' may be interpreted as either narratorial or authorial representation, but the question to whom we can attribute non-narratorial representation turns out to be no less complex.

Comics studies have only just begun to give the problem of non-narratorial verbal-pictorial representation the attention it undoubtedly deserves.[14] Following Philippe Marion's groundbreaking *Traces en cases* (1993), there have been several more recent attempts to come to terms with this mode of representation by positing some kind of 'elusive enunciator' that mainly manifests itself through the traces left in the results of an act of enunciation.[15] While Marion's notion of 'graphiation' as "a set of graphic markers evoking the presence of a drawing instance" (Surdiacourt 2012: 174) may, indeed, help us get a clearer idea of the medium-specific ways in which graphic narrative narrates by emphasizing that its pictures are *drawn*, graphic enunciation theories tend to blur the line between (hypothetical) authors and (implicit) narrators. For the time being, however, it may suffice to stress that the 'elusive enunciators' identified by Marion and others are very different from the narrators-as-narrating-characters that the present chapter primarily examines.[16]

---

14 However, the question to whom we can attribute the audiovisual representation of storyworlds in the feature film has, of course, been extensively discussed in film studies, where the concept of a more or less intangible 'image-maker,' 'grand imagier,' 'enunciator,' 'implied,' 'cinematic,' or otherwise 'elusive' narrator has not only enjoyed astonishing longevity but also generated a great amount of controversy. Cf. e.g., Chatman 1990: 124–38; Metz 1991; Branigan 1992: 86–100; Gaudreault and Jost 1999; Wilson 2007; Gaudreault 2009; and the surveys by Thomson-Jones 2007, 2009.

15 See Marion 1993; Baetens 2001; Groensteen 2010, 2013; Surdiacourt 2012. See also Mikkonen 2015, who takes a more cautious approach to 'narrative agency.'

16 Incidentally, it should be noted that Marion 1993 as well as Baetens 2001 and Surdiacourt 2012 seem to understand the 'graphiator' (as well as the 'monstrator') of a graphic narrative as being closer to some kind of hypothetical author (or 'implied author' or 'author function') than to a narrator-as-narrating-character, which at least Marion explicitly distinguishes from the former. Groensteen, however, not only argues that the distinction between a 'monstrator' and a 'graphiator' is redundant but also assumes the existence of a 'narrator' as "the ultimate authority that is responsible for the selection and organization of all the information that makes up the storytelling" (2010: 14). I do not believe that calling such a 'hypothetical-author-in-disguise' a 'narrator' will prove particularly helpful and, hence, do not agree with Surdiacourt's claim that "Groensteen's model is convincing" (2012: 175).

So, apart from these 'implied-narrators-as-elusive-enunciators,' what different types of narrators-as-narrating-characters can one distinguish in both literary and graphic narrative? As is well known, Genette identifies an 'extradiegetic level' on which a primary 'extradiegetic narrator' is located. That 'extradiegetic narrator' narrates the first-order storyworld (or 'diegetic level'), on which a secondary 'intradiegetic narrator,' who narrates a second-order storyworld (or 'metadiegetic level'), may be located.[17] While this distinction refers to the *absolute* ontological position of a narrator in the system of diegetic levels or sub-worlds that make up what Marie-Laure Ryan would call a 'narrative universe,'[18] Genette discusses the *relative* ontological position of narrators with regard to the story they narrate, as well: heterodiegetic narrators are not part of the story they narrate; homodiegetic narrators are part of that story.[19] Now, there are obvious problems with that distinction, in that it accounts neither for the rather subtle differences of involvement that homodiegetic narrators may exhibit nor for the difference between a narrator who is not part of the story she narrates and a narrator who is not part of the story*world* she narrates.[20] Nevertheless, the distinction itself is certainly useful and can, at least in principle, be retained for narrators in graphic narrative. While the distinction between heterodiegetic and homodiegetic as well as that between overt and covert narrators (mentioned earlier) can be transferred to 'verbal' narrators in graphic narrative without major modification, however, the distinction between extradiegetic and intradiegetic narrators does not apply in the same way to multimodal narrative representations as it does to purely verbal narrative representations.

One of the consequences of limiting the term 'narrator' to refer to 'narrating characters' in the sense sketched above is that, in multimodal narrative in general and graphic narrative in particular, we can encounter intradiegetic narrators without having previously encountered an

---

17 Cf. Genette 1980: 227–34, 1988: 84–95. Genette's use of the prefix 'meta-' to refer to a hierarchical relation more aptly described by the prefix 'hypo-' has been criticized by Bal 1981, whose proposal to use the term 'hypodiegetic' instead was taken up by e.g., Rimmon-Kenan 2002. Considering that Genette's terms still appear decidedly more often, and that using 'metadiegetic' and 'hypodiegetic' interchangeably would only add to the confusion, however, it may be preferable to minimize using these 'technical' terms altogether, instead speaking of first-order storyworlds (narrated by extradiegetic or primary narrators), second-order storyworlds (narrated by intradiegetic or secondary narrators), third-order storyworlds (narrated by tertiary narrators), and so forth. See also Schmid 2010: 67–68.
18 Cf. Ryan 1991: 110–23.
19 Cf. Genette 1980: 243–52, 1988: 96–113.
20 It should be noted, however, that Genette's discussion of this question in *Narrative Discourse* (1980: 243–52) and *Narrative Discourse Revisited* (1988: 96–113) is rather nuanced and cannot be reduced to a simple distinction between heterodiegetic and homodiegetic narrators. Cf. also the brief discussion of narratorial involvement in Schmid 2010: 74–78.

extradiegetic narrator. Hence, it might be helpful to say a few more words about the distinction between extradiegetic and intradiegetic narrators as it applies to graphic narratives. Since intradiegetic narrators cannot be defined as being narrated by extradiegetic narrators in graphic narrative, the core question becomes: is the narrator located within the first-order storyworld or 'outside' of it? And this question, in turn, is connected to a second question: does the graphic narrative provide any information about the specific situation in which a given narrator narrates that can be attributed to a source different from the narrator? The additional criterion proposed here seems necessary since even extradiegetic narrators may, of course, very well provide at least some information about the situation in which they narrate through the way they narrate without thereby locating themselves in the first-order storyworld at all. If there is another source that provides information on the situation in which a given narrator narrates—be it another narratorial voice or the non-narratorial representation that characteristically takes verbal-pictorial form in graphic narrative—, we can usually assume that this very information locates the narrator in question 'in a storyworld of its own.'

Having established some of the more central dimensions of the concept of the narrator, I would now like to examine what types of narrators are used in graphic narrative, paying particular attention to how its specific mediality influences the forms and functions of its narrators.[21] While it would certainly prove fruitful to trace the use of narrators through the rich and varied history of graphic narrative, the present chapter will have to limit itself to discussing what one could consider prototypical instances of how contemporary graphic novels—most if not all of them by American and British authors—use narrators. There is no doubt that this choice may further reaffirm what has been called "the presentist bias of comics studies" (Charles Hatfield, quoted in Gardner 2012: back matter), but contemporary graphic novels do not only tend to employ particularly complex strategies of narrative representation which provide interesting narratological case studies, but are also often highly self-reflexive and well aware of their own history. That being said, a future project that attempts to further 'historicize' and 'transculturize' the argument presented here seems both conceivable and desirable.[22]

---

21 While the present chapter is primarily concerned with authors and narrators in graphic narrative, many of the more general problems of transmedial narratology regarding the transfer of terms and concepts apply. The aim here, as elsewhere, is to acknowledge both the similarities and the differences in the ways conventionally distinct media narrate, or, in this case, use narrators. For a more detailed discussion, see Thon 2014b, 2014c.

22 For a recent, historically-oriented approach to graphic narrative, see e.g., Gardner 2012. For more general—if largely programmatic—demands to 'historicize' narratology, see e.g., Fludernik 2003.

Narratorial Representation and Types of Narrators

Evidently, graphic narratives are representations of stories (and their worlds). Just as evidently, not all parts of these stories (and storyworlds) are narrated verbally by a more or less explicitly represented narrator. Still, graphic narratives in general and contemporary graphic novels in particular use various kinds of narrators-as-narrating-characters. Heterodiegetic narrators, on the one hand, tend to be extradiegetic and are often limited to giving spatiotemporal coordinates, as in the beginning of Alan Moore and Kevin O'Neill's *The League of Extraordinary Gentlemen* series (1999–, see figure 1), but there are extradiegetic heterodiegetic narrators that (subsequently) make more extensive use of their narratorial voice, as in Neil Gaiman's *The Sandman* series (1988–1996, see figure 2).

Figure 1: Alan Moore and Kevin O'Neill, *The League of Extraordinary Gentlemen: Vol. 1* (2002). © DC Comics. All rights reserved.

Figure 2: Neil Gaiman, *The Sandman: Preludes & Nocturnes* (2010).
© DC Comics. All rights reserved.

The notion that readers usually try to attribute verbal narration to some kind of narrating character is important in this context, since this attribution reinforces the reader's shift of attention from the level of representation, where the default mode of representation of verbal narration in the graphic novel would evidently be written, to the level of the storyworld, where the default mode of verbal narration that is being represented seems to be spoken rather than written or thought. However, this general tendency is at least partly subverted in *The League of Extraordinary Gentlemen* and *The Sandman*, since the verbal narration that is attributable to their covert extradiegetic narrators is represented in 'narration boxes' which—through their color and shape—appear to emulate the look of writing paper. Since there are, moreover, no further cues beyond the verbal narration itself that would point toward the (initial) presence of a fictional narrator in both *The League of Extraordinary Gentlemen* and *The Sandman*, one could argue that the verbal narration is actually a form of ('covert') authorial representation. Nonetheless, I would—at least for the time being—prefer to limit speaking of authorial representation to cases were the verbal narration is more or less explicitly attributed not only to a narrating but also to an authoring character.

Homodiegetic narrators, on the other hand, are more easily realized in extradiegetic and intradiegetic varieties, even though deciding which is which may occasionally prove difficult. A prototypical example of a particularly overt extradiegetic homodiegetic narrator can be found in Craig Thompson's *Habibi* (2011), the verbal narration of which clearly locates Dodola's 'narrating I' outside of the first-order storyworld in which her 'experiencing I' is located via deictic markers such as the use of the past tense, while simultaneously giving the reader next to no information about the situation in which the act of narration takes place (see figure 3).[23] While Dodola's 'narrating I' is marked clearly as extradiegetic, then, there is some fluctuation regarding her involvement in the story (or, rather, stories) she tells: the main part of the overall narrative consists of her and her friend/lover Zam's life story, making her narratorial role in these parts homodiegetic. Thompson includes countless shorter religious stories from within the first-order storyworld, however, and the narration of some of these can be attributed to Dodola's 'experiencing I' (which in turn becomes an intradiegetic 'narrating I'), making her oscillate between an extradiegetic homodiegetic and an intradiegetic heterodiegetic narratorial role throughout the graphic novel. Moreover, it is worth noting that Thompson not only extensively uses calligraphic elements to explore

---

23 While not providing explicit information regarding the spatio-temporal location of the 'narrating,' the way in which the narrator narrates and the use of the past tense through her whole narration indicate that the narration takes place some time *after* the narrated events.

Figure 3: Craig Thompson, *Habibi* (2011). © Craig Thompson. All rights reserved.

the importance of writing in Islam and beyond, but that Dodola's 'experiencing I' is also shown as having been taught reading and writing by her husband at a young age and that she subsequently develops a sustained interest in just the relations between writing and religious experience that are explored by the graphic novel. Hence, while the verbal-pictorial representation may not be attributable to Dodola in the same way that the verbal narration is, there are several points in the graphic novel where the latter is self-reflexively intertwined with both an examination of its own status as written speech and the pictorial representation of symbols to such an extent that the distinction between narratorial and non-narratorial representation at least becomes less clear-cut than it usually is in fictional graphic narrative (see e.g., figure 4).[24]

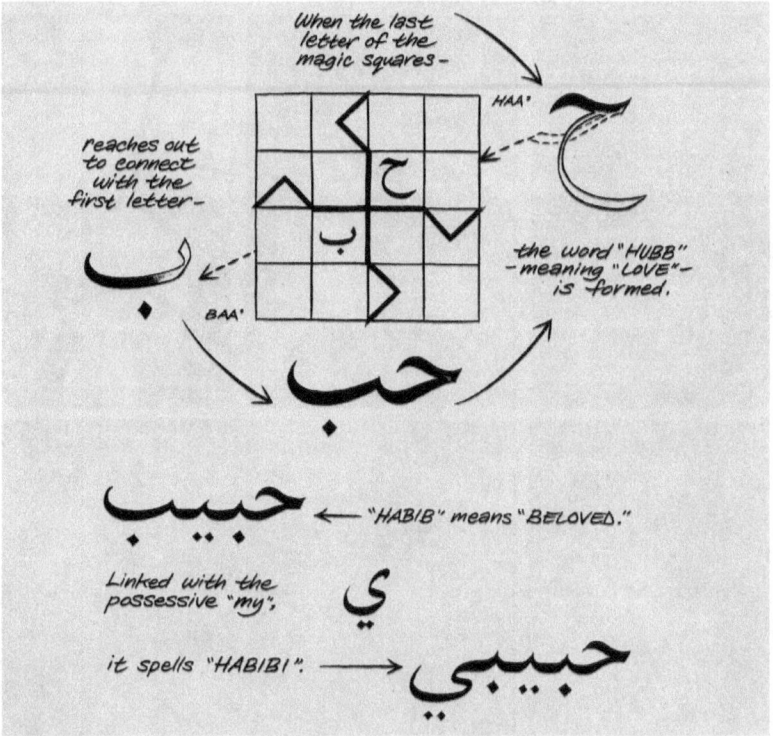

Figure 4: Craig Thompson, *Habibi* (2011). © Craig Thompson. All rights reserved.

---

[24] The possibility of attributing the verbal-pictorial representation to the graphic novel's narrator becomes even more pronounced when Dodola's 'narrating I' presents a "Map of the boat" in which her 'experiencing I' has taken refugee with Zam. That it is, indeed, Dodola who presents the map is indicated by the map's legend, consisting of rudimentary narration, such as "A We cooked here, and slept here. D" or "C The PILOTHOUSE served as lookout," which merge verbal and pictorial elements of the representation.

Despite the complex narratorial structure of *Habibi*, it is usually fairly easy to figure out who is narrating what in which mode at any given point in the narrative. As has already been mentioned, however, this is not always the case in contemporary graphic novels, and the question of whether we should understand a given verbal narration as spoken, written, or thought is closely connected to the question of whether we should understand a given narrator as extradiegetic or intradiegetic. With its variety of narratorial voices (marked through differently colored 'narration boxes'), Gaiman's *The Sandman* series provides a good example of this kind of indeterminacy. In addition to the seemingly written verbal narration that we can attribute to a comparatively covert extradiegetic and heterodiegetic narrator (or, alternatively, understand as a form of 'covert' authorial representation), the series' first volume, *Preludes & Nocturnes* (2010), already introduces a second narratorial voice that can be attributed to the story's main character, Dream of the Endless, who comments on the unfolding story in the present tense (see figure 5).

It seems clear that the verbal-pictorial narration does not represent Dream's 'experiencing I' as actually speaking in these situations (which would, at a first glance, imply an extradiegetic 'speaking' narrator). But the reader can imagine him thinking at least part of the verbal narration in question and, hence, also imagine him to be an intradiegetic 'thinking' narrator. While some parts of the verbal narration that is attributable to Dream could indeed be interpreted in a way that would make him an intradiegetic narrator, then (e.g., "It feels so good to be back... I left a monarch. Yet I return naked, alone... Hungry."), the overall narration once more uses deictic markers to locate Dream's 'narrating I' outside of the first-order storyworld in which his 'experiencing I' is located.[25] While there is still some amount of indeterminacy regarding the location of the 'narrating I' at some points in his verbal narration, then, all in all it seems more plausible to understand him as another extradiegetic—albeit homodiegetic—narrator.[26]

---

25 One of the more interesting parts of Dream's verbal narration is characterized by a switch to the past tense when Dream's 'experiencing I' remembers his journey back to his castle, after having freed himself from his imprisonment: "It was a DARK and STORMY NIGHTMARE... Before my IMPRISONMENT, I knew, the journey would have meant NOTHING to me. I would NOT even have NEEDED to TRAVEL. But WEAKENED and EXHAUSTED, I stumbled through the FRINGES of the DREAMTIME..." Again, though, it is Dream's extradiegetic 'narrating I' that does the narrating, since Dream's intradiegetic 'experiencing I' is so exhausted as to be barely able to talk coherently.

26 The verbal narration in Rorschach's diary that frames much of the overall narration in Alan Moore and Dave Gibbons's *Watchmen* (2005) may be considered an example of an apparent narratorial indeterminacy that works the other way round. Introduced as belonging to a possibly extradiegetic narrator, it later becomes clear that the diary in question is located within the first-order storyworld, rendering the narrator clearly intradiegetic.

Figure 5: Neil Gaiman, *The Sandman: Preludes & Nocturnes* (2010).
© DC Comics. All rights reserved.

Figure 6: Neil Gaiman, *The Sandman: Preludes & Nocturnes* (2010).
© DC Comics. All rights reserved.

Not only do all three graphic novels mentioned so far use extradiegetic narrators—a fairly covert heterodiegetic narrator on the verge of authorial representation in *The League of Extraordinary Gentlemen*, a very overt homodiegetic narrator in *Habibi*, and both a heterodiegetic and a homodiegetic narrator in *The Sandman*—, but they also all use intradiegetic narrators, both heterodiegetic and homodiegetic. While there may be points where it is difficult to distinguish between Dream as an extradiegetic 'speaking' narrator and Dream as an intradiegetic 'thinking' narrator in *The Sandman*, since Gaiman and his various collaborators use formally similar speech balloons/thought bubbles/'narration boxes' for any verbal representation attributable to Dream, there are also various instances of spoken narration that are clearly attributable to Dream as an intradiegetic homodiegetic narrator, where the narrative situation in question is explicitly represented by the verbal-pictorial representation (see figure 6). Similarly, *The League of Extraordinary Gentlemen* and *Habibi* represent intradiegetic narrators explicitly several times, and in different modes of narration, including the letters written by Ms. Murray in the former (rendering her an intradiegetic homodiegetic narrator; see figure 7) and the stories read to Zam by Dodola's 'experiencing I' in the latter (rendering her an intradiegetic heterodiegetic narrator; see figure 8).

Having established that contemporary graphic novels—just like traditional 'monomodal' novels—may use narrators both extradiegetic and intradiegetic as well as both heterodiegetic and homodiegetic, I would like to focus in slightly more detail on the medium-specific aspects of this use of narrators. While graphic novels can, and in fact often do, use verbal narration that we tend to attribute to a narrating character in one way or another, this kind of *narratorial representation* is evidently not the only way in which storyworlds are represented in graphic narrative. Rather, much of the overall narrative is usually conveyed via the verbal-pictorial mode of representation that defines the medium and that can—at least in fictional graphic narratives—usually be understood as a form of *non-narratorial representation*. Not least since narrators in fictional graphic narratives tend not to be represented as being in control of the selection, organization, and presentation of the verbal-pictorial elements of the overall narration, the question of how verbal narratorial representation relates to verbal-pictorial non-narratorial representation seems central to the medium-specific ways in which contemporary graphic novels—as well as graphic narratives in general—use narrators.[27]

---

[27] It may be worth stressing at this point that, at least within the theoretical framework presented in the present chapter, narrators are not (necessarily) 'focalizers' (or *vice versa*). For a more detailed discussion, see Thon 2014b as well as e.g., Branigan 1990: 125–91; Currie 2010: 123–47; Horstkotte and Pedri 2011. See also Mikkonen 2015.

Figure 7: Alan Moore and Kevin O'Neill, *The League of Extraordinary Gentlemen: Vol. 1* (2002). © DC Comics. All rights reserved.

Figure 8: Craig Thompson, *Habibi* (2011). © Craig Thompson. All rights reserved.

There are, of course, graphic novels such as Jeff Smith's *Bone* series (1991–2004) that use a purely verbal-pictorial (or non-narratorial) mode of narration and at least some special cases such as Alan Moore and Kevin O'Neill's *The League of Extraordinary Gentlemen* series or Alan Moore and Dave Gibbons's *Watchmen* series (1986–1987), specific parts of which could be described as exclusively verbal (or narratorial) representation. Nonetheless, it should be emphasized that, even in verbally-dominated works such as *The League of Extraordinary Gentlemen* or *Watchmen* as well as *The Sandman* or *Habibi*, the combination of narratorial and non-narratorial representation is in constant flux. While both the quantitative and the qualitative relations between narratorial and non-narratorial representation can be examined with regard to the overall narrative, then, it often seems more useful to describe these relations on a local level first, i.e., with regard to the stories told by particular narrators. In order to do so, however, one needs to add another, more medium-specific tweak to the established Genettean distinctions between extradiegetic/intradiegetic and heterodiegetic/homodiegetic narrators: in graphic narrative (as well as other kinds of multimodal narrative), narrators can be either framing or non-framing, i.e., their respective verbal narration is either 'illustrated' by the verbal-pictorial representation, or it is not.[28]

The prototypical use of a 'framing' narrator appears to consist of the introduction of a narrator telling a story, followed by the non-narratorial representation illustrating the story as well as adding additional, but largely consistent, information (see e.g., figures 1–3 and 5–8). While some pages of *The League of Extraordinary Gentlemen*, *The Sandman*, and *Habibi* can be described as being verbally-dominated, the relation between narratorial and non-narratorial representation continually shifts through the graphic novels, with stretches of purely verbal-pictorial representation as well as various cases in which the verbal narration of both extradiegetic and intradiegetic narrators is not illustrated by the verbal-pictorial representation at all. Of course, it only makes sense to ask for the qualitative relations between narratorial and non-narratorial representation

---

28 As the possible relations between verbal and pictorial as well as between narratorial and non-narratorial representation span a considerably wider spectrum, speaking of the verbal-pictorial representation's 'illustrative function' might be considered overly reductive. While it is important to note that 'illustration' is not the only function the verbal-pictorial representation can fulfill in relation to a narrator's verbal narration, then, it still seems to be the one most commonly encountered. Cf. also McCloud 1993; Schüwer 2008: 445–58; Hoppeler, Etter, and Rippl 2009; as well as Gabriele Rippl and Lukas Etter's contribution in this volume. Moreover, cf. the discussion within film studies, e.g., Kozloff 1988: 100–09; as well as Chatman 1999; Kuhn 2011: 98–100. It might also be worth emphasizing yet again that there are other kinds of framing that introduce a change of diegetic levels or sub-worlds with regard to the non-narratorial representation; see, once more, Thon 2014b.

if the story in question is conveyed neither in an exclusively verbal manner—which is very rare in the case of extradiegetic narrators, but fairly common in the case of intradiegetic narrators—nor in an exclusively verbal-pictorial manner—which is even rarer as far as the 'illustration' of narratorial representation is concerned, but can, for example, be found in silent strips such as Shaun Tan's *The Arrival* (2006), where the intradiegetic narrator's narration is not presented verbally at all, but rather in the form of purely pictorial panels that further emphasize their pictorial nature by emulating pictures—or polaroids—glued into an album (see figure 9).

Despite these caveats, then, the combination of narratorial and non-narratorial representation in *The League of Extraordinary Gentlemen*, *The Sandman*, and *Habibi* appears to be rather prototypical of how graphic novels narrate not only in terms of the quantitative relations between narratorial and non-narratorial representation but also with regard to their qualitative relations. Throughout all three of these graphic novels, the relation between narratorial and non-narratorial representation can usually be described as (mildly) redundant or complementary, and even though unrelated or downright contradictory combinations are, of course, possible (and do occasionally occur in *The League of Extraordinary Gentlemen*, for example), it seems as if not that many contemporary graphic novels are very keen on realizing that possibility. One way or another, though, the fictional narrators in these graphic novels are usually not represented as being in control of the non-narratorial representation, which brings me back to the question to whom we can attribute the latter (if not to fictional narrators-as-narrating-characters, that is). In other words, 'who's telling the verbal-pictorial parts of the tale?'

Figure 9: Shaun Tan, *The Arrival* (2006). © Shaun Tan. All rights reserved.

Hypothetical Author Collectives and Authoring Characters

It should be clear by now that the presence of a more or less explicitly represented narrator poses its own theoretical as well as methodological problems. David Bordwell has a point (that applies to graphic as well as to audiovisual narratives), though, when he claims that "the interesting theoretical problem involves an implicit, nonpersonified narrator" (1985: 61) and goes on to ask: "Even if no voice or body gets identified as the locus of narration, can we still speak of a narrator as being present in a film? In other words, must we go beyond the process of narration to locate an entity which is its source?" (Bordwell 1985: 61–62). If going beyond what I have, rather programmatically, described as non-narratorial representation is taken to mean that we have to attribute the latter to a narrator, the answer to Bordwell's question is just as evident: it is not necessary to attribute non-narratorial representation to a narrator. Still, it seems to be the case that we generally tend to attribute narration in any medium or semiotic mode to a 'source,' which makes Bordwell's proposal to assume that the narration 'tells itself' somewhat unsatisfactory.

As Jens Eder observes, however, there is a simple alternative to attributing these processes to narrators: "Even if one assumes that spectators understand films as intentionally designed communicative devices […], one does not have to attribute their design to narrators or implied authors, but can also trace it back to the real film makers as authors or author collective" (2008: 616; my translation from the German: "Selbst wenn man davon ausgeht, dass Filme von ihren Zuschauern in der Regel als bewusst gestaltete Kommunikationsmittel verstanden werden […], muss man ihre Gestaltung nicht Erzählern oder impliziten Autoren zuschreiben, sondern kann sie auch auf die realen Filmemacher als Autoren(kollektiv) zurückführen."). In line with my previous argument for an understanding of narrators as narrating characters, then, I follow Eder in arguing that the verbal-pictorial representation of a graphic narrative can usually be attributed not to a (fictional) narrator, but to the author or author collective of the graphic narrative in question. In light of the controversies surrounding authorship within literary theory and beyond, however, some further remarks on what such an attribution entails and how the author(s) in question are best conceptualized seem in order.[29]

---

29 It should also be mentioned at this point that the notion of 'author' proposed here is, of course, significantly broader than 'single author of a literary text,' encompassing a variety of roles and responsibilities involved in creating graphic narrative.

It is no secret that contemporary narratology tends to suffer from a proliferation of 'communicative instances,'[30] and while I am certainly sympathetic to narratological approaches that "opt for not multiplying narrative agents" (Mikkonen 2015: 16), any proposal to attribute the non-narratorial representation to the actual author or author collective will have to address two problems connected to the notion of 'authorship' in graphic narrative. First, there is the problem of *collective authorship*: while a novel usually is the result of several people's work, as well, graphic novels (and graphic narratives in general) are often more visibly created by a team of people with different roles and degrees of authority. Of course, there *are* graphic novels such as Craig Thompson's *Habibi* that have a single author responsible for all the decisions involved in their creation, but the distribution of production roles and artistic responsibility tends to be significantly more complex and often changes as a project develops. Hence, while there are cases where one can identify a single person as the author of a given graphic narrative, the situation is usually not as clear-cut.

Second, there is the problem of *intentionalism*, which is closely connected to the question of what exactly we mean (or should mean) when we say 'author' in the context of literary theory and narratology: following the banishment of the author from the realm of interpretation for fear of the 'intentional fallacy' and its return in the multi-faceted guises of the 'implied author,'[31] this question has been primarily examined in the context of intentionalistic theories of interpretation. While the term 'implied author' has become too vague and varied to be particularly useful by now, some aspects of the (ongoing) debate[32] still seem relevant for coming to terms with the relation between authors and narrators in graphic narrative, without unnecessarily postulating 'implied' instances by insisting that various aspects of a given graphic narrative's design should be attributed to an 'enunciator' different from the work's author(s).

---

30 The standard models of narrative communication in literary texts usually distinguish between at least the 'biographical' or 'actual author,' the 'narrator(s),' and the narrated characters, but sometimes add an 'abstract' or 'implied author.' See e.g., Chatman 1978, 1990; Bal 1997; Rimmon-Kenan 2002. Enunciation theories of audiovisual as well as graphic narrative tend to add additional 'enunciative instances' held responsible for various semiotic modes of representation. See e.g., Gaudreault and Jost 1999; Gaudreault 2009; as well as the works of Marion 1993; Baetens 2001; Groensteen 2010, 2013; Surdiacourt 2012; Mikkonen 2015, the latter of which provides a balanced discussion of the different ways in which 'narrative agency' can be conceptualized.

31 See Wimsatt and Beardsley 1954 [1946]; Booth 1961; Barthes 1977 [1967]; Foucault 2000 [1969]. On the implied author's conceptual history, see also Kindt and Müller 2006.

32 See, for example, the special issue of *Style* (1/2011), in which a number of well-known narratologists—among them Kindt and Müller 2011; Lanser 2011; and Ryan 2011—have revisited the concept of the 'implied author.'

As Tom Kindt and Hans-Harald Müller have noted, "the idea that the implied author stands for images that the authors produce of themselves in their works" has long been part of the concept of the 'implied author' and "can be properly accounted for only in the context of an intentionalistic approach to interpretation" (2006: 180). While I would follow Schmid (and others) in acknowledging that authors do not necessarily need to "have the intention of creating an image of themselves in their work" (2009: 161), it still seems clear that these kinds of authorial self-representations form an integral part of the concept's history. Moreover, it is fairly uncontroversial that "narratives are understood by making inferences to the intentions of their makers," in so far as these inferences are not taken to be "a forensic investigation into a person's motives that involves sifting the evidence of diaries, letters, and the reminiscences of friends" (Currie 2010: 25). The resulting position of *hypothetical intentionalism* is capable of evading both a "biographical drift" and the "model of the 'complete author'" (Baetens 2001: 151) that Jan Baetens identifies as a potential problem in the theory of graphic enunciation developed by Marion (1993) and others.[33]

Of course, the present chapter is not primarily concerned with theories of interpretation, but it is still important to note that if one proposes that readers of a graphic narrative attribute the non-narratorial verbal-pictorial representation to the graphic narrative's author(s), this has very little to do with the real author(s), but rather with the image of these author(s) that the readers have formed in the process of reading.[34]

---

33 For an in-depth discussion of hypothetical intentionalism with regard to the notion of implied authorship, see Kindt and Müller 2006. Incidentally, it could be argued that hypothetical intentionalism does not exclude the possibility of using 'additional evidence' and may, in fact, be compatible with "sifting the evidence of diaries, letters, and the reminiscences of friends" (Currie 2010: 25) in order to strengthen specific interpretations.

34 Here as elsewhere, I am operating with the notion of an 'ideal' reader, which may make it necessary to say a few words on the cognitive reception theories underlying much of the argument in the present chapter. Drawing on general theories of human cognition in order to hypothesize about reception processes is not entirely unproblematic, since these kinds of hypotheses about 'ideal' readers tend to be based primarily on the reading experience of the scholar who does the hypothesizing. As Herman remarks in *Basic Elements of Narrative*, "[t]o be addressed adequately, these questions must be explored via empirical methods of investigation," but in the absence of relevant empirical research, to draw on our "own native intuitions about stories and storytelling, coupled with traditions of narrative scholarship" (2009: 4) and general theories about human cognition seems to be the next best thing. Cf. e.g., Eco 1979: 7–11; Jannidis 2004: 28–33; Eder 2008: 80–106 on the notion of an 'ideal' or 'model' recipient as well as e.g., Branigan 1992; Eder 2003; Herman 2009 for more detailed discussions of the relation between narratology and cognitive reception theories. It might also be worth mentioning the kind of 'reader-response theory' (*Rezeptionsästhetik*) pioneered by scholars such as Iser 1974; Fish 1980; Jauss 1982 as a second influential strand of reception theories, whose rather different approach to reception processes seems no less relevant for the problem sketched above.

Accordingly, while I will refrain from speaking of an 'implied author,' there is still some need for the notion of a "hypothetical or postulated author in the context of hypothetical intentionalism" (Kindt and Müller 2006: 181). In the process of forming hypotheses about a given graphic narrative's author(s), readers also tend to make certain assumptions of a fairly general nature about the processes involved in its creation, and these assumptions are (usually) based on the knowledge they have about the *prototypical* distribution of work, decision-making, and authority according to historically specific, highly conventionalized 'production roles.'[35] It is against this background that readers will process available information regarding *unusual* distributions of work, decision-making, and authority in cases of collective authorship, and, hence, general historical knowledge about prototypical authorial constellation plays an important role in how they imagine a graphic narrative's *hypothetical author collective*.[36]

A brief look at the graphic novels discussed in the preceding section already serves to illustrate the breadth of contemporary graphic narrative's hypothetical author collectives. While *Habibi* is a single-author work which clearly identifies Craig Thompson as the person responsible for (most of) its creation, *The League of Extraordinary Gentlemen* is identified as a collaborative work, with Alan Moore and Kevin O'Neill fulfilling the roles of writer and artist, respectively, as well as several others involved with coloring, lettering, editing, etc. Similarly, *The Sandman* is identified as the result of a collaborative work, but in this case, writer Neil Gaiman has collaborated with a number of different artists over the years, which emphasizes his authority over the whole series, even though the various artists have, each in their own way, evidently influenced the design of the graphic narrative significantly. Incidentally, it should be noted that the seriality of many forms of graphic narrative—including *The League of Extraordinary Gentlemen* and *The Sandman*,[37] but being even more pervasive in newspaper comic strips and comic books—facilitates this kind of personnel change while at the same time making the individual persons fulfilling the various production roles appear less salient.

---

35 See e.g., Duncan and Smith 2009; Stein 2009; Gabilliet 2010; Kelleter and Stein 2012; Uidhir 2012; and the contributions in Williams and Lyons 2010 for a more in-depth discussion of the historical development of prototypical authoring practices in graphic narrative. See also Daniel Stein's contribution in the present volume.
36 See also Kindt and Müller 2006 or Alber 2010 for further discussion of the notion of a 'hypothetical author' as well as reasons for why it is preferable to the 'implied author.'
37 While originally published in serial form, both *The League of Extraordinary Gentlemen* and *The Sandman* are usually understood as (a series of) graphic novels rather than (a series of) comic book issues. For a more detailed discussion of these different formats, see also Christina Meyer's, Julia Round's, and Daniel Stein's contributions in this volume.

While hypothetical author collectives do not necessarily have to be 'fleshed-out' with regard to their individual members, then, there still seem to be quite a few similarities between the representation of authors and the representation of narrators. In his influential discussion of cinematic authorship, Paisley Livingston—a proponent of 'real' intentionalism—emphasizes that he does not subscribe to an "anti-realist notion of authorship" that would result in the construction of a "make-believe persona [...] referred to variously as the 'real,' 'fictional,' 'implied,' or 'postulated' author" (1997: 145). But while an author (or author collective) is usually not accurately described as fictional, she nevertheless "exists not only as a biographical person, or persons, who has created a text, but also as a cultural *legend* created by texts" (Branigan 1992: 87, original emphasis). Just like narrators, then, authors (or author collectives) can be more or less explicitly represented across a range of media and media texts, and these representations are not necessarily accurate or consistent. Keeping in mind the distinction between narratorial representation and authorial representation introduced earlier, however, I propose to distinguish further between, on the one hand, hypothetical author collectives whose individual members can be represented more or less extensively in various peritexts and epitexts, and, on the other hand, the special case of *authoring characters* that are represented within the 'text' itself.

Both *Habibi* and the most recent edition of the various volumes of *The Sandman* include a photograph and a brief biographical note of Craig Thompson and Neil Gaiman, respectively, but the way that peritexts are used to represent the authors of *The League of Extraordinary Gentlemen* is markedly different. While the representation of Craig Thompson and Neil Gaiman is brief but more or less accurate or at least clearly marked as being nonfictional, *The League of Extraordinary Gentlemen* may serve as an example of the use of strongly 'fictionalized' authoring characters that blend into the Victorian setting of the series.[38] The fictional authoring characters of 'Alan Moore' and 'Kevin O'Neill' (among others) are represented in a wealth of peritextual material, including fictional biographies on the back matter of the collected volumes, which are logically inconsistent not only with the actual biographies of Moore and O'Neill but also with each other. Despite the many inconsistencies that

---

[38] It might be misleading to speak of 'fictionalized' authoring characters, as most theories of fiction do not allow for degrees of fictionality. What is meant here is that authorial characters can be represented more or less accurately with respect to the 'actual world' but that their representation can also be marked as being fictional, as is the case in *The League of Extraordinary Gentlemen*. See also Thon 2014a for a brief survey of the notion of fictionality in film and media studies (including comics studies and game studies) as well as Stein 2009 for a discussion of authorial self-representation in graphic narrative and Nancy Pedri's contribution in this volume for a more detailed discussion of graphic memoirs.

seem to indicate a rather playful stance with regard to these fictional self-representations on the part of the actual authors, among other things, the representation of fictional authoring characters might be said to introduce an additional higher-order storyworld in which the creation of the 'proper' graphic narrative is embedded.

So, what elements of the overall narration can be attributed to these kinds of fictional authoring characters? Once more, an examination of the use of verbal and verbal-pictorial representation in *The League of Extraordinary Gentlemen* proves illuminating, as the verbal narration that was described as being attributable to a covert extradiegetic heterodiegetic narrator at the beginning of the series becomes more 'overt' and openly 'authorial' at the end of each of the issues collected in the first volume. Even though in the latter case, the verbal narration can easily be attributed to the fictional authoring characters of 'Alan Moore' and 'Kevin O'Neill' (the former probably being the more salient source despite the verbal narration's use of the first-person plural), however, I would be reluctant to speak of authorial representation here. Rather, it seems as if the kind of fictional authoring characters to be found in *The League of Extraordinary Gentlemen* are closer to fictional narrators than to nonfictional authoring characters, the difference mainly being that the former are represented as being in control not only of the narratorial (or fictional authorial) but also of the non-narratorial representation.

In contrast to the fictional authoring characters of *The League of Extraordinary Gentlemen*, the authoring characters represented in so-called graphic memoirs tend to be largely nonfictional, with Art Spiegelman's *Maus* (1996) providing not only one of the most famous but also one of the more interesting and complex examples of a highly self-reflexive authoring character. It should be noted that Spiegelman's metaphorical depiction of Jews as mice, Germans as cats, Poles as pigs, etc. does not necessarily 'fictionalize' the self-depiction of the autobiographical narrator's 'experiencing I' as a mouse and his 'narrating I/authoring I' as a human wearing a mouse mask, since what is represented here is the nonfictional truth of Spiegelman being Jewish.[39] But of course, the self-representation of Art Spiegelman still differs quite a bit from more realistic (or simply less metaphorical) self-representations in other graphic memoirs or works of graphic journalism such as Joe Sacco's *Palestine*

---

39 While I can only hint at the complex narratorial structure within *Maus*, Spiegelman's work has fortunately received quite a lot of academic attention and probably remains one of the most thoroughly analyzed examples at the intersection of autobiography and comics studies as well as within the emerging field comics narratology. See e.g., Hirsch 1992; Miller 2003; Berlatsky 2011: 145–86 as well as Ewert 2000; McGlothlin 2003; Chute 2006. See also the wealth of additional material collected in Spiegelman 2011.

(2003).[40] In both cases, though, the verbal narration attributable to the authoring characters 'Art' and 'Joe,' respectively, would have to be understood as (nonfictional) authorial representation. Moreover, since both graphic memoirs and works of graphic journalism tend to be realized as single-author works, their authoring characters are usually represented as being in control not only of the verbal narration but also of the verbal-pictorial representation.

Even though some distinctions can be drawn, then, the necessarily brief discussion of authoring characters and authorial representation leads me to tentatively agree with Edward Branigan that "[e]stablishing exact categories for the narrations is usually less important than recognizing pertinent relationships and gradations" (1992: 100). Still, one can observe a prototypical 'division of labor' between (hypothetical) author(s) and (fictional) narrators in most contemporary graphic novels (as well as in other forms of graphic narrative): in the context of fictional graphic narrative, readers will usually attempt to attribute (fictional) verbal narration (or *narratorial representation*) to some kind of (fictional) narrator (even if there are only few cues to such a narrator's presence apart from the presence of the verbal narration itself), while attributing (fictional) verbal-pictorial representation (or *non-narratorial representation*) to the work's hypothetical author collectives in a majority of cases. Against this background, both authorial verbal narration (or *authorial representation*, which needs significantly more cues to be recognizable as *not* being narratorial representation) and 'narratorial' verbal-pictorial representation (that is more or less explicitly represented as being attributable to a fictional narrator or narrator-like entity) should be treated as 'marked cases' when it comes to the question of 'who's telling the tale' in graphic narrative.[41]

---

40 By now, Joe Sacco's works of graphic journalism are comparatively well-researched within comics studies, too. See e.g., Adams 2008: 121–60; Woo 2010; Gadassik and Henstra 2012.

41 Not least since many contributions in the present volume rightly emphasize the importance of historical and cultural contexts for the production and reception of graphic narrative, it should be stressed that the claims I make here regarding the 'division of labor' between authors and narrators are not particularly strong. Since the main aim of the present chapter has been the development of a "method of analysis" (Genette 1980: 23) for narrators in graphic narratives as distinct from a historically oriented account of how graphic narratives have used narrators in different genres and cultures, I do not wish to claim that the kinds of narrators I describe are necessarily present in all contemporary graphic novels, nor do I wish to insinuate that there are no exceptions to the prototypical attributions of narratorial, authorial, and non-narratorial representation to fictional narrating characters, nonfictional authoring characters, and hypothetical author collectives sketched above. As has already been mentioned, a further examination of the historical and cross-cultural development of the use of narrators in graphic narrative—whose differentiation of prototypical uses of narrators could well be based on the heuristic distinctions developed in the present chapter—would certainly prove valuable for comics studies and comics narratology alike.

Works Cited

Aczel, Richard (1998). "Hearing Voices in Narrative Texts." *New Literary History* 29: 467–500. Print.

Adams, Jeff (2008). *Documentary Graphic Novels and Social Realism*. Bern: Peter Lang. Print.

Alber, Jan (2010). "Hypothetical Intentionalism: Cinematic Narration Reconsidered." Jan Alber and Monika Fludernik (eds.). *Postclassical Narratology: Approaches and Analyses*. Columbus: Ohio State UP. 163–85. Print.

Baetens, Jan (2001). "Revealing Traces: A New Theory of Graphic Enunciation." Robin Varnum and Christina T. Gibbons (eds.). *The Language of Comics: Word and Image*. Jackson: UP of Mississippi. 145–55. Print.

Bal, Mieke (1981). "Notes on Narrative Embedding." *Poetics Today* 2.2: 41–59. Print.

— (1997). *Narratology: Introduction to the Theory of Narrative*. 2nd edition. Toronto: U of Toronto P. Print.

Banfield, Ann (1983). *Unspeakable Sentences: Narration and Representation in the Language of Fiction*. Boston: Routledge. Print.

Bareis, Alexander J. (2006). "Mimesis der Stimme: Fiktionstheoretische Aspekte einer narratologischen Kategorie." Andreas Blödorn, Daniela Langer, and Michael Scheffel (eds.). *Stimme(n) im Text: Narratologische Positionsbestimmungen*. Berlin: De Gruyter. 101–22. Print.

Barthes, Roland (1977 [1967]). "The Death of the Author." *Image—Music—Text*. Ed. and trans. Stephen Heath. New York: Hill and Wang. 142–48. Print.

Berlatsky, Eric L. (2011). *The Real, the True, and the Told: Postmodern Historical Narrative and the Ethics of Representation*. Columbus: Ohio State UP. Print.

Booth, Wayne C. (1961). *The Rhetoric of Fiction*. Chicago: U of Chicago P. Print.

Bordwell, David (1985). *Narration in the Fiction Film*. Madison: U of Wisconsin P. Print.

Branigan, Edward (1992). *Narrative Comprehension and Film*. Abingdon: Routledge. Print.

Chatman, Seymour (1978). *Story and Discourse: Narrative Structure in Fiction and Film*. Ithaca: Cornell UP. Print.

— (1990). *Coming to Terms: The Rhetoric of Narrative in Fiction and Film*. Ithaca: Cornell UP. Print.

— (1999). "New Directions in Voice-Narrated Cinema." David Herman (ed.). *Narratologies: New Perspectives on Narrative Analysis*. Columbus: Ohio State UP. 315–39. Print.
Chute, Hillary (2006). "History and Graphic Representation in *Maus*." *Twentieth-Century Literature* 52.2: 199–230. Print.
Currie, Gregory (2010). *Narratives & Narrators: A Philosophy of Stories*. Oxford: Oxford UP. Print.
Duncan, Randy, and Matthew J. Smith (2009). *The Power of Comics: History, Form and Culture*. New York: Continuum. Print.
Eco, Umberto (1979). *The Role of the Reader: Explorations in the Semiotics of Text*. Bloomington: Indiana UP. Print.
Eder, Jens (2003). "Narratology and Cognitive Reception Theories." Tom Kindt and Hans-Harald Müller (eds.). *What Is Narratology? Questions and Answers Regarding the Status of a Theory*. Berlin: De Gruyter. 277–301. Print.
— (2008). *Die Figur im Film: Grundlagen der Figurenanalyse*. Marburg: Schüren. Print.
Eder, Jens, Fotis Jannidis, and Ralf Schneider (2010). "Characters in Fictional Worlds: An Introduction." Jens Eder, Fotis Jannidis, and Ralf Schneider (eds.). *Characters in Fictional Worlds: Understanding Imaginary Beings in Literature, Film, and Other Media*. Berlin: De Gruyter. 3–66. Print.
Ewert, Jeanne (2000). "Reading Visual Narrative: Art Spiegelman's *Maus*." *Narrative* 8.1: 87–103. Print.
Fludernik, Monika (2003). "The Diachronization of Narratology." *Narrative* 11.3: 331–48. Print.
Fish, Stanley (1980). *Is There a Text in This Class?* Harvard: Harvard UP. Print.
Foucault, Michel (2000 [1969]). "What Is an Author?" David Lodge and Nigel Wood (eds.). *Modern Criticism and Theory: A Reader*. 2nd edition. Harlow: Longman. 174–87. Print.
Gabilliet, Jean-Paul (2010). *Of Comics and Men: A Cultural History of American Comic Books*. Trans. Bart Beaty and Nick Nguyen. Jackson: UP of Mississippi. Print.
Gadassik, Alla, and Sarah Henstra (2012). "Comics (as) Journalism: Teaching Joe Sacco's *Palestine* to Media Students." Lan Dong (ed.). *Teaching Comics and Graphic Narratives: Essays on Theory, Strategy and Practice*. Jefferson: McFarland. 243–60. Print.

Gaiman, Neil (2010). *The Sandman: Preludes & Nocturnes*. Vol. 1. Art by Sam Kieth, Mike Dringenberg, and Malcolm Jones III. Colors by Daniel Vozzo. Lettered by Todd Klein. Covers by Dave McKean. Originally published in single magazine form as *The Sandman* #1–8, 1988–1989. New York: DC Comics. Print.

Gardner, Jared (2012). *Projections: Comics and the History of Twenty-First-Century Storytelling*. Stanford: Stanford UP. Print.

Gaudreault, André (2009). *From Plato to Lumière: Narration and Monstration in Literature and Cinema*. Toronto: U of Toronto P. Print.

Gaudreault, André, and François Jost (1999). "Enunciation and Narration." Toby Miller and Robert Stam (eds.). *A Companion to Film Theory*. Malden: Blackwell. 45–63. Print.

Genette, Gérard (1980). *Narrative Discourse: An Essay in Method*. Trans. Jane E. Lewin. Oxford: Basil Blackwell. Print.

— (1988). *Narrative Discourse Revisited*. Trans. Jane E. Lewin. Ithaca: Cornell UP. Print.

Gravett, Paul (2005). *Graphic Novels: Stories to Change Your Life*. London: Aurum. Print.

Groensteen, Thierry (2010). "The Monstrator, the Recitant and the Shadow of the Narrator." *European Comic Art* 3.1: 1–21. Print.

— (2013). *Comics and Narration*. Trans. Ann Miller. Jackson: UP of Mississippi. Print.

Hirsch, Marianne (1992). "Family Pictures: *Maus*, Mourning and Post-Memory." *Discourse* 15.2: 3–29. Print.

Hoppeler, Stephanie, Lukas Etter, and Gabriele Rippl (2009). "Intermedialität in Comics: Neil Gaimans *The Sandman*." Stephan Ditschke, Katerina Kroucheva, and Daniel Stein (eds.). *Comics: Zur Geschichte und Theorie eines populärkulturellen Mediums*. Bielefeld: transcript. 53–79. Print.

Horstkotte, Silke, and Nancy Pedri (2011). "Focalization in Graphic Narrative." *Narrative* 19.3: 330–57. Print.

Iser, Wolfgang (1974). *The Implied Reader: Patterns of Communication in Prose Fiction from Bunyan to Beckett*. Baltimore: Johns Hopkins UP. Print.

Janik, Dieter (1973). *Die Kommunikationsstruktur des Erzählwerks: Ein semiologisches Modell*. Bebenhausen: Rotsch. Print.

Jannidis, Fotis (2004). *Figur und Person: Beitrag zu einer historischen Narratologie*. Berlin: De Gruyter. Print.

— (2006). "Wer sagt das? Erzählen mit Stimmverlust." Andreas Blödorn, Daniela Langer, and Michael Scheffel (eds.). *Stimme(n) im Text: Narratologische Positionsbestimmungen*. Berlin: De Gruyter. 151–64. Print.

Jauss, Hans R. (1982). *Toward an Aesthetic of Reception*. Trans. Timothy Bahti. Introd. Paul de Man. Minneapolis: U of Minnesota P. Print.

Kania, Andrew (2005). "Against the Ubiquity of Fictional Narrators." *Journal of Aesthetics and Art Criticism* 63.4: 47–54. Print.
Kelleter, Frank, and Daniel Stein (2012). "Autorisierungspraktiken seriellen Erzählens: Zur Gattungsentwicklung von Superheldencomics." Frank Kelleter (ed.). *Populäre Serialität: Narration—Evolution—Distinktion. Zum seriellen Erzählen seit dem 19. Jahrhundert*. Bielefeld: transcript. 259–90. Print.
Kindt, Tom, and Hans-Harald Müller (2006). *The Implied Author: Concept and Controversy*. Berlin: De Gruyter. Print.
— (2011). "Six Ways Not to Save the Implied Author." *Style* 45.1: 67–79. Print.
Köppe, Tilmann, and Jan Stühring (2011). "Against Pan-Narrator Theories." *Journal of Literary Semantics* 40.1: 59–80. Print.
Kozloff, Sarah (1988). *Invisible Storytellers: Voice-Over Narration in American Fiction Film*. Berkeley: U of California P. Print.
Kuhn, Markus (2011). *Filmnarratologie: Ein erzähltheoretisches Analysemodell*. Berlin: De Gruyter. Print.
Lanser, Susan S. (1981). *The Narrative Act: Point of View in Prose Fiction*. Princeton: Princeton UP. Print.
— (2011). "The Implied Author: An Agnostic's Manifesto." *Style* 45.1: 153–60. Print.
Livingston, Paisley (1997). "Cinematic Authorship." Richard Allen and Murray Smith (eds.). *Film Theory and Philosophy*. Oxford: Clarendon Press. 132–48. Print.
Marion, Philippe (1993). *Traces en cases: Travail graphique, figuration narrative et participation du lecteur*. Louvain-la-Neuve: Academia. Print.
McCloud, Scott (1993). *Understanding Comics: The Invisible Art*. Northampton: Tundra. Print.
McGlothlin, Erin (2003). "No Time Like the Present: Narrative and Time in Art Spiegelman's *Maus*." *Narrative* 11.2: 177–98. Print.
Metz, Christian (1991). "The Impersonal Encunciation or the Site of Film." *New Literary History* 22.3: 747–72. Print.
Mikkonen, Kai (2015). "Narrative Agency in Comics." Forthcoming. Manuscript kindly made available by the author. 1–26. Print.
Miller, Nancy K. (2003). "Cartoons of the Self: Portrait of the Artist as a Young Murderer—Art Spiegelman's *Maus*." Deborah R. Geis (ed.). *Considering Maus: Approaches to Art Spiegelman's "Survivor's Tale" of the Holocaust*. Tuscaloosa: U of Alabama P. 44–59. Print.
Moore, Alan (2002). *The League of Extraordinary Gentlemen: Vol. One*. Art by Kevin O'Neill. Colors by Ben Dimagmaliw. Lettered by Bill Oakley. Originally published in single magazine form as *The League of Extraordinary Gentlemen*, Vol. 1, #1–6, 1999–2000. London: Titan. Print.

— (2005). *Watchmen*. Illustrated and lettered by Dave Gibbons. Colors by John Higgins. Originally published in single magazine form as *Watchmen* #1–12, 1986–1987. London: Titan. Print.
Nünning, Ansgar (2001). "Mimesis des Erzählens: Prolegomena zu einer Wirkungsästhetik, Typologie und Funktionsgeschichte des Aktes des Erzählens und der Metanarration." Jörg Helbig (ed.). *Erzählen und Erzähltheorie im 20. Jahrhundert: Festschrift für Wilhelm Füger*. Heidelberg: Universitätsverlag Winter. 13–47. Print.
Rajewsky, Irina O. (2010). "Border Talks: The Problematic Status of Media Borders in the Current Debate about Intermediality." Lars Elleström (ed.). *Media Borders, Multimodality and Intermediality*. Basingstoke: Palgrave Macmillan. 51–68. Print.
Rimmon-Kenan, Shlomith (2002). *Narrative Fiction: Contemporary Poetics*. 2nd edition. London: Routledge. Print.
Ryan, Marie-Laure (1991). *Possible Worlds, Artificial Intelligence, and Narrative Theory*. Bloomington: Indiana UP. Print.
— (2006). *Avatars of Story*. Minneapolis: U of Minnesota P. Print.
— (2011). "Meaning, Intent, and the Implied Author." *Style* 45.1: 29–47. Print.
Sacco, Joe (2003). *Palestine*. Originally published as *Palestine* #1–6, 1993–1995. London: Jonathan Cape. Print.
Schmid, Wolf (2010). *Narratology: An Introduction*. Berlin: De Gruyter. Print.
Schüwer, Martin (2008). *Wie Comics erzählen: Grundriss einer intermedialen Erzähltheorie der grafischen Literatur*. Trier: Wissenschaftlicher Verlag Trier. Print.
Spiegelman, Art (1996). *The Complete Maus*. Originally published as *Maus*, Vol. I, 1986 and *Maus*, Vol. II, 1991. New York: Pantheon. Print.
— (2011). *MetaMaus*. New York: Pantheon. Print.
Stein, Daniel (2009). "Was ist ein Comic-Autor? Autorinszenierung in autobiografischen Comics und Selbstportraits." Stephan Ditschke, Katerina Kroucheva, and Daniel Stein (eds). *Comics: Zur Geschichte und Theorie eines populärkulturellen Mediums*. Bielefeld: transcript. 201–37. Print.
Surdiacourt, Stephen (2012). "Can You Hear Me Drawing? 'Voice' and the Graphic Novel." Sibylle Baumbach, Beatrice Michaelis, and Ansgar Nünning (eds.). *Travelling Concepts, Metaphors, and Narratives: Literary and Cultural Studies in an Age of Interdisciplinary Research*. Trier: Wissenschaftlicher Verlag Trier. 165–78. Print.
Tan, Shaun (2006). *The Arrival*. Melbourne: Lothian Books. Print.
Thompson, Craig (2011). *Habibi*. London: Faber and Faber. Print.

Thomson-Jones, Katherine (2007). "The Literary Origins of the Cinematic Narrator." *British Journal of Aesthetics* 47.1: 76–94. Print.
— (2009). "Cinematic Narrators." *Philosophy Compass* 4.2: 296–311. Print.
Thon, Jan-Noël (2014a). "Fiktionalität in Film- und Medienwissenschaft." Tobias Klauk and Tilmann Köppe (eds.). *Fiktionalität: Ein interdisziplinäres Handbuch*. Berlin: De Gruyter. 443–66. Print.
— (2014b). "Subjectivity across Media: On Transmedial Strategies of Subjective Representation in Contemporary Feature Films, Graphic Novels, and Computer Games." Marie-Laure Ryan and Jan-Noël Thon (eds.). *Storyworlds across Media: Toward a Media-Conscious Narratology*. Lincoln: U of Nebraska P. 67–102. Print.
— (2014c). "Toward Transmedial Narratology: On Narrators in Contemporary Graphic Novels, Feature Films, and Computer Games." Jan Alber and Per Krogh Hansen (eds). *Beyond Classical Narration: Transmedial and Unnatural Challenges*. Berlin: De Gruyter. 25–56. Print.
Uidhir, Christy M. (2012). "Comics and Collective Authorship." Aaron Meskin and Roy T. Cook (eds.). *The Art of Comics: A Philosophical Approach*. Malden: Blackwell. 47–67. Print.
Walsh, Richard (1997). "Who Is the Narrator?" *Poetics Today* 18.4: 495–513. Print.
— (2007). *The Rhetoric of Fictionality: Narrative Theory and the Idea of Fiction*. Columbus: Ohio State UP. Print.
— (2010). "Person, Level, Voice: A Rhetorical Reconsideration." Jan Alber and Monika Fludernik (eds.). *Postclassical Narratology: Approaches and Analyses*. Columbus: Ohio State UP. 35–57. Print.
Weiner, Stephen (2010). "How the Graphic Novel Changed American Comics." Paul Williams and James Lyons (eds.). *The Rise of the American Comics Artist: Creators and Contexts*. Jackson: UP of Mississippi. 3–13. Print.
Williams, Paul, and James Lyons (eds.) (2010). *The Rise of the American Comics Artist: Creators and Contexts*. Jackson: UP of Mississippi. Print.
Wilson, George M. (2007). "Elusive Narrators in Literature and Film." *Philosophical Studies* 135.1: 73–88. Print.
Wimsatt, William K., and Monroe C. Beardsley (1954 [1946]). "The Intentional Fallacy." William K. Wimsatt. *The Verbal Icon: Studies in the Meaning of Poetry*. Lexington: Kentucky UP. 3–18. Print.
Woo, Benjamin (2010). "Reconsidering Comics Journalism: Information and Experience in Joe Sacco's *Palestine*." Joyce Goggin and Dan Hassler-Forest (eds.). *The Rise and Reason of Comics and Graphic Literature: Critical Essays on the Form*. Jefferson: McFarland. 166–77. Print.

KAI MIKKONEN
(Helsinki)

Subjectivity and Style in Graphic Narratives

The question of subjectivity in graphic narratives is vast, given the multiple meanings that the term 'subjectivity' suggests. To begin with, we can distinguish between two basic dimensions of subjectivity in graphic narratives, that of an author (or author function) and a character (or a narrator).[1] The cartoonist's subjectivity can be detected in the use and combination of stylistic conventions such as the graphic line, lettering, or the spatial organization of the page. At least traditionally, graphic style has been seen as a kind of signature of the story's creation, the image bearing the signs of its making.[2]

Graphic narratives have a variety of devices available for presenting a character's subjectivity. These include perspectival techniques, narrative voice (external/internal, explicit, implicit, in legends and balloons), the presentation of dialogue and thought (speech and thought balloons), the technique of following (as sentiments and thoughts are revealed through action in a sequence of images), and other means of visual showing such as facial expression, gesture, body language, gaze, and the character's position in the image in relation to other visible objects.[3] Furthermore, a number of combined visual and verbal signs such as metaphorical images and pictograms (*emanata*, *symbolia*) that mark thought, emotion, reaction, and attitude, or onomatopoeia, such as imitatives and interjections, can offer access to a character's mind. Likewise, various aspects of spatial articulation, such as framing, sequencing, breakdown, page layout, and tabulation, can emphasize the attribution of mental functions to particular characters. For example, changes in the frame shape and size can

---

[1] The notion of an author function underscores the fact that graphic narratives are regularly products of multiple authors in cooperation. See also Daniel Stein's and Jan-Noël Thon's contributions in this volume.

[2] Cf. Marion 1993: 249–53; Baetens 2001: 147; Bredehoft 2011: 109–14; Gardner 2011: 54, 66.

[3] On how the character's position (on the page) and expression, as well as style, tone, and color should be part of focalization analysis in picture books, cf. Nikolajeva and Scott 2001: 118. On how sentiments and thoughts are revealed by metaphorical and symbolic images, cf. Groensteen 2011: 135–37, 140.

accentuate a character's mental and emotional experience. Moreover, changes in the visual style, for instance, blurry images or changes on a scale between graphic realism and a simpler cartoon style, can indicate that a certain image is a subjective mental image, such as a fantasy, dream, or memory.[4]

The traditional expectation regarding the relation of these two subjectivities, that of the author and the character, is that they are distinct, one belonging to the actual world of the story's making, and the other to the world of the story. However, as I will show in this chapter, it is possible that the interaction between these dimensions becomes significant in the story, especially in cases where a graphic narrative undermines the expectation of a unified style or closely associates important stylistic features with a particular character's mind.[5] The major emphasis in this chapter is the character's subjectivity in graphic narratives, particularly the presentation of subjective consciousness through narrative perspective (focalization and ocularization) and graphic style. The far-reaching claims I will make about the presentation of subjectivity and consciousness and graphic style should naturally be placed in a wider context of graphic narratives than I present here.[6]

Focalization and Ocularization

The techniques of narrative perspective in comics to which I refer from here on as techniques of ocularization or perceptual focalization involve different formal choices with regard to the position, angle, field, and focus of vision.[7] All of these means can attribute to the image a sense of subjective perception. The most common techniques of subjective focus of perception, in comics as in film (but in different portions and combinations), include the various ways in which the character's

---

[4] Gaudreault and Jost (1990: 128–37) refer to "opérateurs de modalisation" ("modalization operators"), such as flash images, which mark particular images out as mental images in cinema. Cf. also Miller 2007: 106, 119, 122–23.

[5] The question of the relation between two or more authorial subjectivities arises especially in cases where the writer and the cartoonist are different individuals and, subsequently, the verbal and visual narration (and styles) can be attributed to different persons. In Harvey Pekar's autobiographical comics, for instance, the question of the author's and the cartoonists' stylistic coherence and narrative control over the narrative is quite relevant. See Bredehoft 2011.

[6] Nevertheless, the theoretical claims draw from a much wider corpus of graphic narratives I have investigated. See Mikkonen 2008, 2010, 2011a, 2011b, 2012.

[7] In this chapter, I will mainly speak of 'perceptual focalization,' under which I will specifically discuss the representation of visual perception. 'Ocularization' is Jost's 1987 term that I take to be synonymous with my use of 'perceptual focalization.'

positioning in a given image—in relation to the frame and what is shown in the image—suggests a subjective narrative perspective. Such techniques comprise, for instance, the point of view (POV) image (the impression that the reader shares the field of vision with a particular character), the gaze image (showing a picture of a character looking at something), the eye-line image/match cut (a combination of a gaze image that is preceded or followed by a point of view image), the over-the-shoulder image, and the reaction image (a character reacting to what he has just seen).[8] Equally, subjective optical effects, such as an out-of-focus image that is related to someone's mental condition, can be used to create a sense of a perception image,[9] and visual effects or signs of the observer's physical presence, such as a shadow or parts of the body, in the foreground of the image can subjectify the viewpoint. Most of these effects are accentuated by the context of the image sequence and the page layout, where a field of vision may be connected to someone looking or speaking.

Unless the graphic narrative is wordless, the effects of such visual techniques are further accentuated, complemented, and sometimes contrasted by the verbal track of narration. Thus, what usually counts in understanding the degree of subjectivity in focalization in comics is our processing of the interaction between 'focalization markers' at these two levels of narration, the verbal and the visual dimension of narrative representation. This does not mean, however, that verbal narration could not complicate the establishment of perceptual focalization. Particularly in cases of split verbal focalization, in which the same person (or character of fiction) speaks and narrates simultaneously outside and inside the image, the relationship between the visual and the verbal narrative perspective can become quite complex and dynamic. Consider, for instance, Marjane Satrapi's autobiographical story *Persepolis* (2000–2003), in which the autobiographical narrator tells her story alternately in the caption boxes and the balloons, thus alternating between intra- and extradiegetic positions. The different levels of verbal narration allow the autobiographical narrator to relate the story from two different temporal perspectives at once and reflect on both the time of the events and the time of the telling. An even more ambiguous case in this respect occurs in the narratorial commentary in the Italian cartoonist Francesco Tullio Altan's *Ada* series from the 1970s and the 1980s, where the narrator, who performs the role of a kind of viewing persona, continuously comments on the ways in which the characters behave, speak, or appear in the

---

8   See Mikkonen 2010, 2012.
9   Branigan distinguishes the perception shot from the point of view image, suggesting that the perception shot includes an indication of a character's mental condition, "a signifier of mental condition has been *added* to an optical POV" (1984: 80, original emphasis).

images. In this case, the main task of the narrator is to voice subjective opinions and orientate the looking at the images, evaluate the characters, and mimic the sounds in the images.

Altan's *Ada* points out the interdependence between images and words—whenever words are used in comics—and the potential multiplication of their layers of interaction. As *Ada* also reveals, the narrator's viewing 'I' and cognitive operations (verbal evaluation, remarks, and so on) can be quite separate from the act of narration. The distinction of focalization and narration, in other words, has an unusual level of complexity in this example, since the 'impersonal' narrative voice is so constantly present and strongly opinionated.[10] Furthermore, while here the heterogeneous narrator's perception and cognition are intimately linked, this is an obvious deviation from mainstream uses of narratorial voice in third-person graphic narratives that suggests a clear distinction between perceptual and cognitive dimensions of focalization as well as between the inside and the outside of the world of the story.

The distinction between perceptual and cognitive focalization is commonly made in film narratology, where it has been argued that in film narratives the point of perception and the cognitive perspective (or attitude) do not have any obligatory correlation.[11] François Jost (1983: 195, 1987: 21–22), for instance, has pointed out that Gérard Genette's focalization concept refers simultaneously to the act of perceiving and the acts of thinking and knowing, or to the point of perception and the narrator's knowledge of the events in comparison to the characters' knowledge of those events, and that this confusion becomes problematic in the analysis of film narratives, where not all uses of the terms 'perspective' or 'focus of perception' are metaphorical. It follows that the

---

10 The difficulty of the distinction between narration and focalization in visual narratives such as film that show a world, or action, is also reflected in the need, in film studies, to add a third component to the model. Branigan has argued that there are three distinct types of narration in films: narration, action, and focalization. All of them describe "how knowledge may be stated, or obtained" (1992: 105).

11 A similar distinction is common in literary and comics studies, also since Genette's original formulation does not distinguish between focalization as the "focus of perception" or focalization as the "selection of narrative information" (1988: 64, 74). Rimmon-Kenan makes the distinction between three facets of focalization: perceptual, psychological (including cognitive and emotive components), and ideological orientation toward the focalized (the object of focalization). The cognitive component involves such narrative elements as the focalizer's (the subject of focalization) knowledge, memory, conjecture, and belief that may restrict the focalizer's knowledge of the represented world (1983: 79–80). Badman 2010 follows Rimmon-Kenan's distinction in his application of focalization analysis to comics. Horstkotte and Pedri concede that what they call optical perspectivation is "only one dimension within a broader category of focalization that also includes aspects of cognition, ideological orientation, and judgment" (2011: 331). For a discussion of the fundamental contradiction in Genette's theory, see Jesch and Stein 2009.

relation with, and distinction between, perception and thinking (or knowing) is a different kind of problem in visual than in literary narratives. In literary narratives, similar signs—and ultimately the same linguistic markers such as deictic words—reveal acts of subjective perception and cognition. In films and graphic narratives, on the contrary, we have to come to terms with the fact that the image has a certain deictic value in itself (as showing or pointing to something) and that the image implies a spatially determined point of perception. There are various exceptions to the iconic expectation of 'pointing to something,' such as the subjective mental images I have mentioned above or 'abstract' and symbolic images. Furthermore, as Jost (1983) also points out, the degree of the deictic value in a scene or a series of shots in films may be difficult to designate from the images alone. However, the meaning and representation of *perception* must be conceived differently in visual than in literary narratives due to the functions of visual showing, including the showing of deictic relations in space, the literal spatial positioning of the focus of perception, and the spatial impact of the frame.[12] In films, as Jost (2004) argues, perceptual and cognitive focalization can have clearly separate functions, expressing quite different things. The same applies to the multimodal expression of subjectivity in comics, except for the fact that graphic showing differs from the conventions and technologies of showing in cinema, such as the use of camera.[13]

Jost thus distinguishes perceptual focalization (what he calls "ocularization"), meaning the "relation between what the camera shows and what the characters are presumed to be seeing," from cognitive focalization (what he calls "focalization"), designating "the cognitive point of view adopted by the narrative" (2004: 74). Similarly, despite the absence of a camera in graphic narration, the manipulation of the relation between what the image shows (from some perspective) and what some character supposedly sees is an essential means though which comics can create a sense of a subjective vision. Not surprisingly, then, Jost's distinction has been increasingly applied, with varying degrees of theoretical rigor and clarity, to graphic narratives.[14]

However, it is important to specify that Jost does not define focalization (as different from ocularization) purely in cognitive terms but claims that the distinction enables us to focus on a relation between

---

12   Cf. also McFarlane 1996: 27.
13   Multimodality has been defined by Kress and van Leeuwen as "the use of several semiotic modes in the design of a semiotic product or event, together with the particular way in which these mode are combined" (2001: 20).
14   Cf. Miller 2007: 106, 109; Badman 2010; Groensteen 2011. Cf. also Fischer and Hatfield 2011: 80.

perception and knowledge. Focalization is "a complex product of what one sees, what the character is presumed to be seeing, what he or she is presumed to know, what he or she says, and so forth" (2004: 74). In other words, in Jost's definition, focalization concerns the relation between the ocular position that the image postulates, the visual field in the image, and the character's speech, thoughts, and presumed knowledge, while ocularization refers to the visual representation of perception in a literal sense. The analysis of focalization thus addresses the way in which cinema works in several registers at once, combining the visual and the verbal narrative track, to give the reader an illusion of an individual mind, while ocularization characterizes visual information about the point and focus of perception only (and auricularization describes the center of auditory perception).

The ocular position is a prerequisite for the impression of depth in the image. In principle, thus, in comics as in film, it is meaningless to speak of non-ocularized images that would not have a point of perception (however imaginary that may be). Ocularization, however, does not have to belong to anyone or any instance in the storyworld, or in the frame narrative; it can remain fully impersonal and hypothetical. Thus, Jost's category of 'zero ocularization' does not refer to a missing point of perception but to a broad range of perspectival options where the focalizer remains impersonal. Equally, the distinction between external and internal ocularization is potentially misleading in comics because purely internal or purely external points of perception are usually short instances only in this medium. The crucial distinction, then, is not between external, internal, or zero focal positions, but how and to what extent the image, and what is seen in the image, is subjectified by narrative conventions and context and associated with the perception and consciousness of a character in the storyworld.[15]

Jost's categories of narrative perspective in films are useful in the analysis of visual focalization in comics, given that we do not take the distinction between perceptual and cognitive focalization in a mechanistic sense. In their approach to the question of focalization in comics, Silke Horstkotte and Nancy Pedri (2011) have emphasized the need to use the concept of aspectuality or aspectual filtering[16] that would subsume the narrower optical view of focalization to better understand the

---

15 For subcategories of ocularization, cf. Jost 2004: 75–76, 79.
16 Palmer defines the aspectuality of the storyworld as the principle that, "whenever events occur in the storyworld, they are always experienced from within a certain vision," that is, perceived by the characters in that world from a particular perceptual and cognitive aspect (2004: 51–52, 2010: 56). Similarly, fictional minds "exist, or are seen from a certain aspect, within the minds of the other characters in the novel" (2004: 194).

representation of consciousness in graphic narratives. Horstkotte and Pedri's definition of focalization as aspectuality, which takes different cognitive and perceptual processes to be dimensions of aspectual filtering, offers a suggestive and holistic view for analyzing focalization-marking resources and their attribution to characters or narrators in comics. Their claims, pertaining, for instance, to the multi-stage braiding of identical visual material, shifts in visual vocabulary, or the combination of the visual and the verbal track of narrative information in a way that complicates the "possible permutations of narration and focalization" (2011: 350), serve as an important reminder of the myopic dangers of a narratological analysis of focalization in graphic narrative that would limit itself to the construction of the focus of perception alone.[17] However, Horstkotte and Pedri are much less convincing in their argument that a move away from what they call the perspectivation model would develop a better-functioning model of focalization in comics. One reason for this is that the (narratological) uses and functions of the point and focus of perception in comics, and the visual encoding of narrative perspective in this medium, are only partially understood at present. Therefore, it seems imperative that we try to take the question of the perceptual and, more precisely, optical dimension of focalization in comics to its outer limit—to see what can be said about the specificity of comics in terms of narrative perspective—before a more holistic theory of focalization can truly be developed. Secondly, in a medium that is much less reliant on narrator figures than literary prose fiction—even in first-person graphic narratives—it would appear to be important to thoroughly investigate all relevant aspects of visual narrative mediation, including not just the point and focus of perception, but the functions of graphic showing and style, to better understand how minds and worlds are created in comics.

A third reason for focusing on ocularization is that it allows us to recognize some of the formal options and narrative devices that are available to graphic narratives to present minds. The manipulation of the ocular position in comics can, for instance, help to create an effect of ambiguous subjectivity and communal perceptual focalization that would be difficult to imagine in literary narratives in quite the same way. In Lewis Trondheim and Matthieu Bonhomme's *Omni-visibilis* (2010), where the whole storyworld shares the sensory perceptions of the main character-narrator called Hervé, who is an office employee in his thirties, the point

---

17 I am not aware of actual approaches that would attempt to reduce the question of focalization in comics to optical/visual perspective alone—or to what Horstkotte and Pedri call "optical perspectivation" (2011: 331). A much more frequent problem in comics theory is that models of focalization from literary and film studies are introduced to the analysis of graphic narratives without taking the specificities of the medium into account.

of perception sharpens the parody of continuous webcam presence. In *Omni-visibilis*, all people, even from other parts of the world, begin to see through the protagonist's eyes when their eyes are closed, hear what he hears, and feel what he feels. Especially interesting in this light are the point-of-view images in the story: when the main character sees his pursuers through a peephole in the door, this cues the reader to imagine that he or she perceives the world with both the protagonist and the pursuers. Furthermore, it is implied in these images that the people whom the readers see with the main character's eyes can also observe themselves from the same viewpoint. Thus, the experience of communal visual perception reaches new heights of ambiguity. The verbal narrative track is crucial to knowing what exactly is happening, but without the skillful manipulation of the ocular position, the whole point of the parody of webcam presence and paranoid reaction to webcams might be lost.

In films, as Jost (1983: 196) points out, verbal anchoring can easily transform internal into external ocularization or vice versa. The same is true of graphic narratives. However, in a wordless graphic narrative like Finnish cartoonist Tommi Musturi's *Walking with Samuel* (2009, translated as *Sur les pas de Samuel/Walking with Samuel*), shifts in perceptual focalization can be detected by visual clues only. In this story, the reader is suddenly invited to share a perspective that appears to belong to a bird that pecks at the protagonist's eye (see figure 1). In order to understand the viewing position, the reader must compare this image with the surrounding sequence of images and the respective perspectives they offer. Wordless comics can underscore the important role played by image-to-image and scene-to-scene transitions in the representation of perspective in graphic narratives, but they may, equally and efficiently, undermine the degree of deixis in the image, that is, any coherent distinction between a character's consciousness and the fictional world.

Several exceptions to the determined ocular position of a three-dimensional image in graphic narratives exist, such as graphs and symbolic images or polyphasic figurations, but these are usually localized instances and often dependent on the general rule. The case of the polyphase image, where one picture juxtaposes or superimposes different points of movement or time, creating a more or less blurred image, does not challenge the rule, since it depends on the norm from which it is a deviation. Typically, in cases of *effet Marey*,[18] the suggested ocular position,

---

[18] The Marey effect is named after the French physicist Étienne-Jules Marey's (1830–1904) chronophotography. Marey photographed the movements of men and animals several times in a second with his chronophotographic gun, thus allowing the decomposition of movement in elementary phases (recorded on the same image or in several frames of print). For a discussion of more or less blurred polyphase images, see Kolp 1992: 134–37.

as well as the image frame, remains relatively stable, whereas the focus in the image undergoes changes in time, reflecting various paces of a process. By showing that the focus of perception is more or less undetermined, such images accentuate, as in the fight scene between Tintin and Doctor Müller in *L'île noire*, a particularly hectic temporality and/or comical rhythm.

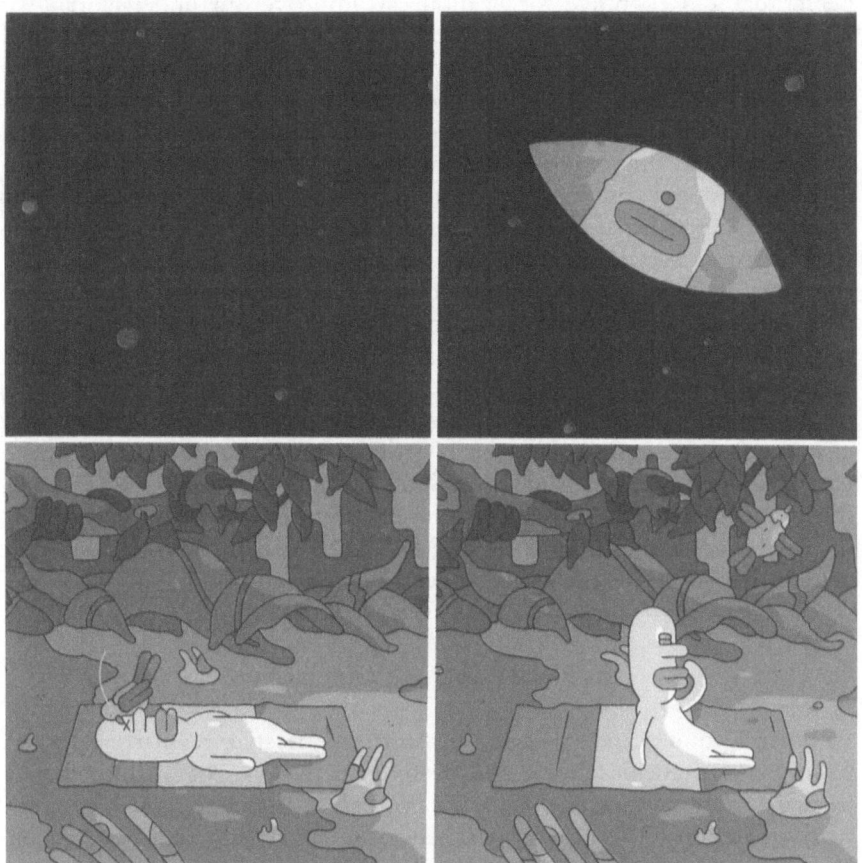

Figure 1: Tommi Musturi, *Walking with Samuel* (2009).
© Tommi Musturi/Huuda Huuda. All rights reserved.

Similarly, a layered page or a double spread, which creates an effect of an ambiguous relationship between the frames and their backdrop, can manipulate the default mode of viewing from a determined point in space. Typically, the technique prompts the viewer to imagine different interrelated viewpoints. This is what happens with what Thierry

Groensteen (2011: 66–67) has called a *multicouche* in shojo manga, a multi-layered page layout typical of this Japanese genre that is especially targeted to girls and women. The same principle applies to split panels that juxtapose different points of perception and fields of vision.

Jost's ocularization concept in itself is not necessary in comics narratology,[19] but a systematic assessment of the distinction between perceptual and cognitive focalization can improve our understanding of the multimodal dimensions of focalization in graphic narratives. Such dimensions include the point of perception in relation to what is seen or shown in the image, the interaction between perceptual and cognitive focalization in a sequence of images, and between visual and verbal focalization. In other words, for the theory of narrative perspective to develop in comics narratology, it is imperative that we investigate how visual perspectives are created and manipulated so that they become wholly or to a certain degree associated with a certain subjective vision or cognitive attitude. Equally, this requires that the criteria that help us determine how and to what extent something that is shown in the image is subjectified, even if the point of perception remains external and impersonal.

In the next section, I will discuss the ways in which graphic style, and in particular stylistic rupture, can contribute to the sense of a subjective narrative perspective. The question of a character's mind style, furthermore, invites us to rethink the relation between graphic style and the source of enunciation or, as this division is also sometimes defined in comics theory, between graphic showing and narration.

Graphic Showing and Graphic Style

In literary studies and stylistics, the concept of style regularly refers to patterns of linguistic choice and preference that can be attributed to a particular author's personal style, a period style, a generic style, or a given work of literature.[20] In its broadest sense, literary style involves all possible linguistic choices in the text, whether lexical, grammatical, phonetic, contextual, choices of figures of speech, or any other. Subsequently, stylistic analysis focuses on these linguistic elements, patterns, and

---

19 Groensteen (2011: 90–91) prefers the notion *foyer perceptif* to ocularization so as to avoid a too-close association with cinematic devices such as the viewfinder, the objective, and the camera eye. However, 'focus of perception' or 'perceptual focus,' which are possible translations of 'foyer perceptif,' would be too limiting for my purposes. Bal's definition of focalization as "the *relation* between the vision and that which is 'seen,' perceived" (1985: 100, emphasis added), is more encompassing.

20 Cf., for instance, Leech and Short 2007: 10–11.

structures, provided that they are foregrounded in the text as having stylistic relevance. In film studies, David Bordwell has defined a film's style similarly as "a system of technical choices instantiated in the total form of the work, itself grasped in its relation to pertinent and proximate stylistic norms" (2008: 378). The stylistically important technical choices can, in Bordwell's (2008: 377) model of functions of style, channel story information (denotative function), convey meanings (thematic function), signal a feelingful quality (expressive function), and exhibit perceptual qualities and patterns (decorative function).

Robert C. Harvey's definition of style as the mark of the maker and as the "visual result of an individual artist's use of the entire arsenal of graphic devices available, including the tools of the craft" (1996: 152), is a traditional conception of graphic style. The scope of this definition is relatively broad as it pertains to all possible devices and formal options available in the medium, from drawing techniques, the use of the brush and the pen, narrative breakdowns and other compositional techniques, to layout style and the overall effect of all these devices, patterns of choices, and preferences. The scope of graphic style would thus extend from the individuality of the graphic trace to the structural organization of mise-en-page, that is, the broad functions of narrative organization, selection, and arrangement of both words and images in the space of a page. The personal manner of holding the pen and the brush, for instance, is central to this definition, and style is clearly understood as something that belongs to the artist, not the world that is depicted.

In French-language comics theory, however, graphic style is frequently defined more narrowly as an instance of a graphic showing, a personal graphic expression, or as "individual graphic writing" (Marion 1993: 251; Groensteen 2011: 92; my translation from the French: "écriture graphique singulière"). Graphic style, in this sense, is a function of the graphic identity of comics,[21] but it does not extend to the broad functions of narrative organization, selection, and arrangement of words and images— functions that these theorists usually relegate to an implicit and higher level 'mega-narrator' (Marion) or "fundamental narrator" (Groensteen 2011: 105; my translation from the French: "le narrateur fondamental").[22]

---

[21] Another theoretical option, however, distinguishes between graphic and other dimensions of style. Lefèvre (2011: 15, 31) divides style in comics into the components of graphic style, the composition (mise-en-scène, framing), and the sequencing of panels. One more alternative, and one closer to the traditional definition, is to equate all visual elements in graphic narratives, including page layout and framing, with graphic style. Cf. Meesters 2010: 217.

[22] For Marion (1993: 193–94), the *narrator* is responsible for the framing of the images and the panel and page setup; thus, the narrator's activity is roughly equivalent to editing or montage in film composition. Groensteen (2007: 95) derives his notion of *narrateur*

Philippe Marion's (1993: 33, 35–36, 193–94) distinction between *graphiation* and *monstration*, which describes two distinct operations of what he calls graphic enunciation and to which he attributes different agents of narration, the *graphiateur* and the *monstrateur*, is relevant in this respect. In Marion's theory, *monstration* in the images is transitive, directed toward the figures of the story, and it involves the act of showing figures and events with an intention to create a sense of a narrative. *Graphiation*, in contrast, is reflexive (or 'autoreferential'), directed to the graphic trace and gesture, and ultimately the artist's subjectivity.[23]

One advantage of the narrower focus on graphic style is that it allows us to pose the question of style as a more specific question of enunciation: to what or whom do we attribute graphic style? This is not simply a pragmatic question of attributing particular graphic features to a particular author, cartoonist, or a colorist, but it involves the complex issue of the relation between graphic style and meaning, for instance, the functions of style in terms of the presentation of the characters' mental life. One highly interesting area of investigation in this respect is stylistic heterogeneity and change—a question that both Marion (1993: 262–67) and Groensteen (2007: 98–100, 2011: 102, 124–29) have highlighted in their approaches and that Gert Meesters (2010: 232–33) foregrounds in his analysis of Olivier Schrauwen's and Dominique Goblet's graphic narratives.

A common effect resulting from the use of heterogeneous graphic styles in one narrative, as Groensteen (2011: 125) argues, is that style is no longer conceived of as a simple mark of the maker and that, subsequently, drawing demands to be regarded as a subtle medium that offers an infinite variety of expressive possibilities. Therefore, what may happen when an artist uses multiple styles in one work, as the French cartoonist Winshluss does in his adaptation of Carlo Collodi's *Pinocchio* (2008), is that graphic style becomes both marked and opaque and points to the way in which the characters and their world (and their speech/thought) are *graphically*

---

fondamental from Gaudreault's (1988) film narratology, arguing, in his *La bande dessinée mode d'emploi*, with a different emphasis from *Système de la bande dessinée 1 & 2*, that all basic composites of the medium, such as framing, page layout, and color, should be counted as style in a broad sense, that is, style as a media performance (*une performance médiatique*).

23 Cf. Marion 1993: 36. A difficult problem that characterizes Marion's and Groensteen's theories of graphic enunciation is the multiplication of narrative agents, namely, the positing of various agents responsible for different functions such as verbal narration and graphic showing. Marion distinguishes between a monstrateur and a *graphiateur*. However, Groensteen (2011), who sees that this distinction as superfluous, distinguishes between *je montrant* (a graphic shower that is responsible for showing the images) and *je récitant*, on the one hand, and *narrateur actorialisé* (narrator as a character) and the fundamental narrator, on the other hand. All of these roles are set within a strict hierarchical structure where the narrator as a character is subjected to the graphic shower in the images while both of these agents are subjected to the fundamental narrator.

rendered. In his version of *Pinocchio*, for instance, Winshluss draws Jiminy Cockroach's tale in a markedly simpler and more spontaneous style, as monochromatic strips, thus perhaps emphasizing the impulsive characteristics of this alcoholic aspiring writer figure. Subsequently, a potential outcome of stylistic heterogeneity and overtness, as Marion argues, is that it can lead the reader to deny the mimetic "pseudo-evidence" (1993: 265) of the images and, subsequently, perhaps better grasp the consistence of their graphic trace. Thus, we may presuppose that graphic style can evoke the question of subjective narrative perspective, prompting the reader to speculate whether the focus of perception and the cognitive attitude belongs to a character, a narrator, or the author.

Think, for example, how the three basic colors—blue, yellow, and red—in Tommi Musturi's *Walking with Samuel* function as a fundamental element of the protagonist's world and are also used to illustrate the expressive potential of color in graphic narratives in general. Throughout the narrative, the three colors are featured in a flag/towel that Samuel carries with him while he also invents multiple new uses for this object. The three colors have the synesthetic quality of representing various sensory impressions and perceptions such as liquid (water or alcoholic beverage), smell (flatulence), sound (bird's song and Samuel's flute-playing emanate the same colors), light (colors in a prism, fire and the sun), and smoke (from Samuel's cigarette). Moreover, these colors can indicate changes in perceptual focalization and distance. In what is a potential reference to the source of the stylistic choices, the colors are also manipulated by the hands of a 'maker' figure who is perhaps the cartoonist's alter ego. The three basic colors thus present, simultaneously, the character's multisensory experience, the metamorphic quality of his world, and the image maker's stylistic choices.

Mind Styles in Graphic Narratives

Graphic style has various potential functions: it marks the maker, a period, a genre, a particular work, or a contextual artistic reference; furthermore, it connotes the cartoonist's intonation, approach, and perception of the world and creates specific effects such as realism, dream, memory, humor, or suspense. Graphic style is an important element in constructing a fantastic world in such texts as Winsor McCay's *Little Nemo* (1905–1914) or Fred's *Philémon* (1965–1986). In these two classic fantasy comics, stylistic features such as vibrant colors and the changing panel shapes stress the dreamlike inconsistency of Slumberland and the unreality of the letter islands of the Atlantic Ocean. McCay's and Fred's stylistic innovations and explorations of the spatial possibilities of the medium are inseparable from the worlds and the characters that their series depict.

Yet another function of graphic style is that it dramatizes a particular character's world-view, perception, and habit of thought. In other words, a narrative can invite the reader to interpret that certain choices of graphic style, stylistic rupture, or heterogeneity need to be attributed to an individual consciousness in the storyworld (rather than the author). The association between graphic style and a character's mind also has the potential to imply, as I will show shortly, that the character's worldview has profoundly affected the way in which the narrative is told and organized.

A useful notion for thinking about the functions of graphic style in such cases is *mind style*. In literary stylistics, the notion of mind style is derived from Roger Fowler, who introduced the term to designate "any distinctive linguistic representation of an individual mental self" (1977: 103) in his stylistic analysis of prose fiction. More precisely, for Fowler, mind style is a realization of a narrative perspective, and it is particularly detectable in clusters of linguistic features or techniques that give an impression of an author's or a character's world view. Geoffrey B. Leech and Mick Short have later developed Fowler's notion, referring to it as the way in which prose style creates "a particular cognitive view of things" (2007: 28) that belongs either to a writer, a narrator, or a character. When a certain mind style can be attributed to a narrator or a character this means that the writer slants the readers toward a particular narrator's or character's "mental set" (Leech and Short 2007: 151).[24] The basic premise in these theories is that all systematic linguistic choices or patterns, such as lexical choices and patterns, figurative language, or conversational behavior, may reflect style and, subsequently, the workings of individual minds.[25]

Thus, the concept of mind style has roughly the same meaning as what I have described as cognitive focalization in the present chapter, or as what Alan Palmer has called 'aspectuality.'[26] All of these notions—mind style, cognitive focalization, and aspectuality—allow us to focus on certain

---

[24] Semino has pointed out that the term 'mind style' is ambiguous "as to whether it refers to linguistic patterns in texts ('style') or to the characteristics that we attribute to particular (fictional) minds by interpreting linguistic patterns in texts" (2007: 169). She adds that there are problems at the "normal" end of mind style, meaning cases where linguistic style appears to remain natural and uncontrived, and thus "the concept seems to lose its usefulness, and to become equivalent to the more general notion of 'style'" (2007: 169).

[25] For Leech and Short's definition of style, cf. Leech and Short 2007: 31–32.

[26] See Palmer 2004, 2010. Cf. also Semino 2011: 418–20. Stockwell (2011: 289–90) has suggested that Palmer's theory of thought representation has the potential to reinvigorate the concept of mind style.

textual markers as cues of a character's mental set or world view and, moreover, to interpret these markers in relation to an evolving consciousness frame. In contradistinction to the other notions, however, the concept of mind style provides us with a focus on the *stylistic* dimensions of narrative. This is important in the sense that any systematic investigation of the presentation of minds in graphic narratives needs to incorporate the question of visual mediation in its diverse forms and must relate this question to the analysis of linguistic patterns such as vocabulary, grammar, transitivity, speech representation, metaphor, conversational behavior, and deictic choices—given that the graphic narrative has words. Furthermore, the interaction between visual and verbal styles and their combined forms can function as a marker of a mind style in its own right. The study of mind styles in graphic narratives thus refers to those (fictional or authorial) minds to which we can attribute cognitive functions by way of linguistic, visual, and combined linguistic-visual patterns, techniques, and other cues. Such patterns and techniques, furthermore, need to be foregrounded as stylistically important. I envision that the analysis of perceptual focalization, or ocularization, can function as an important dimension in this investigation, enabling us to better define what we mean by 'visual' and 'cognitive' forms of mental functioning in comics, and to identify graphic markers and patterns of perceptual focalization that have potential cognitive value.

Let us think of some examples of character-bound stylistic choices in which style contributes in a significant way to a sense of a character's mental state. One remarkable aspect, for instance, about the stylistic heterogeneity in David Mazzucchelli's much-discussed graphic novel, *Asterios Polyp* (2009), is the function of graphic style as a means of characterization. The various visual styles, such as expressionist, realist, or romantic style, abstract or mimetic style, and the changing colors and hues in the narrative correspond intimately to the characters' personalities and emotional states, or in some cases to specific events. Therefore, the various graphic styles and colors are *metaphorically* attributed to given characters, connoting their world view, experience, or emotional state.[27] Furthermore, the association between graphic style and the characters' minds suggests that the individual minds have affected the way in which the narrative is visually told and organized. The situation clearly breaks with the conventional attribution of graphic style to an author and creates a unique form of multi-styled (and multi-perspective) visual narration.

---

27 Fischer and Hatfield refer to *Asterios Polyp* by way of Palmer's notion of aspectuality to point out how conflicts between the protagonist Asterios and his wife Hana "are visually represented as non-compatible ways of seeing the world" (2011: 77).

Local stylistic changes or ruptures may also create an illusion of direct access to a character's mind. For instance, Manu Larcenet's *Blast* (2009–), a still ongoing series about the homeless ex-writer and murder suspect Polza Mancini, includes various instances of local stylistic rupture. These ruptures, accompanied by the surprise effect of color, represent a complex inner experience in the narrator-protagonist's mind. In these moments, which the narrator Polza Mancini calls "blasts," the black-and-white story incorporates children's color drawings (the images are drawn by Larcenet's children Lilie and Lenni).[28] The drawings constitute a kind of color explosion as if these colors were emanating from the narrator's mind. They first emerge around Polza's head and then spread all over the space of the image, sometimes superimposed on Polza's body (see figure 2). This suggests that the color images are something that only Polza sees in his lonely moments. However, whether Polza literally sees these images remains ambiguous. While Polza occasionally seems to be looking at the drawings and even lifts his hands toward them, the images are also shown around his body and on top of him when he has his eyes closed (see figure 3). The drawings are, furthermore, associated with other figurations in his mind, such as a hallucination of the Moai statues, which frequently occur in connection with these experiences.

Figure 2: Manu Larcenet, *Blast* 2 (2011). © DARGAUD. All rights reserved.

---

28 Larcenet also uses color in two passages in *Blast 2*, where color indicates a simple flashback.

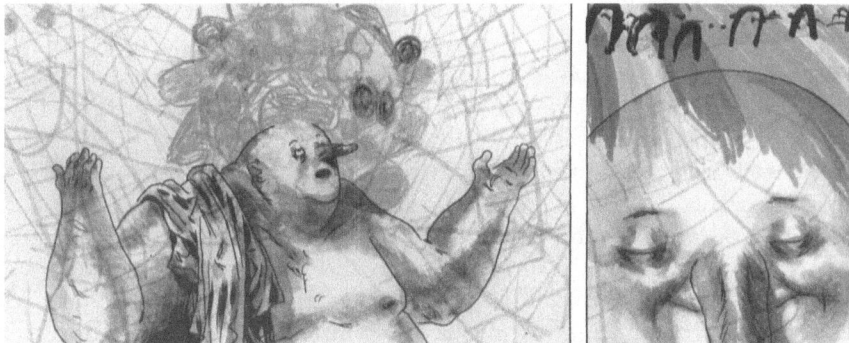

Figure 3: Manu Larcenet, *Blast* 2 (2011). © DARGAUD. All rights reserved.

The stylistic contrast that the color drawings create with the rest of the narrative dramatizes the power of the experience, giving the readers a glimpse of the protagonist's inner perception and tumult. The vivid colors and the distinctly childish style of the drawings separate the blast sensations from his everyday experience. The narrator's verbal descriptions specify their meaning. Polza Mancini explains that the blasts involve sensations of fullness and of the instant, accompanied by a sudden clarity of vision, as if the whole world appeared to him without morality or any preconception. The blasts are, as he specifies, an out-of-body experience of incredible lightness that allows him to hover over the ground, constituting a kind of rebirth or an 'intimate apocalypsis' that, moreover, implies a profound sense of union with nature.[29]

The verbal narrative track in *Blast* contributes significantly to a sense of a 'continuing-consciousness frame'[30] in these scenes, thus deepening the reader's understanding of the character's experience. Marion (1993: 156–57) has pointed out that color in comics can contribute extensively to the development of an array of sensations, evoking a sensation of the real, while color may also have a predominantly expressive and poetic function, presenting a high tenor of the graphic trace. The scenes of color explosion and stylistic rupture in Larcenet's *Blast* series rely on both of these functions (referential and poetic) at once. Something similar happens in

---

29 In an interview in which he discusses the meaning of the blast scenes, Larcenet also explains his fascination with children's drawings "without a code" that he compares to drawings by mentally disabled persons: "J'ai eu l'occasion de travailler dans un hôpital psychiatrique et d'observer les dessins des malades et c'est aussi passionnant que ceux des enfants. Ce sont des dessins qui n'ont pas de codes" (Larcenet 2011b: n.p.).

30 Palmer's 'continuing-consciousness frame' is "the ability to take a reference to a character in the text and attach to it a presumed consciousness that exists continuously within the storyworld between the various, more or less intermittent references to that character" (2010: 10).

Marc-Antoine Mathieu's black-and-white graphic narrative *La Qu...* (1991), in which the color explosion at the end of the narrative marks the passage between the world of dreams and the world of reality. Both Larcenet's and Mathieu's works employ the sudden eruption of color as a means by which to represent a character's inner experience.[31] The use of this device in *Blast*, however, is more systematic and accompanied by a stylistic rupture.

The concept of mind style provides us with an analytical frame for studying cases in which graphic style and an individual character's consciousness are intimately associated. Nevertheless, the limitations of this notion become apparent in wordless graphic narratives in which the question of how to ascribe states of mind to characters remains open in a profound sense.[32] For instance, Musturi's *Walking with Samuel* underscores the difficulty of drawing a coherent distinction between a character's consciousness and the fictional world, since it is challenging, if not impossible, to evaluate how much of what we see in the images is subjective. Beyond his muteness, the mystery of Samuel's mental functioning is further emphasized by his nearly expressionless face and lack of gestures. Due to sleeping, physical effort, or (perhaps) excitement over the course of the narrative, only some minute changes occur in his pupil-less eyes; the rare gestures he makes when he dances remain minimal (see figure 4). Furthermore, the storyworld, and sometimes the protagonist's body, is metamorphic and destabilized. On the one hand, Samuel seems to be able to live through the erosion of his world while, on the other hand, his body is at times manipulated and literally remolded by huge hands that suddenly appear. The six dictums that are listed at the end of the book and that comprise the only words in the narrative (beyond the title) might represent Samuel's world view. Equally, they may also constitute the author's interpretation of his character and the story. The dictums, such as "Do not be afraid," are followed by Samuel's gradual disappearance into the whiteness of the page.

---

31 On how color can function in a perception structure and character narration in films and how the origin of the color may be *metaphorically* attributed to characters, cf. Branigan 1984: 94–95.

32 Groensteen (2011: 137) poses a similar question about the interpretive challenges in wordless comics to anchor images to a subjectivity, including the difficulty in knowing whether what one sees in the images emanates from the reality or the imagination.

Figure 4: Tommi Musturi, *Walking with Samuel*.
© Tommi Musturi/Huuda Huuda. All rights reserved.

Conclusion

The present chapter has focused on medium-specific features of graphic narratives, involving the questions of the point and focus of perception as well as graphic style and mind style, which pose important challenges to the analysis of subjectivity in this medium.[33] I have underscored the role of perceptual focalization in the context of a more comprehensive understanding of narrative perspective. In order to develop the study of focalization in this multimodal narrative medium, we need to examine the interaction between perceptual and cognitive focus, as well as the relation between verbal narration and graphic style.

I have also shown how the notion of mind style can be applied to graphic narratives where aspects of style reflect a narrator's or a character's world-view. The graphic narratives that have served as my examples suggest, through stylistic changes and ruptures, that these changes are consistent with a given individual character's mind, emotional state, or mental state. Some of these narratives further prompt us to imagine that elements of graphic style emanate from the character-narrator.[34] At the same time, it is important to realize that the application

---

[33] See my earlier work on comparable challenges, Mikkonen 2008, 2010, 2011a, 2011b, 2012. Herman 2011 has formulated a similar concern about how medium-specific properties of graphic narratives impinge on methods of consciousness representation.

[34] I emphasize the importance of imagination here and do not claim that the narrators of *Asterios Polyp* and *Blast* are or become agents who are responsible for stylistic choices because graphic style is metaphorically associated with their consciousness and experience. What these examples suggest is a kind of thought game that invites the reader to question the distinction between the character-narrator and the agent—however we wish to name that agent—responsible for stylistic choices. I find Wilson's reading of Ernst Lubitsch's

of the concept of mind style can easily be challenged in a number of cases. The concept may lose its usefulness when graphic style appears to remain so uncontrived that it is hard to distinguish it from a generic norm, for instance, or in postmodern and unnatural narratives in which the world-creating narrative is revealed to be unreliable, as well as in wordless graphic narratives. Such narratives have the potential to undermine the ascription of states of mind to characters since it may be difficult to draw a coherent distinction between a character's consciousness and the fictional world. In other words, the challenge is to know the degree of subjectivity of vision from images alone.

The questions of narrative perspective and the function of graphic style in graphic narratives are closely related to the general problems of enunciation (source of narration), narrative agency, and narratorial idiom. The importance of first-person narratives in contemporary graphic storytelling has perhaps been one of the factors that has inspired proponents of comics theory to rethink their premises in the recent years. As Horstkotte and Pedri (2011) suggest, in analyzing graphic narratives it can be highly productive to differentiate between narration and focalization (understood in both visual and cognitive senses), especially when a character's experience and perception are embedded within a narrator's reporting discourse. Yet again, since it may be difficult to agree on what exactly would be an 'implicit' narrator, or an 'impersonal' heterodiegetic narrator, in this narrative medium,[35] the distinction between focalization and narration in comics must be given some serious medium-specific attention. Traditionally, graphic narratives are relatively independent of narrator figures in third-person narration, in which narrators appear only intermittently or not at all. In some cases, the tasks that narrators traditionally fulfill in literary narratives are carried out by the narrator (if there is one) through different means of focalization and various stylistic devices in graphic narratives. However, there are other crucial components of narrative mediation beyond the activities of narration and focalization. My underlying argument has been that we need to pay attention to the various visual and spatial features of graphic showing, or *monstration*, which interact with the activities of narration and the many dimensions of focalization.[36]

---

film *Trouble in Paradise* and his discussion of 'cinematic narrator' (which Wilson rejects) to be analogous to these examples. Wilson argues that the camera work and the editing in Lubitsch's film are exceptional because they create a strong impression of personification by seeming to be "consistently guided by someone with the sensibility of a prurient voyeur keen to know what is going on behind the closed doors" (Wilson 1986: 136).

35 See also Mikkonen 2010, 2011.
36 See also Deleyto 1991, who argues that in film narratology, one needs to consider the activities of representation and (nondiegetic) music, not just narration and focalization.

Works Cited

Altan [Francesco Tullio-Altan] (1988). *Ada nella jungla*. Milano: Glénat Italia. Print.

Badman, Derik A. (2010). "Talking, Thinking, and Seeing in Pictures: Narration, Focalization, and Ocularization in Comics Narratives." *International Journal of Comic Art* 12.2: 91–111. Print.

Baetens, Jan (2001). "Revealing Traces: A New Theory of Graphic Enunciation." Robin Varnum and Christina T. Gibbons (eds.). *The Language of Comics: Word and Image*. Jackson: UP of Mississippi: 145–55. Print.

Bal, Mieke (1985). *Narratology: Introduction to the Theory of Narrative*. Toronto: U of Toronto P. Print.

Bordwell, David (2008). *Poetics of Cinema*. New York: Routledge. Print.

Branigan, Edward (1984). *Point of View in the Cinema: A Theory of Narration and Subjectivity in Classical Film*. Berlin: Mouton. Print.

— (1992). *Narrative Comprehension and Film*. Abingdon: Routledge. Print.

Bredehoft, Thomas A. (2011). "Style, Voice, and Authorship in Harvey Pekar's (Auto) (Bio) Graphical Comics." *College Literature* 38.3: 97–110. Print.

Deleyto, Celestino (1991). "Focalisation in Film Narrative." *Atlantis* 13.1–2: 159–77. Print.

Fischer, Craig, and Charles Hatfield (2011). "Teeth, Sticks, and Bricks: Calligraphy, Graphic Focalization, and Narrative Braiding in Eddie Campbell's *Alec*." Jared Gardner and David Herman (eds.). *Graphic Narratives and Narrative Theory*. Special issue of *SubStance* 40.1: 70–93. Print.

Fowler, Roger (1977). *Linguistics and the Novel*. London: Methuen. Print.

Gardner, Jared (2011). "Storylines." Jared Gardner and David Herman (eds.). *Graphic Narratives and Narrative Theory*. Special issue of *SubStance* 40.1: 53–69. Print.

Gaudreault, André (1988). *Du littéraire au filmique*. Paris: Klincksieck. Print.

Gaudreault, André, and François Jost (1990). *Le récit cinematographique*. Paris: Éditions Nathan, Collection Nathan-Université.

Genette, Gérard (1988). *Narrative Discourse Revisited*. Trans. Jane E. Lewin. Ithaca: Cornell UP. Print.

Groensteen, Thierry (1999). *Système de la bande dessinée*. Paris: PU de France. Print.

— (2007). *La bande dessinée: Mode d'emploi*. Liège: Les Impressions Nouvelles. Print.

— (2011). *Bande dessinée et narration: Système de la bande dessinée 2*. Paris: PU de Paris. Print.

Harvey, Robert C. (1996). *The Art of the Comic Book: An Aesthetic History*. Jackson: UP of Mississippi. Print.

Herman, David (2011). "Storyworld/Umwelt: Nonhuman Experiences in Graphic Narratives." Jared Gardner and David Herman (eds.). *Graphic Narratives and Narrative Theory*. Special issue of *SubStance* 40.1: 156–81. Print.

Horstkotte, Silke, and Nancy Pedri (2011). "Focalization in Graphic Narrative." *Narrative* 19.3: 330–57. Print.

Jesch, Tatjana, and Malte Stein (2009). "Perspectivization and Focalization: Two Concepts—One Meaning? An Attempt at Conceptual Differentiation." Peter Hühn, Wolf Schmid, and Jörg Schönert (eds.). *Point of View, Perspective, and Focalization: Modeling Mediation in Narrative*. Berlin: De Gruyter. 59–77. Print.

Jost, François (1983). "Narration(s): en deçà et au-delà." *Communications* 38: 192–212. Print.

— (1987). *L'Œil-Caméra: Entre film et roman*. Lyon: PU de Lyon. Print.

— (2004). "The Look: From Film to Novel. An Essay in Comparative Narratology." Robert Stam and Alessandra Raengo (eds.). *A Companion to Literature and Film*. Malden: Blackwell. 71–80. Print.

Kolp, Manuel (1992). *Le langage cinématographique en bande dessinée*. Brussels: Éditions de l'université de Bruxelles. Print.

Kress, Gunther, and Theo van Leeuwen (2001). *Multimodal Discourse: The Modes and Media of Contemporary Communication*. London: Arnold. Print.

Larcenet, Manu (2009). *Blast 1. Grasse Carcasse*. Paris: Dargaud. Print.

— (2011a). *Blast 2. L'apocalypse selon Saint Jacky*. Paris: Dargaud. Print.

— (2011b). Interview by Agnès Deyzieux. *Le cas des cases*, Apr. 8. Web.

— (2012). *Blast 3. La tête la première*. Paris: Dargaud. Print.

Leech, Geoffrey N., and Mick Short (2007). *Style in Fiction: A Linguistic Introduction to English Fictional Prose*. 2nd edition. London: Longman. Print.

Lefèvre, Pascal (2011). "Some Medium-Specific Qualities of Graphic Sequences." Jared Gardner and David Herman (eds.). *Graphic Narratives and Narrative Theory*. Special issue of *SubStance* 40.1: 14–33. Print.

Marion, Philippe (1993). *Traces en cases: Travail graphique, figuration narrative et participation du lecteur*. Louvain-la-Neuve: Academia. Print.

Mathieu, Marc-Antoine (1991). *Julius Corentin Acquefacques, prisonnier des rêves: La Qu...* Vol. 2. Paris: Delcourt. Print.

Mazzucchelli, David (2009). *Asterios Polyp*. New York: Pantheon. Print.

McFarlane, Brian (1996). *Novel to Film: An Introduction to the Theory of Adaptation*. Oxford: Clarendon. Print.

Meesters, Gert (2010). "Les significations du style graphique." *Textyles, revue des lettres belges de langue française* 36–37: 519–26. Print.

Mikkonen, Kai (2008). "Presenting Minds in Graphic Narratives." *Partial Answers* 6.2: 301–21. Print.

— (2010). "Le narrateur implicite dans la bande dessinée: La transformation du *style indirect libre* dans deux adaptations en bandes dessinées de *Madame Bovary*." *Image & Narrative* 11.4: 185–207. Web.

— (2011a). "The Implicit Narrator in Comics: Transformations of Free Indirect Discourse in Two Graphic Adaptations of *Madame Bovary*." *International Journal of Comic Art* 13.2: 473–87. Print.

— (2011b). "Graphic Narratives as a Challenge to Transmedial Narratology: The Question of Focalization." Daniel Stein, Christina Meyer, and Micha Edlich (eds.). *American Comic Books and Graphic Novels*. Special Issue of *American Studies/Amerikastudien* 56.4: 637–52. Print.

— (2012). "Focalisation in Comics: From the Specificities of the Medium to Conceptual Reformulation." *Scandinavian Journal of Comic Art* 1: 69–95. Web.

Miller, Ann (2007). *Reading Bande Dessinée: Critical Approaches to French-Language Comic Strip*. Bristol: Intellect. Print.

Musturi, Tommi (2009). *Walking with Samuel*. Helsinki: Huuda Huuda. Print.

Nikolajeva, Maria, and Carole Scott (2001). *How Picturebooks Work*. New York: Garland. Print.

Palmer, Alan (2004). *Fictional Minds*. Lincoln: U of Nebraska P. Print.

— (2010). *Social Minds in the Novel*. Columbus: Ohio State UP. Print.

Rimmon-Kenan, Shlomith (1983). *Narrative Fiction: Contemporary Poetics*. New York: Routledge. Print.

Semino, Elena (2007). "Mind Style Twenty-Five Years On." *Style* 41.2: 153–73. Print.

— (2011). "Deixis and Fictional Minds." *Style* 45.3: 418–40. Print.

Stockwell, Peter (2011). "Changing Minds in Narrative." *Style* 45.2: 288–91. Print.

Trondheim, Lewis, and Matthieu Bonhomme (2010). *Omni-visibilis*. Paris: Dupuis. Print.

Wilson, George M. (1986). *Narration in Light: Studies in Cinematic Point of View*. Baltimore: Johns Hopkins UP. Print.

Part II

Graphic Narrative beyond the 'Single Work'

NANCY PEDRI
(St. John's, Newfoundland)

Graphic Memoir: Neither Fact Nor Fiction[1]

One! Hundred! Demons!, a collection of seventeen short "autobifictionalography" (Barry 2002: 5) stories by Lynda Barry about her problematic adolescence, opens with a two-panel page portraying the author-protagonist sitting at her desk, brush in hand, asking: "Is it autobiography if parts of it are not true? Is it fiction if parts of it are?" (2002: 7).[2] The introduction's direct challenge to authority through questions of mediation and veracity touches the heart of the issue at hand: to what extent can one distinguish between fact and fiction in graphic memoir, and is it theoretically attractive to do so? If, as Barry suggests, facts are altered when translated into representation and if "'telling the truth' in memoir is not always a straightforward process" (Versaci 2007: 57), then how is it that memoirs are able to create "in readers the expectation that they are told about something—for example, a series of life-changing events—that has actually occurred more or less as presented" (Böger 2011: 604)? What are some of the multimodal narrative strategies or operative conventions put in place to impart to readers graphic memoir's "special reality" (Eisner 2008b: xi)?

Memoir, it is argued, claims to, and is thus expected to "depict the lives of real, not imagined, individuals" (Couser 2012: 15). Memoir communicates as accurately as possible through self-representation a self and a life that exist or existed in the real world. Its writing can thus be said to be governed by what David Davies, expanding on the theories of Kendall L. Walton and Gregory Currie, calls the fidelity constraint, a constraint that makes readers "assume that the author has included only events she believes to have occurred, narrated as occurring in the order in

---

[1] Despite its growing popularity and the large outpour of graphic memoir, no consensus has been reached as to how to refer to this graphic narrative subgenre. Graphic memoir is referred to as 'autographics' by Whitlock 2006, 'comic book memoir' by Versaci 2007, 'autography' by Gardner 2008, 2012, 'autographic memoir' by Watson 2011, 'graphic novel memoir' by Chaney 2011c, and 'autobiocomics' or 'autobioBD' by Miller and Pratt 2004. Graphic memoir also belongs to the spectrum of 'out-law' genres of autobiography proposed by Kaplan 1992.

[2] For a discussion of how these two panels establish Barry's sincerity, cf. Chaney 2011c: 22.

which she believes them to have occurred" (Davies 2007: 46).[3] Although the memoir's overriding constraint is fidelity so that readers are asked to believe instead of make-believe the narrative's content,[4] it is rare, especially today, to read a memoir that does not also betray a fictive intent. Not only do memoirs openly adopt many recognizable authenticating strategies, but they also draw attention to gaps and omissions, to doubt and invention. Many comingle fact and fiction, self-critically using literary techniques to tell 'real' stories about people's lives. Even though memoirs are nonfictional, then, they differ from other works of nonfiction in that, while fidelity is the overarching constraint, most memoirists relax this constraint to produce a desired effect on readers.[5]

To postulate memoir as nonfiction and, at the same time, appreciate its fictive intent impacts questions of memoir's representation and its readers' appreciation of facts. Walton, for instance, specifies that although facts are made and not found, "[e]very piece of discourse or thought which aspires to truth has a reality independent of *itself* to answer to, whatever role sentient beings might have in the construction of this reality" (1990: 102). This claim is echoed by Marie-Laure Ryan, who clarifies that whereas readers contemplate the textual world of fiction as "an end in itself," they "evaluate [that of nonfiction] in terms of its accuracy with respect to an external reference world known to the reader through other channels of information" (2001: 92). So, although a certain "leeway or looseness with the facts is expected" (Yagoda 2009: 2), as is the inevitable mediation and subsequent constructedness of self through representation, memoir is bound by a claim, if not an obligation, to present a "compelling and authoritative and close-to-the-bone honest" (Yagoda 2009: 241) account of a real person. This obligation, in turn, is met by readers, who turn to it with an eye for truth.[6]

Graphic memoir has been theorized as differing "from text autobiographies in several ways, tending towards self reflexivity and often

---

3   As Davies explains, chronological presentation means that the "narrated events be *represented as occurring* in the order in which the author believes them to have actually occurred" (2007: 191, note 13, original emphasis).
4   Several theorists who distinguish between fiction and nonfiction do so in terms of intention and what kind of response the text prompts in readers: whereas nonfiction asks readers to believe the text's content, fiction asks them to make-believe or imagine its content. See Currie 1990; Walton 1990; Lamarque and Olsen 1994; Davies 1996, 2001, 2007; Lamarque 1996.
5   Davies (2007: 48) makes a similar argument in relation to Mailer, Capote, and Morrison.
6   For an overview of how the concept of authorial intention has governed theories of autobiography, and a strong critique against it, cf. Anderson 2001: 1–6, 123. For a structuralist position of truthfulness in memoir, specifically AIDS memoirs, cf. Chambers 1998: 1–4. For a sustained analysis of how autobiography and its subgenres, including memoir, are susceptible to the burdens of proof, see Egan 2011.

featuring metafictional elements that point to ideas of the self as a construct" (Williams 2011: 356). While this argument is difficult to support when keeping theories of fiction in mind, it has gained currency among those who claim that the fictive intent is inherent in the comics medium. Some argue that since the "formal grammar [of graphic narratives] rejects transparency and renders textualization conspicuous" (Chute 2008: 457) and thus "everything in [its] represented world is very overtly *as if*" (O'Neill 1994: 99, original emphasis), the graphic memoir's proposed (and expected) factual portrayal of self is openly caught up in the cartoon image's constructed and interpretative quality.[7] Cartooning, the argument goes, renders overt the inevitable subjective register of self-representation, openly operating under the pretense that all that is presented was "transformed through somebody's eye and hand" (Wolk 2007: 118).[8] Although much can be said to weaken claims that fictionality is inherent to the medium of comics, these readings serve to illustrate the complex reading demands born from complementing the fidelity constraint with more general interests in storytelling.

Credibility: Authority and Doubt

The telling of one's self, whether through recall or direct witnessing, is a task that is often fraught with perils and doubts that pose a challenge for both authority and accuracy. *Fun Home: A Family Tragicomic* is Alison Bechdel's memoir about her closeted homosexual father who most likely committed suicide when she was an adolescent and her realization at that time of her homosexuality. Bechdel's narrator sustains that in her dysfunctional family, described by her as "a mildly autistic colony" (2006: 139), each member had only his or her own self. To support her interpretation of how her family functioned as a group of individualistic loners, she briefly mentions her father's "solipsistic circle of self" and then examines her "own compulsive propensity to autobiography" (Bechdel 2006: 140), which concretely manifested itself in the form of diary writing. The task of writing the self, however, soon proves difficult (if not

---

7   Gardner argues that "[t]he comics form necessarily and inevitably calls attention through its formal properties to its limitations as juridical evidence—to the compressions and gaps of its narrative (represented graphically by the gutterspace between the panels) and to the iconic distillations of its art" (2008: 6).
8   Verano (2006: 326) describes the narrative universe of comics as the world of the fictional signifier; Versaci holds that "the comic book projects unreality to some degree because every comic book is a drawn version of the world and, therefore, not 'real'" (2007: 12); Round 2010 supports this view in her examination of the blurring of fact and fiction in Alan Moore and Eddie Campbell's *From Hell* (1989–1996).

impossible) for Alison, who struggles with fundamental questions of knowledge and representation of self.

In her attempt to follow her father's advice to "just write down what's happening" (Bechdel 2006: 140) in her diary, the narrator somewhat surprisingly realizes that "the minutely-lettered phrase *I think* begins to crop up between [her] comments" (Bechdel 2006: 141, original emphasis). This intensely self-reflexive gesture exposes her awareness that the 'facts' about her life are merely what she perceives to be true, that her narrative and the past experiences that give rise to it are relentlessly framed by her own aspectuality.[9] The panels accompanying this realization show how the young Alison inserts this statement of doubt after every declaration she makes, including the most seemingly insignificant ones such as making popcorn (see figure 1). The narrative text accompanying a vertically long panel of Alison making popcorn explains her obsessive fixation as resulting from "a sort of epistemological crisis" (Bechdel 2006: 140). She asks herself how she knew "that the things [she] was writing there were absolutely, objectively true?" (Bechdel 2006: 140). She then admits: "All I could speak for was my own perceptions, and perhaps not even those" (Bechdel 2006: 140). Uncertain as to where the truth lies and whether she could ever know it, Alison questions her own ability to be sincere or, at the very least, sincere enough to capture, with the aid of an undoubtedly faulty memory, the factual details of her life.

The protagonist's confusions, interpretive difficulties, and mental turmoil are not as apparently exposed in the visual track. Whereas the verbal track betrays the narrator's desire to communicate the truth and, at the same time, her realization of the impossibility of reaching such a goal since she can relate only what she perceives to be truthful and maybe not even that, given the limitations of writing, the visual track is littered with visuals supporting the declarations she has made in her diary (such as, making popcorn, reading *Hardy Boys*, and writing in her diary). The visual track is authoritative in its declarative statements: the hesitation at the center of the verbal track is nowhere to be seen in the visual track. Even when depicting diary entries that become more and more laden with doubt—she replaces "I think" with a shorthand version that looks like a sort of circumflex or an upside-down "V" that became so ubiquitous that her diary is almost illegible[10] (see figure 2)—the visual track does not

---

9   Palmer introduces the term 'aspectuality' to account for how events in a storyworld "are always experienced from within a certain vision" (2004: 51–52). For an extended analysis of how aspectual filtering impacts meaning in graphic narrative, see Horstkotte and Pedri 2011. See also Kai Mikkonen's contribution in this volume.

10 Cf. Bechdel 2006: 143. For an extended discussion of this symbol in *Fun Home*, cf. Gardner 2008: 1–6; Chute 2010: 186–93.

Graphic Memoir: Neither Fact Nor Fiction 131

waver in its depictions of what is claimed (and doubted) in the diary entries. This incongruity between the verbal and the visual leaves readers to ask, along with Alison, where the truth lies.[11]

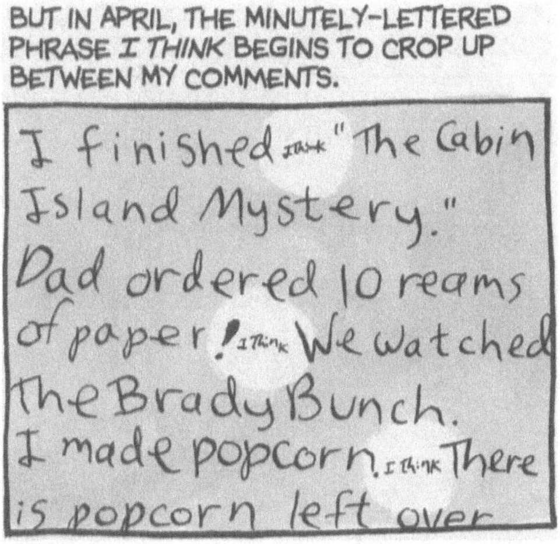

> BUT IN APRIL, THE MINUTELY-LETTERED PHRASE *I THINK* BEGINS TO CROP UP BETWEEN MY COMMENTS.
>
> I finished saw "The Cabin Island Mystery." Dad ordered 10 reams of paper! I think We watched The Brady Bunch. I made popcorn. I think There is popcorn left over

Figure 1: Alison Bechdel, *Fun Home: A Tragicomic* (2006). © Alison Bechdel. All rights reserved.

> THINGS WERE GETTING FAIRLY ILLEGIBLE BY AUGUST, WHEN WE HAD OUR CAMPING TRIP/INITIATION RITE AT THE BULLPEN.
>
> Dad got a dead person. We came to the Bull pen. Bill Hat came with us. We went for a walk. It got dark we saw falling stars.

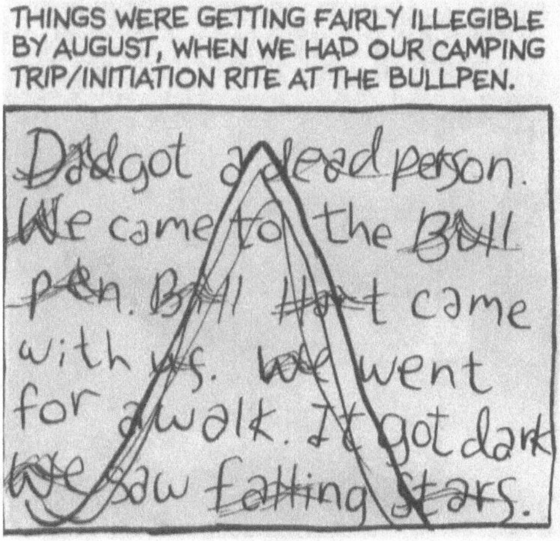

Figure 2: Alison Bechdel, *Fun Home: A Tragicomic* (2006). © Alison Bechdel. All rights reserved.

---

11 This is not to suggest that the visual depicts all that the older Alison narrates in the text boxes. Instead, the visual is confined only to what a younger Alison narrates in her diary entries.

132   Nancy Pedri

Fun Home's visual track, however, is not without its gaps and omissions. When Alison recalls a camping trip at the Bullpen, she marvels that her "notes on it are surprisingly cursory. No mention of the pin-up girl, the strip mine, or Bill's .22. Just the snake--and even that with an extreme economy of style" (2006: 143). As if in imitation of that economy of style, the large comics panel accompanying the verbal text depicts a young Alison with two other children staring at a garbage-ridden body of water from which a partially drawn snake is drinking (see figure 3).

Figure 3: Alison Bechdel, *Fun Home: A Tragicomic* (2006). © Alison Bechdel. All rights reserved.

All of the other details, so matter-of-factly exposed by an older Alison, who functions as an extradiegetic narrator in the present who writes and draws of her past self, do not figure in the comics panel. A text box within the panel specifies: "Again, the troubling gap between word and meaning. My feeble language skills could not bear the weight of such a laden experience" (2006: 143). Here, the narrator acknowledges her own doubts as an artist, admitting, if even implicitly, that uncertainty, 'untruthfulness,' and artifice are inevitable features of remembering and creating. The implications of these words for memoir's factual representation of self echo across *Fun Home*, which incorporates into its narrative an extended discussion on Alison's struggle to put the story into words and images. Implied in them is that so much of her life cannot be adequately, accurately represented. Her story, she admits to readers, is riddled with gaps and fissures, doubts and uncertainties.

Taken together, the initial incongruity between the written and the visual tracks,[12] which are immediately followed by a cartoon sequence where the two are more in sync,[13] situates the narrator's dilemma of telling the truth squarely within narration, that is, squarely within the very process of representation.[14] What is verbally and visually thematized across these four pages (and throughout *Fun Home*) is that in graphic memoir, "the power of memory must always share the act of self-representation with the devices of fiction" (Gardner 2008: 6). To highlight the union of fact and fiction in graphic memoir is to suggest that fact and truth telling have little to do with reference. Instead, here they rest, at least in part, in openly confronting that the real, the remembered, and the subjective share center stage with fictional creativity.

In doubting the truthfulness of her own account and her ability to transcribe her life into words and images, Bechdel's narrator intimately connects her subjective (re)interpretation to both the telling of self and personal experience, the storyworld and lived reality. Her reflections on, and enactment of, the conflicted process of self-representation contribute to establishing a relation of trust between the narrator and her readers. Fact and truth telling prove to rest on the closeness between the narrative assertions and "*the way we, as readers, believe the actual world to be*" (Davies 2007: 61, original emphasis).[15] Thus, the narrator builds credibility by questioning her writing while she writes, by recognizing that the very act of making sense of her self and her history is part of the problem. The second-guessing of her own perspective actually closes the gap between the author's historical presence and the Alison she has constructed as the narrator of her story. It also seeks to elicit in readers a complex narrative

---

12 Cf. Bechdel 2006: 140–41.
13 Cf. Bechdel 2006: 142–43.
14 Quite surprisingly, it is Alison's mother who teaches her to overcome the compulsion to scribble over all she writes, encouraging her to stand behind what she writes. Cf. Bechdel 2006: 149.
15 For a similar argument, cf. Mooij 1993: 125–48.

response that secures belief in the narrative's content.[16] It does so by asserting common, real-experience understandings of the impossibility to fully know and represent the self.

To render transparent her own anxiety about being able to respect the fidelity constraint and abide by memoir's "preference for the literal and verifiable" (Gilmore 2001: 3) is one of the key strategies adopted by this and other graphic memoirs to communicate nonfictionality. The memoir's narrative authority is thus left intact; indeed, the narrator's credibility is enhanced through the admittance of doubt, of not knowing for sure if the event unfolded as it is being told. Working within the fidelity constraint, doubt feeds the readers' need to know not only what happened, but also how it is perceived to have happened as well as how the narrator/author struggles to communicate faithfully that subjective perception.

Authority and doubt thus unite to ensure credibility. That they are both caught up in the very fabric of graphic memoir's commitment to accuracy is a central theme in Art Spiegelman's *Maus* (1986, 1991), a two-volume graphic memoir of the author's engagement with his father Vladek's Holocaust survival and its narrative. Throughout *Maus*, the fictionality of its verbal and visual telling is repeatedly highlighted by Artie, who serves as both the extradiegetic verbal narrator (in text boxes) of the 1980s storyline in which he interviews his father in New York about his Holocaust experience (the intradiegetic storyline) and the visual narrator—i.e., drawer or graphiator—of the extra- and intradiegetic narratives. Indeed, concerns of how subjective filtering inevitably infringes upon all aspects of the storyworld are so ubiquitous in *Maus* that Linda Hutcheon observes that it "always reminds us of the *lack* of transparency of both its verbal and visual media. Its consistent reflexivity [...] point[s] to the utter non-objectivity of the historian or biographer" (1997: 306).

A brief analysis of an instance where *Maus*'s visual track communicates the narrator's doubt will serve to complement and emphasize the argument that evincing doubt and non-objectivity does not necessarily threaten credibility. A three-panel series relating the destiny of an Auschwitz prisoner addresses the narrator's doubt as to the facts of Vladek's eyewitness account by way of a shading technique (see figure 4). The episode is introduced in the context of Vladek's telling of the endless roll calls in Auschwitz. The page opens with two panels that span its width, depicting long rows of prisoners. The first illustrates the prisoners' anonymity: all in striped prisoner garb, the crowd of prisoners is one great mass of undistinguishable faces. The second, slightly taller panel zooms in

---

16 Lehman (1997: 164–93) offers a similar reading in relation to Tim O'Brien's nonfictional work.

on a portion of the group, making it possible to discern individual faces—some mice, some pigs. In it, a 'mouse' prisoner steps forward to protest to the guard: "I don't belong here with all these Yids and Polacks! I'm a **German** like you!" (Spiegelman 1991: 50, original emphasis). In the next row, comprised of a symmetrical pair of panels, doubt about the prisoner's identity is visually expressed, a doubt that can be attributed to Artie, the visual narrator—or drawer—of Vladek's telling.

Figure 4: Art Spiegelman, *Maus: A Survivor's Tale. II: And Here My Troubles Began* (1991). © Art Spiegelman. All rights reserved.

In the first panel, the prisoner is a mouse against a black background. The drawing is a medium close-up, showing the character's head and upper body down to about his waist. A jagged-edged speech balloon indicates that the prisoner is shouting: "I have medals from the Kaiser. My **son** is a soldier!" (Spiegelman 1991: 50, original emphasis). In the second panel of the pair, Artie in the foreground asks Vladek, "Was he *really* a German?" (Spiegelman 1991: 50, original emphasis). Visually, doubt as to the prisoner's identity is represented with a heavily shaded replica of the previous panel in the background, with a meaningful substitution of the prisoner's mouse head with a cat head.[17] The repetition of the two panels with the visual changes coupled with Artie's question and Vladek's

---

[17] That Spiegelman draws Jews as mice, Germans as cats, Poles as pigs, and so on has received much attention since its publication. Hathaway, for instance, argues that "Spiegelman's choice to draw animals rather than human figures, visibly and immediately alerts the reader to the work's constructedness" (2011: 252). Loman examines the "translation of the cat-and-mouse metaphor from the American context to the European" (2006: 552); Saraceni sees Spiegelman's use of the animal metaphor as "a mockery of the very racial claims that the Nazis promulgated" (2001: 453).

assertion of not knowing indicates hesitation between two possible truths, which would necessitate different visual representations.[18]

Maus's performance of doubt does not weaken credibility in the narrative's authority; instead, it unites authority with a questioning process that is all too familiar to readers. By reflecting on the difficulties and acknowledging the possible gaps and omissions of remembering and knowing for certain, graphic memoir reminds readers that what they are reading is a very human story, one in which the narrator is not a super, all-knowing being, but rather an ordinary person telling his life in his own terms as best he can.

Degrees of Abstraction: Photographs and Cartoons[19]

Like most comics genres, graphic memoir is "a hybrid word-and-image form in which two narrative tracks, one verbal and one visual, register temporality spatially" (Chute 2008: 452). It goes without saying that this multimodal form of life writing is "different from both written life narrative and visual or photographic self-portraiture" (Watson 2011: 124). It also goes without saying that graphic memoir is far more complex than the straightforward comingling of two modes of representation. Most graphic memoirs combine different writing styles and fonts in their verbal track, as well as different styles and types of images in their visual track. Representational shifts in either track raise fundamental questions about how to interpret the visual as well as about the power of the visual to relay affect.[20] Variation in the graphic memoir's visual track also introduces a change in the degree of visual abstraction, thus raising a different set of questions as to how the factual can accommodate the interpretative initiatives signaled by such changes.

An analysis of the evermore popular comingling of cartoons and photographic images in graphic memoir is particularly suited for understanding how graphic memoir works within and against common (mis)conceptions informing visual representation in order to secure

---

[18] In addition, the juxtaposition of these two images exposes the shortcomings of the animal imagery, which does not account for the complexities informing identity—such as that of an assimilated German Jew.

[19] This section is a version of "Cartooning Ex-Posing Photography in Graphic Memoir" (Pedri 2012).

[20] Eisner argues that "[t]he style of lettering and the emulation of accents are the clues enabling the reader to read it with the emotional nuances the comics storyteller intended. This is essential to the credibility of the imagery" (2008a: 61).

belief.[21] Cartooning and photography have been theorized as opposite types of images vis-à-vis their degree of abstraction, that is, in relation to how closely they resemble their real-life counterparts.[22] Unlike photographic images that are said to have a necessary "relationship to objective reality," cartoon images betray a "relationship to the subjectivity of the artist: a drawn image implies that someone drew it" (Woo 2010: 175). The photographic image is readily approached as "an imprint or transfer of the real" (Krauss 1981: 26) since most readers privilege photography's mechanical processes of production and thus fail to see or overlook the traces of authorship in its product. The cartoon image, on the other hand, has a history of being perceived to be obviously handcrafted, "eminently self-reflexive and autoreferential" (Marion quoted in Baetens 2001: 149).

This perceived difference between the two types of images—the "stylized" quality of cartoons and the "realist" (Beaty 2006: n.p.) quality of photographs—has grave implications for the representation of fact (and fiction) in graphic memoirs that use both modes of representation. If one considers that photographs, as W. J. T. Mitchell indicates, "seem to involve a different sort of 'ethic' from that associated with drawings and paintings" (1986: 61), then one would expect photographs in graphic memoir to provide a more factual, accurate visual rendition of the author's self than the crafted cartoon images alongside which they work. Photographs, it must stressed, are governed by an "assumption that the camera makes it possible to obtain as sharp, clear, and lifelike an image as possible of what appears in front of the lens" (Azoulay 2008: 150). This assumption, which Ariella Azoulay claims is actually "an agreement among the citizens of the citizenry of photography [...] concerning access to what is imprinted on the photograph" (2008: 150), brings readers to expect that photographs in graphic memoir function as they often are believed to function in purely verbal memoirs: providing "evidence of the author's lived reality beyond the way that she or he may manipulate it in words" (Edwards 2011: 80).

Surprisingly, however, when reproduced in graphic memoirs, photographic images can serve not to confirm that what is being related—identity, self, personal experience—is real or factual or accurately portrayed. Indeed, the comingling of cartooning and photography in graphic memoir's visual track often "eradicate[s] any clear-cut distinction

---

21 Groensteen (2007: 41–3) comments on the use of photography in comics without, however, stopping on the actual reproduction of photographic images in the comic universe. For an extended examination of the use of photography in Emanuel Guibert's *Le Photographe*, see Pedri 2011.
22 Cf. McCloud 1994: 29.

between documentary and aesthetic" (Hirsch 2011: 25). As Marianne Hirsch suggests in relation to the use of photographs in *Maus*, "[i]n moving from documentary photographs—perhaps the most referential representational medium—to cartoon drawings of mice and cats, Spiegelman lays bare the levels of mediation that underlie *all* visual representational forms" (1997: 25).[23] In addition to blurring boundaries separating the documentary and the aesthetic, the inclusion of photographs in graphic memoir can accentuate a commonality between photographic and cartoon images that is often theoretically and practically overlooked: both are representations or, to borrow from Walton, both induce an imagining. A 1958 photographic image of Spiegelman with his mother (see figure 5) introduces a four-page graphic memoir "Prisoner on the Hell Planet: A Case History" (1986: 100–03) that recounts his mother's suicide and the author's mental breakdown ten years later as he struggles to come to terms with her suicide.[24] Framed by a thick black drawn wavy line and captioned in the same hand as the embedded memoir's cartoon panels, the photograph is held up at an angle by a cartoon drawing of a hand. The drawn frame, caption, and hand

Figure 5: Art Spiegelman, *Maus: A Survivor's Tale. I: My Father Bleeds History* (1986).
© Art Spiegelman. All rights reserved.

---

23 Hutcheon makes a more general observation when she argues that "however documentary or realist [*Maus*'s] mode [...,] it always reminds us of the *lack* of transparency of both its verbal and visual media" (1999: 11).
24 "Prisoner on the Hell Planet" was first published in 1973 in *Short Order Comix*.

graphically signal the transposition of the photographic image into the comic universe. They also indicate its status as a hand-crafted, hand-selected artifact, one that gains meaning within a particular context.

By blatantly transposing the photographic image into the cartoon universe, a universe that announces itself as the product of a "graphiator responsible for graphic line, composition, framing, and layout" (Miller 2011: 244–45), the cartoon hand accentuates the photographic image's fictionality.[25] It announces that what is shown in the photograph is not to be believed to be true, but rather imagined to be so. The hand's similarity (despite its slightly lower degree of abstraction) to the drawn hand at the bottom of the comic page that holds open "Prisoner on the Hell Planet" further suggests that all visual representations are subject to the interpretative maneuvers of those who create them (see figure 6). Just as the photographic image works alongside the cartoon image to accentuate the workings of a creative mind, so too do the cartoon images highlight the photographic image's fictionality. Through their comingling, readers are reminded that *Maus* "is no doubt accurate, but it is anything but objective" (Mordden 1992: 94). In this way, readers are made aware that what they are holding—"Hell Planet" and *Maus*—is, to put it bluntly, "Art's story" (Mordden 1992: 94).[26]

The union of photography and cartooning in *Maus* (and in other graphic memoirs) exposes the historical experience supposedly captured in the photographic image as always actualized by its narrative presentation. Hence, their union in *Maus* enacts and confirms the meeting of fact and fiction, thus shedding light on how graphic memoir works to secure belief. Tellingly, Spiegelman conceives of the meeting between what he calls the real and the creative as "a point of discovery" or "a moment of collision" that gives "the biggest charge" (1995: n.p.). The overt comingling of fact and fiction brings readers to confront their union as generating a continuous assessment of their own expectations and assumptions in relation to the author's intention of fidelity. Readers are thus made aware of their own role in believing the narrated events.

---

25 Banner (2000: 133) argues that the photographs in *Maus* serve as documentary evidence; Hirsch (2011: 32) confirms their archival status; Oliver suggests that the photographic images in *Maus* provide "a contrast [to the cartoon drawings] that reminds the reader about the ghastly reality of the historical events narrated in the novel" (2009: n.p.).

26 The filtering through Artie's consciousness of all elements—fictional or nonfictional—that comprise the narrative is so strong that despite a lack of evidence either in the photographic image or in the surrounding information (the caption, the drawn frame, or the drawn hand holding it) asserting that it is, in fact, an image of Artie and his mother, few readers would question its link of correspondence to the author. Critics who have asserted that the photograph is of Artie and his mother include Hirsch (1997: 31, 2011: 29) and Rothberg (1995: 679).

Figure 6: Art Spiegelman, *Maus: A Survivor's Tale. I: My Father Bleeds History* (1986).
© Art Spiegelman. All rights reserved.

Oftentimes, the inclusion of photographic images in graphic memoirs also makes readers aware that the author's views of self that have been transcribed verbally and visually are not necessarily what can be literally seen and captured photographically. *Cancer Vixen* (2006), a graphic memoir by Marisa Acocella Marchetto that tells the story of her struggle with breast cancer, opens with an ultrasound photograph (see figure 7) accompanied by a bright yellow-green cartoon arrow verbally specifying that somewhere in the middle of the image is "the tumor" (2006: 1). Despite most readers' familiarity with this type of photographic image, it is difficult to determine what dark or light shadow actually is the tumor, especially before taking note of the dark sphere carefully delineated by four crosses in the top portion of the ultrasound photograph. The arrow that points to the ultrasound clarifies that "it looks like a black hole" (Marchetto 2006: 1). With its explicatory note and modifying specification, the cartoon arrow, and not the ultrasound photograph, represents the portion of life, the actual event, covered in *Cancer Vixen*.[27]

That cartooning is more apt than photography to detailing the protagonist's personal struggle with breast cancer is particularly evident when, on the following page, the tumor is visually represented in cartoon form as an oddly shaped lump just above Marisa's left breast (Marchetto

---

[27] Cf. Yagoda, who distinguishes memoir from autobiography by specifying that "'memoir' has been used by books that cover the entirety *or* some portion of [a life]" (2009: 1).

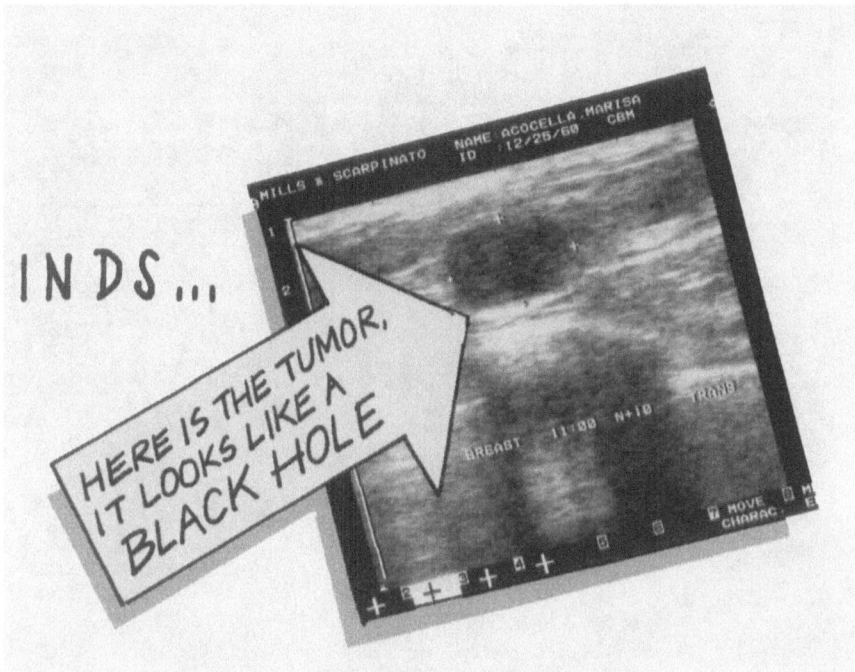

Figure 7: Marisa Acocella Marchetto, *Cancer Vixen* (2006).
© Marisa Acocella Marchetto. All rights reserved.

2006: 2). The close-up of the lump in two sequential panels portrays it from two different angles: that of the doctor examining Marisa and that of Marisa looking down at it from the examination table. Marisa's perspective of the lump and its makeup is further accentuated two pages later with the introduction of a round purple-colored background cartoon panel in which a group of cancer cells with green malignant faces, pinched eyes, and protruding red tongues are imaged (see figure 8).

Each cell is depicted as a one-armed face, disparagingly shooting the middle finger. A short verbal footnote accompanied by a yellow cartoon arrow pointing to the round panel indicates that what is being represented is "possible cancer cells, an artist's rendition" (Marchetto 2006: 4). A second footnote wrapped around the bottom of the panel specifies that the rendition is "magnified 3 gazillion times" (Marchetto 2006: 4), thus self-reflexively adopting (and adapting) the scientific language that usually accompanies medical images such as the ultrasound photograph that opened the memoir.

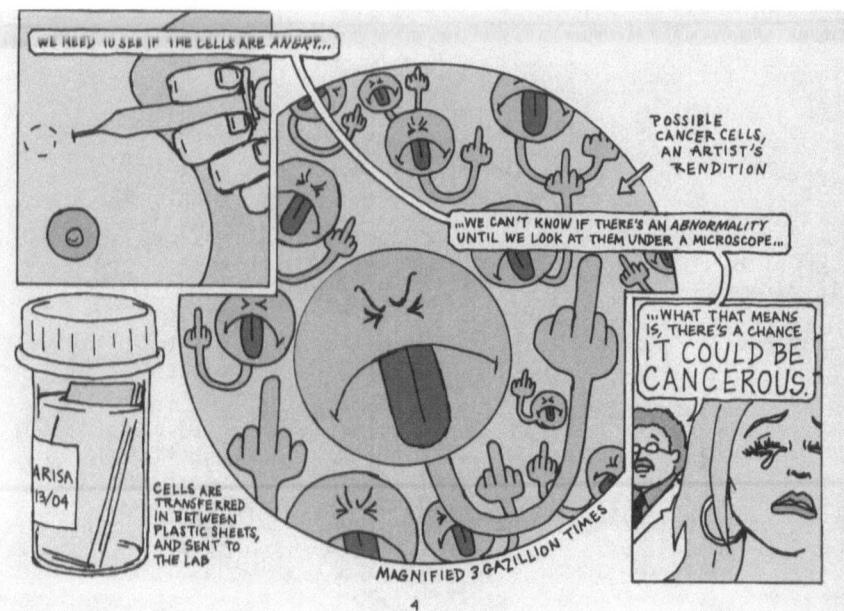

Figure 8: Marisa Acocella Marchetto, *Cancer Vixen* (2006).
© Marisa Acocella Marchetto. All rights reserved.

Unlike that and similar medical photographs, the cartoon renditions of cancer cells in Marchetto's graphic memoir situate the cancer's meaning in lived, personal experience by blatantly, overtly offering up for consideration Marisa's subjective perspective of, and reaction to, her cancer. The open interpretative stance of her cartoon images embraces the subjective, acknowledging its role in accurately communicating the real experience represented in *Cancer Vixen*. Indeed, when considered alongside the introductory ultrasound photograph, the cartoon renditions of the tumor represent the reality the author *feels* to be true, and not the attributes of cancer that can be scientifically (or objectively) *seen*.

The inclusion of the ultrasound photograph alongside cartoon drawings of the same tumor stands to indicate two opposite visual poles of abstraction, the photographic and the cartoon image. However, their union exposes the photograph as being the least informative of the two types of images and void of emotive charge, thus working against common assumptions informing the photograph's appreciation as factual evidence. Consequently, the "difference between what is shown and how something is shown" (Mikkonen 2010: 81) that is characteristic of graphic memoir is raised for explicit consideration. As the addition of the cartoon arrow and its specifications as well as the repeated use of the cartoon green-faced artist's rendition of the tumor throughout *Cancer Vixen*[28] suggest, graphic memoir secures belief in readers by charging the representation of reality (even that of a photographic image) with the value it has for the character and not by confirming any presumed referential claims to an unqualified real.

The demystification of photographic objectivity is also apparent when photography and cartooning come together in *Mom's Cancer* (2006), Brian Fies's graphic memoir of his family's experience with their mother's metastatic lung cancer.[29] In this memoir, cartoon text penciled on a photographic image critically disrupts the perception that a medical photograph (in this case, an M. R. I. scan) accurately shows "a dying brain tumor" (Fies 2006: 79). Instead of the M. R. I. scan, the author reproduces a black-and-white photograph of the M57 "nebula in the constellation Lyra" on a full page and titles it "A Universe Inside her Head" (Fies 2006: 79) (see figure 9).

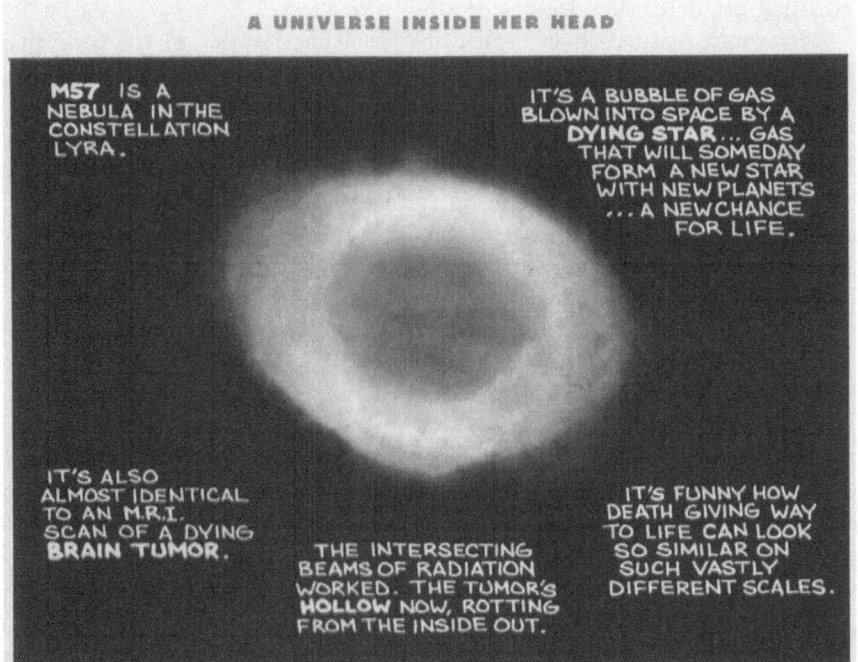

Figure 9: Brian Fies, *Mom's Cancer* (2006). © Brian Fies. All rights reserved.

---

28 Cf. Marchetto 2006: 89, 123, 208.
29 For a discussion of how the myth of photographic objectivity has been propagated, see Pedri 2008.

Across the photograph's black top margin, white printed writing specifies that what we see is "a bubble of gas" produced by a "dying star ... gas that will someday form a new star with new planets" (Fies 2006: 79). Across its bottom margin, a parallel narrative written in the same hand clarifies that the image is "almost identical to an M. R. I. scan of a dying brain tumor" and observes, "it's funny how death giving way to life can look so similar on such vastly different scales" (Fies 2006: 79). The cartoon writing emphasizes that the photograph of the nebula looks surprisingly similar to the narrator's mother's brain tumor captured photographically by medical scans. By reproducing the nebula photograph in lieu of the actual M. R. I. scan of the dying tumor and suggesting that the two are interchangeable, the narrator sets in motion the demystification of claims to objective reality that medical photographs are reputed to have. The suggestion that to a non-specialized audience a photograph of a bubble of gas looks similar to one of a tumor within a graphic memoir about that very tumor aligns belief with the fanciful, constructed, fictional workings of a subjective mind.[30]

Recently, theorists have argued that subjective truth (i.e., the truth that lies with the representation) and not historical truth or truth that requires dates, facts, and research distinguishes memoir from autobiography.[31] Within the cartoon universe of these and other graphic memoirs, the inclusion of photography forges the articulation of a complex truth, one where the "creative treatment of actuality" (Grierson 1933: 8) is held under serious consideration and the documented treatment of actuality under scrutiny. Thierry Groensteen argues that cartooning has the "power to generate a depiction that [...] will manifest, if the cartoonist wants it, the same qualities of precision and veracity as the adjacent [photographic] documented parts" (2007: 42). These examples illustrate that in graphic memoir cartooning often supersedes the photographic in its manifestation of those very qualities.

The inclusion of photographic images in graphic memoir does something more than highlight the privileged status of subjective truth in life writing that translates into "a kind of subjective camera" (Miller and Pratt 2004: n.p.) in graphic memoir. It actually helps expose the authorial

---

[30] Three cartoon renditions of the brain tumor, before treatment, are included at the beginning of *Mom's Cancer* (cf. Fies 2006: 4). The visual renditions are not accompanied by words. For an analysis of the use of photography in psychoanalysis, see Rose 1986; for a historical-cultural overview of the use of photography in the sciences, including medicine, cf. Marien 2006: 32–44, 143–51, 209–16; for an analysis of photography in medicine, see Ruddick 1982; Auger 1984; Dermer 1999; Van Dijck 2005. For bibliographic sources of the role of photography in medicine, cf. Lenman 2005: 726.

[31] Cf. Yagoda 2009: 3.

subject position as intrinsically linked to its cartoon self.³² When photography and cartooning come together in these and other graphic memoirs, the perception of self and the representations to which it gives rise may be considered more truthful (and, thus, more real) than the extradiegetic, real self, pictured in the photographic image. It follows that a diegetic self, and not a real self, is the focal point and the filtering mind of graphic memoir. Such a self often sidesteps or undermines that which is verifiably true to revel instead in the way "[it] perceive[s], remember[s], and make[s] sense out of [its life]" (Chaney 2011b: 3).

Accuracy: Real World⇔Interpretive Distortion

The privileging of a diegetic self in graphic memoir is why style, which is so personal and subjective, actually betrays important truths about the storyworld represented. "The fact of style as a narrative choice—and not simply a default expression—," Hillary Chute specifies, "is fundamental to understanding graphic narrative (as it is, of course, to understanding, say, prose, poetry, and painting)" (2010: 146). Every graphic memoir has its own particular pictorial and lettering style that "encourage readers to see the story as the author's personal expression" (Versaci 2007: 44). And although much can be said about how that style triggers recognition and appreciation, what is important to accentuate in a discussion on fact and fiction in graphic memoir is that style actually presents readers with a particularly personal vision of what is remembered as having been experienced. Style, then, speaks not so much to what is seen and remembered, but rather to the subjective interpretation of the facts or what some call the "'cartooning as interpretation' effect" (Wolk 2007: 121).

When considered in this light, even the most impressionistic or abstract cartoon style fails to threaten the commitment to fidelity that governs graphic memoir. *Epileptic* (2005), David B.'s graphic memoir of growing up with a brother who suffers epileptic seizures and parents who go to great pains to find a cure for him, is perhaps one of the most visually impressive and challenging graphic memoirs about illness published in recent years.³³ In a letter that serves as the book's foreword,

---

32 Cf., for instance, Lynda Barry's cartoon scribbles with which she 'defaces' the photographic portraits reproduced on the cover pages of four short stories, "Common Scents" (2002: 50–51), "Resilience" (62–63), "Magic" (98–99), and "Lost and Found" (206–07).

33 *Epileptic* was first published in French as *L'Ascension du Haut Mal* as a series of six volumes from 1996 to 2003. For a recent analysis of disease in *Epileptic*, see Engelmann 2010.

his sister writes: "You've laid down, in the panels of this book, the shadows of our childhood. My recollections are neither as detailed nor as precise as yours. You've always been concerned about the correct detail, about faithful reconstruction" (2005: n.p.). Besides emphasizing that *Epileptic* is David's story as remembered by him, this foreword also foregrounds the narrative's accuracy, confirming its adherence to nonfiction's fidelity constraint.

What becomes apparent upon reading the book, however, is that as the disease becomes graver (or, David grows into a deeper awareness of it), the cartoon drawings are more and more abstract and metaphorical (and, thus further removed from realist aesthetics). As Douglas Wolk notes, "[t]he artwork in *Epileptic* tracks [David's] perceptions, becoming increasingly elaborate and design-heavy" (2007: 140) as his family begins to collapse under the disease's demands. For instance, dreams become more frequent, with their psychedelic backgrounds and imaginary creatures that betray David's "difficult process of self-discovery" (Tabachnick 2011: 105); his brother Jean-Christophe figures more often as beastly and contorted; his brother's epilepsy takes on the shape of a long-mouthed serpent with a body that twists into all sorts of contortions, often carrying Jean-Christophe with it. With these and other metaphorically charged images, the divide between David's reality and his imagining of that reality begins to weaken.

As we "visit the inside of David B.'s head" (B. 2005: 278), we come to realize that the use of metaphorical representation is the best way he can communicate the turmoil of his experience. He admits as much: "I want to tell the whole story. My brother's epilepsy, the physicians, macrobiotics, spiritualism, the gurus, the communes. But I don't know how to draw it. And I don't yet realize that it'll take me another 20 years to get there" (B. 2005: 291). The year is 1979, and David is living in Paris, writing and drawing. The large panel accompanying this confession depicts Jean-Christophe entangled in the epilepsy serpent-like creature, confirming that *Epileptic* is the product of that twenty-year struggle (see figure 10).

Here, David B.'s graphic animalization of illness is embroiled in a "self-reflexivity [that] unveils the text's constructedness" (Chaney 2011a: 141). However, as can be guessed at this point, neither the metaphorical cartoon images nor *Epileptic*'s self-reflexive strategies render that which is narrated fictional. On the contrary, they provide an accurate account of David's experience, if we understand this to mean that readers accept the metaphorical images as adequately expressive of the emotions and emotional responses as the memoirist/protagonist understands them to

Figure 10: David B., *Epileptic* (2005). © David B. All rights reserved.

have been.³⁴ The use of metaphorical images confirms that his brother's disease and its effect on David's family are best deciphered subjectively. Like other visual metaphors, they "can only 'mean' according to the mind that makes [them] 'mean'" (Reizenstein 2007: 324). As with the comingling of photography and cartooning, in this and other metaphorically charged graphic memoirs, the craftsmanship of cartooning proves to be particularly equipped to address the ins and outs of personal experience. Indeed, Wolk maintains that cartooning's "chief tools are distortion and symbolic abstraction" (2007: 120). In graphic memoir, these tools are put to good use. They expose the interior landscape of characters and thus carry readers into the particular details of the mental processing of hard facts. Indeed, *Epileptic* can be said to guide

> readers who are used to reality as it can be captured by photographs into the profoundly different way [David] perceives the world, partly by relating the specific experiences that led him there and partly by representing everything not as his eye apprehends it but as his consciousness alters it. (Wolk 2007: 141)

The metaphorical images, born from David's imagination, unite real world experience with interpretive distortion and, consequently, persuade readers as to the accuracy of his point of view. The fidelity constraint is thus left intact.

---

34 On metaphor and truth, see Ankersmit and Mooij 1993. For an overview of critical approaches to metaphor and its relation to truth, cf. Mooij 1993: 171–86.

Well, then…

The melding of fact and fiction, where one cannot be easily distinguished from the other, bestows graphic memoir with "imaginative strength, or plausibility" (Coovadia 2009: 1), indeed, the type of authority that Imraan Coovadia attributes to literature. Surprisingly, these authors postulate an accurate, believable self within and across representation by adopting strategies that foreground fictionality. As argued, they make provocative use of storytelling techniques that acknowledge, critique, and ultimately embrace the very impossibility of the truthful representation of self in which they are absorbed. By so forcibly asserting the inherent problematics of representing the real and suggesting that a truthful account of self is out of reach within a genre that is governed by the fidelity constraint, graphic memoirs dismantle factual/fictional divisions. Indeed, they make it theoretically unattractive to distinguish between fact and fiction for the graphic memoir's strength to foster belief in their telling resides with the abolishment of such boundaries through the foregrounding of the subjective viewpoints, memory filters, or emotive charges operative in the representation of self.

The incongruence between the real and its cartoon representation that has been central to the present chapter's analysis points to the creative interplay between an individual, private self and its representation in the public realm of graphic memoir to dismantle notions of self (and reality) as anything other than always mediated and assumed, and not given. What ultimately comes to light is the central role of the subjective in graphic memoir's commitment to the accurate portrayal of a self and its life. Counterintuitively, the consideration of how fact and fiction meld by way of a variety of narrative strategies and operative conventions has revealed that in graphic memoir a diegetic self, and not the author's intention or other extradiegetic promises, gains the reader's belief. Such thinking would require understanding the fidelity constraint as secured through storytelling strategies that take into consideration readers' common expectations and assumptions to secure belief.

Works Cited

Anderson, Linda (2001). *Autobiography*. London: Routledge. Print.
Ankersmit, F. R., and J. J. A. Mooij (eds.) (1993). *Knowledge and Language*. Vol. III: *Metaphor and Knowledge*. Dordrecht: Kluwer. Print.
Auger, Derek (1984). "Medicine: The Role of the Photographer." *British Journal of Photography* 131: 977–78. Print.

Azoulay, Ariella (2008). *The Civil Contract of Photography*. New York: Zone Books. Print.
B., David (2005). *Epileptic*. New York: Pantheon. Print.
Baetens, Jan (2001). "Revealing Traces: A New Theory of Graphic Enunciation." Robin Varnum and Christina T. Gibbons (eds.). *The Language of Comics: Word and Image*. Jackson: UP of Mississippi. 145–55. Print.
Banner, Gillian (2000). *Holocaust Literature: Schultz, Levi, Spiegelman, and the Memory of the Offence*. London: Valentine Mitchell. Print.
Barry, Lynda (2002). *One! Hundred! Demons!* Seattle: Sasquatch. Print.
Beaty, Bart (2006). "*Le Photographe* Vol. 3, Emmanuel Guibert." *The Comics Reporter*, Dec. 14. Web.
Bechdel, Alison (2006). *Fun Home: A Family Tragicomic*. Boston: Houghton Mifflin. Print.
Böger, Astrid (2011). "Conquering Silence: David Small's *Stitches* and the Art of Getting Better." Daniel Stein, Christina Meyer, and Micha Edlich (eds.). *American Comic Books and Graphic Novels*. Special issue of *Amerikastudien/American Studies* 56.4: 603–16. Print.
Chambers, Ross (1998). *AIDS Diaries and the Death of the Author*. Ann Arbor: U of Michigan P. Print.
Chaney, Michael, A. (2011a). "Animal Subjects of the Graphic Novel." *College Literature* 38.3: 129–49. Print.
— (2011b). "Introduction." Michael Chaney (ed.). *Graphic Subjects: Critical Essays on Autobiography and Graphic Novels*. Wisconsin: U of Wisconsin P. 3–9. Print.
— (2011c). "Terrors of the Mirror and the *Mise en Abyme* of Graphic Novel Autobiography." *College Literature* 38.3: 21–44. Print.
Chute, Hillary (2008). "Comics as Literature? Reading Graphic Narrative." *PMLA* 132.2: 452–65. Print.
— (2010). *Graphic Women: Life Narrative and Contemporary Comics*. New York: Columbia UP. Print.
Coovadia, Imraan (2009). *Authority and Authorship in V. S. Naipaul*. New York: Palgrave Macmillan. Print.
Couser, Thomas G. (2012). *Memoir: An Introduction*. Oxford: Oxford UP. Print.
Currie, Gregory (1990). *The Nature of Fiction*. New York: Cambridge UP. Print.
Davies, David (1996). "Fictional Truth and Fictional Authors." *British Journal of Aesthetics* 36: 43–55. Print.
— (2001). "Fiction." Berys Gaut and Dominic Lopes (eds.). *The Routledge Companion to Aesthetics*. London: Routledge. 263–74. Print.
— (2007). *Aesthetics and Literature*. London: Continuum. Print.

Dermer, Rachelle A. (ed.) (1999). *Medicine and Photography*. Special issue of *History of Photography* 23. Print.

Edwards, Natalie (2011). "The Absent Body: *Photography* and Autobiography in Hélène Cixous's *Photos de racines* and Annie Ernaux and Marc Marie's *L'Usage de la photo*." Natalie Edwards, Amy L. Hubbell, and Ann Miller (eds.). *Textual and Visual Selves: Photography, Film, and Comic Art in French Autobiography*. Lincoln: U of Nebraska P. 79–97. Print.

Egan, Susanna (2011). *Burdens of Proof: Faith, Doubt, and Identity in Autobiography*. Waterloo: Wilfrid Laurier UP. Print.

Eisner, Will (2008a). *Graphic Storytelling and Visual Narrative: Principles and Practices from the Legendary Cartoonist*. New York: Norton. Print.

— (2008b). "Introduction." *To the Heart of the Storm*. New York: Norton. xi. Print.

Engelmann, Jonas (2010). "'Picture This': Disease and Autobiographic Narration in the Graphic Novels of David B and Julie Doucet." Mark Berninger, Jochen Ecke, and Gideon Haberkorn (eds.). *Comics as a Nexus of Cultures: Essays on the Interplay of Media, Disciplines and International Perspectives*. Jefferson: McFarland. 45–59. Print.

Fies, Brian (2006). *Mom's Cancer*. New York: Abrams ComicArts. Print.

Gardner, Jared (2008). "Autography's Biography, 1972-2007." *Biography* 31.1: 1–26. Print.

— (2012). *Projections: Comics and the History of Twenty-First-Century Storytelling*. Stanford: Stanford UP. Print.

Gilmore, Leigh (2001). *The Limits of Autobiography: Trauma and Testimony*. Ithaca: Cornell UP. Print.

Grierson, John (1933). "The Function of the Producer: 2. The Documentary Producer." *Cinema Quarterly* 2.1: 7–9. Print.

Groensteen, Thierry (2007). *The System of Comics*. Trans. Bart Beaty and Nick Nguyen. Jackson: UP of Mississippi. Print.

Hathaway, Rosemary V. (2011). "Reading Art Spiegelman's *Maus* as Postmodern Ethnography." *Journal of Folklore Research* 48.2: 249–67. Print.

Hirsch, Marianne (1997). *Family Frames: Photography, Narrative and Postmemory*. Cambridge: Harvard UP. Print.

— (2011). "Memory and Postmemory." Michael A. Chaney (ed.). *Graphic Subjects: Critical Essays on Autobiography and Graphic Novels*. Madison: U of Wisconsin P. 17–44. Print.

Horstkotte, Silke, and Nancy Pedri (2011). "Focalization in Graphic Narrative." *Narrative* 19.3: 330–57. Print.

Hutcheon, Linda (1997). "Postmodern Provocation: History and 'Graphic' Literature." *Torre: Revista de la Universitad de Puerto Rico* 2.4–5: 299–308. Print.
— (1999). "Literature Meets History: Counter-Discoursive 'Comix.'" *Anglia: Zeitschrift für Englische Philologie* 117.1: 4–14. Print.
Kaplan, Caren (1992). "Resisting Autobiography: Out-Law Genres and Transnational Feminist Subject." Sidonie Smith and Julia Watson (eds.). *De/Colonizing the Subject*. Minneapolis: U of Minnesota P. 115–38. Print.
Krauss, Rosalind (1981). "The Photographic Conditions of Surrealism." *October* 19: 3–34. Print.
Lamarque, Peter (1996). *Fictional Points of View*. Ithaca: Cornell UP. Print.
Lamarque, Peter, and Stein H. Olsen (1994). *Truth, Fiction and Literature: A Philosophical Perspective*. Oxford: Oxford UP. Print.
Lehman, Daniel W. (1997). *Matters of Fact: Reading Nonfiction Over the Edge*. Columbus: Ohio State UP. Print.
Lenman, Robin (ed.) (2005). *The Oxford Companion to the Photograph*. Oxford: Oxford UP. Print.
Loman, Andrew (2006). "'Well Intended Liberal Slop': Allegories of Race in Spiegelman's *Maus*." *Journal of American Studies* 40.3: 551–71. Print.
Marchetto, Marisa A. (2006). *Cancer Vixen: A True Story*. New York: Alfred A. Knopf. Print.
Marien, Mary W. (2006). *Photography: A Cultural History*. London: Laurence King. Print.
McCloud, Scott (1994). *Understanding Comics: The Invisible Art*. New York: Harper Perennial. Print.
Mikkonen, Kai (2010). "Remediation and the Sense of Time in Graphic Narratives." Joyce Goggin and Dan Hassler-Forest (eds.). *The Rise and Reason of Comics and Graphic Literature: Critical Essays on the Form*. Jefferson: McFarland. 74–86. Print.
Miller, Ann (2011). "Autobiography in *Bande Dessinée*." Natalie Edwards, Amy L. Hubbell, and Ann Miller (eds.). *Textual and Visual Selves: Photography, Film, and Comic Art in French Autobiography*. Lincoln: U of Nebraska P. 235–62. Print.
Miller, Ann, and Murray Pratt (2004). "Transgressive Bodies in the Work of Julie Doucet, Fabrice Neaud, and Jean-Christophe Menu: Towards a Theory of the AutobioBD." *Belphegor* 4.1: n.p. Web.
Mitchell, W. J. T. (1986). *Iconology: Image, Text, Ideology*. Chicago: U of Chicago P. Print.
Mooij, J. J. A. (1993). *Fictional Realities: The Uses of Literary Imagination*. Amsterdam: John Benjamins. Print.

Mordden, Ethan (1992). "Kat and Maus." *The New Yorker*, Apr. 9. 90–96. Print.

Oliver, Antonio (2009). "The *Shoah* and the Second Generation: Graphical Representation. The Unusual Structure of *Maus*." http://www.oocities.org/soho/veranda/2207/maus/tut2.html. Web.

O'Neill, Patrick (1994). *Fictions of Discourse: Reading Narrative Theory*. Toronto: U of Toronto P. Print.

Palmer, Alan (2004). *Fictional Minds*. Lincoln: U of Nebraska P. Print.

Pedri, Nancy (2008). "Documenting the Fictions of Reality." *Poetics Today* 29.1: 155–73. Print.

— (2011). "When Photographs Aren't Quite Enough: Reflections on Photography and Cartooning in *Le Photographe*." *ImageTexT: Interdisciplinary Comics Studies* 6.1: n.p. Web.

— (2012). "Cartooning Ex-Posing Photography in Graphic Memoir." *Literature and Aesthetics* 22.2: 248-66. Print.

Reizenstein, Ben (2007). "Perspicuous Opacity: Marianne Moore and Truth in a Fallen World." *Cambridge Quarterly* 36.4: 317–37. Print.

Rose, Jacqueline (1986). *Sexuality in the Field of Vision*. London: Verso. Print.

Rothberg, Michael (1995). "'We Were Talking Jewish': Art Spiegelman's *Maus* as Holocaust Production." *Contemporary Literature* 35.4: 661–87. Print.

Round, Julia (2010). "'Be Vewy, Vewy Quiet. We're Hunting Wippers': A Barthesian Analysis of the Construction of Fact and Fiction in Alan Moore and Eddie Campbell's *From Hell*." Joyce Goggin and Dan Hassler-Forest (eds.). *The Rise and Reason of Comics and Graphic Literature: Critical Essays on the Form*. Jefferson: McFarland. 188–201. Print.

Ruddick, Ray F. (1982). "The Role of the Medical Photographer in Forensic Medicine." *British Journal of Photography* 129: 170–71. Print.

Ryan, Marie-Laure (2001). *Narrative as Virtual Reality: Immersion and Interactivity in Literature and Electronic Media*. Baltimore: Johns Hopkins UP. Print.

Saraceni, Mario (2001). "Seeing beyond Language: When Words Are Not Alone." *CAUCE* 24: 433–55. Print.

Spiegelman, Art (1986). *Maus: A Survivor's Tale*. I: *My Father Bleeds History*. New York: Pantheon. Print.

— (1991). *Maus: A Survivor's Tale*. II: *And Here My Troubles Began*. New York: Pantheon. Print.

— (1995). "Art Spiegelman: Lips." Interview with Harvey Blume. *Boston Book Review*, June 1. Web.

Tabachnick, Stephen E. (2011). "Autobiography as Discovery in *Epileptic*." Michael A. Chaney (ed.). *Graphic Subjects: Critical Essays on Autobiography and Graphic Novels*. Madison: U of Wisconsin P. 101–16. Print.

Van Dijck (2005). *The Transparent Body: A Cultural Analysis of Medical Imaging*. Seattle: U of Washington P. Print.

Verano, Frank (2006). "Invisible Spectacles, Invisible Limits: Grant Morrison, Situationist Theory, and Real Unrealities." *International Journal of Comic Art* 8.2: 319–29. Print.

Versaci, Rocco (2007). *This Book Contains Graphic Language: Comics as Literature*. New York: Continuum. Print.

Walton, Kendall L. (1990). *Mimesis as Make-Believe: On the Foundations of the Representational Arts*. Cambridge: Harvard UP. Print.

Watson, Julia (2011). "Autographic Disclosures and Genealogies of Desire in Alison Bechdel's *Fun Home*." Michael A. Chaney (ed.). *Graphic Subjects: Critical Essays on Autobiography and Graphic Novels*. Wisconsin: U of Wisconsin P. 123–56. Print.

Whitlock, Gillian (2006). "Autographics: The Seeing 'I' of the Comics." Hillary Chute and Marianne DeKoven (eds.). *Graphic Narrative*. Special issue of *Modern Fiction Studies* 52.4: 965–79. Print.

Williams, Ian (2011). "Autography as Auto-Therapy: Psychic Pain and the Graphic Memoir." *Journal of Medical Humanities* 32.4: 353–66. Print.

Wolk, Douglas (2007). *Reading Comics: How Graphic Novels Work*. Cambridge: DaCapo. Print.

Woo, Benjamin (2010). "Reconsidering Comics Journalism: Information and Experience in Joe Sacco's *Palestine*." Joyce Goggin and Dan Hassler-Forest (eds.). *The Rise and Reason of Comics and Graphic Literature: Critical Essays on the Form*. Jefferson: McFarland. 166–77. Print.

Yagoda, Ben (2009). *Memoir: A History*. New York: Riverhead. Print.

DANIEL STEIN
(Siegen)

Superhero Comics and the Authorizing Functions of the Comic Book Paratext

Introduction

While the past few decades have seen an astonishing boom in comics theory and criticism, questions concerning the serial creation, publication, and reception of comics have rarely been at the center of analysis.[1] Indeed, the seriality of comics constitutes one of the major blind spots in the rapidly expanding field of comics studies, despite the fact that serial forms of storytelling have shaped the development of this popular medium, as well as individual formats and genres, perhaps more than any other narrative principle.[2] Making any kind of sweeping claims about overcoming this particular blind spot would, of course, be foolish, and to even try to answer all of the many pressing questions related to issues of seriality in comics in a single chapter would certainly be condemned to resounding failure. This is why I want to take a much more narrow focus in this chapter, a focus that will allow me to conduct a narratological analysis of serial American comic books with the degree of historical specificity and analytical scrutiny they deserve as popular artifacts that have made a significant imprint on modern American culture (and beyond).[3] In fact, I will limit my inquiry rather radically to one genre and format (the superhero comic book), a single character (Batman), a specific

---

1 An early version of this chapter was presented at the "Interdisciplinary Methodology: The Case of Comics Studies" conference in Bern on Oct. 15, 2011. I thank the organizers of the conference, Stephanie Hoppeler, Lukas Etter, and Gabriele Rippl, as well as the participants for their critical feedback. This chapter is part of my current book project "Authorizing Superhero Comics: On the Evolution of a Popular Serial Genre" and emerges from a joint research project with Frank Kelleter in the DFG-Research Unit "Popular Seriality—Aesthetics and Practice" (Göttingen).
2 Recent publications such as Heer and Worcester 2009, Eder, Klar, and Reichert 2011, and Smith and Duncan 2012 do not offer any systematic analysis of seriality in comics. On the phenomenon of popular seriality, see the essays in Kelleter 2012; on comics as a popular medium, see Stein, Ditschke, and Kroucheva 2009.
3 This focus is sanctioned by the early emergence and cultural significance of American comic strips and superhero comic books, both of which are prime examples of popular serial storytelling. See also Stein, Meyer, and Edlich 2011.

time period (the 1940s to the 1960s), and one particular element of the narrative apparatus (paratextual constructions of author fictions and negotiations of their functions). This does not mean, of course, that attempts to trace different forms of serial storytelling throughout American comics history are necessarily futile.[4] It is also not intended to suggest that questions of seriality and authorship could not be addressed in the contexts of other comics traditions.[5] And it should not be taken to imply that it would be impossible to develop a transcultural or transnational theory of graphic narratives and comics authorship.[6] What it does signal, however, is that if we want to take comics seriously not just as serial narratives but as cultural objects that exert agency—as objects that make others do things—we must be willing to zero in on the very specific mechanisms through which particular comics have generated specific author fictions and functions at particular moments in time. Narratological analysis, in my view, is most convincing when it minds the historicity of the narratives and artifacts it studies. Rather than merely asking on a formal level how narratives and artifacts communicate meaning, we must also ask what kinds of cultural work they perform: not just what they are, but also what they do and how they do it; which meanings they enable at concrete historical moments and how they participate in the very creation of what we call history and culture.[7]

As the phrase 'make others do things' indicates, I take a central cue from Bruno Latour's Actor-Network-Theory, especially the suggestion that objects have agency: that they are not only employed by human actors but that they themselves make specific actions possible or impossible, likely or unlikely, thinkable or unthinkable. I also subscribe to Latour's notion that we should "follow the actors," human as well as non-human, and let them "deploy the full range of controversies in which they are immersed" (2005: 79, 68). I do so because I believe that popular serial narratives have a profound tendency to develop their own theories of seriality.[8] In that sense, I view the superhero comic book not as what Latour perceives as an "intermediary" that simply "transports, transfers, [or] transmits" creative content, genre conventions, and information

---

4   For a successful attempt, see Gardner 2012. On serial comic strips, see also Hayward 1997: ch. 2; Kelleter and Stein 2009; on serial comic books, see Eco 2004 [1962]; Dittmer 2007; Wüllner 2010; Denson 2011; Kelleter and Stein 2012; Stein 2014.
5   See Becker 2010; Saika 2011.
6   See Ecke 2013; Stein 2013, 2014. On the transnational exchanges that have shaped American comics, see Denson, Meyer, and Stein 2013.
7   On the notion of cultural work, see Tompkins 1985; on the cultural work of superhero comics, see Kelleter and Stein 2012.
8   For a more elaborate treatment of the theory of popular seriality, see the introduction to Kelleter 2012.

about authors without affecting them, but as an active "mediator," "an original event" that always "creates what it translates" (1993: 77-78). I maintain that superhero comic books actively participate in the construction of their narrative apparatus because they "authorize, allow, afford, encourage, permit, suggest, influence, block, render possible, [or] forbid" (Latour: 2005: 72) specific ways in which a series propels itself toward ever new iterations and variations of an accumulating archive of stories in search of expanding readerships. As such, comics "provide a vast playground to rehearse accounts of what makes us act" (Latour 2005: 55), including practices and mediations of comics authorship that emerge from evolving conflicts over who is authorized to create legitimate new installments of an ongoing series.[9]

As Michel Foucault has famously argued, our understanding of authorship generally results from "specific discursive practices" that create "systems of valorization" whereby the "relationship [...] between an author and a text [... and] the manner in which a text apparently points to this figure who is outside and precedes it" (2001 [1969]: 1622, 1623) is continually managed and authorized. Foucault does not talk specifically about popular culture, of course, and he certainly does not have in mind the kind of multi-authored, monthly issued, and decade-spanning type of serial storytelling that has shaped the history of American superhero comic books when he suggests that the discursive construction of authorship performs a particularly significant function for serial texts. But when he notes that the author "constitutes a principle of unity in writing where any unevenness of production is ascribed to changes caused by evolution, maturation, and outside influence" and that this "author serves to neutralize the contradictions that are found in a series of texts" (Foucault 2001 [1969]: 1630), he does point to one important function of authorship discourses that is especially poignant in popular forms of serial storytelling: to stabilize the inherently unstable project of narrative continuation from installment to installment and to answer the conflicting desires for authorial unity and heterogeneous author figures behind proliferating, sprawling, and often contradictory narrative styles and contents.

We thus encounter a nexus between the sprawling potential of serial storytelling and discourses of authorship as a means of managing the narrative consequences of this sprawl. In his narratological assessment of popular genre stories, Umberto Eco connects this nexus with the generative principle of serial storytelling: the "dialectic between order and

---

9   Studies of comics authorship include Brooker 2001, 2012; Carpenter 2005; Stein 2009; Gabilliet 2010; Williams and Lyons 2010; Zani 2010; Smith 2012; Uidhir 2012. An early, largely biographical example, is Sheridan 1942.

novelty, [...] between scheme and innovation," or repetition and variation (1990: 91). While Foucault largely marginalizes the role of the reader, Eco's model distinguishes between two types of readers: the 'naïve' and the 'smart' reader. The naïve reader is "the victim of the strategies of the author who will lead him little by little along a series of provisions and expectations"; the smart reader "evaluates the work as an aesthetic product" and "enjoys the seriality of the series" by recognizing its narrative strategies (1990: 92). While this distinction may be criticized on different levels, it is obviously short-sighted when it comes to popular forms of serial storytelling and their reception. For one, I would argue that the very dynamic of repetition and variation that structures serial storytelling also structures the reading practices through which followers of superhero comics and other types of serial narratives make meaning. More often than not, the serial reader is both naïve and smart at the same time (though perhaps to varying degrees), appreciating the repetitiveness of an ongoing series and enjoying the familiarity of certain characters, settings, drawing styles, and story structures as much as treasuring the variations, additions, and revisions that keep a series interesting and allow it to move forward.

Secondly, Eco's reader tends to be someone who merely consumes a series and has little impact on its continuing production: "The series consoles us (the consumers) because it rewards our ability to foresee: we are happy because we discover our ability to guess what will happen," he alleges, noting further:

> We do not attribute this happy result to the obviousness of the narrative structure but to our own presumed capacities to make forecasts. We do not think, "The author constructed the story in a way that I could guess the end," but rather, "I was so smart to guess the end in spite of the efforts the author made to deceive me." (1990: 86)

Today's aficionados of popular seriality are usually much more advanced than this statement implies, evaluating not just the seriality of a series but also reflecting and commenting on their own significance as consumers and commentators whose actions have consequences for a series' continuation. Thus, today's serial readers are generally aware of their double position as simultaneously (and willingly) naïve and smart readers, acting as the kinds of "amateur narratologists" that Jason Mittell (2006: 38) has discussed in the context of contemporary serial American television and as producers of their own discourses and creators of (serial) artifacts. As such, readers of popular serial stories frequently seek to transcend their status as largely passive recipients and actively comment, question, and challenge ongoing series in order to participate in their future development.¹⁰

Superhero comics do not just allow such readerly activism; their serial production and reception necessitates and thrives on such activism. Comic books are active mediators in the Latourian sense, then, because they raise very particular questions: Who can legitimately author an ongoing series? Who can authoritatively interpret a series' history? Who can propose dominant interpretations of its current state? As I will explain below, comic books have developed their very own set of answers, too. One such answer relates to the ways in which comic book series negotiate fictions and functions of authorship. If we agree with Foucault that discursive constructions of comic book authorship orchestrate relations between serial texts and their producers in ways that create an overarching sense of serial cohesiveness and continuity, then we must venture beyond Eco's differentiation between naïve and smart readers in favor of a more active understanding of comics readership and a more dynamic notion of comics authorship.

Such a critical maneuver is supported by Jared Gardner (2012), who proposes that comics generally motivate heightened degrees of authorial engagement *and* reader involvement. Discussing the sequential spacing of comic narratives and their amalgamation of images and words, Gardner notes the "unique affordances" (2012: 193) through which comics involve their readers in active processes of meaning making. Comics "depend on and privilege an audience not only projecting its own storytelling into the text but also always potentially picking up a pen [...] and creating the story themselves" (Gardner 2012: xiii). Readers are usefully conceived as always potential and sometimes actual authors here, but what goes unmentioned is a particular space in comic books that has functioned as a prime mediator in the construction, negotiation, and authorization of comics authorship: the space between the actual comic book stories themselves (i.e., the text into which readers project their own ideas by imaginatively filling in the gutter spaces between panels or by working the interface between words and images) and the world outside of the comic book, where readers may draw their own comics or create their own comic-book related stories.

---

10 Examples of smart readers of serial entertainment who reflect on their double position as willingly naïve consumers of popular culture and as smart readers of cultural artifacts who turn their readings into creative commentary about these artifacts are the producers of Batman and Spider-Man video spoofs that highlight the work of amateur narratology. For further analysis, see Stein 2012.

Gérard Genette (1997: 1-2, original emphases) labels this space the paratext and defines it as follows:

> More than a boundary or a sealed border, the paratext is, rather, a *threshold*, or [...] a "vestibule" that offers the world at large the possibility of either stepping inside or turning back. It is an "undefined zone" between the inside and the outside [...]. Indeed, this fringe, always the conveyor of a commentary that is authorial or more or less legitimated by the author, constitutes a zone between text and off-text, a zone not only of transition but also of *transaction*.

It is this very transaction at the fringes of the text, at this diffuse space of uncertain authorial legitimization and ambiguously authorized expression that has functioned as a particularly significant mediator in the evolution of the American superhero comic book.

Of course, paratextual transactions have been prominent in American serial narration since at least the nineteenth century, when city mysteries, magazine fiction, and dime novels were among the most widely received and most heavily negotiated publications, and when, at the tail end of the century, newspaper comic strips emerged in the pages of mass-printed tabloid newspapers. Even in the twentieth century, comic strips, film serials, and science fiction magazines thrived on the ability to turn their textual fringes into productive contact zones between producers and consumers, authors and readers. And while these productive transactions are certainly not limited to the realm of popular culture, they profit from the relatively low entry level that popular publications offer to their readers. After all, pretty much anybody can ask questions about a plot development or character trait and make suggestions about future installments he or she wishes to see. It is true that, as stories accumulate and paratextual discourses acquire their own histories, such questions and suggestions must generally display a certain amount of series knowledge and reading competence in order to be taken seriously, but I would still argue that writing a letter to an editor about a comic book differs substantially in terms of the cultural capital necessary to establish a legitimate claim from critiquing a modernist poem or avantgarde painting habitually invested with the auratic powers of high art. Moreover, it is the very seriality of comic books that tends to trigger such responses. Serial storytelling means serial reading, which, in turn, entails a heightened emotional (because continued, invested, and always tenuous) engagement with ongoing stories and expanding storyworlds as well as a sense of intimacy between readers and texts that stems from the close integration of serial narratives into the personal lives and lifeworlds of their dedicated readers.[11]

---

11 See especially Kelleter 2011.

Paradigmatic examples from the realm of American superhero comic books are the editorials and letter columns that have offered instructions and discussions about how to read and author serial comics. These paratextual spaces not only allow for, but actually necessitate, ongoing and indeed serial debates about plot developments, the gestation of complex narrative universes (or storyworlds[12]), specific aspects of setting (from Metropolis to Gotham in DC Comics[13]), the evolving characterization of superheroes and villains,[14] and themes from the rather simple good vs. evil stories of the genre's early years to the morally conflicted narratives of the darker graphic novel period since the 1980s and 1990s.[15] Moreover, such spaces have generated extensive exchanges between the official comic book producers, represented, for instance, by the company logo, superhero trademark, copyright notices, authorial signatures, and editorial commentary, and the receivers of the stories, those who buy and read the magazines and frequently become active participants in the serial construction of comic book narratives by writing letters to the editor, producing fanzines, and thus claiming authorial competences themselves.

Authorial Origin Stories: From Peritext to Epitext

American comic books possessed a rather low cultural esteem and were associated with notions of cheap entertainment and assembly-line production throughout the first few decades of their existence. From the beginning, however, their producers counteracted the widespread assumption that what they offered to their readers in monthly installments were merely formula stories told by anonymous, insignificant authors.[16] When the first Batman story appeared in *Detective Comics* #27 (May 1939), for instance, it signaled its authorship status through a "Rob't Kane" signature on the first page as well as the company logo and the title of this popular series on the cover. But *Batman* #1 (spring 1940) already communicated a more complex notion of authorship, indicating that the

---

12   On fictional universes and transmedia storyworlds, see Ryan and Thon 2014; on managing and authoring vast serial narratives, see Harrigan and Wardrip-Fruin 2009.
13   Setting generally functions as a spatial anchor for continued investments with, and debates about, ongoing stories, authorial collaborations, and comics reception. See Uricchio 2010.
14   For narratological explorations of fictional characters, see Eder, Jannidis, and Schneider 2010.
15   On the different phases of the superhero genre, see Klock 2003; Jenkins 2010; for different approaches to the genre history of the American superhero comic, see Coogan 2006; Duncan and Smith 2009; Lopes 2009; Ndalianis 2010. For a film- and television-centered analysis of authorial paratexts, see Gray 2010.
16   On superhero comics as formula stories, see Blythe and Sweet 2002.

series had gained a readership specifically interested in this superhero, his history, and his creators. Here, then, the notion of comic book authorship solidifies, and author fictions begin to take center stage: a "Bob Kane" signature is displayed on the actual cover of the comic book. Inside, readers are introduced to Batman's origin story, which supplies the character with the childhood trauma—the murder of his parents—that will motivate his endless fights against crime. As writer and editor Dennis O'Neil once observed, "The origin is the engine that drives Batman" (Pearson and Uricchio 1991: 25), and in order to be fully effective, this engine must be fueled by repeated iterations and revised reiterations of its basic elements: by the kinds of novelties, variations, and innovations that Eco locates at the roots of all forms of serial storytelling and that proliferate prodigiously in the realm of popular seriality.

If serial characters are driven by evolving origin stories, comics authorship is indebted to its very own tales of origin. In *Batman* #1, Bob Kane is introduced as the "creator of THE BATMAN!" in a one-page biography titled "Meet the Artist!" (see figure 1). This biography is the first of many following paratextual projections of Batman's authorship. The photograph of Kane that shows him at work at the drawing board in his studio provides readers with an image of where and by whom the stories are created. Kane looks directly at the camera and thus also at the reader, intimating a potentially personal relationship between author and reader: "READERS, meet Bob Kane," the opening sentence states. Here, then, the author is not merely implied, but verbally described and visualized rendered.[17] This author biography further emphasizes the originality of Kane's creation, seeking to preempt any discussion of Kane as a popular copycat—of DC's earlier and massively successful Superman, for instance, or of comic books more generally as a mass-produced form of storytelling assembled from a smorgasbord of cultural sources (film serials, movies, newspaper strips, pulp fiction, and so forth): "Bob is certainly not a copyist; his work shows a definite originality and freshness." Thus, the text mixes a romantic notion of inspired authorial creativity with an understanding and public acknowledgement of comic book production as a skilled, and speedy, artisanal process that leads to a marketable and thus successfully novel, or fresh, product.

---

[17] Gardner (2012: 74–75) discusses a similar biographical piece about Jerry Siegel and Joe Shuster from *Superman* 1 (summer 1939). The ambiguity of Wayne C. Booth's implied author concept as "an intentional product of the author in or qua the work or [...] an inference made by the recipient about the author of the work" (Kindt and Müller 2006: 8) foregrounds the diffusely authorized and negotiated nature of emerging projections of comic book authorship. Most of the sources I will cite throughout this chapter are not paginated; in order to increase readability, I cite page numbers when available but omit all "n.p." references.

MEET THE ARTIST!

READERS, meet Bob Kane, creator of THE BATMAN! Realizing that people like to know something about the men who draw their favorite cartoon-strips, we induced Bob to sit down at a typewriter and dash off a few pertinent facts about his life. He complained that a drawing-board—and not a typewriter—was his natural means of artistic expression, but he did manage to hammer out a sort of synopsis about himself.

On top of that, we felt that we should have a picture of Bob to grace this page. We asked him to bring us one. "Sure," he said, "I'll take care of that." But as the days went by, and publication date came nearer and nearer, we still had no picture. Finally we had to sit Bob down at a drawing board, hold him there until a photographer could be called in from another floor of the building—and we finally got our picture!

Bob Kane was born twenty-four years ago in New York City, and has spent most of his life in the big town. As you might expect, his primary interest has always been in drawing. His work has appeared in a long list of national magazines. For some time Bob was a straight "comic" artist, specializing in drawings of a humorous nature. When the trend swung toward the adventure type of drawing, Bob was quick to see that therein lay his future, and though the abrupt change in drawing technique necessitated plenty of hard labor on his part, the phenomenal success of THE BATMAN is proof enough that Bob was capable of making the transition. It hasn't been easy, and it isn't easy even now. Anyone who thinks a comic artist has an easy life should take a look at Bob Kane's working-schedule. It's an unusual week which doesn't find Bob at the drawing board on seven consecutive days. The saving grace about it all is the fact that he enjoys his work, though he does admit that he might like to have a little vacation come summer—three days in a row, or something like that.

Bob has spent a good deal of time in the North woods, hunting and fishing (before THE BATMAN took up all his time, of course). He loves outdoor life in all its phases. For a time he worked as seaman on a boat plying South American waters, and he says that he feels that this contact with all sorts of people, plus the satisfaction of seeing parts of the world absolutely foreign to the environment of New York, has been of great help to him in humanizing the characters which he draws.

Bob is certainly not a copyist; his work shows a definite originality and freshness which has attracted many fervent fans. He studies constantly, striving always to improve his work. If he has a free hour or two, he is very likely to spend it at one of the local medical colleges studying anatomy, for he well realizes that only by a thorough knowledge of bone and muscle structure is an artist able to inject into his drawings the true expression of action and motion which is so necessary to this type of art.

Bob Kane has worked hard, is still working hard, and will continue to work hard to give you just the sort of thing which you have come to expect in THE BATMAN. We predict ever-increasing success for both the artist and the creation of his facile pen. And they both deserve that success!

—THE EDITOR

Figure 1: *Batman* #1 (spring 1940). © DC Comics. All rights reserved.

Comic book authors are geniuses, according to this biography, precisely because they can produce riveting stories and fascinating superhero figures fast and thus supply their readers with a steady flow of satisfactory entertainment. What is more, the focus of this biography may be on Kane as a comics creator, but the tone and narrative perspective complicate the image of singular authorial creation. While Kane "did manage to hammer out a sort of synopsis about himself," the text is actually written by a self-identifying "editor" who "induced" Kane to "dash off a few pertinent facts about his life" and then converted the autobiographical raw material into a biographical peritext.[18] This process mirrors the way in which the comics themselves were produced, with writers and artists hammering out serial stories and editors authorizing the final versions for their "many fervent fans" (whose status as "fans" elevates them from the role of mere consumers by casting them as particularly dedicated and loyal connoisseurs).[19] While the notion of collaborative production is implied, the twin fictions of superhero origins and singular authorial creation remain largely intact, even though readers are signaled that comics authors are hired and inspired professionals who work fast in order to meet, and ideally supersede, the expectations of both their editors and their readers.

Only a few years later, a second origin story extended these authorial projections. The serial superhero's growing narrative universe apparently called for an expanding universe of authorship as well. What was a surprising new bestselling product in 1940 had evolved into a mainstream genre read by large segments of the American population only a few years later. While Batman's origins and Kane's biography had been presented as two distinct pieces in *Batman* #1 (the hero's textual origins being supplemented with the author's peritextual origin story), "The True Story of Batman and Robin: How a Big-Time Comic Is Born!" in *Real Fact Comics* #5 (Nov.–Dec. 1946) synthesized them into one extended comic book origin story (see figure 2). According to Genette's nomenclature, the *Real Fact Comics* book was part of the superhero's epitext since it was not

---

[18] On the distinction between peritext (material surrounding the text proper within the same artifact) and epitext (material closely connected with a text but printed outside of the artifact in question), cf. Genette 1997: 344.

[19] The distinction between reader and fan is important since the majority of comic book buyers have been readers whose involvement in comics culture did not necessarily extend beyond acts of purchasing, reading, perhaps collecting and discussing comics with friends. Fans tend to be more active, for instance, by writing letters to editors, organizing and attending conventions, producing fanzines, hosting comics-related websites, and so forth. Historically, however, American comics readers have been particularly active and highly organized as fans. See Sabin 1993: ch. 5; Pustz 1999; Brown 2001; for an insider's view, see Schelly 1999; on fandom cultures more generally, see Jenkins 1992, 2006; Hills 2002.

Superhero Comics and the Authorizing Functions of the Comic Book Paratext 165

Figure 2: "The True Story of Batman and Robin: How a Big-Time Comic Is Born!" *Real Fact Comics* #5 (Nov.–Dec. 1946). © DC Comics. All rights reserved.

materially appended to the Batman comic books but nonetheless part of Batman's wider cosmos. The extension from text (Batman's origin story) and peritext (the author biography in *Batman* #1) to the expitext of *Real Fact Comics* follows a central dynamic of popular serial storytelling, where proliferating stories, characters, and settings are accompanied by an increasing demand for author fictions that contain the potentially unruly sprawl of serial narration. Long-running serial narratives usually generate not only vast narrative universes and intersecting storyworlds (multiverses) but also metaverses that organize the proliferating information by establishing classificatory systems, critical terminologies, popular canons, and powerful author fictions.[20]

"The True Story of Batman and Robin: How a Big-Time Comic Is Born!" depicts Kane as a comics figure behind the drawing board. He is presented as an artist working within a specific setting (his studio) and institutional structure (the offices of DC Comics). In addition, the notion of collaborative production no longer remains implied. The narrative refers to the "expert editorial guidance" Kane had received when he first created *Batman*, and readers actually get to see a comic book rendition of an editor. While Kane had already been described as an employee of DC Comics in *Batman* #1, he is now much more clearly shown as one creative element in the larger production structures at DC Comics whose work must be approved by an editor wielding a substantial degree of control over it. After all, "The True Story of Batman and Robin" is not an autobiographical comic; it was drawn by Win Mortimer, and the narrative perspective is explicitly authorial, rather than first-person: "Let us drop in at the studio of talented young Bob Kane." Furthermore, the offer to collaborate in the serial storytelling is made explicit in a scene that directly authorizes readers as serial authors. In this scene, readers learn that the suggestion that had allegedly sparked off the creation of Batman's teenage sidekick Robin had come from a fan who had expressed his desires in a personal letter to Bob Kane: "I would like to see Batman have a partner … someone who can share the secret of his identity." Finally, Batman and Robin appear as characters on the same storyworld level as Bob Kane but also as fictional comic book characters in the comic strip he draws. On the story level, they meet their creator, who has left his extratextual position as a comics artist and has transformed into a comics character. When Batman and Robin thank Kane "for bringing us to life" and Kane thanks the fans "for your interest and wonderful friendship," the comic book paratext (or epitext, in this case) is publicly acknowledged as the place where authorial and readerly projections must vie for the

---

20   See Kelleter and Stein 2012.

legitimization of the whole discursive community involved in the production and reception of a superhero comic and where every decision concerning a series must be publicly authorized.

Letter Pages as Serial Paratexts: Authorizing Comics Authorship

As my remarks about *Batman* #1 and *Real Fact Comics* #5 have indicted, questions of authorship and the authorization conflicts they generate with particular force in the realm of serial popular culture appeared early on in the history of the superhero genre.[21] But they attained a new dimension with the introduction of letter columns in the late 1950s and 1960s, a time when an older generation of readers began to embrace superhero comics as a serial genre whose history was worth preserving by amassing collections, creating archives, researching backstories, reconstructing production histories, and developing a critical vocabulary with which the merits and weaknesses of particular works, authors, and the genre at large could be adequately discussed.[22] In Foucault's nomenclature, one function of comic book authorship, publicly debated and eventually fully credited, was to create 'systems of valorization' according to which particular styles and stories could be attributed to individual creators, criticized, and, over time, canonized. Such heightened reader involvement was enabled and amplified by the "Letters to the Bat-Cave" section, which first appeared in *Batman* #125 (Aug. 1959) and functioned as an authorial mediator, reshaping the nature of comic book authorship by fostering the projection of new author fictions. The letters page implemented the notion that readers could and should act upon their desire to project their ideas from the extratextual world into the material space of the comic book by entering the printed paratextual discourse about their favorite series at a time when all Batman stories were still officially signed by Bob Kane.[23]

---

21 On authorization conflicts in superhero comics, see Kelleter and Stein 2012; for a general view, see Bennett 2005: ch. 2; Donovan, Fjellestad and Lundén 2008.

22 As serially produced artifacts, comic books encourage practices of collecting, archiving, and canonizing. See Gardner 2012: ch. 5 as well as Henry Jenkins's analysis (in this volume) of the archival, ephemeral, and residual practices triggered by serial comics. In the context of the Batman series, the epochal change was signaled by DC's introduction of a revamped "New Look" Batman.

23 In *Detective Comics*, the parallel series that featured Batman stories, the letters pages appeared later (#327, May 1964). My investigation takes off from Brooker's reading of DC's letter columns in the 1960s. Brooker speaks of DC's "cultivation of [an] 'authorship' discourse" and concludes that "[t]he boundaries between comic author and fan, writer and reader, have always been thin and often dissolve entirely" (2001: 253). I conducted my research on the *Batman* letter columns of the 1960s in the Comic Art Collection at

The very first letter column in *Batman* #125 begins with a reader's comment. "I've been a BATMAN fan for many years," Larry Graff writes, "and I would like to make a suggestion. How about a page of letters for your readers?" Such a page "would give readers a chance to make suggestions of their own." The answer—"We agree with you, Larry, and so do many of your fellow BATMAN fans, who have suggested the same idea to us"—is supplied by a nameless editor who will, from now on, play the role of the moderator always at the service of his audience.[24] The existence of this letter and the fact that DC printed it as the opening salvo in an ensuing exchange between comic book producers and consumers makes a compelling argument about the evolution of the superhero genre from the 1940s, when comic book communication was largely directed at readers, to the 1960s, when this communication begins to flow back and forth between comic book producers and their readers. As a long-running superhero series, *Batman* now has a history, and this history can be explored and discussed by dedicated readers whose long-term reading practices will eventually aggregate into consolidated forms of comics fandom and whose activities will no longer remain confined to the act of reading. Graff's letter, in that sense, constitutes a paratextual practice in a double sense: it transforms Graff from a reader into a published author (if only of a fan letter), and it announces an officially sanctioned notion of reader participation in DC's serial storytelling. The letter columns will, from now on, function as a public forum in which readers may make suggestions about their favorite series, and while the letter discourse will generally be controlled by those who publish the comics (a point that is not specified in the editorial response, for obvious reasons), it will afford readers a say—or the feeling of having a say—in the future course of *Batman* (Graff's phrase "of their own" further signals a sense of ownership earned through the repeated purchase and reading of comic books).

If the letter columns transformed readers into authors of letters and implied co-authors of future stories, they also turned editors into readers of fan mail.[25] Questions such as "what's your favorite, fans?" (*Batman*

Michigan State University in July 2011 and want to thank Randy Scott for his generous help and advice.

24 Superman comics had featured letters since 1958. Gabilliet suggests that the introduction of letter columns created "a new type of proximity between readers and publishers" (2010: 53). DC editors like Mort Weisinger, Jack Schiff, and Julius Schwartz, who encouraged fan practices like letter writing and fanzine publication, had themselves been part of science-fiction fandom in the 1920s and 1930s (cf. Gabilliet 2010: 53).

25 Brooker notes that "the two concepts of comic book 'author' and 'fan' evolved in tandem" (2001: 249). Brown views comic book readers as "active textual participants [...] organize[d] into loosely structured interpretive communities" (2001: 58). The creators of continuity newspaper comic strips such as Sidney Smith (*The Gumps*) and Milton Caniff

#150, Sept. 1962) and "what's your choice, reader?" (*Batman* #151, Nov. 1962) were significant because they communicated a strong sense of collaborative stewardship by comic book producers who publicly believed that they would benefit from the mutual exchange of ideas—however contrived or manipulative such publicly expressed notions may have actually been—that was to shape much of the discourse in the letter columns.[26] What is more, the editor occasionally delegated his editorial authorities: "This is your department, with a minimum of editorial interference," we read in *Batman* #190 (Mar. 1967); "make this page your own"; "what would you do if you were the editor of *Batman*?"; "It's your right to write, [...] so don't muff out on this [...] chance to break into print," we learn in *Batman* #189 (Feb. 1967). These calculated rhetorical gestures are obviously part of a marketing strategy rather than actual transpositions of editorial power, but they have consequences: they invoke a reader who has a right to be a published author and potential editor—a right that, once granted, can and will also be legitimately demanded.[27]

The authorship discourse in the "Letters to the Bat-Cave" column began with relatively simple assertions such as "Bob Kane must have had a job on that one" (*Batman* #163, May 1964) or "a John Broome sounding title—right?" (*Batman* #167, Nov. 1964). But it quickly morphed into detailed discussions of individual styles and authorial voices that were informed by the writers' personal interaction with DC editors outside of the official letter columns as well as within the pages of specific fanzines.[28] As a letter by Mike Friedrich that appeared in *Batman* #181 (June 1966) indicates, readers eagerly displayed the expert and inside knowledge that only years of reading comic books and investigating their production

---

(*Terry and the Pirates*) had been especially apt at cultivating a public and private exchange with their followers. See Hayward 1997: ch. 2; Gardner 2012: ch. 2.

26 Marvel took its own approach to authorship negotiations, including Stan Lee's editorials ("Stan's Soapbox") as well as celebrations of Marvel's bullpen (the fictionalized space in which Marvel writers, artists, and other employees worked) in the "Marvel Bullpen Bulletins." These peritexts painted portraits of the Marvel staff and the doings at the bullpen that treated comic book producers as part of an extended cast of comic book characters whose quasi-superheroic powers allegedly allowed them to create the best comics on the market. The editorials are collected in Cunningham 2009; for analysis, cf. Pustz 1999: 48–60; see also Kelleter and Stein 2012.

27 Some of the letters were certainly invented by DC staff; we also know very little about the criteria for the selection of actual letters. Cf. Barker: "[L]etters are selected, and often for early editions solicited or ghostwritten. They are not produced by some 'natural sampling' of readers' responses. [...] They are a part of the self-image of the comic. They present that self-image, and help to encourage the right kind of future response from readers" (1989: 47).

28 The *Alter Ego* fanzine featured letters from writers like Otto Binder and Gardner Fox, artists like Kurt Schaffenberger, and editors like Mort Weisinger in its own letter columns. Cf. Thomas and Schelly 2008: 138–39.

processes could garner in order to distinguish themselves from less knowledgeable followers:

> I'm sure a new writer has joined the *Batman* bullpen. The style of writing is completely different from either Fox, Herron, or Broome, the three mainstays. It might be the veteran Bill Finger, but I doubt it. The story had everything that *Batman* needs to have a story that clicks: (1) Plenty of action; (2) very good art; (3) practically a pun per panel; (4) very good supporting characters; (5) a good, though not outstanding villain. My guess for the authorship is Nelson Bridwell.

Friedrich speaks as an educated interpreter, critic, and chronicler of Batman comics here, as someone who can tell a veteran writer not officially credited in DC's comics (Finger, in this case) apart from newer writers like Nelson Bridwell. Another letter writer, Ken Hodl, puts a name to the back-and-forth about the authorship of *Batman* in the same issue:

> Guess the author, eh? Well, I have some sneaky suspicions but I'll go about it in a scientific manner. Since it's not Fox, Finger, Broome, or Herron, it would have to be either Kanigher, Hamilton, or Drake. I will rule out Arnold Drake for the reason that the story was a bit too wild, as far as violence is concerned. Mr. Drake also lacks the reality in his stories which this one had in tremendous proportions. Edmond Hamilton [...] and Robert Kanigher are both likely suspects, but with Kubert (who does most of his fine work for RK) doing some *Batman* covers now, I'd just have to put my money down on Robert Kanigher.

These are the paratextual beginnings of an authorship discourse that ventures beyond merely identifying specific creators. The letter writer's "scientific manner" points to the recognition of individual drawing styles and authorial voices.[29] And if the comics were no longer seen as being produced by a singular "Bob Kane" but by a heterogeneous group of collaborators whose input could be recognized and judged on the basis of its artistic merits or entertaining qualities, several new practices beyond the mere reading of comics become feasible: devising portraits of, and conducting interviews with, individual writers and artists; lobbying for the assignment of particular authors and artists to specific story arcs; criticizing some creators and celebrating others and thereby privileging certain story developments while disavowing others, and so forth. In the 1960s and 1970s, these practices facilitated the emergence of comic book fandoms (including comic book conventions) and a budding fanzine culture that would morph into professionalized forms of comics journalism such as *The Comics Journal, Amazing Heroes*, or *Wizard* by the 1980s and 1990s and finds its expression in today's digital environment of online blogs, websites, and forums, not to mention the massive popularity of comics conventions such as the annual San Diego Comic-Con.

---

29 For a more skeptical view, cf. Brooker 2001: 257–58.

All of these practices make themselves heard in the letters, and they suggest an increase in self-proclaimed authority among those who read and write about comics. "I consider myself a fairly good authority on *Batman*," Mike Friedrich writes in *Batman* #166 (Sept. 1964), a claim that is publicly rewarded when he crosses the paratextual threshold from being a letter writer operating in the border zone between the world outside of the comic book and its textual inside by becoming the actual author of one of the stories in *Batman* #200 (Mar. 1968).[30] This border-crossing role-reversal is remarkable as it represents a serious case of adolescent wish fulfillment, an act of authorial empowerment that is preordained by years of fictional comic book stories depicting the metamorphosis from ordinary human being to superhuman hero. The socially unobtrusive fan is magically transformed into his second-ultimate dream fantasy. He may not have become a superhero, but he has established himself as the next best thing: the author of superhero stories. Friedrich, for instance, was hired by DC Comics in the late 1960s and moved on to become a writer for Marvel a few years later. This transformation is possible because long-running serial stories pose a central problem to any author, however officially legitimated or institutionally authorized: how to master the steadily growing history of a series, its often convoluted plot developments and expanding character constellations, as well as changes in style, tone, and setting, so as to be able to produce convincing, legitimate, and authoritative new installments. In other words, comic book authors have to be avid readers, if not fans, and even then, they will have a hard time competing with the collective knowledge of comic book readers. In addition, over the years, the most dedicated readers will amass a collective serial memory, with detailed knowledge about the most arcane elements of the series' past, and they may also acquire skills that qualify them either as authors of future stories or as apt critics of the ongoing serial storytelling.

With readers like Friedrich and the many others who wrote letters, published fanzines, and organized (or at least attended) comic book conventions, it was no longer feasible for superhero comics to tell simple episodic stories. The 1960s therefore saw the emergence of a new serial form of storytelling. If earlier stories had largely taken place in an "oneiric climate" (Eco 2004 [1962]: 153) in which previous stories had no or only little consequence for present and future installments, they now attain a serial memory, increasingly feature longer story arcs, and connect the

---

30 Friedrich's transformation from reader to author is mentioned in the author credits and in the last panel of "The Cry of Night Is 'Sudden Death!'" as well as on the final page of the comic book, which features a "Dialogue Between Two Batmaniacs Upon Batman Reaching Issue 200" (Friedrich and fanzine editor Biljo White).

storyworlds of different superheroes within a larger intra-company fictional universe. Frank Kelleter and I have described this change as a transition from a linear form of seriality represented, in its ideal type, by professionally produced series with simple episodic structures that seek to close themselves off from acts of creative appropriation by their recipients, to a form of multilinear seriality, which we understand as parallel and overlapping, often transmedially organized serial universes that possess a narrative memory and are produced by professional and increasingly by non-professional actors.[31] By 1966, Batman did not just appear in *Detective Comics* and *Batman*, where he was subjected to a stylistic overhaul labeled "the new look" by DC, but also in comic book series like *The Brave and the Bold* and *Justice League of America*, fanzines like *Batmania* (discussed below), as well as the popular ABC live-action television series starring Adam West. In the *Batman* comics themselves, this change was mediated by repeated attempts to engage readers in narrative meaning making, for instance by asking them to decode narrative clues, encouraging them to guess the authors of the stories, and, in some cases, even directly calling on them to intervene in the trajectory of a serial plot. As a note beneath the final panel of "The Million Dollar Debut of Batgirl" (*Detective Comics* #359, Jan. 1967) reads: "Will the new Batgirl appear again? That depends on you, readers! Write and let us know!"[32]

In the *Batman* comics of the 1960s, then, textual and paratextual mediations of authorship functions take place at the exact moment in which Bob Kane is no longer responsible for the series and is supplanted by new artists and writers under the artistic direction of Carmine Infantino, who had asked editor Julius Schwarz to print his name instead

---

31 Cf. Kelleter and Stein: "Lineare Serialität zeichnet sich idealtypisch durch professionell hergestellte mit einfachen Episoden- oder Fortsetzungsstrukturen aus, die sich gegen kreative Aneignung durch ihre Adressaten weitgehend abzuschließen versuchen. Multilineare Serialität bezeichnet im Idealtyp parallele und überlappende, oft medienübergreifend organisiert und mit narrativem Gedächtnis ausgestattete serielle Universen, die durch professionelle und zunehmend auch nicht-professionelle Akteure produziert werden" (2012: 264). Examples are stories that draw upon the readers' knowledge of the series' history and their engagement with ongoing parallel series (including team-ups and crossovers), intersecting character constellations and plotlines. "Gotham Line-Up!" (*Detective Comics* #328, June 1964), for example, features butler Alfred because "Batman and Robin are on a case out of town with Superman"; in "Whatever Will Happen to Heiress Heloise?" (*Detective Comics* #384, Feb. 1969), Batman fights alone because "Robin [is] off on a Teen Titans case."

32 It seems that crime fiction, with its in-built emphasis on decoding mysteries, collecting hidden information, and interpreting clues is particularly prone to popular serialization. Examples from Anglo-American popular culture include the genre of the city mysteries in the antebellum period, the fan phenomenon of Sherlock Holmes from the late nineteenth century until today, the hard-boiled pulp magazine fiction of the 1920s and beyond, comics from *Dick Tracy* to *Sin City*, and a host of serial television shows.

of the Kane signature as early as 1964, thus indicating that fictions of authorial unity should no longer be hidden behind the Bob Kane label.[33] Therefore, actual changes in the authorship as well as a new consciousness among comic book authors and long-time readers, both of whom had begun to claim their own authority over the past, present, and future of the series, necessitated new mediations of comic book authorship. The letters pages constituted one form of collaborative mediation of the change at DC Comics from the era of singular author fictions and its attendant anonymous system of comics production to an era of explicit authorial attribution (first on covers, then on the stories, starting with *Batman* #204, Aug. 1968). They took part in a broader history of transactions between comic book producers and comic book consumers that affected the change from linear to multilinear storytelling and prepared the ground for the long story arcs and complex continuity demands of superhero comics in the coming decades.

A second noteworthy type of mediation welded the paratextual discourse of the letters pages to the actual Batman stories. Several stories from the 1960s thematize questions of authorship within their diegetic worlds. In one such story, Batman must solve a case regarding a mystery novel written by an anonymous author. In "The Perfect Crime—Slightly Imperfect" (*Batman* #181, June 1966), Commissioner Gordon claims, "No publisher would dare bring out a book under [mystery author Kaye Day's] name if you hadn't written it." In another story, "The Million Dollar Debut of Batgirl," Barbara Gordon (aka Batgirl) looks at books in a library that carry the names Infantino and Greene (both authors of this particular story) on their spines. It is plausible to read these stories as instances in which previously anonymous comic book authors announce their newfound prominence within the pages of the stories they are creating. But such authorial self-inscription also took on more explicit forms when readers encountered instances of explicit intradiegetic self-authorization. The first example appeared in "The Secret War of the Phantom General" (*Detective Comics* #343, Sept. 1965). Here, the narrative is interrupted by a panel that shows "the writer of this story" (John Broome, who remains unnamed) at work at his typewriter, warning readers "that you're in for a startling surprise" (see figure 3). The writer appears a second time on the next page, encouraging an analytical approach to comics reading that sanctions the types of amateur criticism published in the fanzines of the times when he expresses happiness about having gotten "that flashback out of the way." Both panels emphasize not just the fact that this story

---

33 Cf. Brooker 2001: 252. On comic book fictions of authorial unity, see Kelleter and Stein 2012; the author as label is conceptionalized in Niefanger 2002.

was written by a particular author, whose fictive representation readers could see looking back at them from the comic book page and whose explicit presence was no longer confined to the paratextual realm, but also that comics authors labored under constant pressure: we see an editorial note stating "deadline 3/9/65" in the background of the first panel, and an image of what seems to be a deadline-enforcing editor on the wall punctuated by darts in the second.

A later story, "The Strange Death of Batman" (*Detective Comics* #347, Jan. 1966), is even more elaborate. It introduces the writer Gardner Fox at his workplace as he has just finished one story and is lying down to think up a speculative "what-if" scenario (see figure 4). In this instance, the visualization and intradiegetic depiction of comics authorship responds to the comic book paratext since readers would have known Gardner's name from the letters page, but it also foregrounds the core mechanics of serial storytelling: the what-if mode of narrative invention and serial variation that would be popularized by Marvel's series of the same title from the 1970s onwards and that had been present in DC Comics' own Imaginary Stories since the 1940s.

Fanzines and Comic Book Authorization

Such explicit representations of authorship followed from, and they also further encouraged, the growth of comic book fandom and the emergence of a fan discourse outside of the company-controlled confines of comic book pages and letter columns. In fact, we are dealing with a paratextual discourse spreading into two directions simultaneously: into the stories themselves as well as beyond the superhero's textual confines into the realm of the epitextual world of fanzines. These developments were generally supported by the major publishers because they secured the future of a serial genre hard-pressed to keep its readership involved and fulfill a consistent, if not always increasing, demand for new stories. DC thus promoted fan clubs and fanzines like *Batmania* in letter columns by printing plugs like the following: "HOT TIPS FROM BATMAN'S HOTLINE: One of the Nation's largest *Batman* fan clubs, the BATMANIANS, has announced that it is issuing a new club fanzine called BATMANIA. A free copy and full club particulars are available for 10c postage from B.J. White, 407 Sondra Avenue, Columbia, Missouri. We highly recommend it" (*Batman* #169, Feb. 1965).[34] Yet as a later letter by Tom Fagan in

---

[34] I was able to study all issues of *Batmania* at the Terry and Edwin Murray Special Collection at Duke University in North Carolina in July 2011 and want to thank research services librarian Elizabeth Dunn for coordinating my activities at Duke.

Figure 3: John Broome and Carmine Infantino, "The Secret War of the Phantom General," *Detective Comics* #343 (Sept. 1965). © DC Comics. All rights reserved.

Figure 4: Gardner Fox and Carmine Infantino, "The Strange Death of Batman," *Detective Comics* #347 (Jan. 1966). © DC Comics. All rights reserved.

Batman #180 (May 1966) indicates, the activities of the Batmanians also created new authorization conflicts that were the logical outcome of the editor's initial recognition of a fellowship of Batman fans and the increase in readerly claims to authoritative knowledge of the series:

> We *Batmanians* have grouped together to promote *Batman*. Our membership is presently close to a thousand persons [...]. Our slogan—*For Batman we accept nothing as impossible!* I would like to invite anyone wishing to join the *Batmanians* to write directly to Biljo White [...]. The *Batmanians* are going places and we want all *Batman* fans alongside us.

DC featured this self-advertisement without any apparent hesitations, even though it issued a strong claim to a kind of authority that was no longer located exclusively in the hands of the publisher. Appealing to strength in numbers and formulating rather ambitious goals, Fagan underscored the power of new players in the field of superhero comics and their will to challenge those who officially produced *Batman*. And indeed, the permeability of the letters page as a paratextual border zone was illustrated quite forcefully by Bob Butts's related threat in *Batman* #186 (Nov. 1966): "If you refuse to elaborate on *Poison Ivy's* 'perfect crime' I swear by the mighty *batmobile*, I'll come to your offices with half of fandom to picket and protest!" Fagan, Butts, and fellow letter writers represent the kinds of 'active audiences' that Jennifer Hayward traces to the continuity newspaper comic strips of the 1930s and 1940s and the 'serial pleasures' that, according to Jared Gardner, follow from the ongoing interaction between comic strip producers and readers and that ultimately lead to the comic book 'fan addicts' of the 1950s and 1960s.[35]

Yet the question remains how the *Batmania* fanzine (and, by implication, other fanzines) extended the superhero discourse, broadened the spectrum of authorization conflicts, allowed for the creation of new author roles, and thereby propelled the genre evolution of superhero comics toward longer storylines, sprawling character constellations, increasingly complex narrative universes, and interacting trajectories among different series. *Batmania* presented itself as a response to the revamped Batman of the early 1960s, which had updated the character and its look for a new generation of readers. As Biljo White explained in the first issue (July 1964): "I decided now that Editor Julius Schwartz is presenting a 'new look' Batman, it would be a good time to start a genuine BATMAN movement. In order to promote my ideas on advancing this movement, I have prepared this first issue of BATMANIA—the fanzine

---

35 Hayward (1997: ch. 2) discusses the author-reader interaction surrounding Milton Caniff's *Terry and the Pirates*; Gardner (2012: ch. 2 and 3) looks at a variety of strips from Bud Fisher's *Mutt and Jeff* to Sidney Smith's *The Gumps* and EC Comics fandom. On EC Comics 'fan-addicts,' see also Adler-Kassner 1997–1998; Pustz 1999: 36–43.

especially for BATMAN fans." The fanzine's stated objective was "to join together those who enjoy reading and collecting the stories of Batman." The wording of these statements, especially their emphasis on comics fandom as a joint movement of emotionally invested readers and collectors, implies a democratic legitimization for a just cause. The fanzine thus offered a serial public forum for those whose only outlet had been the comic book letter columns. In that sense, it enacted the transformation from the letter column as an officially controlled peritext to a far less controlled, and potentially competing, space—the fanzine as epitext—at the very moment in which DC was trying to establish Batman's new look.

But while *Batmania* presented itself as critical, it was not antagonistic or even subversive. In an editorial titled "The Batmania Philosophy," White explained how he had solicited editor Julius Schwartz's "blessing" and referred to his own authorial role as that of a "faned" (= fan editor) in analogy to the professional editorship at DC (*Batmania* #12, Oct. 1966). What is more, the first issue of *Batmania* was explicit about its legal status. It used copyrighted material on the cover but acknowledged National Publications (DC Comics) as the owner, announcing above another image: "Permission to publish and use the name 'BATMANIA' has been granted by National." This symbiotic relationship between the respective producers of comic books and fanzines was rewarded by repeated references to "Batmaniancs" within the Batman comics and even to Biljo himself when a character was named after the fanzine editor in one story.[36] Thus authorized, the fanzine repeatedly appealed to those working at DC. White's "Open Letter to Editor Jack Schiff" in issue #3 (Jan. 1965) spoke from the position of a well-informed and well-connected fanzine writer who could appeal to public sentiment to make his case: "I've been informed by many fans that they have written you for more stories of this type"; "I would like to make known a few opinions of loyal Batmanians and myself." In an "Open Letter to Julius Schwartz," Tom Fagan addressed issues of authority again: "Maybe to an editor the fans are annoying because of their constant demand for attention to detail and their frequent, sharp criticisms of poor story line and art work. But let's face it. The fans are an outspoken vocal group of a far wider representation of readers than editors care to admit" (*Batmania Annual* 1967).

---

36 See "Hunted or—Haunted" (*Detective Comics* #376, June 1968); "The Man Who Radiated Fear" (*Batman* #200, Mar. 1968).

Figure 5: Biljo White, cover illustration, *Batmania* #15 (May 1967). All rights reserved.

In addition to challenging the decisions of DC editors directly and demanding a say in the development of Batman stories, fanzines also extended—and thus further diversified, and indeed serialized—the fictions and functions of comic book authorship. The cover of *Batmania* #15 (May 1967) is a good case in point (see figure 5). It depicts Biljo White at the drawing board, sketching away as an interested Batman is looking over his shoulder, thinking: "Wonder what he'll put on the cover this time." Superheroes like Batman cannot ignore what is going on in fanzines like *Batmania*, this self-reflexive cover suggest, and White is not just the cover artist of this issue but also a competent copier of DC's official Batman, as the visual rendition of the superhero indicates.

Batmania featured editorials, critical essays, historiographic research, fan fiction, and various visual renditions of Batman, all of which established the roles of fanzine editor, writer, and artist as legitimate contributors to the expanding universe of Batman stories and its surrounding discourses. Examples include artwork by Bill Ryan in issue #1 that humorously explored how Batman might have looked had he been drawn by various famous cartoonists, or critical essays such as Stephen Harrell's "What Has the 'New Look' Done for Batman?" (*Batmania Annual* 1967). Significantly, some of these presentations were collaborative and participatory, substantiating the assumption that popular serial stories, and comics in particular, favor shared authorial responsibilities and tend to disperse creative authority to different factions of authors and readers: the very first story in *Batmania* #1, "The New Look," was authored "by BILJO WHITE and BATMAN FANS from COAST-TO-COAST"; *Batmania* #15 even proposed a line of special issues created entirely by readers where "You will be the editor!"

However, fanzines rarely completely toppled the distinction between officially authorized comics authors and amateur artists or fan writers. Instead, we see the elevation of comic books from a low, throwaway type of youth entertainment to a revered form of cultural expression that offered many different actors a stake in their symbolic power. This process was accompanied by increasing efforts to make sense of how DC's Batman comics were actually created and by whom. As George Pacinda writes in his article "Those Behind Batman" (*Batmania* #6, Oct. 1965):

> With the advent of the "New Look" Batman there came praise for all concerned. There was praise for the editor, that fine genius who was mainly responsible for the change. There came credits to the writer, a master of scripting. The honor call continued with the pencil-artist, a true craftsman of delineation. Next came praise for the inker, an able and talented artist. Since these people are so well known, especially here in the pages of BATMANIA, I have purposely avoided listing them. […] But […] there are others.

These 'others' include those who letter the comics, proofread them, and do the actual printing. "Suppose we trace a comic, a BATMAN comic, to see how it comes into being," Pacinda suggests and then provides a step-by-step description of the production process.[37] Pacinda's article was published in October 1965, and it is remarkable that the serialized authorship discourse, which had begun with the introduction of the letter columns only a few years earlier, had clearly moved beyond the "guessing-the-author" game.[38] The article also produced a new author role: that of the enlightened critic as a mediating agent who stands in personal contact with those who are making comics, knows how they work, and presents his findings to "[t]he better educated fans."

The productive powers of the comic books paratext became especially apparent when such 'educated fans' were no longer satisfied with communicating in writing and sought out the producers of superhero comics in person during comic conventions that, in turn, reentered the paratextual space as they were covered by fanzines. The comics conventions were an extratextual manifestation of reader expectations and projections of comics authorship as well as evidence of the comics industry's realization that courting fans and sampling their opinions would benefit their business objectives. *Batmania* #7 (Nov. 1965) reported on the New York convention of 1965 ("Con-Cave Coming") and reconstructed the debate about the original authorship of Batman: "[Bill] Finger's comments filled in the history of Batman's success as a continually popular comic book character. Finger related how he had scripted the first Batman story, working in close conjunction with Bob Kane." The editor's note—"Tom Fagan has prepared an article on Bill tentatively entitled, 'Bill Finger, Man Behind A Legend', which is based upon a personal conversation with the writer during the ComicCon"—clearly points to the dispersal of author responsibilities: "Kane" actually stands for the contributions of many different writers and artists in the serial history of the character whose work was only now being recognized and whose efforts had been written out of Batman's history through earlier authorial fictions such as Kane's biography in *Batman* #1 and *Real Fact Comics* #5.

As Fagan's report of a later convention in *Batmania* #14 (Feb. 1967) illustrates, questions of authorship were at the forefront of the comic book discourse: "Why aren't artist and writer credits given in the Batman comic book sagas, asked a Batmanian. [Editor Julius] Schwartz explained

---

37 The most thorough historical analysis of American comic book production is Gabilliet 2010: part 2; for discussions among writers and artists, see Eisner 2001.

38 In *Batman* #206 (Nov. 1968), Joe Rusnak writes: "Figuring out the authors of stories isn't much fun now. The fad should soon be dying out because it's getting too easy," to which the DC editor responds: "[T]he author-guessing fad has run its course. From now on we're giving author (and artists) credit along with each story." Uricchio and Pearson interpret this new editorial policy as reflecting an "increasing valorization of comic book authorship, further encouraging fans to take an auteurist perspective of the production process" (1991: 188).

he had been giving these recently in letter-page paragraphs. He also stated that Bob Kane's contract with National [DC Comics] might stipulate Kane's name appear on Batman stories since Kane was the originator." While Kane's legal authority seemed somewhat uncertain,[39] Finger's remarks about his own role in the history of the series attained special relevance because they undermined the established authorial origin story behind the *Batman* series: "Finger, when called upon, told how he came up with the name of Robin for Batman's youthful companion when the strip was only a few month's [sic] old. On the start of Batman from the beginning, it was Finger's suggestions that added cowl, cape and gauntlets to the Batman costume."

Not surprisingly, Finger's remarks and their dissemination throughout the world of fanzines demanded a response from various sources, all of which laid claim to an authorial voice that possessed a substantial degree of authority. One of these responses was fan writer and editor Jerry Bails's "If the Truth Be Known or 'A Finger in Every Plot,'" which appeared in *Capa-alpha* #12 (Sept. 1965). Like Fagan's piece in *Batmania*, this exposé raised not just the question of who had actually authored the initial Batman character but also asked who was able to make his case in which form and forum. If DC Comics had presented the myth of solitary creation (albeit under editorial tutelage) in the 1940s, fanzine writers like Fagan and Bails now begin to act as investigative journalists and hobby historians who present their findings in settings they themselves control. Bails left little doubt about the close collaboration that he believed had led to the creation of Batman: "Bill is the man who first put words in the mouth of the Guardian of Gotham. He worked from the very beginning with Bob Kane in shaping and reshaping Comicdom's first truly mortal costumed character." But rather than reduce the complexity of author involvements, such authorization conflicts produced even more authors and more author roles. They diversified authorial practices and increased the pool of actors who could legitimately claim authorship status as much as they instigated new ways of managing the proliferation of author functions, enriching older fictions of comic book authorship with new origin stories.

Bails's exposé is a case in point. It spawned Bob Kane's "Open Letter to All 'Batmanians' Everywhere," which Kane sent out to be printed in *Batmania*.[40] Kane writes: "Now, Biljo, I'd like to emphatically set the

---

[39] The narrative implications of legal restrictions and considerations for superhero comics are discussed in Gaines 1991: ch. 7; Packard 2010. Even today, Batman comics, television cartoons, movies, and computer games carry the byline "Batman created by Bob Kane."

[40] The letter was dated Sept. 14, 1965, and eventually appeared in the *Batmania Annual* of 1967.

record straight, once and for all, about the many 'myths' and 'conjectures' that I read about myself and my creation, 'Batman,' in your 'Fanzine' and other publications [...]. I, Bob Kane, am the sole creator of 'Batman.'" And then: "The truth is that Bill Finger is taking credit for much more than he deserves, and I refute much of his statements [...]. The fact is that I conceived the 'Batman' figure and costume entirely by myself, even before I called Bill in to help me write the 'Batman.' I created the title, masthead, the format and concept, as well as the Batman figure and costume." Kane speaks as a professional author here, as the institutionally backed inventor of Batman. He does acknowledge that Finger co-wrote the early stories, but he locates the act of original creation before their first encounter, which makes Finger a hired gun rather than a genuine creator figure. But Kane has to make his claim plausible for a readership that has become increasingly aware of various forms of authorial collaboration and is critical of traditional author fictions. What we see here, then, is a shift in interpretive authority and the emergence of new actors with new competences. Batman fans are no longer passive readers, and neither are they mere letter writers; they are authors of critical essays and use their newfound authority to complicate Kane's authorial status. Now, a writer like Bails can retroactively inscribe Finger's authorship into the historiography of the series and thereby establish himself as an authority on comics history.

Once constituted, such authority is difficult to contain. Kane tried to control his author image but was forced to do so by appointing another fanzine writer as its protector (and thus authorizing yet another author and creating yet another author function). Sarcastically referring to Bails as "the self-appointed authority on Batman," Kane then makes White the "unofficial guardian of pertinent Batmania folklore." Kane obviously missed the double irony inherent in this statement. It remains unclear, for one, how an "unofficial guardian" might effectively overrule the verdict of a "self-appointed authority." If authority may either be bestowed upon someone by a higher order or power (and would then be more or less official, which White's authority is explicitly not) or earned on its own strength (which means that authorities can be self-appointed if they can legitimatize themselves within a discourse community), neither White's nor Bails's claim to the correct view of Batman's authorship is *per se* more authoritative than the other. The reason for this unresolved tension is already (and apparently unintentionally) implied in Kane's statement: if Batman's existence in popular culture is equated with the workings of folklore (a much-cited and certainly debatable equation), then any attempt to pin down his original or most authoritative authorship is rendered moot from the start. At least in the original sense of the word, folklore is a prominent example of serial storytelling, but its imperatives run counter to the very romantically charged notions of individual authorship and the modern legal understanding of copyrighted and trademarked production that undergird Kane's claim to being the sole creator of Batman.

Conclusion

My reflections on the serial fictions and functions of authorship in American superhero comics in this chapter have obviously been reductive. To single out one character, one genre, and one time period cannot do justice to the wealth and complexity of the many issues involved. Moreover, I have, largely out of necessity, ignored questions of authorship construction through individual drawing styles, narrative voices, intraserial retcons, metanarratives, and various other kinds of mechanisms through which superhero comics have moved beyond Eco's dialectic of author-controlled repetition and variation and toward a more diversified process that William Uricchio and Roberta Pearson have labeled "containment and refraction" (1991: 211).[41] What I do want to suggest in conclusion, however, is that the notion of the threshold may offer a compelling metaphor for further investigation, especially if we want to pursue the assumption that the sequential structuring of comics narratives and the serial organization of ongoing stories serve as openings, or gaps, for projections, mediations, transactions, and other kinds of productive and creative maneuvers through which those who produce and read comics struggle to achieve closure where serial comics must, by their very nature, remain unclosed, always ready for a new installment or variation as long someone is buying. After all, in order to decipher the full-scale workings of serial storytelling in comics at specific historical moments, we would have to consider a range of thresholds performing very actively as mediators: the gutter as the threshold between panels; the multimodal or intermedial threshold between image and text; as well as various other types of thresholds among texts, peritexts, and epitexts; between individual installments and accumulating series; between superhero comics and other genres; between comics genres and other media; and between different nationally conceived comics traditions in our rapidly globalizing world.

---

41 For further investigation, see Stein 2013, 2014.

Works Cited

Adler-Kassner, Linds (1997–1998). "'Why Won't You Just Read It?' E.C. Comic Book Readers and Community in the 1950s." *Reader: Essays in Reader-Oriented Theory, Criticism, and Pedagogy* 38–39: 101–27. Print.

Barker, Martin (1989). *Comics: Ideology, Power and the Critics*. Manchester: Manchester UP. Print.

Becker, Thomas (2010). "Enki Bilal's 'Woman Trap': Reflections of Authorship under the Shifting Boundaries between Order and Terror in the Cities." Jörn Ahrens and Arno Meteling (eds.). *Comics and the City: Urban Space in Print, Picture and Sequence*. London: Continuum. 265–78. Print.

Bennett, Andrew (2005). *The Author*. London: Routledge. Print.

Blythe, Hal, and Charlie Sweet (2002). "The Superhero Formula." *Storytelling: A Critical Journal of Popular Narrative* 2.1: 45–59. Print.

Brooker, Will (2001). *Batman Unmasked: Analysing a Cultural Icon*. London: Continuum. Print.

— (2012). *Hunting the Dark Knight: Twenty-First Century Batman*. London: I. B. Tauris. Print.

Brown, Jeffrey A. (2001). *Black Superheroes, Milestone Comics, and Their Fans*. Jackson: UP of Mississippi. Print.

Carpenter, Stanford W. (2005). "Truth Be Told: Authorship and the Creation of a Black Captain America." Jeff McLaughlin (ed.). *Comics and Philosophy*. Jackson: UP of Mississippi. 46–62. Print.

Coogan, Peter (2006). *Superhero: The Secret Origin of a Genre*. Austin: MonkeyBrain. Print.

Cunningham, Brian (ed.) (2009). *Stan's Soapbox: The Collection*. New York: Marvel Comics. Print.

Denson, Shane (2011). "Marvel Comics' Frankenstein: A Case Study in the Media of Serial Figures." Daniel Stein, Christina Meyer, and Micha Edlich (eds.). *American Comic Books and Graphic Novels*. Special issue of *Amerikastudien/American Studies* 56.4: 531–53. Print.

Denson, Shane, Christina Meyer, and Daniel Stein (eds.) (2013). *Transnational Perspectives on Graphic Narratives: Comics at the Crossroads*. London: Bloomsbury. Print.

Dittmer, Jason (2007). "The Tyranny of the Serial: Popular Geopolitics, the Nation, and Comic Book Discourse." *Antipode* 39.2: 247–68. Print.

Donovan, Stephen, Danuta Fjellestad, and Rolf Lundén (eds.) (2008). *Authority Matters: Rethinking the Theory and Practice of Authorship*. New York: Rodopi. Print.

Duncan, Randy, and Matthew J. Smith (2009). *The Power of Comics: History, Form and Culture*. New York: Continuum. Print.

Ecke, Jochen (2013). "Warren Ellis: Performing the Transnational Author in American Mainstream Comics." Shane Denson, Christina Meyer, and Daniel Stein (eds.). *Transnational Perspectives on Graphic Narratives: Comics at the Crossroads*. London: Bloomsbury. 163–79. Print.

Eco, Umberto (1990). "Interpreting Serials." *The Limits of Interpretation*. Bloomington: Indiana UP. 83–100. Print.

— (2004 [1962]). "The Myth of Superman." Jeet Heer and Kent Worcester (eds.). *Arguing Comics: Literary Masters on a Popular Medium*. Jackson: UP of Mississippi. 146–64. Print.

Eder, Barbara, Elisabeth Klar, and Ramón Reichert (eds.) (2011). *Theorien des Comics: Ein Reader*. Bielefeld: transcript. Print.

Eder, Jens, Fotis Jannidis, and Ralf Schneider (eds.) (2010). *Characters in Fictional Worlds: Understanding Imaginary Beings in Literature, Film, and Other Media*. Berlin: De Gruyter. Print.

Eisner, Will (2001). *Will Eisner's Shop Talk*. Milwaukie: Dark Horse Comics. Print.

Foucault, Michel (2001 [1969]). "What Is an Author?" Vincent B. Leitch (ed.). *The Norton Anthology of Theory and Criticism*. New York: Norton. 1622–36. Print.

Gabilliet, Jean-Paul (2010). *Of Comics and Men: A Cultural History of American Comic Books*. Trans. Bart Beaty and Nick Nguyen. Jackson: UP of Mississippi. Print.

Gaines, Jane M. (1991). *Contested Culture: The Image, the Voice, and the Law*. Chapel Hill: U of North Carolina P. Print.

Gardner, Jared (2012). *Projections: Comics and the History of Twenty-First-Century Storytelling*. Stanford: Stanford UP. Print.

Genette, Gérard (1997). *Paratexts: Thresholds of Interpretations*. Trans. Jane E. Lewin. Cambridge: Cambridge UP. Print.

Gray, Jonathan (2010). *Show Sold Separately: Promos, Spoilers, and Other Media Paratexts*. New York: New York UP. Print.

Harrigan, Pat, and Noah Wardrip-Fruin (eds.) (2009). *ThirdPerson: Authoring and Exploring Vast Narratives*. Boston: MIT Press. Print.

Hayward, Jennifer (1997). *Consuming Pleasures: Active Audiences and Serial Fictions from Dickens to Soap Opera*. Lexington: Kentucky UP. Print.

Heer, Jeet, and Kent Worcester (eds.) (2009). *A Comics Studies Reader*. Jackson: UP of Mississippi. Print.

Hills, Matt (2002). *Fan Cultures*. New York: Routledge. Print.

Jenkins, Henry (1992). *Textual Poachers: Television Fans and Participatory Culture*. New York: Routledge. Print.

— (2006). *Fans, Gamers, and Bloggers: Exploring Participatory Culture*. New York: New York UP. Print.

— (2010). "'Just Men in Tights': Rewriting Silver Age Comics in an Era of Multiplicity." Angela Ndalianis (ed.). *The Contemporary Comic Book Superhero*. New York: Routledge. 16-43. Print.

Kelleter, Frank (2011). "Serienhelden sehen dich an." *Psychologie Heute* 38.4: 70-75. Print.

— (ed.) (2012). *Populäre Serialität: Narration—Evolution—Distinktion. Zum seriellen Erzählen seit dem 19. Jahrhundert*. Bielefeld: transcript. Print.

Kelleter, Frank, and Daniel Stein (2009). "*Great, Mad, New:* Populärkultur, serielle Ästhetik und der frühe amerikanische Zeitungscomic." Stephan Ditschke, Katerina Kroucheva, and Daniel Stein (eds.). *Comics: Zur Geschichte und Theorie eines populärkulturellen Mediums*. Bielefeld: transcript. 81–117. Print.

— (2012). "Autorisierungspraktiken seriellen Erzählens: Zur Gattungsentwicklung von Superheldencomics." Frank Kelleter (ed.). *Populäre Serialität: Narration—Evolution—Distinktion. Zum seriellen Erzählen seit dem 19. Jahrhundert*. Bielefeld: transcript. 259–90. Print.

Kindt, Tom, and Hans-Harald Müller (eds.) (2006). *The Implied Author: Concept and Controversy*. Berlin: De Gruyter. Print.

Klock, Geoff (2003). *How to Read Superhero Comics and Why*. London: Continuum. Print.

Latour, Bruno (1993). *We Have Never Been Modern*. Trans. Catherine Porter. Cambridge: Harvard UP. Print.

— (2005). *Reassembling the Social: An Introduction to Actor-Network-Theory*. Oxford: Oxford UP. Print.

Lopes, Paul (2009). *Demanding Respect: The Evolution of the American Comic Book*. Philadelphia: Temple UP. Print.

Mittell, Jason (2006). "Narrative Complexity in Contemporary American Television." *The Velvet Light Trap* 58: 29–40. Print.

Ndalianis, Angela (ed.) (2010). *The Contemporary Comic Book Superhero*. New York: Routledge. Print.

Niefanger, Dirk (2002). "Der Autor und sein Label: Überlegungen zur fonction classificatoire Foucaults (mit Fallstudien zu Langbehn und Kracauer)." Heinrich Detering (ed.). *Autorschaft: Positionen und Revisionen*. Stuttgart: Metzler. 521–39. Print.

Packard, Stephan (2010). "Copyright und Superhelden: Über die Prägung populärer Mythologie durch textuelle Kontrolle." Claude D. Conter (ed.). *Justitiabilität und Rechtmäßigkeit: Verrechtlichungsprozesse von Literatur und Film in der Moderne*. Amsterdam: Rodopi. 109–26. Print.

Pearson, Roberta E., and William Uricchio (1991). "Notes from the Batcave: An Interview with Dennis O'Neil." Roberta E. Pearson and William Uricchio (eds.). *The Many Lives of the Batman: Critical Approaches to a Superhero and His Media*. New York: Routledge. 18–32. Print.

Pustz, Matthew J. (1999). *Comic Book Culture: Fanboys and True Believers*. Jackson: UP of Mississippi. Print.

Ryan, Marie-Laure, and Jan-Noël Thon (eds.) (2014). *Storyworlds across Media: Toward a Media-Conscious Narratology*. Lincoln: U of Nebraska P. Print.

Sabin, Roger (1993). *Adult Comics: An Introduction*. London: Routledge. Print.

Saika, Tadahiro (2011). "How Creators Depict Creating Manga: Mangaka Manga as Authenticating Discourse." Jaqueline Berndt (ed.). *Intercultural Crossovers, Transcultural Flows: Manga/Comics*. Kyoto: imrc. 99–109. Print.

Schelly, Bill (1999). *The Golden Age of Comic Fandom*. Seattle: Hamster Press. Print.

Sheridan, Martin (1942). *Comics and Their Creators: Life Stories of American Cartoonists*. Boston: Hale, Cushman and Flint. Print.

Smith, Matthew J. (2012). "Auteur Criticism: The Re-Visionary Works of Alan Moore." Matthew J. Smith and Randy Duncan (eds.). *Critical Approaches to Comics: Theories and Methods*. New York: Routledge. 178–88. Print.

Smith, Matthew J., and Randy Duncan (eds.). (2012). *Critical Approaches to Comics: Theories and Methods*. New York: Routledge. Print.

Stein, Daniel (2009). "Was ist ein Comic-Autor? Autorinszenierung in autobiografischen Comics und Selbstporträts." Stephan Ditschke, Katerina Kroucheva, and Daniel Stein (eds.). *Comics: Zur Geschichte und Theorie eines populärkulturellen Mediums*. Bielefeld: transcript. 201–37. Print.

— (2012). "Spoofin' Spidey—Rebooting the Bat: Immersive Story Worlds and the Narrative Complexities of Video Spoofs in the Era of the Superhero Blockbuster." Kathleen Loock and Constantine Verevis (eds.). *New Perspectives on Film Remakes, Adaptations, and Fan Productions: Remake|Remodel*. Basingstoke: Palgrave Macmillan. 231–47. Print.

— (2013). "Of Transcreations and Transpacific Adaptations: Investigating Manga Versions of Spider-Man." Shane Denson, Christina Meyer, and Daniel Stein (eds.). *Transnational Perspectives on Graphic Narratives: Comics at the Crossroads*. London: Bloomsbury. 145–61. Print.

— (2014). "Popular Seriality, Authorship, Superhero Comics: On the Evolution of a Transnational Genre Economy." Marcel Hartwig, Evelyne Keitel and Gunter Süß (eds.). *Media Economies: Perspectives on American Cultural Practices*. Trier: Wissenschaftlicher Verlag Trier. 133–57. Print.

Stein, Daniel, Stephan Ditschke, and Katerina Kroucheva (2009). "Birth of a Notion: Comics als populärkulturelles Medium." Stephan Ditschke, Katerina Kroucheva, and Daniel Stein (eds.). *Comics: Zur Geschichte und Theorie eines populärkulturellen Mediums*. Bielefeld: transcript. 7–27. Print.

Stein, Daniel, Christina Meyer, and Micha Edlich (eds.) (2011). *American Comic Books and Graphic Novels*. Special issue of *Amerikastudien/American Studies* 56.4: 501–29. Print.

Thomas, Roy, and Bill Schelly (eds.) (2008). *Alter Ego: The Best of the Legendary Magazine*. Raleigh: TwoMorrows. Print.

Tompkins, Jane (1985). *Sensational Designs: The Cultural Work of American Fiction*. New York: Oxford UP. Print.

Uidhir, Christy M. (2012). "Comics and Collective Authorship." Aaron Meskin and Roy T. Cook (eds.). *The Art of Comics: A Philosophical Approach*. Malden: Blackwell. 47–67. Print.

Uricchio, William (2010). "The Batman's Gotham City™: Story, Ideology, Performance." Jörn Ahrens and Arno Meteling (eds.). *Comics and the City: Urban Space in Print, Picture and Sequence*. London: Continuum. 119–32. Print.

Uricchio, William, and Roberta E. Pearson (1991). "'I'm Not Fooled by That Cheap Disguise." Roberta E. Pearson and William Uricchio (eds.). *The Many Lives of the Batman: Critical Approaches to a Superhero and His Media*. New York: Routledge. 182–213. Print.

Williams, Paul, and James Lyons (eds.) (2010). *The Rise of the American Comics Artist: Creators and Contexts*. Jackson: UP of Mississippi. Print.

Wüllner, Daniel (2010). "Suspended in Mid-Month: Serialized Storytelling in Comics." Joyce Goggin and Dan Hassler-Forest (eds.). *The Rise and Reason of Comics and Graphic Literature: Critical Essays on the Form*. Jefferson: McFarland. 43–55. Print.

Zani, Steven (2010). "It's a Jungle in Here: Animal Man, Continuity Issues and the Authorial Death Drive." Angela Ndalianis (ed.). *The Contemporary Comic Book Superhero*. New York: Routledge. 233–49. Print.

GABRIELE RIPPL AND LUKAS ETTER
(Bern)

Intermediality, Transmediality, and Graphic Narrative[1]

Introduction

Over the past decades, various types of graphic narrative, such as comic strips, comic books, and graphic novels, have enjoyed an enthusiastic popular reception.[2] While the exploits of superheroes like Superman and Batman have long fascinated readers, licensing and merchandising have made comic books and graphic novels more widely known to the general public than ever. Their popularity may result from the fact that they are prone to what Jay David Bolter and Richard Grusin (2000) call 'remediation,' to transmedial storytelling and diversification: many of the novels, movies, animated cartoons, and video games launched today are based on graphic narratives. While graphic narratives are transmedial phenomena due to their remediation potential, they are also intermedial narratives based on words and images that collaborate to relate stories. Whereas writer-artists like Art Spiegelman and Chris Ware are responsible for both the words and pictures of their works, the bulk of graphic narratives are produced by creative teams consisting of writers, scripters, and plotters to outline the complete story, and pencilers, inkers, and colorists to render the story in visual form. Examples are Neil Gaiman, Alan Moore, and Frank Miller, who collaborate with well-known graphic artists such as Dave McKean, Dave Gibbons, and Bryan Talbot.

Comic strips, comic books, and graphic novels can be read as stories due to the sequential nature of their panels[3]: closure, i.e., the readers' ability and constant activity to bridge the gutters that divide the single static pictures, helps to create narrativity. Since graphic narratives combine word and image to tell stories, they are ideal test cases for a discussion of

---

1   Lukas Etter has contributed the examples from primary sources; Gabriele Rippl is responsible for all other parts of this article.
2   The term 'graphic narrative' was introduced by Hillary Chute and Marianne DeKoven in 2006. There are additional formats outside the English-speaking world, such as Japanese manga and French-Belgian albums, which would equally qualify as 'graphic narratives.' For further analysis, see the chapters by Jaqueline Berndt, Pascal Lefèvre, and Jan Baetens and Steven Surdiacourt in this volume.
3   See Eisner 1985; McCloud 1993.

inter- and transmedial strategies of storytelling. After a brief analysis of the terminology pertinent to our discussion, we move on to examine theoretical concepts such as intermediality and transmedial narratology in order to gauge how fruitful these concepts are when applied to a variety of graphic narratives. As will be demonstrated, the results of intermediality research (1) are especially relevant for investigations into how word-image combinations collaborate in graphic narratives to tell stories, and (2) they have paved the way for new approaches in narratology, namely, transmedial ones that investigate the narrative potential of different media, their narrative limitations, and their affordances.

Terminology: Graphic Narrative as Art Form, Genre, or Medium?

In Henry John Pratt's recent article "Narrative in Comics" (2009), he defines comics as narratives telling stories by a sequence of pictures with speech balloons. While some critics have argued that non-narrative comics, like non-narrative film and literature, are possible,[4] the majority of comics are read with the expectation that a story unfolds, which is why Pratt considers comics "a predominantly narrative medium" (2009: 107) whose literary as well as pictorial narrative dimensions he then explores. He does so with a shifting terminology, variously calling comics a medium, an art form, a code, and a genre. As a hybrid art form, he suggests, "comics have both literary and *pictorial* narrative dimensions: it is a *hybrid* art form that employs narrative strategies closely connected to literature, on the one hand, and other pictorial media, on the other" (Pratt 2009: 107, original emphases).

Pratt's inconsistent terminology demonstrates a general problem centered around the term 'medium' and its many different definitions. Narratologist Marie-Laure Ryan (2004) has discussed the question 'What are media?' in the context of a transmedial narratology,[5] trying to bridge the diverging positions held by different academic communities. There is consensus on the view that all media, be it a printed text or a digital photo, function as intermediaries that allow for the production, distribution, and reception of semiotic signs, thus enabling communication. Yet it is far more difficult to define and classify media: sociologists, philosophers, literary historians and new media theorists all have deviating ideas about what exactly a medium is. What is more, while in the English-speaking world the term 'media' refers most often to mechanical, electronic, and

---
4   See Meskin 2007.
5   See also Ryan 2014; Ryan and Thon 2014; Thon 2014b.

digital (mass) media such as photography, telephone, radio, film, TV, video, and the Internet, and while media studies tend mainly to investigate the social systems and cultural institutions on which the technologies of mass communication are based, for German-speaking academic communities, the investigation into medium/media and mediality is a more encompassing and diversified field that includes a general media theory.[6] In this tradition, 'medium' refers in a very general sense to the material side of the sign, i.e., its carrier[7]—it is that which mediates (cf. the etymology of the Latin term *medius* which means 'middle' and 'intermediate,' and *Vermittler* in German)—, and the focus is on the question of how this material side of the sign/semiotic system is involved in the production of narrative meaning.

In connection with narratological issues, it is important to note that different media such as oil painting, music, digital photography, and film "are not hollow conduits for the transmission of messages but material supports of information whose materiality, precisely, 'matters' for the type of meanings that can be encoded" (Ryan 2004: 1–2). Instead, "a medium is a category that truly makes a difference about what stories can be evoked or told, how they are presented, why they are communicated, and how they are experienced" (Ryan 2004: 18). Following Ryan, we may distinguish between at least three different approaches to media: (1) semiotic approaches such as that of Gotthold Ephraim Lessing (1984 [1766]) and Werner Wolf (1999, 2002), who have looked into codes and sensory channels that support various (verbal, visual, and musical) media; (2) material and technological approaches that focus on how the semiotic types are supported by media[8]; and (3) cultural approaches that are interested in social and cultural aspects of the media as well as in the network of relations among media. While many scholars in media theory today disregard semiotic categories when discussing media and prefer to call them 'modes' and a combination of modes 'multimodal,'[9] we believe that Ryan is right when pointing out that semiotically based media such as music and two-dimensional images cannot be ignored: "modes of signification play a major role in distinguishing media from each other. There is simply no way to build a media system without taking semiotic criteria into consideration. Moreover, 'mode' is just as difficult to define as medium" (2014: 4–5).

---

6 See Voigts-Virchow 2005; Rippl 2012.
7 See Rippl 2005.
8 Cf. Ryan 2005: 15; see also Ryan 2014.
9 See Kress and van Leeuwen 2001.

"Image-language combinations," i.e., "combinations of still pictures and text," such as emblems and graphic narratives, are "spatio-temporal media" (Ryan 2005: 19). But it is very hard to decide where the medium ends and genre begins. Due to the problematic terminology sketched above, it is worthwhile to ruminate on Ryan's following suggestion:

> Whereas genre is defined by more or less freely adopted conventions, chosen for both personal and cultural reasons, *medium* imposes its possibilities and limitations on the reader. [...] Genre conventions are genuine rules specified by humans, whereas the constraints and possibilities offered by media are dictated by their material substance and mode of encoding. (2005: 19)

Are graphic narratives, then, a hybrid medium that narrates stories by correlating words and sequences of still images, or should they rather count as a genre? How, indeed, do terms and concepts such as mode, code, channel, and art form relate to other terms, such as genre and medium? Labeling graphic narratives a 'medium' is somewhat problematic because they actually involve two basic media which they combine, word and image, and these two media or representational semiotic codes are not present independently, but interact in very complex ways on the page in order to tell a story. Something is not a type of comics/graphic narrative "if the prose is independent of pictures [... or] if the written story could exist without any pictures and still be a continuous whole" (Harvey 1995: 75). Labeling graphic narratives a 'hybrid art form' likewise raises questions: it sounds defensive (as if one had to insist that graphic narratives are an art form rather than a popular mass medium). And why should the rather vague term 'hybrid' be used instead of the adjective 'intermedial,' which refers to widely accepted typologies and is based on a rich reservoir of research in intermediality and inter- and transmedial narration? One may conclude that graphic narratives range between the two categories, depending on the angle from which they are looked at: according to semiotic approaches, graphic narratives are representational codes based on two media, words and pictures; according to cultural, material, and technical approaches, the graphic narratives' semiotic types, word and picture, are based on the medium of the printed book. We suggest a combined approach which—in analogy to film—understands graphic narrative as a medium that is able to tell stories through the combination of word and image. However, graphic narrative can also be considered as a genre which encompasses several subgenres such as the comic strip, the comic book and the graphic novel.

Intermediality

As stated above, the programmatic results of intermediality research are highly relevant for an exploration of graphic narratives. Intermediality studies is a field of research that for more than three decades has dealt with interrelations between different media. Intermediality researchers (1) are interested in differences between media but also in their collaborations and networks as well as their functions across cultures and through history; (2) they consider intermediality studies as 'democratic,' i.e., they do not deal exclusively with art forms and highbrow culture, but also with popular mass culture products and the new media; (3) they question the applicability of verbal models to all cultural manifestations.[10] Werner Wolf and Irina O. Rajewsky have presented typologies that make distinctions among different intermedial phenomena. According to Rajewsky, the current debate reveals two basic understandings of intermediality, "a broader and a narrower one, which are not in themselves homogeneous. The first concentrates on *intermediality as a fundamental condition or category* while the second approaches *intermediality as a critical category for the concrete analysis of specific individual media products or configurations*" (2005: 47, original emphases). Rajewsky's literary conception of intermediality in the latter and narrower sense encompasses three subcategories, but single medial configurations will match more than just one of the three subcategories:

(1) Media combination (also called multi-media, pluri-media as well as mixed media) such as opera, film, theater, performances, illuminated manuscripts, comics, computer installations, etc. In this subcategory, intermediality is "a communicative-semiotic concept, based on the combination of at least two medial forms of articulation" (2005: 52).[11]

(2) Medial transposition, e.g., film adaptations, novelizations, etc. This category is production-oriented; the intermedial quality "has to do with the way in which a media product comes into being, i.e., with the transformation of a given media product (a text, a film, etc.) or of its substratum into another medium" (2005: 51).

(3) Intermedial references, for instance references in a literary text to a piece of music (the so-called musicalization of fiction, the imitation and evocation of filmic techniques such as dissolves, zoom shots, montage editing, etc.); descriptive modes in literature that evoke visual effects or refer to specific visual works of art (so-called ekphrasis). Intermedial references contribute to the overall signification; like the first category,

---

10 See Rippl 2005.
11 It is this category of intermediality that today is often referred to as 'multimodal'; cf. Kukkonen 2011: 35-37.

they are of a communicative-semiotic nature, but they involve by definition only one medium.[12]

According to Werner Wolf, intermediality applies in its broadest sense to any transgression of boundaries between media and thus is concerned with "'heteromedial' relations between different semiotic complexes" (2005: 252). Wolf understands media as conventionally distinct means of communicating cultural content, which are specified principally by the nature of their underlying semiotic systems (involving verbal language, pictorial signs, music, etc. or in cases of 'composite media' such as film, a combination of several semiotic systems); their technical or institutional channels are merely secondary. He differentiates between

- *intramediality*, which involves only one medium, so there is no transgression of media boundaries;
- *transmediality*, which describes such phenomena that are non-specific to individual media (motifs, thematic variation, style, narrativity etc.) and appear across a variety of different media;
- *intermediality*, which is subdivided into two variants of intermedial relations/references. The involvement with another medium may take place explicitly, "whenever two or more media are overtly present in a given semiotic entity" (Wolf 2005: 254), or covertly, i.e., indirectly (e.g., musicalization of fiction or ekphrasis, i.e., visualization of fiction/poetry). For many critics the mere thematization of another medium is not enough, and they reserve the term 'intermediality' for an evocation of certain formal features of another medium; this category includes a change of medium (e.g., the film adaptation of a novel), or combination of media ("multi-" or "plurimediality" [Wolf 2005: 253–55]: ballet, opera, film, comic strips, technopaignia).

Rajewsky's and Wolf's typologies help us to investigate the medial specificities of graphic narratives, particularly how word and image interact in various complex ways to tell stories. We can further build on the work of Martin Schüwer and others who have started to explain how the static images of graphic narratives and the unique blend of graphic and verbal signs are able to construct a fictive world full of movement, space, and its own time structure and, while being related to the medium of film, still follow their own medial rules. Both graphic novels and novels are generally published in book form; their use of medial carrier/s, however, differs greatly: while novels tell stories by using one medium, namely writing, graphic novels usually combine two media, sequences of static pictures and integrated textual parts, in order to narrate.

---

12   See Rajewsky 2010; Rippl 2012.

Schüwer—with frequent reference to Benoît Peeters (1991)—discusses the word-image interactions in comics/graphic narratives in great depth and presents several examples in which either the verbal or the visual element dominates the graphic narrative. Provided a specific graphic narrative is the product of collaboration, either the penciler or the scenarist can be perceived to be the dominant creative force.[13] Whereas graphic narratives without visual elements do not exist, there are examples completely devoid of text. Several effects can be achieved in such cases. Pantomimic sequences of images may either just appear "natural" (Schüwer 2008: 320; our translation from the German: "gewisser Natürlichkeit"), or they may establish a contrast to text-based passages in the same work and express, e.g., moments of trauma or alienation.

In graphic narratives, the combination of text and pictures—the fact that the "image and the dialogue give meaning to each other" (Eisner 1985: 59)—is the vital element of storytelling. It is therefore important to note that processes of decoding/reading are based on the different perception modes of both sign systems, on reading sequentially and on looking at the panel and the graphic narrative page as a whole.[14] Equally important is another characteristic, namely, that writing is usually represented through lettering, i.e., handwriting remediated through print. In graphic narratives, writing in general possesses more iconic freedom than in literary texts (except in *technopaignia* and other experimental forms) in order to express intonation, pitch, atmosphere, and so forth, and it also features as a visual carrier of meaning. Sequential and simultaneous modes of reception allow the reader to turn the two-dimensional fragments (panels and the gaps between them) into three-dimensional space and static pictures into movement. Since the sequences of pictures in graphic narratives are invested with a successive power and thus transcend the static quality of a single picture, they in fact invite us to question Lessing's (1984 [1766]) influential differentiation between words and images.

In graphic narratives, word and image correlate and compete in a plethora of ways. What has been said so far relates to Rajewsky's first category, media combination or media hybridity, i.e., to the fact that graphic narratives commonly combine two media, text and image, and are hence *per se* intermedial phenomena. However, graphic narratives' specific intermediality is by no means restricted to this category and to the word-picture combinations in individual panels. In fact, intermediality in graphic narratives can be discussed in a different way by using Rajewsky's categories 2 and 3.

---

13 Cf. Schüwer 2008: 315.
14 See Schnackertz 1980; Schüwer 2002; Saraceni 2003.

The graphic narrative *V for Vendetta* (1988), written by Alan Moore and penciled by David Lloyd, lends itself as an example of Rajewsky's second intermedial category of medial transposition (or change of medium). *V for Vendetta* started as a black-and-white cartoon in the magazine *Warrior* in 1982 and was later completed and edited as a full-color graphic novel by DC Comics. In 2005, James McTeigue produced a commercially successful movie adaptation of the graphic narrative. Based on the screenplay, Stephen Moore wrote a homonymic novel, which was released in 2006. The filmic adaptation (what Rajewsky calls medial transposition)[15] led to a vocal dissent among the creators of the graphic narrative and those of the movie.[16] As James Reynolds and others have pointed out, the movie *V for Vendetta* does not substantially add characters or plotlines—it has a tendency to reduce both.[17] In fact, McTeigue's movie has gone so far in simplifying the plot that Moore ended up publicly distancing himself from it. Even critics cautious not to fall prey to the "morally loaded discourse of fidelity" (Hutcheon 2006: 7), frequently encountered when any sort of film adaptation is discussed, acknowledged that the movie reduced significantly the original plot of the 10-installment graphic narrative, as well as its political explosiveness. This is why *V for Vendetta* invites us to reflect upon transmedial narratology and graphic narratives. While probably no other major movie adaptation has caused such publicly expressed irritation by the original's author as was the case with Alan Moore and *V for Vendetta*, the question has nonetheless been the same for the full legion of screenwriters and directors venturing to make adaptations of graphic narratives: what are the central problems we face when adapting/transposing a graphic narrative to other media, and what are the medial idiosyncrasies of graphic narratives that pose challenges? Future investigations into aspects of graphic narratives' inter- and transmediality are needed, especially close readings of lesser-known graphic narratives, in order to learn more about the many intricate ways in which word and image collaborate and compete in this specific medium.

---

15 Transmedial storytelling should not be confused with Jenkins's concept of "transmedia storytelling," defined as a strategy to reach "a more integrated approach to franchise development than models based on urtexts and ancillary products" (2006: 293). The concept is applicable to stories that unfold across multiple media platforms, i.e., to cases where the creators of a plot focus on their collaborative endeavors across several media *from the very beginning* (see also Ryan and Thon 2014).

16 The fact that *V for Vendetta*'s penciler David Lloyd was not irritated by the movie version in the same way as Alan Moore was has gained much less publicity (see Keller 2008; Reynolds 2009).

17 Cf. Reynolds 2009: 128.

There is also a wide range of intermedial references (Rajewsky's third category and Wolf's third category of covert intermediality) in experimental as well as non-experimental graphic narratives: formal features of other media like film and music are imitated by the means of graphic narratives. They can take on functions similar to ekphrasis and musicalization strategies in fiction. An example can be found in a passage from Jason Lutes's *Berlin: City of Smoke* (2008), in which the Vallotton-style black-and-white depiction of a jazz clarinetist takes place in 44 panels over more than two full pages. This proliferation of panels has the effect of pausing the action; by means of small variations in the musician's posture the effect of rhythm and of musicality is created within a two-dimensional sequence of drawings (see figure 1).[18]

Figure 1: Jason Lutes, *Berlin: City of Smoke* (2008). © Jason Lutes. All rights reserved.

Another example of intermedial reference is Nathan Schreiber's graphic narrative *Power Out* (2009), for which the Internet functions as the medium to be imitated (see figure 2). This intermedial reference may also be described as remediation, a landmark of today's media ecology, which Bolter and Grusin have defined as "the formal logic by which new media refashion prior media forms" (2000: 273). According to Bolter and Grusin, a medium "is that which remediates. It is that which appropriates the techniques, forms, and social significance of other media and attempts

---

[18] On Lutes's visual and verbal aesthetics in *City of Smoke*, including the Vallotton-style, see Etter 2013.

Figure 2: Nathan Schreiber, *Power Out* (2009). © Nathan Schreiber. All rights reserved.

to rival or refashion them in the name of the real" (2000: 65). New visual technologies, such as computer graphics and the World Wide Web, present themselves as

> refashioned and improved versions of other media. Digital media can best be understood through the ways in which they honor, rival, and revise linear-perspective painting, photography, film, television, and print. […] What is new about new media comes from the particular ways in which they refashion older media and the ways in which older media refashion themselves to answer the challenges of new media. (Bolter and Grusin 2000: 14–15)

Schreiber's example convincingly shows that remediation is not a one-directional process of new media refashioning prior media forms, but also a process in which established media represent newer media forms. Remediation can easily be aligned with concepts like adaptation. Especially when adaptation is to a different medium, which is the case with filmic adaptations of texts, remediation may serve as a synonym for adaptation.

Nevertheless it is "hardly reconcilable with conceptions of intermedial subcategories like medial transformation, media combination, or medial references" for the very reason that remediation

> necessarily implies a tendency to level out significant differences both between the individual phenomena in question and between different media with their respective materiality; differences that come to the fore as soon as detailed analyses of specific medial configurations, their respective meaning-constitutional strategies, and their overall signification are at stake. (Rajewsky 2005: 64)

While Bolter and Grusin use "*ekphrasis*, the literary description of works of visual art" (2000: 45, original emphasis), as a non-digital example of remediation, they ignore the fact that ekphrasis is closely connected with the *paragone*, the contest between the arts, which does not level the medial differences between words (literature) and pictures (e.g., painting) but in fact depends on them.

Inter- and Transmedial Narratology

As has already been mentioned, graphic narratives are rewarding objects for intermedial and transmedial investigation. Since most research on graphic narratives today focuses on individual works and series, generally applicable theories of inter- and transmedial narration as well as an inter- and transmedial narratological terminology and methodology have to be developed further in connection with the specific means of graphic storytelling. Obviously, narration takes place in novels, films, and graphic narratives alike, and it can therefore be considered as a transmedial phenomenon.[19] But it is important to account for the specificities of the respective medium in which an idea or story is expressed.[20] The medium as the carrier of the signs is never transparent or 'innocent'; its internal structural and medial laws define the ways in which the categories of time and space are used. Generally speaking, one can say that the tellability of any given narrative may depend intimately on the resources and the constraints of a given medium, just as each medium has particular affinities for certain themes and certain types of plot: "You cannot tell the same type of story on the stage and in writing, during conversation and in a thousand-page novel, in a two-hour movie and in a TV serial that runs for many years" (Ryan 2004: 356).

Werner Wolf triggered the debate with a groundbreaking article in 2002 that systematically investigated the narrative potential of music, paintings, and of picture series by bringing together the findings of

---

19 Cf. Rajewsky 2002: 13.
20 See also Wolf 2002; Ryan 2004; Walsh 2006.

intermediality studies and literary narratology, thus developing a new intermedial narratology. On the basis of formal (chronology, repetition, teleology, causality/cohesion) and thematic indicators (tellability and singularity),[21] he has discriminated *genuinely narrative* genres, such as novels that are based on predominantly verbal media (written and oral text) and whose recipients do hardly participate in narrativization, from works that indicate narration, such as picture series and mono- or polyphase pictures. According to Wolf, the narrative potential is low whenever a considerable input to the production of narrativity is required from the recipient.[22] In other words, prototypical narration in a novel requires a minimal narratavizing activity on the part of the recipient, whereas instrumental music demands a maximum.[23] Comic strips hold a middle position on Wolf's scale.[24] Thus, intermedial narration is based on the insight that narrativity is a transmedial cognitive frame. While most classical narratology has "disregarded the interrelation between narrativity and media, [...] [p]ostclassical narratology has started to dismantle th[e] hegemony of narrator-transmitted narratives and has emphasized the transmedial nature of narrativity as a cognitive frame applicable to ever 'remoter' media and genres" (Wolf 2011: 145).

Wolf defines transmedial narratology as the study of narrativity in works of art outside the literary text, such as painting, sculpture, instrumental music.[25] By developing a flexible concept of medium, he accounts for the material effects of a medium and "thus mediates between the positions of media determinism and media relativism" (Fludernik and Olson 2011: 16). If narratology leaves behind concepts such as that of the narrator and the preoccupation with the verbal medium and focuses instead on prototypical and cognitive aspects of narrativity, a transmedial reconceptualization of narrative becomes possible. What is necessary, however, is a compromise between the descriptions of media as mere conduits, on the one hand, and a 'the-medium-is-the-message view,' on the other. The latter "places the medium in such a strong position that a medium-independent conception of narrativity in cognitive and prototypical terms becomes impossible, for if media are the ultimate reality, cognitive frames become negligible" (Wolf 2011: 165–66). Wolf (2011: 166, original emphasis) suggests conceiving of

---

21 Cf. Wolf 2002: 47–51.
22 Wolf 2002: 96.
23 Wolf 2002: 95.
24 Cf. Hoppeler, Etter, and Rippl 2009: 96.
25 Cf. Wolf 2011: 158.

the function of media in transmedial narratology [...] in a more flexible way as influencing, but not *a priori* as determining, narrativity and narrative content. [...] As applicable to transmedial narratology, medium is a conventionally and culturally distinct means of communication; it is specified not only by technical or institutional channels (or a channel) but also and primarily by its use of one or more semiotic systems to transmit its contents, in particular within the public sphere; according to the nature and format of their constituents, different media have different capabilities for transmitting as well as shaping narratives.

Wolf concludes that narrative, like all cognitive macro-frames, can be realized in more than one medium. This implies that narrativity is to a large extent (but never completely) medium-independent and hence a transmedial phenomenon.

As has become clear, transmediality and transmedial storytelling are comparatively recent concepts that made their first prominent appearance in the field of narratology in the early 2000s. In addition to Wolf, Marie-Laure Ryan's pioneering work has also greatly helped to propel academic interest in transmedial storytelling. Ryan differentiates between a text "being a narrative" and it "possessing narrativity" (2004: 9) and between narrative as "a textual act of representation" and "a mental image—a cognitive construct—built in by the interpreter as a response to the text" (9) that allows for transmedial narratological approaches: any work of art can be considered to possess narrativity provided that the recipient can elicit a narrative script from it. No matter which medium, language, image, sound, or gesture is involved, according to Ryan, they are all able to narrate a story (but not equally well). Ryan frequently uses the terms "remediation" and "transmedial narration" (2004: 31–32) as synonyms. In that sense, transmedial means that a story told in one medium can later be retold in a different medium, but due to medium specificities, the result will never be the same. Even so, the recipient will be capable of distinguishing a narrative thread. Ryan lists nine phenomena of remediation, among them the "representation of a medium within another medium by either mechanical or descriptive means" (2004: 33), such as ekphrasis in novels; the representation of performance arts or TV shows in movies; a medium "imitating the techniques of another" (2004: 33), such as cinematic and musical techniques in novels; the "[i]nsertion of a medium in another," for example, texts in paintings, movie clips in computer games or photos in novels, remediation, i.e., transmedial strategies that have the potential to enhance a work's ability to tell stories; and "[t]ransposition from a medium into another" (2004: 33), such as transpositions of novels into movies, computer games based on literary works, illustrations of stories.

When we turn to graphic narratives, it was Jeanne C. Ewert (2005: 72) who called for a narratological method specific to comics/graphic narrative that

> must take into account both textual and graphic elements in the panels, a challenge for critics habituated to text-based narrative. Images must contain details that propel the story forward, saving (literal) page space that would otherwise be required for textual exposition. Transitional elements which move the narrative from one scene to the next, visual elements which condense or elide textual or verbal elements, and framing devices which negotiate between temporalities of the verbal/textual narration, all contribute to a complex narrative method.

Since 2005, narratologists aware of the pertaining 'media-blindness' of traditional narratology have started to carry out a considerable amount of critical work related to questions of mediality.[26] They agree that what is necessary is a medium-specific, i.e., an inter- and transmedial theory of narrativity for graphic narratives, a theory that takes into account the collaborative and competitive interplay of *words and images* (including onomatopoetic elements, graphic symbols and lettering); *time dimensions* (which encompass three levels: the individual panels, the panel sequence, and the page layout[27]); *depictions of space and bodies* (which again comprehend the three levels of individual panels, the panel sequence, and the page layout); subjectivity and *focalization*[28]; as well as the (sometimes very complex, nested) *structures of communication*, which may include metaleptic instances.[29] Martin Schüwer (2008) was one of the first scholars embarking on precisely this project and set himself the task of elaborating a way of analyzing comics that is founded in postclassical narratology, informed by cultural concerns and encompassing comics' central features.

How Graphic Narratives Narrate: Text-Picture Relationships and Their Narrative Potential

Some theoreticians of graphic narrative believe in the crucial role of the pictures in storytelling.[30] Others, however, subordinate the pictorial to the verbal elements.[31] Robert C. Harvey's criteria for the formal and aesthetic evaluation of comics are governed by elements of verbal-visual blending.

---

26 For examples see Herman 2004, 2009; Ryan 2006, 2014; Wolf 2011; Ryan and Thon 2014; Thon 2014a, 2014b.
27 See Groensteen 2007; Schüwer 2008.
28 See Horstkotte and Pedri 2011; Mikkonen 2011; Thon 2014a.
29 See Wolf 2005; Fehrle 2011.
30 See Stocker 1986; Groensteen 2007.
31 See Abbott 1986.

Hence he favors those comics in which word and image are as complementary as possible; he only allows for wordless or 'pantomime' comics as the exception that proves the rule.[32] In order to discuss the narrative potential of the wide range of word-image correlations in single panels as well as in sequences, we have developed a typology of five text-picture relationships in graphic narratives (Hoppeler, Etter, and Rippl 2009: 65). This typology modifies Scott McCloud's (1993) earlier suggestions. It should be pointed out, however, that what follows are heuristic categories without clear-cut distinctions:

(1) *word specific combinations*, "where pictures *illustrate*, but don't significantly *add* to a largely *complete* text" (McCloud 1993: 153)
(2) *alternating combinations*, meaning panels in which image and text alternate in propelling the story
(3) *montage*, "where words are treated as integral *parts* of the picture" (McCloud 1993: 154)
(4) *parallel combinations*, where "words and pictures seem to follow very different courses—without *intersecting*" (McCloud 1993: 154)
(5) *picture specific combinations*, "where words do little more than add a *soundtrack* to a visually told sequence" (McCloud 1993: 153)

Added to Wolf's scale of transmedial narrativity, the narrative potential of the individual text-picture combinations in graphic narratives becomes evident, involving different degrees of narrativization by the recipient (see figure 3).

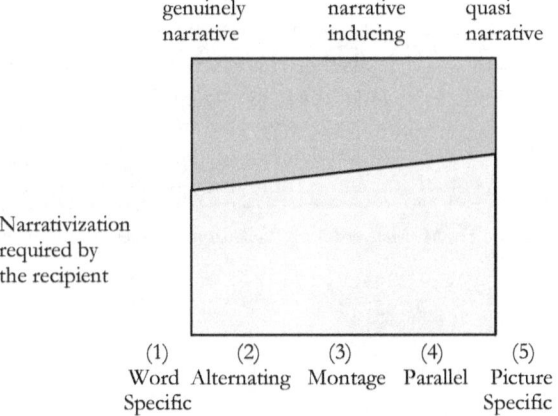

Figure 3: The Narrative Potential of Graphic Narratives (Hoppeler, Etter, and Rippl 2009: 66).

---

32 See Harvey 1994, 1996; for more recent publications on comics and intermediality, see Dittmar 2011; Bachmann, Sina, and Banhold 2012.

Combination Type 1: Word Specific

In single panels, *word specific combinations* can often be found primarily where no images are needed since the text alone has sufficient narrative potential. Hence this category 1 is close to Wolf's category of prototypical/genuine narration in which the amount of narrativization required by the reader is relatively low. A good example is Alison Bechdel's memoir *Are You My Mother?* (2012), many panels of which contain nothing but text. The narrative independence of these panels is often highlighted by other 'text-only' panels on the same page, which do not represent a narrator's voice but rather reproduce actual *paper-bound* texts that are part of the diegesis, such as letters from the protagonist's mother that are excerpts of (presumably) larger texts (see figure 4). They require a higher degree of narrativization by the reader than the first category of text-only panels, i.e., those containing nothing but what the narrator has to 'say.' Whereas the narrator's panels (the first category) would clearly belong to type 1 in our scheme, the reproduction of excerpts from larger paper-bound texts include the text's materiality and are therefore closer to type 3 (montage).

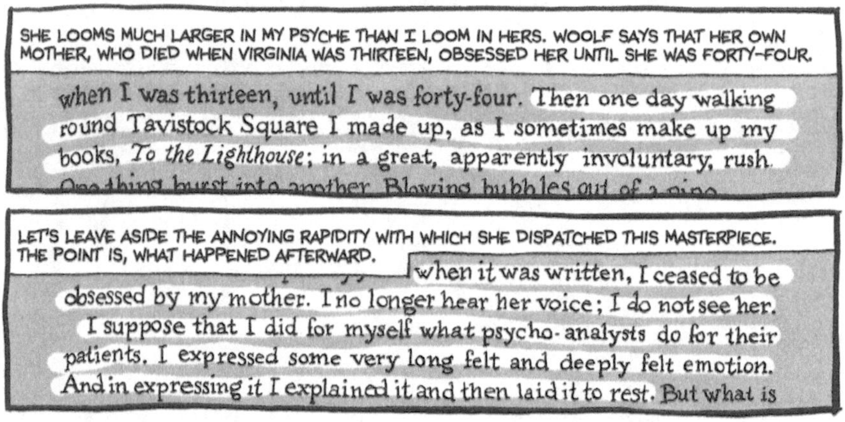

Figure 4: Alison Bechdel, *Are You My Mother?* (2012). © Alison Bechdel. All rights reserved.

Combination Type 2: Alternating

By *alternating combinations* we mean panels in which image and text alternate in pushing forward the narration. In this type, a higher contribution from the recipient is needed to propel the story. The most obvious example can be found in the "desperation device" (Eisner 1985: 26), i.e., speech balloons.[33] While speech balloons are considered a characteristic feature of graphic narratives and are usually discussed in depth in systematic monographs on the topic, the lettering itself is something largely underrepresented in such analyses.[34] Early newspaper comics such as the *Katzenjammer Kids* (1897–) as well as early European comics series such as Hergé's *Tintin* (1929–1976) made use of speech bubbles which are comparatively neutral in nature. These bubbles were filled with black text on white background, usually capital sans-serif letters written in straight horizontal lines. In this way, the bubble was intended as a 'parallel' device to the figurative drawings of a panel.

Figure 5: David B., *Black Paths* (2011). © David B. All rights reserved.

Using freer ways of placing speech-bubble text, authors of later graphic narratives have found ways to highlight their individual drawing style and mise-en-pages. Among Western artists with highly recognizable lettering styles are Molly Crabapple, Nicolas Mahler, Peter Bagge, and

---

33 Cf. Schüwer 2008: 326, 361.
34 Jean-Matthieu Méon is currently working on a publication on lettering.

Debbie Drechsler. Idiosyncratic lettering can also be found in the comics by Kati Rickenbacher and Vanessa Davis, who are less concerned with the traditional *horizontal* nature of the text. This freedom can go so far that some of their characters occasionally have to 'lean back' awkwardly in order to give way to huge ameboid speech bubbles. While in these cases the dominance of the speech bubbles highlights the mediality of the graphic narrative and decreases the reader's willingness to 'suspend disbelief,' other artists have used abundant and stratified speech bubbles within one panel as a specific narrative device—either to indicate the oversupply of simultaneous speech acts[35] (see figure 5) or to add a narrator's layer of comment to the character's utterance, rendering the latter almost indecipherable and thereby highlighting that its significance is subservient to that of the narrator's comments.[36]

Combination Type 3: Montage

Midway between the genuinely narrative and the quasi-narrative media, our third category, *montage*, comes into play. McCloud uses this term to denote the integration of text into an image. Examples can be found both where letters are integrated into a narrative and where they are used (partly or fully) in their iconic quality.[37] Some authors of graphic narratives take this potential to a meta-level, properly exemplifying it, as for instance Paul Karasik and David Mazzucchelli's *City of Glass* (1994) and Mike Carey and Peter Gross's *The Unwritten* (2009–).[38] The iconic use of letters is widespread among authors of graphic narratives and not only known thanks to such prominent headings as the ones found in Will Eisner's *Spirit* installments (1940–1952). It has even been used as an inspiration for entire narratives: French comics author Fred has based his album series *Philémon* (serialized since 1965) on a character whose adventures take place on a number of fictitious islands, each one of which has the shape of a letter and which together form the word "Océan Atlantique" (see figure 6). The fact that textual elements are turned into iconic elements and forms that are primarily looked at and not read demonstrates that graphic narratives question the clear division between words and pictures.

---

35 Cf. David B. 2011: 30.
36 Cf. Clowes 2011: 42.
37 Cf. Schüwer 2008: 53.
38 On this meta-level in *City of Glass*, cf. Schüwer 2008: 303; for extended analysis of *The Unwritten*, see Christina Meyer's contribution in this volume.

Figure 6: Fred, *Philémon: L'intégrale* (2011). © Fred. All rights reserved.

Combination Type 4: Parallel

Our fourth category, the *parallel combination*, subsumes those cases where text and image (seem to) diverge, which may result in an intensification of the reader's narrativization activity. Inevitably, the reader will attempt to construe the narrative coherence of whatever he or she confronts. A genuinely parallel combination in which little sense can be made of the connection between text and drawing in the same panel is unlikely. The closest we get to it is the suggestion of the 'empty' gaze, such as that frequently found in the Tibetan adventures Cosey presents in his album series *Jonathan* (2009).[39] Panels with a less action-oriented visual content are better suited to such parallel combinations. Nylso is a pertinent example in this context. In his *Jérôme et le lièvre* (2004), he draws a simple black-and-white character who makes a long journey through nature. Over the course of more than thirty panels, this character wanders across beaches and meadows, while reciting aloud a text by Paul Nizon which compares the process of walking to that of keeping a diary. While the choice of topic, i.e., the comparison, may create at least a vague connection between word and image on the page as a whole, no such connection can be found in the single panels: the content of the speech bubbles does not directly relate to the action depicted (see figure 7).

---

[39] Generally speaking, Cosey seems to conceive of his *Jonathan* series in close proximity to what Wolf places at the right-hand side of his scheme, namely, instrumental music. On the first page of a single installment, the author-artist suggests a 'soundtrack'—groups such as Pink Floyd and Tangerine Dream—to be listened to during the reading process.

Figure 7: Nylso, *Jérôme et le lièvre* (2004). © Nylso. All rights reserved.

Combination Type 5: Picture Specific

The last category in the transition from the graphic narrative to monophase single image is what we call *picture specific combinations*. Authors of graphic narratives can either partly or entirely dispense with text. This fifth category is a vast one. Examples in which readers can relatively easily construe narrative coherence can be found in comic strips consisting of single-line (e.g., Carl Anderson's *Henry*) or single-page (e.g., Antonio Prohías's *Spy vs. Spy*) pantomimic episodes. Many authors of manga produce long pantomimic sequences with detailed successions of the protagonist's movements. The size of the present-day manga industry and its high degree of labor division allows for a vast production of pages in both weekly and monthly series, resulting in some of these pantomimic graphic narratives approximating McCloud's experiment of a roll of film laid out instead of projected.[40]

'Depriving' a panel sequence of verbal language can, of course, be used to very particular effect. In comics series where the verbal element is relatively dominant, readers confronted with such a deprivation will not only need to employ a "more intensive process of combination and deduction" (Schüwer 2008: 320; our translation from the German: "höhere Kombinations- und Deduktionsleistung"), but will also feel the particular effect of 'silence' when going through the respective panels. An example can be found in a September 2001 episode of Alison Bechdel's monthly strip *Dykes to Watch Out For*. The subtle humor of this series has always been heavily based on the *verbal* sarcasm of its protagonists. After eight years of producing the single-page weekly strips, in September 2001 Bechdel drew an episode in which all the characters are silent. They are depicted in the moments when they learn about the attacks on the Twin Towers. The 'silent' atmosphere of this episode shows the characters in a profound state of shock. The progression from panel to panel is a flash-like tour through the entire group of characters, dispersed as they are throughout the city, and it requires a high degree of reader participation, as well as a certain amount of knowledge of the context, to make sense of this 'jumping' panel series.[41]

Wordless panel sequences are used to particularly good effect in those graphic narratives which, in the tradition of Winsor McCay's *Little Nemo in Slumberland* (1905–1914), have a surreal or quasi-surreal plot. Examples are the works of Moebius or Geof Darrow, but also some dream-like episodes in the works of Chris Ware. However, it is undoubtedly abstract comics that demand the highest level of narrativization amongst all types of graphic narratives. In this relatively recent form of experimenting with the genre, abstract (or almost abstract) geometrical forms are placed on a page in such a way as to suggest a sequence of panels, provoking the reader to see in them a type of narrative (see figure 8).[42]

---

40 Cf. McCloud 1993: 7–9; Pratt 2009: 114; cf. also Schodt 2007: 24.
41 Cf. Bechdel 2008: 267.
42 Cf. Baetens 2011: 95.

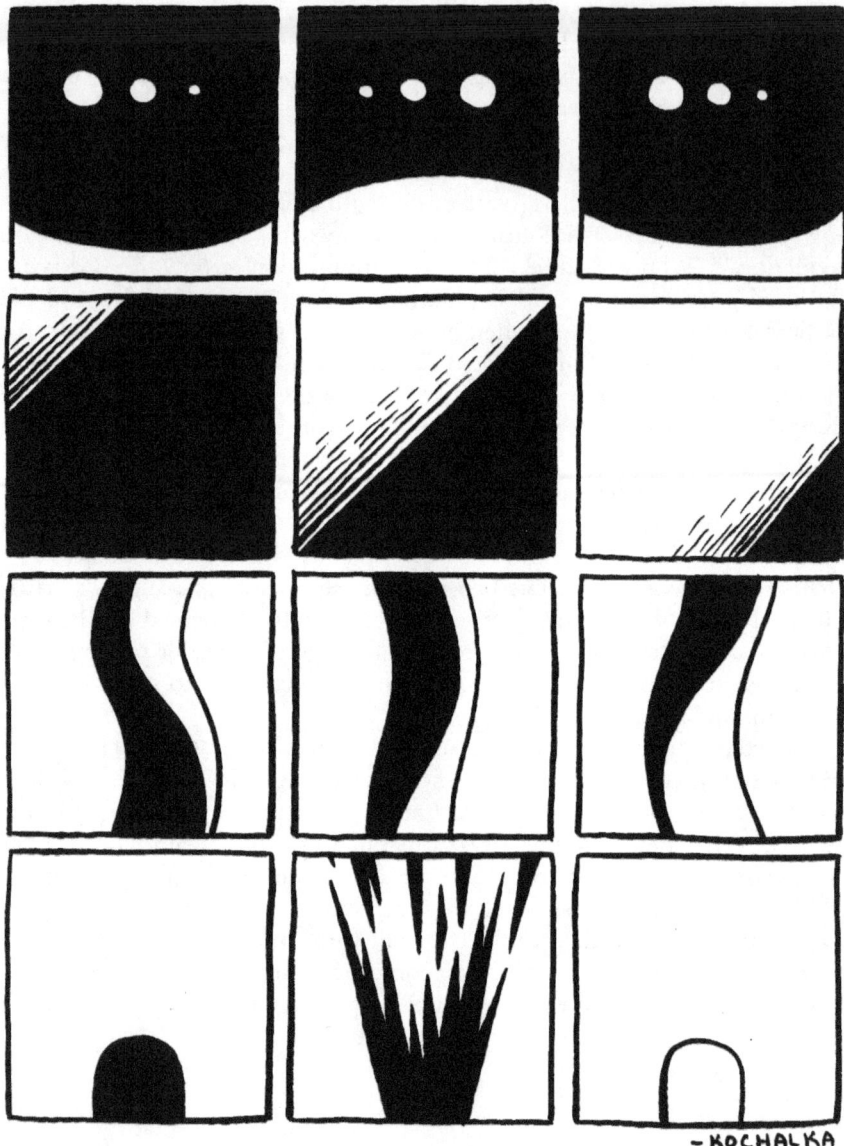

Figure 8: James Kochalka, [No title] (2009), published in Molotiu 2009 (n.p.).
© James Kochalka. All rights reserved.

Conclusions

Postclassical narratologists such as Ryan and Wolf are interested in developing a transmedial narratology that is based on the insight that narrativity is a cognitive macro-frame to be activated in different media. They are, however, very much aware of the fact that the narrative potential of different media, i.e., the limits and affordances inherent to specific media, varies. We have discussed the results of intermediality studies and combined them with recent theoretical results from transmedial narratology in order to develop a more specific terminology and typology that help explain the wide range of intermedial relationships in graphic narratives and their transmedial narrative potential. The fields of intermediality studies, transmedial and interdisciplinary narratology, comics studies, media studies as well as semiotics have developed diverging terminologies, methodologies, and concepts, but we hope to have demonstrated how these approaches can be combined in a fruitful way.

Works Cited

Abbott, Lawrence L. (1986). "Comic Art: Characteristics and Potentialities of a Narrative Medium." *Journal of Popular Culture* 19.4: 155–76. Print.

B., David (2007). *Par les Chemins Noirs*. Paris: Futuropolis. Print.

— (2011). *Black Paths*. London: SelfMadeHero. Print.

Bachmann, Christian A., Véronique Sina, and Lars Banhold (eds.) (2012). *Comics Intermedial*. Bochum: Ch. A. Bachmann Verlag. Print.

Baetens, Jan (2011). "Abstraction in Comics." Jared Gardner and David Herman (eds.). *Graphic Narratives and Narrative Theory*. Special issue of *SubStance* 40.1: 94–113. Print.

Bechdel, Alison (2008). *The Essential Dykes to Watch Out For*. Boston: Houghton Mifflin. Print.

— (2012). *Are You My Mother? A Comic Drama*. Boston: Houghton Mifflin. Print.

Bolter, Jay D., and Richard Grusin (2000). *Remediation: Understanding New Media*. Cambridge: MIT Press. Print.

Chute, Hillary, and Marianne DeKoven (2006). "Introduction: Graphic Narrative." Hillary Chute and Marianne DeKoven (eds.). *Graphic Narrative*. Special issue of *Modern Fiction Studies* 52.4: 767–82. Print.

Clowes, Daniel (2011). *Mr. Wonderful*. New York: Pantheon. Print.

Cosey (2009). *Jonathan: Intégrale*. Vol. 1–3. Brussels: Le Lombard. Print.

Dittmar, Jakob (2011). "Grenzüberschreitungen: Integration von Technikdokumentation und dreidimensionalen Bildern in fiktionale Comics." Thomas Becker (ed.). *Comic: Intermedialität und Legitimität eines popkulturellen Mediums*. Bochum: Ch. A. Bachmann Verlag. 147–58. Print.

Eisner, Will (1985). *Comics and Sequential Art: Principles and Practices from the Legendary Cartoonist*. New York: Norton. Print.

Etter, Lukas (2013). "The 'Big Picture' as a Multitude of Fragments: Jason Lutes's Depiction of Weimar Republic Berlin." Shane Denson, Christina Meyer, and Daniel Stein (eds.). *Transnational Perspectives on Graphic Narratives: Comics at the Crossroads*. London: Bloomsbury. 229–41. Print.

Ewert, Jeanne C. (2005). "Comics and the Graphic Novel." David Herman, Manfred Jahn, and Marie-Laure Ryan (eds.). *Routledge Encyclopedia of Narrative Theory*. London: Routledge. 71–73. Print.

Fehrle, Johannes (2011). "Unnatural Worlds and Unnatural Narration in Comics? A Critical Examination." Jan Alber and Rüdiger Heinze (eds.). *Unnatural Narratives—Unnatural Narratology*. Berlin: De Gruyter. 210–45. Print.

Fludernik, Monika, and Greta Olson (2011). "Introduction." Greta Olson (ed.). *Current Trends in Narratology*. Berlin: De Gruyter. 1–33. Print.

Fred (2011). *Philémon: L'intégrale*. Vol. 1–5. Paris: Dargaud. Print.

Groensteen, Thierry (2007). *The System of Comics*. Trans. Bart Beaty and Nick Nguyen. Jackson: UP of Mississippi. Print.

Harvey, Robert C. (1994). *The Art of the Funnies: An Aesthetic History*. Jackson: UP of Mississippi. Print.

— (1995). "An Interview with Scott McCloud." *The Comics Journal* 179: 53–81. Print.

— (1996). *The Art of the Comic Book: An Aesthetic History*. Jackson: UP of Mississippi. Print.

Herman, David (2004). "Toward a Transmedial Narratology." Marie-Laure Ryan (ed.). *Narrative across Media: The Languages of Storytelling*. Lincoln: U of Nebraska P. 47–75. Print.

— (2009). *Basic Elements of Narrative*. Chichester: Wiley-Blackwell. Print.

Hoppeler, Stephanie, Lukas Etter, and Gabriele Rippl (2009). "Intermedialität in Comics: Neil Gaimans *The Sandman*." Stephan Ditschke, Katerina Kroucheva, and Daniel Stein (eds.). *Comics: Zur Geschichte und Theorie eines populärkulturellen Mediums*. Bielefeld: transcript. 53–79. Print.

Horstkotte, Silke, and Nancy Pedri (2011). "Focalization in Graphic Narrative." *Narrative* 19.3: 330–57. Print.

Hutcheon, Linda (2006). *A Theory of Adaptation*. New York: Routledge. Print.
Jenkins, Henry (2006). *Convergence Culture: Where Old and New Media Collide*. New York: New York UP. Print.
Karasik, Paul, and David Mazzucchelli (1994). *Paul Auster's City of Glass*. New York: Avon. Print.
Keller, James R. (2009). *'V for Vendetta' as Cultural Pastiche: A Critical Study of the Graphic Novel and Film*. Jefferson: McFarland. Print.
Kress, Gunther, and Theo van Leeuwen (2001). *Multimodal Discourse: The Modes and Media of Contemporary Communication*. London: Arnold. Print.
Kukkonen, Karin (2011). "Comics as a Test Case for Transmedial Narratology." Jared Gardner and David Herman (eds.). *Graphic Narratives and Narrative Theory*. Special issue of *SubStance* 40.1: 34–52. Print.
Lessing, Gotthold E. (1984 [1766]). *Laocoön: An Essay on the Limits of Painting and Poetry*. Trans. E. A. McCormick. Baltimore: Johns Hopkins UP. Print.
Lutes, Jason (2008). *Berlin: City of Smoke*. Montreal: Drawn & Quarterly. Print.
McCloud, Scott (1993). *Understanding Comics: The Invisible Art*. New York: Harper Perennial. Print.
Meskin, Aaron (2007). "Defining Comics?" *Journal of Aesthetics and Art Criticism* 65: 369–79. Print.
Mikkonen, Kai (2011). "Graphic Narratives as a Challenge to Transmedial Narratology: The Question of Focalization." Daniel Stein, Christina Meyer, and Micha Edlich (eds.). *American Comic Books and Graphic Novels*. Special issue of *Amerikastudien/American Studies* 56.4: 637–52. Print.
Molotiu, Andrei (ed.) (2009). *Abstract Comics: The Anthology*. Seattle: Fantagraphics. Print.
Moore, Alan, and David Lloyd (1988). *V for Vendetta*. New York: DC Comics. Print.
Nylso (2004). *Jérôme et le lièvre*. Poitiers: FLBLB éditions. Print.
Peeters, Benoît (1991). *Case, planche, récit: Comment lire une bande dessinée*. Tournai: Casterman. Print.
Pratt, Henry J. (2009). "Narrative in Comics." *Journal of Aesthetics and Art Criticism* 67: 107–17. Print.
Rajewsky, Irina O. (2002). *Intermedialität*. Tübingen: A. Francke. Print.
— (2005). "Intermediality, Intertextuality, and Remediation: A Literary Perspective on Intermediality." *Intermédialités* 6: 43–64. Print.

— (2010). "Border Talks: The Problematic Status of Media Borders in the Current Debate about Intermediality." Lars Elleström (ed.). *Media Borders, Multimodality and Intermediality*. Houndmills: Palgrave Macmillan. 51–68. Print.
Reynolds, James (2009). "'Kill Me Sentiment': *V for Vendetta* and Comic-to-Film Adaptation." *Journal of Adaptation in Film and Performance* 2.2: 121–36. Print.
Rippl, Gabriele (2005). *Beschreibungs-Kunst: Zur intermedialen Poetik angloamerikanischer Ikontexte (1880-2000)*. München: Fink. Print.
— (2012). "Film and Media Studies." Martin Middeke, Timo Müller, Christina Wald, and Hubert Zapf (eds.). *English and American Studies*. Stuttgart: Metzler. 314–32. Print.
Ryan, Marie-Laure (2004). "Introduction." Marie-Laure Ryan (ed.). *Narrative across Media: The Languages of Storytelling*. Lincoln: U of Nebraska P. 1–40. Print.
— (2005). "On the Theoretical Foundations of Transmedial Narratology." J. Christoph Meister (ed.). *Narratology beyond Criticism: Mediality—Disciplinarity*. Berlin: De Gruyter. 1–23. Print.
— (2006). *Avatars of Story*. Minneapolis: U of Minnesota P. Print.
— (2014). "Story/Worlds/Media: Tuning the Instruments of a Media-Conscious Narratology." Marie-Laure Ryan and Jan-Noël Thon (eds.). *Storyworlds across Media: Toward a Media-Conscious Narratology*. Lincoln: U of Nebraska P. 25–49. Print.
Ryan, Marie-Laure, and Jan-Noël Thon (2014). "Introduction: Storyworlds across Media." Marie-Laure Ryan and Jan-Noël Thon (eds.). *Storyworlds across Media: Toward a Media-Conscious Narratology*. Lincoln: U of Nebraska P. 1–21. Print.
Saraceni, Mario (2003). *The Language of Comics*. London: Routledge. Print.
Schnackertz, Hermann J. (1980). *Form und Funktion medialen Erzählens: Narrativität in Bildsequenz und Comicstrip*. München: Fink. Print.
Schodt, Frederik (2007). *Dreamland Japan: Writings on Modern Manga*. Berkeley: Stone Bridge. Print.
Schreiber, Nathan (2009). *Power Out*. Brooklyn: Canal. Print.
Schüwer, Martin "Erzählen in Comics: Bausteine einer plurimedialen Erzähltheorie." Vera Nünning and Ansgar Nünning (eds.). *Erzähltheorie transgenerisch, intermedial, interdisziplinär*. Trier: Wissenschaftlicher Verlag Trier. 185–216. Print.
— (2008). *Wie Comics erzählen: Grundriss einer intermedialen Erzähltheorie der grafischen Literatur*. Trier: Wissenschaftlicher Verlag Trier. Print.
Stocker, Karl (1986). "Comics: Eine Verbindung von Zeichensystemen. Ein Plädoyer gegen Pauschalurteile." Annemarie Verweyen (ed.). *Comics*. Köln: Rheinland. 51–63. Print.

Thon, Jan-Noël (2014a). "Subjectivity across Media: On Transmedial Strategies of Subjective Representation in Contemporary Feature Films, Graphic Novels, and Computer Games." Marie-Laure Ryan and Jan-Noël Thon (eds.). *Storyworlds across Media: Toward a Media-Conscious Narratology*. Lincoln: U of Nebraska P. 67–102. Print.

— (2014b). "Toward a Transmedial Narratology: On Narrators in Contemporary Graphic Novels, Feature Films, and Computer Games." Jan Alber and Per Krogh Hansen (eds.). *Beyond Classical Narration: Transmedial and Unnatural Challenges*. Berlin: De Gruyter. 25–56. Print.

Voigts-Virchow, Eckart (2005). *Introduction to Media Studies*. Stuttgart: Klett. Print.

Walsh, Richard (2006). "The Narrative Imagination across Media." Hillary Chute and Marianne DeKoven (eds.). *Graphic Narrative*. Special issue of *Modern Fiction Studies* 52.4: 855–68. Print.

Wolf, Werner (1999). *The Musicalization of Fiction: A Study in the Theory and History of Intermediality*. Amsterdam: Rodopi. Print.

— (2002). "Das Problem der Narrativität in Literatur, bildender Kunst und Musik: Ein Beitrag zu einer intermedialen Erzähltheorie." Vera Nünning and Ansgar Nünning (eds.). *Erzähltheorie transgenerisch, intermedial, interdisziplinär*. Trier: Wissenschaftlicher Verlag Trier. 23–104. Print.

— (2005). "Intermediality." David Herman, Manfred Jahn, and Marie-Laure Ryan (eds.). *Routledge Encyclopedia of Narrative Theory*. London: Routledge. 252–56. Print.

— (2011). "Narratology and Media(lity): The Transmedial Expansion of a Literary Discipline and Possible Consequences." Greta Olson (ed.). *Current Trends in Narratology*. Berlin: De Gruyter. 146–80. Print.

GREG M. SMITH
(Atlanta)

Comics in the Intersecting Histories of the Window, the Frame, and the Panel

Before the nineteenth century, media had only a fairly limited capacity to tell stories using pictures and words. By the end of that century and the beginning of the next, two popular media arose that could provide such narratives: film and comics. Although both audiovisual and graphic narrative have engaged in considerable interaction and their formal similarities are widely acknowledged, the written histories of these visual storytelling media usually proceed in fairly independent fashion.[1] Comics history tends to be specialized, written for those who are interested specifically in that medium. The best comics historians[2] do put comics into their social/industrial context, but such medium-specific histories have had little impact on the broader story we tell about how mainstream narrative media develop their narrative and expressive capabilities. Most scholars examining how windows and frames become narrativized—most directly Anne Friedberg (2006), Mary Ann Doane (2002), André Bazin (1967), and Stephen Kern (2003), but also two of the humanities' most influential thinkers, Walter Benjamin (1968) and Gilles Deleuze (1986, 1989)—leave out comics, and so their depiction of the age of mechanical reproduction or the nature of consciousness or the story of modern time and space has a particularly cinematic bias.

This chapter takes the now fairly familiar broad history of this development as a starting point, integrating the conceptual precursors for both film and comics. As both media learned to tell stories, they relied on conceptual foundations created by earlier representational visual media. Although this chapter eventually arrives at modern storytelling media and their formal capacities, I begin with a long 'flashback' examining how primarily non-narrative forms of expression created deeper cultural logics. As Western perception experimented with Renaissance painting, the camera obscura, photography, motion pictures, and computerized media,

---
1 See Smith 2011.
2 For example, Kunzle 1973, 1990; Gabilliet 2010.

it relied on and nuanced our understandings of several foundational concepts: the window, the frame, perspective, realism, and the observer. To this list of conceptual building blocks, I will add the history of the panel, a neglected presence in the typical retelling of visual media history but an important component of comics. These abstract concepts were given formal expression by particular concrete media at different historical moments, and so I will pay attention to how historical media reconfigured the logic of the window, the frame, and the panel.

The concepts of the window and the frame have dominated our understanding of how pictorial media narratively present space and time, while the concept of the panel dominates our theoretical understanding of comics.[3] Examining comics as the *other* modern arrangement of the intersecting logics of window, frame, and panel helps provide theoretical alternatives to the cinematic tradition of realistic image capture that dates back to the Renaissance. Interweaving the long transmedia histories of windows, frames, and panels will help us see how comics develop their particular narrative and expressive capacities in conversation with other media. Comics emerge in the late nineteenth century as a distinctively new narrative reconfiguration of much older representational concepts.

Against this background, this chapter articulates concepts from transmedial narratology,[4] tracing them across history rather than focusing on the media options available at a specific moment. My approach shares certain commonalities with Jared Gardner's (2012) narratologically grounded account of comics' historical engagement with fan culture and interactivity across media, but my account begins earlier, focusing on longstanding media practices that become fundamental to comics.[5] The concepts I emphasize here are different from Gunther Kress and Theo van Leeuwen's (2001) notion of a narrative mode, a specific semiotic grammar developed through the interaction of cultural meanings, technological affordances/limitations of a medium, and artistic practice.[6] To one way of thinking, then, the concepts of window, frame, and panel are 'narrower' than a narrative mode; they are components of how comics, film, and paintings convey expression and meaning. Viewed from another perspective, however, these concepts are 'broader' than any single narrative mode; they are shared intermedially across historically developed

---

3 See McCloud 1993; Groensteen 2007.
4 See Herman 2004, 2009; Ryan 2005, 2006; Wolf 2005.
5 Other key works taking a narratological approach to comics are Ewert 2000; Lefèvre 2000; Groensteen 2007.
6 In Kress and van Leeuwen's (2001) usage, a 'medium' is the material expression of an expressive/communicative semiosis. A 'mode' is a set of semiotic capabilities that is not bound to a physical medium.

forms.⁷ In a third sense, these concepts are inflected by particular physical instantiations of media technology; they change as specific technologies give them new expressive capacities. They function at times as metaphor and at other times as physical properties. To a new medium, the concepts of windows, frames, and panels are a usefully orienting inheritance from older media; they help us make sense of the newer expressive form and allow us to see the novel difference presented by the new medium. At the same time, new media have the opportunity to alter our understandings of what constitutes a window, a frame, or a panel. In Mieke Bal's (2002) sense, therefore, these concepts travel.⁸ Their journeys are marked by physical media at key defining historical moments, but they are not bound by any particular medium or a specific narrative mode. At times they float with the abstraction of metaphor, while at other times they act like grounded physical properties of a medium. The present chapter retells the interrelated histories of these concepts as they congealed into recognizable narrative modes of visual storytelling called 'film' and 'comics,' each with distinctive expressive affordances and constraints.

The Window, the Frame, and Renaissance Technologies of Representation

In an age where 'windows' are as often virtual as they are physical, it is easy to forget that the window began as a simple opening in a structure's wall. The window mediated between indoors and outdoors, letting in a moderated portion of the outer world into the domestic sphere. The window was not solely a visual phenomenon; it let in not only sunlight but also smells (fresh air or otherwise) from outside. Coverings such as shutters, curtains, and eventually glass could moderate how much the external weather (or hostile invaders) intruded into the private space. The window served multiple functions, and the visual aspects of the window only became primary with the technological innovation of transparent glass, a relatively recent phenomenon in the window's long history. A Renaissance innovation, transparent glass transformed the window into a barrier that more firmly bracketed off the outdoor world, allowing only light to enter, and the window took on more of the metaphoric function we associate with it today as a 'window on the world.' The window became more like a frame, an enclosure for looking.⁹

---

7   See Kress and van Leeuwen 2001; Wolf 2002; Grishakova and Ryan 2010; Rajewsky 2010.
8   In fact, Bal 2002 cites 'framing' (in the fuller sense) as one of her traveling concepts.
9   Friedberg 2006 also tells the history of windows and frames 'from Alberti to Microsoft,' paying more attention to the ways that these concepts have been used metaphorically (by

The frame itself began as a way to clearly demarcate a portion of the wall as 'art.' Framed art is a step away from painting directly on the exhibition surface (as in murals), which necessarily limits the painter's mobility. The frame arose in conjunction with the new technology of the canvas, which encouraged the painter to move into the physical world to capture visual sensations that could be brought back into interior living spaces. Once inside, those canvases were framed, which helped set art apart as something distinct from the practical world, separating it from decoration on useful objects.

Although the frame itself might be aesthetically pleasing, it is of a different material (both physically and conceptually) than the artwork itself. The frame announced that its contents required a particular kind of aesthetic attention that everyday objects did not. The frame performs a kind of 'work,' and thus a 'framework' is a way of seeing an object, a perspectival reorientation of our perception.[10] Its work can serve narrative purposes (when mobilized by film or comics, for instance), but it can be purely representational, as well.[11] This work is always aesthetic, however. A frame helps to position art as a realm apart from the rest of the real world, an arena where aesthetic considerations reign supreme.

Western painting engages in a long dialogue about these two conceptions of art. The notion of the frame emphasizes the painting as a two-dimensional object, as a composition of line, shape, and color arranged on a flat surface that is different from the wall. On the other hand, by thinking of art as more like a window, we foreground the cues that make painting seem more three-dimensional, as if painting could present the image of objects in a created 'space' on the other side of the canvas. The Renaissance developed techniques that emphasized the appearance of three-dimensionality. Central perspectival systems created depth cues that prompted spectators to see painting as presenting a more 'realistic' representation of space.[12] Advancing understandings of optics

---

Heidegger and Deleuze, among others). Friedberg also integrates the history of the screen into her account.

10 Goffman's (1974) account of how the metaphorical 'frame' organizes experience has been particularly influential. See also Wolf 2006.
11 Recent narratology has discussed how representational forms contain the seeds of narrativity that can become narrative. See Jannidis 2003; Ryan 2005; Altman 2008; Abbott 2009. This is admittedly true; it is also true that such forms can still be seen *as* representation, that they need not necessarily be transformed into narrative.
12 Several Renaissance painters contributed to the early development of central perspective, particularly Masolino da Panicale and Masaccio but also Fra Angelico and Andrea Mantegna, leading to the High Renaissance work of Raphael and Leonardo da Vinci. Damisch 1994 and Andersen 2006 provide more detailed discussion of the history of visual perspective. Most of the theoretical discussion around realism focuses on central Albertian perspective, though this is not the only perspective system. For a discussion of alternative

provided more tools (both technical and conceptual) for painters to create a more 'objective' sense of space to populate. In particular, the grid became a useful tool for translating three-dimensional space into cues. The grid breaks down the vista in front of the painter into a set of smaller areas whose cues could be duplicated on a flat surface. Isolating a limited section of the whole view to be depicted had a flattening effect, which helped the painter to translate that segment into two-dimensional cues on a portion of the flat canvas. Reconstructing those fragments in the painting (while eliminating the guiding set of frames provided by the grid) helped the painting achieve the illusion of a more objective depiction grounded in scientific principles. The frame (as part of the grid) allowed the Renaissance painter to more rationally structure the spatial representation, so that when the grid disappears and the canvas is framed on the wall, the system of perspective returns the spectator to the visual logic of the window.

The camera obscura, another frequently discussed Renaissance technology of seeing, turns the objective window into a visual screen. Using a small opening to project a large image of the surrounding world onto the wall, this technology brings the visuals from outdoors into the interior space, but with certain distinctive characteristics. The camera obscura's visual representation is a projection, a representation composed entirely of light that temporarily covers the wall's flat surface instead of a permanent depiction in paint. The camera obscura also captures movement in the exterior world and projects that instantaneous vista into the domestic sphere. Of course, the view of the moving world is available by simply looking through a window, but bringing that projected image inside called for a different form of perception. The Renaissance camera obscura transformed the quality of attention through a combination of scientific optics and aesthetic positioning, giving a sense of the objective universe re-presented for our perusal. As recent art history scholarship has argued, this projection itself could be used as a tool to help painters translate three-dimensional space into two-dimensional Renaissance perspective, allowing painters to trace guide lines over the projected image onto the painting/drawing surface.[13]

This history is not solely about technologies of expression, as Jonathan Crary's (1990) work has reminded us; this is also a history of a changing conception of the observer. The Renaissance perspectival system requires a relatively distanced perceiver who interprets the painted/drawn cues as giving a fairly 'objective' sense of space. Crary points out that the

---

perspectival systems and their importance to cinematic space, see Bordwell 1985: ch. 1 and 7.
13   See Steadman 2001.

viewer of the camera obscura becomes disembodied, that it becomes a position rather than a person.[14] The identity of the perceiver does not matter, since anyone can make sense of the perspective cues. The classical Renaissance perspective painting (even an early one such as Masolino's 1427 *St. Peter Healing a Cripple and the Raising of Tabitha*) fixes that position in a single observation point from which a single moment in time/space is represented. We accept this frozen, fixed position when we occupy the spectator position. Although depth cues in the real world change as we move in space, they do not in a central perspective Renaissance painting. We understand the spatiotemporal logic of the painting, realizing that it emanates from an unmoving location of inscription portraying an artificially still slice of the world.

This logic is more than just technological; it is conceptual and extends beyond individual technologies of seeing. Today we tend to view windows and frames as self-apparent building blocks of representational art, but as my remarks in this section remind us, these concepts have histories. Renaissance technologies and artistic practices privileged the visual aspect of the window, activating a historical vector that emphasizes a three-dimensional view of represented space. The 'new technologies' of frame and canvas in the Renaissance offered a mixed set of affordances. The canvas encouraged the artist to travel into the world to capture images; when those images were brought indoors and displayed on a wall, the frame-work encouraged us to see the enclosed artwork as distinct from the surrounding two-dimensional display space. Revisiting the premodern past of these foundational concepts and teasing apart their representational vectors will help us see how later media (particularly film and comics) reconfigure aspects of these histories when presented with the challenge of visual storytelling.

The Photograph and the Cinema as Window and Frame

The story of Western aesthetic vision typically follows the logics of the frame and the window as newer media forms developed. Photography emerged as a mechanical means of creating objective still images of the world with minimal human intervention at the point of image capture. The ephemeral spectator once again examines a single frozen moment presented in two dimensions within the fixed aspect ratio of the frame, except this time the image's realism is linked to an understanding of the camera's mechanical properties. An instant of objective time/space, like

---

14 Friedberg 2006 provides an alternative reading.

that on display in the camera obscura, is taken out of the stream of time and preserved as a visual archive, thus foregrounding the photograph's indexicality.

Nineteenth century advances in technology enabled us to capture smaller and smaller slices of time, with experiments in chronophotography (such as those by Muybridge and Marey) allowing us to see aspects of motion that occur too quickly for the human eye to observe. These pictures generated considerable scientific and popular interest when placed on display in magazines. The photographs in these motion studies were not intended to be seen as single independent views but as a sequence of images, each one of them in a standard mechanically produced aspect ratio. The reader compares one image to another to make sense out of the whole. Chronophotography takes us one mechanical step away from the privileged single view that has dominated this history so far, and Scott Bukatman (2012) has noted the complex borrowings between chronophotography's side-by-side sequences of images and the multiple panels of Winsor McCay's comic *Little Nemo in Slumberland* (1905–1914). Chronophotography uses a fixed viewer perspective to gain rational control over the unseen processes of movement. As Bukatman argues, McCay's *Little Nemo* evokes the visual conventions of the chronophotograph while subverting the rationalist impulse with an animating force in the form of the dreaming child.

The tension in chronophotography between stillness and motion,[15] between single and multiple views, can be resolved in two different ways. If readers can move their attention across a sequence of non-indexical images, this results in comics (as we shall see). And if indexical chronophotographs are projected on top of each other,[16] the illusion of motion pictures results. This movement adds another lifelike quality, thus further privileging its function as a 'window on the world.' Although the economics of production control encouraged early filmmakers to shift their focus away from documentary actualities (where filming conditions were less predictable) to fiction films (where shooting could be more rationally controlled), film retained a sense of indexicality in capturing live action taking place in front of the camera. Bazin (1967) emphasized the cinema's ability to 'embalm time' as its distinguishing characteristic, even in fiction filmmaking, which came to dominate both cinema practice and theory. The cinema clearly animates the sequential still photographs on a filmstrip, but animation of drawings remained a minority practice because

---

15 Such explorations of stillness and movement gave birth to a broad range of gizmos that straddled the line between scientific instruments and toys, a line that could be fairly blurry in the nineteenth century, as Prince 2010 notes.
16 With an intermittent start-and-stop motion at at least 16 images per second.

of how difficult it is to industrialize motion drawings in ways that duplicate a realistic sense of smooth movement.[17] Mainstream film became a particular kind of one-way window for the disembodied spectator, creating a voyeuristic view of a diegetic world that unfolds for us without acknowledging us. Film actors quickly learned not to look at the camera because such glances would acknowledge both the audience and the mechanism of filmmaking, both of which should remain 'invisible' if the illusion of the voyeuristic window is to be maintained.

Cinematic projection further emphasized the window over the frame, since the frame boundary in film was a property of the physical projection facility itself. The content varied from film to film, but the frame itself did not vary in aspect or size. Irises and mattes could alter the shapes and sizes of film depictions, but those alterations occurred within the standard frame size, with certain isolated exceptions such as *Napoleon* (Abel Gance, 1927). Instead of the frame being an object created separately from the image to call attention to the image as art, in the cinema the frame was a property created by the apparatus of the image, a border between onscreen and offscreen space that rarely called attention to its presence.

The cinema therefore activates a very particular sense of 'window' in the history of vision. Although it technically depends on the fundamentals of chronophotography (and thus shares something with comics' sequentiality), the cinema experientially foregrounds the single window, encouraging the disembodied observer to see a realistic view of the captured world on display. Projecting those captured images made the frame appear to be more a technical fact than an actively working boundary. The technological and expressive logics of live action cinema privileges a specific historical version of the window. As we will see in the next section, this is not the only viable trajectory of the window in representation. Comics rely on multiple concepts of windows when they configure these logics to tell stories.

---

17 Comics artist Winsor McCay's work in animation is an example of early nonindustrialized processes in animation. McCay drew every frame of his pioneering *Gertie the Dinosaur* (1914) himself, an extraordinarily work-intensive method. Mainstream animation moved away from a solo artisanal process toward a more efficient model with many workers and strict division of labor. For a comprehensive overview of shifts in animation practice, see Bendazzi 1995.

Different Windows

The emphasis on indexicality in the historical vector leading from Renaissance art to photography and film/television participates in what Bazin (1967) calls the 'myth of total cinema,' the notion that these media will progress toward an increasingly detailed realistic depiction of the world. The more contemporary fantasy of 'virtual reality' acknowledges the appeal of the frame disappearing entirely as we step through the window into an immersive environment. Widescreen, IMAX, and 3-D film participate in this visual regime, attempting to envelop our peripheral vision in stimuli so that there is no frame bounding our perception. Although 3-D computer games are bounded by the frame, they provide motion and depth cues that allow us to move past the voyeuristic, fixed, invisible spectator position that can only observe. Interactive gaming enables our onscreen avatar to move about the depicted world, which appears to respond to commands that we initiate. Viewed in the context of media development toward the goal of increased sensory immersion in a single view,[18] the frame becomes a historical necessity that was grounded in the limitations of particular media technologies that new media can discard as the window's spatial logic becomes dominant.

One difficulty with this story is that our primary use of the 'window' in new media is less apparently the outgrowth of this historical impulse. Windows on computers are frequently used in conjunction with other windows, allowing us to multitask among several different activities and views. Those views are often far from 3-D vistas; although these windows can contain images that pull the viewer's eye into the composition, they frequently present 2-D depictions of data without perspectival depth cues. Rather than showing us a window whose surface appears to be a transparent portal to another environment, computer windows often are blatantly opaque. These windows can vary in size and shape as we reconfigure them according to our individual purposes, creating a media environment that is multiply fractured, not singularly arresting. One reason that contemporary new media seem new is that they appear to violate the narrative of the single unified view through a transparent medium, replacing it with overlapping layers composed of different media forms in multiple windows that are monitored rather than being immersive. The 'postmodern condition' can be seen as an adaptation to, and adeptness at, multiple sign processing, relying on our training as single-view spectators but fracturing those subject positions using multiple windows/frames/images.

---

18 For an overview of the discussion of 'immersion' in gaming, see Thon 2008.

In telling this image-driven history, it is easy to leave the written text aside because it seems to function as non-visual representation. Text, of course, is read through an operation of our eyes, but its representative power comes from looking past the visual form of the letters themselves to the meanings conveyed by those words. So although the mass-produced novel was a historically important portable technology of narrative immersion, text tends to appear as a source for visual media to adapt, not as a visual medium in its own right. Thus the history of text is the history of its content: works of literature, for instance, or important stories in newspapers and magazines. These texts can be reformatted without seeming to do too much violence to their representation, as in physical reprints or in online archives of periodicals that store text without attention to the original layout. Print forms such as advertising where text and image work together are usually given separate treatment in history, although arguably print advertising provides a model of using overlapping media layers, an important component of the computer window. To an image-driven history, text can appear to be an outlier (a label applied to a painting, onscreen film credits created by a third party) rather than a crucial component of the representation. This is why, to theorists less focused on comics, an integration of text layers into visual media seems like a bold example of what Jay David Bolter and Richard Grusin (1999) call 'remediation' as they detail how new media integrate previously separate forms.[19]

New media seem particularly new because their windows seem outside the legacy of the Renaissance perspective window that has dominated the history of mainstream media for so long. These new windows are often opaque rather than transparent; they can vary in size/shape instead of using a fixed aspect ratio; they may be viewed in conjunction with each other instead of singly; they can integrate nonnaturalistic objects such as text. They can emphasize their two-dimensional aspects as well as their virtual three-dimensionality. In other words: they can act as frames as well as windows.

This multiplicity is usually seen as part of computerized media's capacity to incorporate other media forms into their amalgamation. But the history outlined here reveals this 'new' media form as a reconfiguration of elements in the long intertwined history of windows and frames. Today's computerized windows privilege a different set of historical vectors than the increasingly indexical window in representation, reminding us that this privileged history is not the only one. Given our

---

19 Recent narratological work on multimodality repositions media as an interlacing network of narrative modes. See Kress and van Leeuwen 2001; Page 2012. Comics clearly operate as a multimodal combination of words and pictures.

familiarity with the computer window, it is now easier to reclaim neglected aspects of that history and see how other media make use of them. The visual structure of comics, for instance, is not simply a footnote to the dominant historical arc of film/television/new media. Comics represent a different activation of the mobile concepts of frame and window in conjunction with an important third concept: the panel.

The Panel and the Moving Line in Comics

The logic of the panel is related to the tradition of single narrative image that selects a particular moment from a familiar mythological/religious story. The single selected scene requires the viewer to know the story (Theseus and the Minotaur, Isaac's sacrifice) so that we can fill in the narrative antecedents and consequents around the depicted moment. The logic of the panel asks the viewer to see such moments (the Stations of the Cross, for instance) as members of a set. The panel, like the frame, delimits a particular portion of a surface (a wall, a door, a folding screen) as containing a picture. Unlike the frame, however, the panel is necessarily a component part of an artistic whole; although it can be viewed on its own, the panel is meant to be seen in conjunction with other panels. The panel, unlike the transparent window, tends to be opaque or at least translucent (in the case of stained glass, that alternate form of window). Since such panels are meant to be viewed together, they create stronger possibilities for narrative elaboration.

Narrative image-making expanded to evoke more generic, less particular secular stories, using stock characters in familiar situations (often in allegories where the characters are explicitly labeled by text). Such familiar (and often racialized/ethnic) stereotypical characters became important in the history of cartooning in Western mass media, both in single drawing editorial cartoons and in early multiple panel comics.[20] These early cartoons provided a different kind of 'realism' than the tradition of the photograph and the motion picture. Appearing in newspapers along with written accounts of contemporary life and events, these cartoon drawings expressed a similarly journalistic impulse to capture the outside world using a non-mechanical form of transcription, one that acknowledged the intervention of the artist but that captured

---

20 Early American comics such as Richard Felton Outcault's *Hogan's Alley* (1895–1898) and *Poor Lil' Mose* (1901–1902) were an extension of newspaper political cartooning's emphasis on racial/ethnic Others in the urban public sphere (see Havig 1988). Such nineteenth-century images can still cause controversy today, as Thomas Nast's cartoons did recently (see Dooley 2012).

impressions for disposable consumption, a form that was imbedded in the flow of daily events rather than being taken out of that time stream and preserved for posterity.

Such drawings used the more intimate language of caricature, a different expressive mode from the more formally detailed styles of realist painting. Caricature developed as an 'insider' practice, as artists created purposefully exaggerated representations for their private amusement within artists' circles.[21] Because caricature did look so different from the naturalistic style displayed in formal gallery settings, it gained a following of its own when it emerged from the private setting. Certain audiences were attracted to the intimacy, the speedy line, the lack of finished polish, and the personal style on display in caricature. The line itself became an explicitly expressive element that was a recognizable (and therefore marketable) marker of an artist's 'touch.' Because of their simplicity, drawings in caricature/cartoon style seemed to betray the artist's 'personality,' and characters recurring in such drawings seemed to become imbued with a sense of their own personality. Thus contemporary drawings of urchins in *Hogan's Alley* gave rise to the Yellow Kid, and recurring appearances by a conniving lazy man made Ally Sloper a merchandising phenomenon.[22] The recurring character appearing in a long-running series of gags (as in George Herriman's *Krazy Kat*, 1913–1944) or in a continuing serial narrative (as in Frank King's *Gasoline Alley*, 1918–) becomes a key pleasure of the comic strip,[23] and those characters are repeatedly given life ('animated,' in a sense) by both the expressive moving line of the cartoonist and the reader's eye filling in the incomplete drawings as they appear daily in the newspaper. The daily newspaper of the late nineteenth century provided caricature with the right technology for circulating images that appeared a bit 'sketchy' compared to the more densely composed, time consuming process of naturalistic painting. In the penny press, such images circulated across class lines and literacy levels, providing intimate glimpses of contemporary urban life, imbued with an artist's 'personality' instead of the scientific gaze captured by a machine.

In moving from the single cartoon image to the comic strip, comics began to accentuate the logic of the panel in conjunction with aspects of the frame and the window. Comics do use depth cues developed in Renaissance perspective, but they can vary in their deployment. A comic can provide a richly detailed sense of the world, following the logic of the

---

21 See Varnedoe and Gopnik 1990.
22 For more on *Hogan's Alley*, see Couch 2001. For details on Ally Sloper and the marketing of this early comics character, see Sabin 2003.
23 Frank King's *Gasoline Alley* particularly emphasized its seriality by matching its diegetic time to 'real world' time, having the characters age as the strip continued through the years.

window. Unlike film, which mechanically captures whatever details are placed in front of the camera, comics drawn with a cartoony line can opt to sketch characters against minimal or no background. Comics, therefore, can choose to rely on the more two-dimensional logic of the frame or to evoke the three-dimensional aspects of the window, depending on how much of the perspectival system each panel chooses to adopt.[24] Even when comics panels rely on strong depth cues, the drawn line remains pronounced, emphasizing the intervention of the artist's hand over any indexical attachment to the real world. Partly because of the intimate appeal of a cartoony drawing style, partly because of the industrial pace of producing comics for daily/weekly/monthly consumption, and partly because of technical limitations in image reproduction on newsprint (which limited the amount of detail that even 'photorealist" comics artists such as Alex Raymond could pack into a panel),[25] comics developed a historical emphasis on the line as a central pleasure,[26] a marker of recognizable artistic style, and an indicator of a comic character's 'personality.'

Privileging the drawn line within the comics panel frequently leads to attention to the panel border. Since the panel border is itself a drawn line, it becomes readily apparent that there is a kind of basic equality between the line that encloses the panel (providing a frame) and the depictive lines within that panel. Unlike painting, the frame in a comics panel is of the same material as the artwork it encloses. Unlike film, that frame changes size and shape as the expressive/narrative needs of the comic varies. This combination of factors encourages many comics artists to pay particular attention to the panel border. Although artists in every medium are attracted to reflexive play with the material aspects of form, comics creators, dating from the early days of *Little Sammy Sneeze* (1904–1906) and *Krazy Kat*,[27] seem particularly drawn to acknowledgment of the frame, partially because the comics artist must redraw the frame again and again as he/she works, unlike the filmmaker, who has the frame's shape specified by the mechanical apparatus.

Although comics images themselves are static, their component lines capture a kind of movement, with the artist's hand movement across the

---

24 See Karin Kukkonen's chapter in this volume.
25 Alex Raymond became known for his detailed work on comic strips such as *Flash Gordon* (1934–1943) and *Rip Kirby* (1946–1956). The photorealist tradition in comics continues today, most notably in the artistry of Alex Ross (*Marvels*, 1994; *Kingdom Come*, 1996).
26 Gardner 2011 privileges the line as fundamental to comics.
27 McCay's *Little Sammy Sneeze* regularly featured a child whose unruly sneezes exploded the comic strip panel border (see Bukatman 2012: ch. 1). Herriman's *Krazy Kat* is an acknowledged modernist classic that experimented with and reformatted the landscape of the entire comics page (see Stein 2012).

panels guiding how the reader's eye traverses the page. All visual art is deeply concerned with managing the perceiver's eye. One of film's great advantages is that it presents literal movement of images onscreen, and it controls our perception of that motion through figure movement, pace, and editing. One shot replaces another onscreen, and viewers must make sense of the moving stream of visual and auditory information without being able to alter the procession. Individual shots contain the image of duration, which is a central insight for Deleuze, who sees the cinema as a model for the workings of consciousness itself. According to Deleuze (1986, 1989), the contents of our consciousness are less like still images and more like cinematic shots that capture movement. Memory is selective, but it selectively archives mental objects that imbed both time and space within. Consciousness both selects (in other words, frames) its constructs and animates them as moving shots.

Comics present an alternative reconfiguration of time and space from the cinematic model that Deleuze privileges. The comic panel acts both as a still image and a shot, a capture of duration. The figures are frozen in a selected moment of action, but in a typical panel with speech balloons, diegetic time elapses as the characters speak their lines. Comics have developed other techniques for capturing duration within the single panel, some distinctive (such as speed lines), some shared with narrative painting (the staging of multiple actions within the same image). In other words, the still comic panel also acts like a shot, an unfolding of time, except this duration is more under the reader's control, depending on the reader's pace and attention.[28] Reading a comic panel takes time; as we parse its space and follow the movements of its lines, we convert the still image into narrative time. As our eye moves from panel to panel (Scott McCloud [1993] sees such transitions as the defining characteristic of comics), we interpret the juxtapositions of panels on a page as an architecture of time. These juxtapositions are different from the deployment of shots in cinematic editing, where the pace is dictated by the filmmaker. In comics, one can linger over a panel and compare it with previous images in the sequence, which are physically and temporally available on the page, unlike the film shot, which is snatched away from us. A good comics artist guides the reader by using cues (such as level of detail) to give a comic a sense of pace, but still the basic traversal of the comics page is in the reader's hands. The interactive control of image speed and sequence that digital technologies promise today have their equivalencies in comics. The link between comics and interactive media, as Gardner (2012) argues, is

---

28 McCloud (1993: ch. 4) examines in detail how comics panels depict duration (like a shot in cinema) as opposed to the capturing of an instant in still photography.

not simply that they share similar visual vocabularies with film (presenting us with shots that capture action); comics' material properties provide an early model of how we can negotiate narratives in a way that is guided by the maker but which ultimately is controlled by the reader.

Comics encourage a different form of interaction than either film or new media. While presenting a sequential narrative, comics allow and encourage what Benjamin (1968) describes as 'contemplation.' Benjamin both mourns and celebrates the loss of the contemplative aspect of auratic art in the age of mechanical reproduction. In the film theater, we cannot hold the image close to linger over its beauty because each image is placed on the 'conveyor belt' of motion pictures. In comics, however, the physical juxtaposition of panels on a page along with the seductive personality of the drawn line allow us to revisit, examine, and contemplate the framed images. An individual reader can parse the panels of a strip in purely linear fashion, extracting the narrative content as a series of windows on the storyworld, but he or she can also handle the tangible object of the printed page in ways that the distant screen cannot be grasped, allowing the reader the possibility of image contemplation that Benjamin argues becomes more difficult to do in the modern age of mechanical reproduction.[29] Comics certainly circulate through technologies of mechanical image reproduction, and so they necessarily lose the aura of the original that Benjamin explores. However, because they are not indexical in the same way that live action film is, because they give readers the opportunity to handle images and examine lines at their own pace, comics open up possibilities for contemplation that Benjamin associates with pre-modern eras of Western art. Comics, therefore, present a different configuration of modern time and space. While a cartoony style of pared-down drawing facilitates our quick traversal of the image, the physical control over the image and its juxtaposition and the 'personal' quality of the line allow comics to fill duration in the reader's consciousness in ways that Benjamin and Deleuze never fully considered in their stories of media and modern time/space.

---

29 Groensteen focuses on the layout of panels on the page (mise-en-page) as distinctly different from the cinema (2007: section 1.11: 91–102).

The Difference of Comics

Seen from the contemporary viewpoint, where film, television, and new media such as computer games dominate the practice of visual storytelling, it is easy to lose sight of comics. However, in this chapter I wish to reposition comics as a theoretical and historical 'road not taken' by the trajectory of more popular narrative media. They are a specific configuration of the logics of window, frame, and panel that arose at a particular moment in modern history. Live action film presented space and time indexically, providing a 'window on the world' that foregrounded the spectacle of movement. Film also was a projection onto a screen that did not call attention to the frame itself; the frame was a mechanical feature of the apparatus that remained a constant size and shape regardless of the content. The cinema created a single viewing position in front of the singular window/frame, and it changed the presented image within that frame while keeping the same spectator position. It is therefore hard to hold the cinematic image close so that the spectator can contemplate the image. Cinema controlled the experience of time for the spectator in ways that evoked the mechanized time of modernity.

Instead of foregrounding an indexical capture of the world, comics privilege the indexical trace of the artist's hand, encouraging us to retrace the line's movement with our eyes across the still image. Like much new media, text is integrated into the comics frame to become a non-indexical element of signification. The frame is composed of the same material as the image it encloses, and it changes size and shape in relation to the image content, which encourages formal play for both artist and reader. The reader controls the pace of the image presentation, allowing contemplation of both the images and their juxtapositions, following the logic of the panel. This freedom to move our attention back and forth across panels is much more like the interactivity and multitasking associated with new media, except that in comics these juxtaposed windows are narrativized.

Interweaving the histories of the frame, the window, and the panel helps us see that film, television, digital media, and comics each present particular configurations of these intermedial components. In the contemporary narrative economy, it is hard for comics to compete with other visual narrative delivery systems. And yet comics retain some distinct advantages over film, television, and games because of how they use windows, frames, and panels to provide a sense of personal expression without requiring the advanced technology of later media.

Works Cited

Abbott, H. Porter (2009). "Narrativity." Peter Hühn, John Pier, Wolf Schmid, and Jörg Schönert (eds.). *Handbook of Narratology*. Berlin: De Gruyter. 309–28. Print.
Altman, Rick (2008). *A Theory of Narrative*. New York: Columbia UP. Print.
Andersen, Kirsti (2006). *The Geometry of an Art: The History of the Mathematical Theory of Perspective from Alberti to Monge*. New York: Springer. Print.
Bal, Mieke (2002). *Travelling Concepts in the Humanities: A Rough Guide*. Toronto: U of Toronto P. Print.
Bazin, André (1967). "The Myth of Total Cinema." *What Is Cinema?* Vol. 1 Trans. Hugh Gray. Berkeley: U of California P. 17–22. Print.
Bendazzi, Giannalberto (1995). *Cartoons: One Hundred Years of Cinema Animation*. Bloomington: Indiana UP. Print.
Benjamin, Walter (1968). "The Work of Art in the Age of Mechanical Reproduction." *Illuminations: Essays and Reflections*. Trans. Harry Zohn. New York: Schocken. 217–51. Print.
Bolter, Jay D., and Richard Grusin (1999). *Remediation: Understanding New Media*. Cambridge: MIT Press. Print.
Bordwell, David (1985). *Narration in the Fiction Film*. Madison: U of Wisconsin P. Print.
Bukatman, Scott (2012). *The Poetics of Slumberland: Animated Spirits and the Animating Spirit*. Berkeley: U of California P. Print.
Couch, N. C. Christopher (2001). "The *Yellow Kid* and the Comic Page." Robin Varnum and Christina T. Gibbons (eds.). *The Language of Comics: Word and Image*. Jackson: UP of Mississippi. 60–74. Print.
Crary, Jonathan (1990). *Techniques of the Observer: On Vision and Modernity in the Nineteenth Century*. Cambridge: MIT Press. Print.
Damisch, Hubert (1994). *The Origins of Perspective*. Trans. John Goodman. Cambridge: MIT Press. Print.
Deleuze, Gilles (1986). *Cinema 1: The Movement-Image*. Minneapolis: U of Minnesota P. Print.
— (1989). *Cinema 2: The Time-Image*. Minneapolis: U of Minnesota P. Print.
Doane, Mary Ann (2002). *The Emergence of Cinematic Time: Modernity, Contingency, the Archive*. Cambridge: Harvard UP. Print.
Dooley, Michael (2012). "Editorial Cartoonist Thomas Nast: Anti-Irish, Anti-Catholic Bigot?" *Imprint*, Jan. 4. Web.
Ewert, Jeanne (2000). "Reading Visual Narrative: Art Spiegelman's *Maus*." *Narrative* 8.1: 87–103. Print.

Friedberg, Anne (2006). *The Virtual Window: From Alberti to Microsoft.* Cambridge: MIT Press. Print.

Gabilliet, Jean-Paul (2010). *Of Comics and Men: A Cultural History of American Comic Books.* Trans. Bart Beaty and Nick Nguyen. Jackson: UP of Mississippi. Print.

Gardner, Jared (2011). "Storylines." Jared Gardner and David Herman (eds.). *Graphic Narratives and Narrative Theory.* Special issue of *SubStance* 40.1: 53–70. Print.

— (2012). *Projections: Comics and the History of Twenty-First-Century Storytelling.* Stanford: Stanford UP. Print.

Goffman, Erving (1974). *Frame Analysis: An Essay on the Organization of Experience.* New York: Harper and Row. Print.

Grishakova, Marina, and Marie-Laure Ryan (eds.) (2010). *Intermediality and Storytelling.* New York: De Gruyter. Print.

Groensteen, Thierry (2007). *The System of Comics.* Trans. Bart Beaty and Nick Nguyen. Jackson: UP of Mississippi. Print.

Havig, Alan (1988). "Richard F. Outcault's 'Poor Lil' Mose': Variations on the Black Stereotype in American Comic Art." *Journal of American Culture* 11.1: 33–41. Print.

Herman, David (2004). "Toward a Transmedial Narratology." Marie-Laure Ryan (ed.). *Narrative across Media: The Languages of Storytelling.* Lincoln: U of Nebraska P. 47–75. Print.

— (2009). *Basic Elements of Narrative.* Chichester: Wiley-Blackwell. Print.

Jannidis, Fotis (2003). "Narratology and the Narrative." Tom Kindt and Hans-Harald Müller (eds.). *What Is Narratology? Questions and Answers Regarding the Status of a Theory.* Berlin: De Gruyter. 35–54. Print.

Kern, Stephen (2003). *The Culture of Time and Space: 1880–1918.* Cambridge: Harvard UP. Print.

Kress, Gunther, and Theo van Leeuwen (2001). *Multimodal Discourse: The Modes and Media of Contemporary Communication.* London: Arnold. Print.

Kunzle, David (1973). *The Early Comic Strip: Narrative Strips and Picture Stories in the European Broadsheet from c.1450 to 1825.* Berkeley: U of California P. Print.

— (1990). *The History of the Comic Strip: The Nineteenth Century.* Berkeley: U of California P. Print.

Lefèvre, Pascal (2000). "Narration in Comics." *Image & Narrative* 1.1: n.p. Web.

McCloud, Scott (1993). *Understanding Comics.* Northampton: Kitchen Sink. Print.

Page, Ruth (ed.) (2012). *New Perspectives on Narrative and Multimodality.* New York: Routledge. Print.

Prince, Stephen (2010). "Through the Looking Glass: Philosophical Toys and Digital Visual Effects." *Projections* 4.2: 19–40. Print.
Rajewsky, Irina O. (2010). "Border Talks: The Problematic Status of Media Borders in the Current Debate about Intermediality." Lars Elleström (ed.). *Media Borders, Multimodality and Intermediality.* Basingstoke: Palgrave Macmillan. 51–68. Print.
Ryan, Marie-Laure (2005). "On the Theoretical Foundations of Transmedial Narratology." J. Christoph Meister (ed.). *Narratology beyond Literary Criticism: Mediality—Disciplinarity.* Berlin: De Gruyter. 1–23. Print.
— (2006). *Avatars of Story.* Minneapolis: U of Minnesota P. Print.
Sabin, Roger (2003). "Ally Sloper: The First Comics Superstar?" *Image & Narrative* 4.1: n.p. Web.
Smith, Greg M. (2011). "Surveying the World of Contemporary Comics Scholarship: A Conversation." *Cinema Journal* 50.3: 135–47. Print.
Steadman, Philip (2001). *Vermeer's Camera: Uncovering the Truth behind the Masterpieces.* Oxford: Oxford UP. Print.
Stein, Daniel (2012). "The Comic Modernism of George Herriman." Jake Jakaitis and James F. Wurtz (eds.). *Crossing Boundaries in Graphic Narrative: Essays on Forms, Series and Genres.* Jefferson: McFarland. 40–70. Print.
Thon, Jan-Noël (2008). "Immersion Revisited: On the Value of a Contested Concept." Olli Leino, Hanna Wirman, and Amyris Fernandez (eds.). *Extending Experiences: Structure, Analysis, and Design of Computer Game Player Experience.* Rovaniemi: Lapland UP. 29–43. Print.
Varnedoe, Kirk, and Adam Gopnik (1990). "Comics." *High and Low: Modern Art and Popular Culture.* New York: Abrams. 153–230. Print.
Wolf, Werner (2002). "Intermediality Revisited: Reflections on Word and Music Relations in the Context of a General Typology of Intermediality." Suzanne M. Lodato, Suzanne Aspden, and Walter Bernhart (eds.). *Word and Music Studies: Essays in Honor of Steven Paul Scher on Cultural Identity and the Musical Stage.* Amsterdam: Rodopi. 13–34. Print.
— (2005). "Metalepsis as a Transgeneric and Transmedial Phenomenon: A Case Study of the Possibilities of 'Exporting' Narratological Concepts." J. Christoph Meister (ed.). *Narratology beyond Literary Criticism: Mediality—Disciplinarity.* Berlin: De Gruyter. 83–107. Print.
— (2006). "Introduction: Frames, Framings, and Framing Borders." Werner Wolf and Walter Bernhart (eds.). *Framing Borders in Literature and Other Media.* Amsterdam: Rodopi. 1–40. Print.

Part III

Genre and Format Histories of Graphic Narrative

JARED GARDNER
(Columbus)

A History of the Narrative Comic Strip

The sequential comic as we know it was born in the illustrated magazines of the late nineteenth century, emerging slowly and unevenly as a solution to narrative problems presented by the single-panel cartoon that dominated its pages. As the popularity of illustrated magazines and the cartoon increased, so did the ambition of cartoonists to tell stories. Sequential graphic narrative precedes the emergence of the modern comic strip by decades, of course, appearing for example in the "progress" series of William Hogarth in the eighteenth or in Wilhelm Busch's picture stories in the nineteenth century.[1] But the cartoon of the illustrated magazine remained largely fixed by the rules of the cartoon: a single panel with accompanying text affixed below.

Granted growing real estate in the illustrated magazine in the final decades of the nineteenth century, some cartoonists began to experiment with sequential graphic narratives that largely eschewed text entirely, with the exception of a title. Pioneers in this form in the illustrated magazine would include Johann Bahr in Germany, Caran D'Ache in France, and F. M. Howarth in the United States.[2] Liberated from the fixed single panel and the body of text below, here the stories told could be more complex and dynamic than the single panel cartoon could possibly allow. But even as the illustrated magazines of the 1880s and 1890s began to offer more examples of sequential graphic short narratives, several of the features we will come to associate with the twentieth-century comic strip are missing: combinations of text and image, dialogue balloons, recurring characters, and ongoing serial narratives.[3]

When sequential comics moved into the colored newspaper supplements at the turn of the twentieth century, however, all of these missing features emerged and established themselves with remarkable

---
1 See Kunzle 1973; on the transition from single-panel cartoon to the comic strip, see also Gardner 2010.
2 See Gordon 1998: ch. 1.
3 For the classic definition of comics, cf. Waugh 1991 [1947]: 14; see also Silke Horstkotte's contribution in this volume.

speed, especially when compared to similar developments in the conventions of other new narrative forms, such as those taking place in film at the same time. In the United States, we see this transformation clearly in the work of Frederick Burr Opper, who at the time of the emergence of the newspaper comic strip had already secured his place as one of the most prominent cartoonists of the illustrated magazines. Working for *Puck* magazine since 1880, Opper had, over the course of twenty years, never used speech balloons, very rarely incorporated text into the panels of sequential cartoons, and—with the exception of the racial and ethnic stereotypes so often deployed by nineteenth-century cartoonists—he had not used recurring characters at all. However, after being hired away in 1899 by William Randolph Hearst, the middle-aged Opper's approach to cartooning changed dramatically. When his *Happy Hooligan* began appearing in the Sunday supplements of Hearst syndicate papers in early 1900, it had all of the elements of the comic strip firmly in hand.[4]

For thirty-two years, *Happy Hooligan* told essentially the same story, with minor variations along the way. Each week, Happy—a tramp with a generous heart and a tin can for a hat—would head out hoping to do the right thing; and each week he would end up beaten, evicted, or arrested, mistaken for the 'hooligan' his appearance and his name suggested. And the following Sunday, Happy would set out, ready to do it all again. While the basic pattern of the story remained largely intact for the run of the strip, from early on, Opper began experimenting with loosely structured ongoing narratives that carried beyond the single installment, such as Happy's constant search for stable employment. The earliest extended narrative in the strip was one that would be used by many comic strips in decades to come: the trip around the world. In 1904, Happy and his brothers set off on a whirlwind trip, visiting several countries over the course of several months. Obviously, part of the great pleasure of the series is that wherever Happy goes, his fate remains unchanged: he winds up in prison in England or Spain just as surely as he did in America. Like other pioneering comic strip artists of this generation, Opper recognized early on that his narrative form was ultimately the loop, the repeated fragment—in a sense the story of the modern industrial city. This was also a form that was being explored by the other new narrative medium to emerge at the turn of the century, film.[5] Like the earliest comic strips, early film was premised on the narrative loop, short stories of modern life that could be rewound, slowed down, replayed.

---

4   Cf. Harvey 1994: 9–10.
5   For further analysis, see Gardner 2012: ch. 1.

Not surprisingly, early film borrowed heavily from the comic strip for several vital features as it explored its narrative possibilities, and *Happy Hooligan*, along with *Buster Brown* (from 1902 onwards) by the pioneering newspaper cartoonist Richard Felton Outcault, was one of the first subjects for series films featuring recurring characters. Of course, as I discuss at length in *Projections: Comics and the History of Twenty-First-Century Storytelling* (2012), driven by different industrial histories and scenes of reception, film and the comic strip would soon begin moving in different directions—narrative film toward the 'evening's entertainment' (Koszarski 1999) and the comic strip toward increasingly complex open-ended serial narratives that defined the twentieth-century newspaper.

Winsor McCay's *Little Nemo*, which began its run in the *New York Herald* in 1905 and ran until 1914, told the story of a boy who is transported each night to adventures in Slumberland. Each episode would be interrupted by poor Nemo falling out of bed and waking himself up (often at a climactic moment in the evening's adventures), but he would return the following night to his proper place in the ongoing narrative— the storyworld of Slumberland having stuck, like a needle on one of the recently-introduced phonograph records. As Scott Bukatman describes the narrative "poetics of slumberland," "this dialectic between wild kinesis and perfectly rendered stasis has its analogue in the overarching narrative of *Little Nemo*: the cosmic journeys across time and space counterbalanced by the insistent return to the bed from which no one has moved at all" (2012: 31). This dialectic plays on what was by 1905 already starting to become visible as the road-not-taken in the emerging conventions of narrative film. Even as we continue to see traces of the fragment of 'perfectly rendered stasis' in pioneering narrative films like *The Great Train Robbery* (Edwin S. Porter, 1903), which follows up on the frenetic climactic shootout with a final shot of an outlaw we thought dead (at least within the narrative logic of the film) staring fixedly at the audience as he fires directly into the camera. A decade earlier, as Tom Gunning (1989) has described, the earliest projected films played with the tension between the still and moving images in laying the foundations for the 'aesthetics of astonishment' that defined the so-called primitive films of the first generation. As film now began to move toward the illusion of *continuous* movement (and more urgently for an industry desperate to secure an anarchic audience's attention) and projection, it was left to the comic strip to explore the dialectic between kinetic movement and framed stillness— as well as between the loop and the open-ended storyline.

Unlike *Happy Hooligan*, the larger story of *Little Nemo* moved forward in time, as Nemo traveled through a series of extended adventures in Slumberland and developed traits—courage, devotion—and relationships over time. But like Happy, Nemo always ended up in roughly the same place—usually on the floor by his bed. While never receiving the audience it deserved, *Nemo*'s influence nonetheless cannot be underestimated. *Nemo* was the first strip to offer consistent characters in an ongoing, open-ended serial narrative. And McCay was also one of the very first to explore the visual narrative possibilities of the Sunday page, whose vast expanses allowed him to tell his story in much more complicated and varied ways than were found in the earliest comic strips like *Happy Hooligan*. Breaking from the largely uniform and neatly sequential panels of the conventional strip, McCay explored the ways in which panel size and shape could serve as tools for conveying varied stretches of time or states of mind. And while his carefully numbered panels served to remind the reader of the 'proper' order in which the story unfolded, his pages were composed in such a way as often to create a tension between this official order and the eye's tendency to follow the kinetic movement around the page in very different directions.

McCay's inventiveness as a graphic storyteller was, of course, aided by the size of his stage. The space which he had to work was 51 x 42 cm, and McCay used that space with a remarkable efficiency. But this same format that afforded such an ideal playing field for McCay's visual imagination was also part of what militated against *Nemo*'s success in finding the audience it deserved. The weekly installments of the Sunday strip created a disjunction between the *daily* adventures of the character—who returned each night to his proper place in the unfolding story—and the *week*-long wait of the reader waiting for the next installment. This disjunction would ultimately be overcome only by the emergence of an entirely new format for narrative comics, the daily comic strip that emerged in late 1907 in the *San Francisco Chronicle* with Bud Fisher's *A. Mutt* (later *Mutt and Jeff*).

A. Mutt initially followed the daily fortunes of Mutt at the racetrack as he bet on horses running that day. The reader was then encouraged to return the next day to see how Mutt fared in his wagers. Printed on the sports pages, the first successful daily strip combined the news of the previous day's racing results with the story of the effects of the success or (more often) failure on Mutt's bet within the same page. Unlike McCay's Sunday page, however, Fischer had a much smaller space to tell his story, and he was limited to a fixed pattern of panels running left to right. But Fisher's formula essentially co-opted the rest of the sports page to create an interactive daily experience that invited readers not only to move between the racing news and Mutt's adventures, but to weave both into the daily rhythms of their own lives.

Given the phenomenal popularity of the formula Fisher created (or, more accurately, adapted from an earlier experiment by Clare Briggs called

A. Piker Clerk[6]), it was inevitable that the strip would soon be called to a larger stage than a local paper could provide. Once William Randolph Hearst acquired *Mutt and Jeff*, Fisher had to abandon his local sports page formula. The solution Fisher came up with was to go from interacting with the news, to actually *being* the news. In 1908, a manhunt was launched for Mutt for robbing $2.60 from a payphone (a crime that would eventually result in Mutt's first meeting with his long-time companion, Jeff). Now the daily suspense of the strip lay not in finding out whether the horse Mutt had bet on would win, but in following the headlines that splashed across the strip itself describing the state of the manhunt or the trial to follow. And, as time went on, the adventures of Mutt and Jeff would be frequently reported in papers across the nation as if they *were* news, even on the front page of papers.

Numerous other daily comic strips would quickly emerge to attempt to duplicate the remarkable success of *Mutt and Jeff*, and by 1912, the daily strip had a page of its own within many newspapers around the country, beginning with Hearst's *Evening Journal*. Among the innovative and influential strips that emerged in the early 1910s were *The Family Upstairs*, where George Herriman's Krazy Kat character would be born in 1910, Cliff Sterrett's *Polly and Her Pals* (1912–1958), and *Bringing Up Father* by George McManus (1913–2000). All of these strips launched in Hearst's syndicate, and for a time Hearst had what amounted to a monopoly on the new format of the daily strip. But in 1917, a rival publisher, Joseph Medill Patterson, determined to create a daily comic strip page to rival Hearst. Beginning with *The Gumps* by Sidney Smith (1917–1959), Patterson's *Chicago Tribune* became the birthplace of the defining comic strips of the next generation, including *Gasoline Alley* (1918–), *Little Orphan Annie* (1924–2010), *Dick Tracy* (1931–1977), and *Terry and the Pirates* (1934–1946). Patterson's initial idea—and one that would be perfected by Smith in the *Gumps* and Frank King in *Gasoline Alley*—was to offer serial strips about ordinary people, with a household presided over by one of the self-important windbags Patterson referred to as "gumps" (Walker 2005: 75). Smith's strip featured a middle-class family living in a modest home in the Chicago area, while King's strip initially focused on the growing fascination of working- and middle-class readers with automobile culture. But in both cases, the strips soon moved beyond the modest limits of their original mandate to include a range of other topics increasingly being featured on the big screen of the film industry, recently settled into Hollywood, California, and into the narrative conventions of the classical

---

6   Cf. Harvey 1994: 46.

Hollywood system.[7] Beginning in 1918, Smith began to break up the daily domestic adventures of Andy and Min Gump with ongoing narratives focused on mystery, melodrama, and adventure, and by 1921, the strip had emerged as a daily soap opera whose cliffhangers were reported on the front page of daily newspapers and whose mysteries solicited thousands of letters of advice from engaged readers. That same year, *Gasoline Alley* introduced the foundling Skeezix to the story, opening up new topics for both comedy and melodrama.

In both cases, the formula was clear. Mixing the genres so popular on the Hollywood screen—domestic comedy, physical comedy, melodrama, adventure, and mystery—the strips offered a coherent and ongoing open-ended serial that promised, unlike the 'evening's entertainment' at the emerging 'picture palaces' of the 1920s, to continue indefinitely into the future. As the first major newspaper publisher to embrace the film serials of the 1910s, Patterson knew first-hand that the comic strip serial could offer something else that the film serial could not: the possibility of interacting directly with the unfolding story, asking questions, making suggestions, and even (as when Smith killed off his beloved character Mary Gold in 1929) expressing shock and outrage. When Uncle Bim becomes engaged to the scheming Widow Zander in 1922, Smith regularly makes space in his strip for letters from readers offering opinions as to whether he should let the marriage take place or not. When Skeezix is kidnapped in 1924, newspapers around the country reported sightings by readers of the missing child. As with *Mutt and Jeff*, the line between 'news' and 'comics' was deliberately blurred in these stories, but here readers were explicitly invited to write in with suggestions and solutions to the mysteries, enjoying the doubled and seemingly irreconcilable knowledge that the strips were fiction created by the cartoonists to whom they addressed their correspondence and the fantasy that the characters were in fact real people whom they had come, through the daily installments of the narrative, to 'know.'

It is important to keep in mind that all of these early strips were addressed first and foremost to adult readers. Smith often would use his Sunday pages for storylines completely independent of his daily strip featuring Andy Gump's eldest son Chester, adventures clearly geared more toward younger readers. But from *Mutt and Jeff* through *Gasoline Alley* the assumption was that daily strips were read by adults and rarely followed regularly by younger readers. That would begin to change in the mid-1920s, however, and the *Tribune* was once again at the center of that important transformation with the launching of *Little Orphan Annie* in

---

7 See Bordwell, Staiger, and Thompson 1985.

1924. Here Harold Gray used a formula similar in many ways to that of Smith and King, but with a child protagonist at the center of the story, courting a new audience opened for the daily strip. Gray began to move away from the domestic comedy systematically, focusing instead on extended adventure narratives of kidnappings, travel, and international criminals. Unlike Smith, for example, who would interrupt even his most baroque melodramas for a day or two of physical comedy, Gray focused exclusively on crafting continuous extended narratives that rarely if ever lost sight of the primary thread of the plot. The result was the emergence of the adventure strip as it would come to dominate the form in the late 1920s and 1930s.

Other strips started to move in similar directions at around this time. For example, Roy Crane's *Wash Tubbs*, which had begun in 1924 as a gag-a-day strip, focused on a diminutive would-be Romeo, transformed itself after a few months into an adventure strip, ultimately featuring the heroic Captain Easy and moving Wash into the role of comic sidekick. In 1928, *Tarzan* and *Buck Rogers* begin, moving the adventure strip into the exotic- and other-worlds that would become its primary setting for much of the 1930s and 1940s. And in 1934, Milton Caniff's *Terry and the Pirates* and Alex Raymond's *Flash Gordon* both launched, after which the dominance of the adventure strip seemed complete.

Caniff is widely regarded as the master of the adventure strip, bringing to his stories a commitment to visual and historical realism, a complex set of multi-dimensional characters, and a focus on both younger and older readers. He also restored to the adventure strip some of the romance and melodrama that had been central to the strips of his youth, and he was equally committed to the adult and younger reader. But among all his contemporaries, Caniff was also the most cinematic in terms of his sense of framing and lighting. One can see in *Terry* both the epitome of the visual storyteller in the daily strip as well as the growing influence of Hollywood storytelling and style on the comic strip form. Increasingly subscribing to the rules codified over the previous generation in American cinema, the adventure strip of the 1930s favored visual realism, consistent characters, logical 'cause-and-effect' storytelling, and the construction of a voyeuristic relationship to the story being told. Outside of *Krazy Kat* (by the mid-1930s in its last decade) or Ernie Bushmiller's *Nancy* (which launched in 1933), violations of the fourth wall and direct appeals to the readers to serve as co-creators of the narrative were increasingly rare in the 1930s and 1940s.

In one vital way, however, the serial comic strip remained distinct from narrative film: the stories in the comic strip had no predetermined end. But by the 1930s, the open-ended serial was no longer unique to comics. Beginning with the nightly adventures of *Amos 'n' Andy* in 1928, serial radio had emerged to capitalize on the formula first developed in the comic strip (it is telling that *Amos 'n' Andy* was originally to have been a radio adaptation of *The Gumps*[8]). By the 1930s, radio's popularity and profitability as a narrative form had surpassed the comic strip and was rivaling even Hollywood. The *Tribune*'s daily strips were quickly adapted to radio form: *Little Orphan Annie* in 1930, *Dick Tracy* in 1934, and *Terry and the Pirates* in 1937.

If radio provided a new outlet for newspaper syndicates to profit on their properties and on the public's appetite for open-ended serials, it also dramatically changed the relationship between readers and their daily comic strips. The kind of response that greeted Smith's killing off of Mary Gold in 1929 would have been almost unimaginable by the end of the 1930s, reserved instead for a similar tragedy in a radio soap opera. The three or four panels of an ongoing serial comic strip each day now had to compete with the disembodied voice in the living room for half an hour each day. And for Depression-era audiences fortunate enough to own a radio, the daily installments of the radio serial came free (courtesy of commercial sponsors whose products were sold as the stories were told), unlike the daily newspaper, and actively sought to recreate the sense of audience ownership and interaction with serial storytelling that had once been the exclusive domain of the comic strip.[9]

It is hard not to look back to the earliest narrative experiments with the comic strip form at the turn of the century, when Happy Hooligan was a household name with some sense of nostalgia. The comic form, inherently elliptical and fragmented, invites and even requires the reader to become active agents in meaning making. As Chris Ware has put it, comics are "not in any way a passive medium. The material is inert unless you're regarding it" (quoted in Ball and Kuhlman 2010: 86). Part of the reason readers became so passionately attached to early comics was because of this investment of imaginative energy and narrative energies— the active filling in of all that cannot be represented in the panels on the page: sounds, detail, the action between the panels, etc. While such filling in is central to all meaning making in narrative across media, the fundamental *inefficiency* of comics as a narrative medium and its foregrounding in the formal space of the gutter between panels, the work required by the 'gap' arguably entails from the outset a different level of investment than any other narrative form.

---

8   Cf. Henderson 1988: 158.
9   See Razlogova 2011: ch. 4.

Radio obviously tells stories without support of visual information, but from early on, radio programs worked to provide visual supplements, with, for example, publicity photographs of Freeman Gosden and Charles Correll in blackface as Amos and Andy, or Virginia Payne in character as radio soap opera star Ma Perkins. But as more and more radio serials came to be adapted from comic strips, they brought with them from the comic pages the visual information to fill in a consistent outline of the characters in listeners' minds. As the profitability of serial radio peaked during the late 1930s and early 1940s, serial comics came under pressure from their syndicates to focus on coherent, unified adventure stories easily translated to the medium of radio.

Even as radio and film continued to exert a growing influence on comic strip storytelling in the 1930s, by the end of the decade a new and ultimately more transformative medium had arrived which would change forever the influence of the comic strip as a narrative medium. On April 18, 1938, the first issue of *Action Comics*, featuring a super-powered alien from another planet, hit newsstands and created a phenomenon that would be unparalleled until the arrival of television a decade later. The comic book format had been used for a few years in the U.S., primarily featuring reprinted newspaper comics and generating relatively little interest on the part of readers. The birth of the superhero adventure comic book changed everything, as if overnight, and even as newspaper cartoonists and publishers looked on disdainfully, a new and powerful industry emerged in the 1940s that would rob newspaper comics of much of the young audience they had come to depend on since the mid-1920s.

It goes without saying that *Superman* and the idea of the 'superhero' emerged in important ways directly from the newspaper adventure strips like *Flash Gordon*, *Buck Rogers*, and *Captain Easy*.[10] And so the question needs to be raised: what was it that the comic book was able to offer readers that the newspaper comic strip did not? It is a challenging question in some ways, since the vast majority of early comics books were relatively poorly drawn and written, and the comic book emerged at a time when the art of the newspaper comic strip was arguably at its very highest. Clearly 'quality,' however defined, was not at the heart of the appeal of comic books.

Part of the answer to that question (and perhaps the major part) requires a return to the interactive and engaged reader of *The Gumps* from the 1920s. For years, fans of serial comic strips had been putting together their own collections, scrapbooks assembled against the ephemerality of the daily newspaper. Inevitably missing installments, readers would write

---

10   Cf. Daniels 1998: 11.

in to the newspaper or the cartoonist, hoping to acquire the missing strips. And just as inevitably, they were rebuffed or, more likely, ignored. There were exceptions, of course. The publisher Cupples and Leon, for example, released several slim reprint volumes of *Mutt and Jeff, The Gumps*, and *Little Orphan Annie* in the 1920s, forerunners of the modern comic book. But for the most part, the syndicates ignored the potential of a reprint market and, more urgently, the expressed desire on the part of their readers to possess their serial stories in volumes that could be owned, reread, collected. In the face of growing competition from serial radio, one might have imagined that the syndicates would have recognized this as something they could provide to their readers that radio in the 1930s could not. However, it would be the serial comic book that would emerge to fill that need, ultimately taking with it the adventure strip that had dominated the comic strip form for a generation.

Storytelling in the comic strip changes dramatically in the postwar period following the rise of the comic book and the new narrative medium of the day, television. Charles Schulz's *Peanuts* (1950-2000) perhaps best epitomizes the new comic strips of the new era. The real estate afforded to a daily comic strip had shrunk dramatically after the start of the Depression, and it would shrink again in the late 1950s, such that by 1958 the average newspaper printed a daily comic strip in roughly half the space that had been allotted to *Mutt and Jeff* a half-century earlier. With diminished readerly attention—the comic strip simply no longer commanded the devoted serial readership of *The Gumps*— and a shrinking physical space, comics such as *Peanuts* moved away from serial adventure and physical comedy and turned inward. In a striking move away from the cinematic realism of Caniff's work, Schulz pursued a minimalist approach to his art and focused on the development of characters whose inner lives and philosophical questions were where the real drama lay. This was a storytelling designed to confront the very different landscape on which the postwar comic strip operated.

In many ways, of course, it was also a return to the narrative loop of *Happy Hooligan*. Charlie Brown will never kick the football; the tree will always get his kite. The immigrant tramp has been replaced by a Midwestern suburban kid, certainly, but like *Happy*, this is a story one can pick up at any point in its fifty-year run with little risk of the kind of narrative disorientation that would take place if trying to do the same with *The Gumps* or *Terry and the Pirates*. And over the course of these fifty years, few other U.S. strips would attempt to take on the kind of narrative and generic complexity that was at work at the height of the open-ended serial strips of the 1920s and 1930s.

The exceptions, however, often prove the general rule. Garry Trudeau's *Doonesbury* launched in 1970, initially focusing on a group of students at Walden College. Over the past four decades, it has developed one of the most complicated universes of characters and genealogies in the history of serial comics. Like *Gasoline Alley*, the characters in *Doonesbury* age in something approximating 'real time,' and like *Mutt and Jeff*, the strip incorporates real political events and contemporary political figures into its universe. From early on, *Doonesbury* worked consciously to meld the serial comic strip with the editorial cartoon, a fact that many editors have used as an excuse to banish the strip from the daily comics page. It remains today, in many respects, *sui generis* and has secured few if any meaningful heirs in the U.S. despite its tremendous success.

Lynn Johnston's *For Better or For Worse*, which launched in 1979, worked even more faithfully with the notion of characters aging in chronological time along with its readers, and like earlier open-ended serial strips, it actively combined genres, especially domestic comedy, melodrama, and social commentary. Tom Batiuk's *Funky Winkerbean* (1972–) has followed a similar formula for the last twenty years of its run. But these strips remain relatively isolated refugees from another era, strips that were in many ways throwbacks in terms of their approach to comics storytelling even in the 1970s when they began.

That there are so few examples of narratively ambitious strips in the U.S. newspapers in recent decades is not surprising. A century earlier, the comic strip had emerged as the first new narrative medium of the twentieth century. The history of the comic strip as a narrative medium over the course of the century is arguably the story of the impact of new players on the field: film, radio, the comic book, and television. Each of these new media had forced the comic strip to reconsider its audience and the rules by which it told stories. By the end of the 1990s, of course, there was one last new medium on the scene, one that promises to bring about the end of the comic strip as we have known it for more than a century. And yet, even as traditional print newspapers collapse in the new media economy of the Internet, there remains reason to believe that the comic strip might possibly survive the transformation to the digital landscape.

The late 1990s witnessed an explosion of webcomics dedicated to open-ended serial storytelling, many of which continue today. Many of these strips focused on characters and interests that were not being covered comprehensively in the mainstream press, and certainly not in newspaper comics, such as gaming culture (Jerry Holkins and Mike Krahulik's *Penny Arcade*, 1998–) or graduate school and science research (Jorge Cham's *Piled Higher and Deeper*, 1997–). Few of even the longest running webcomics thus far have shown much ambition in terms of developing ongoing narrative, however, and even webcomics with recurring characters often explicitly eschew narratives that require multiple installments to tell. *Penny Arcade*, for instance, refers disparagingly to ongoing serial narrative as the "dreaded *Continuity*" (Holkins 2002: n.p., original emphasis). The vast majority of webcomics focus on one-shot gags, and many do not even make use of recurring characters.

The reasons for this are fairly clear. At a time when few webcomics have succeeded in securing a loyal and consistent readership, there is little faith that digital comics could possibly succeed as a medium for serial storytelling. It may well take the final end of the newspaper comic strip and the serial comic book before a platform emerges to bring readers hungry for this serial storytelling together with creators working in the comic strip format. For now, the serial comic strip—the form that first explored the possibilities of open-ended seriality—remains in limbo waiting for the Winsor McCay or Bud Fisher of the digital comic strip to enter the scene, and for a William Randolph Hearst for the twenty-first century to lay the foundations of a business model that will allow the narrative comics of the Internet age to develop and thrive.

Works Cited

Ball, David M., and Martha B. Kuhlman (2010). *The Comics of Chris Ware: Drawing Is a Way of Thinking*. Jackson: UP of Mississippi. Print.

Bordwell, David, Janet Staiger, and Kristin Thompson (1985). *The Classical Hollywood Cinema: Film Style and Mode of Production to 1960*. New York: Columbia UP. Print.

Bukatman, Scott (2012). *The Poetics of Slumberland: Animated Spirits and the Animating Spirit*. Berkeley: U of California P. Print.

Daniels, Les (1998). *Superman: The Complete History*. San Francisco: Chronicle. Print.

Gardner, Jared (2010). "Same Difference: Graphic Alterity in the Work of Gene Luen Yang, Adrian Tomine, and Derek Kirk Kim." Frederick Luis Aldama (ed.). *Multicultural Comics: From* Zap *to* Blue Beetle. Austin: U of Texas P. 132–47. Print.

— (2012). *Projections: Comics and the History of Twenty-First-Century Storytelling*. Stanford: Stanford UP. Print.

Gordon, Ian (1998). *Comic Strips and Consumer Culture, 1890–1945*. Washington, D.C.: Smithsonian Institution P. Print.

Gunning, Tom (1989). "An Aesthetic of Astonishment: Early Film and the (In)credulous Spectator." *Art and Text* 34: 31–45. Print.

Harvey, Robert C. (1994). *The Art of the Funnies: An Aesthetic History*. Jackson: UP of Mississippi. Print.
Henderson, Amy (1988). *On the Air: Pioneers of American Broadcasting*. Washington, D.C.: Smithsonian Institution P. Print.
Holkins, Jerry (2002). "Das Olskoolen Part 1." *Penny Arcade*, Mar. 6. Web.
Koszarski, Richard (1990). *An Evening's Entertainment: The Age of the Silent Feature Picture, 1915–1928*. New York: Scribner. Print.
Kunzle, David (1973). *The Early Comic Strip: Narrative Strips and Picture Stories in the European Broadsheet from c.1450 to 1825*. Berkeley: U of California P. Print.
Razlogova, Elena (2011). *The Listener's Voice: Early Radio and the American Public*. Philadelphia: U of Pennsylvania P. Print.
Walker, Brian (2005). *The Comics before 1945*. New York: Abrams. Print.
Waugh, Coulton (1991 [1947]). *The Comics*. Jackson: UP of Mississippi. Print.

PASCAL LEFÈVRE

(Leuven and Brussels)

Narration in the Flemish Dual Publication System: The Crossover Genre of the Humoristic Adventure

The role of formats is often neglected in narratological research. Yet, as this chapter argues, publication formats determine many aspects of published stories. Material conditions such as the size of the paper, temporal properties such as daily or weekly publication, and editorial concerns such as regulations concerning content, style, or public reception can impact the particular shapes and forms of graphic narratives. As I have argued in the past, every publication format contains an aesthetic system with a set of norms that offers a bounded set of alternatives to the individual creator of comics.[1] In other words, every publication format or system (such as the daily strip, the Sunday page, the comic book, the European album, or the 'mangazine') uses particular conventions concerning the dimensions of the publication, the arrangement of panels, drawing styles, and narrative structures.

Popular comics series have been published in various publication formats. This chapter analyzes a specific example of the interaction between two publication formats, the Flemish dual publication system of daily newspaper and album series, through a case study of the most popular Flemish comic strip series, *Suske en Wiske*. The chapter focuses on a particular period (the 1950s and 1960s) in which this series was especially popular, and it argues that two quite different publication formats shaped the ways in which the comic strip narrative was constructed.[2] It further considers the extent to which the development of a crossover genre, the humoristic adventure story, is an outcome of the dual publication system.

---

1   See Lefèvre 2000. For related analyses, see Lefèvre 1995, 2006, 2011.
2   For a detailed analysis of the strip during this time period, see also my dissertation (Lefèvre 2003).

Publication Formats for Graphic Narratives

Though European graphic narratives from the nineteenth century onwards preceded the artistic and commercial boom of American comic strips at the beginning of the twentieth century, it was foremost the American model (with speech and thought balloons) that would shape the development of the comics medium in the following decades. In the colorful Sunday supplements of the American newspapers, the so-called Sunday Pages, artists delivered weekly episodes of a comics series with recurring protagonist(s). A few years later, daily comics of just one tier in black and white became widespread in the American dailies. Both publication formats (Sunday and daily) have been evolving for over more than a century.[3] They may have recently lost a great deal of their impact, but, in essence, they are still present in thousands of publications worldwide. Though both publication formats were imitated during the early twentieth century in diverse places such as Mexico, Japan, and France, various countries have developed their own publication formats. Think of the success of the new manga monthlies and weeklies in postwar Japan, the boom of comics weeklies in various Western European countries in the 1930s and 1950s, the success of comic books in the United States since the late 1930s, and the breakthrough of one-shots for adults (widely known as graphic novels) in Europe and the USA since the late 1970s.

Even in a small region such as Flanders, the Dutch-speaking part of Belgium, a particular combination of two publication formats was forged and perfected as part of a commercially attractive dual publication system. It involved a daily installment consisting of two tiers in a newspaper (published as one long tier over the total width of the newspaper page until 1966) and a collection of daily tiers in one album of a fixed number of pages. From the start, it was decided that, since the series would be published in album format by offset printing, the total amount of pages must be a multiple of 8, 16, or 32. Therefore, the classic format for albums in Belgium was 48 or 64 pages, but the album publisher of *Suske and Wiske* chose 56 pages, also a multiple of 8. Each page consisted of 4 equal tiers, which amounted to a total of 220 tiers for an album. If an album consisted of 56 pages (one title page and 55 pages with the tiers), it would take 110 daily installments (of two tiers) to publish a complete story. This meant that an author had to tell a self-contained story in 220 tiers or on an average of 660 panels (because a tier consisted usually of 3

---

[3] On the evolution of the American comic strip, see also Jared Gardner's contribution in this volume.

panels). Thus, the length of the story was imposed by the album format, while the installment length of 2 tiers a day was imposed by the traditional way of publishing continuity comics in daily newspapers. But these specific publication formats had additional consequences. For one, in order to keep the newspaper reader interested, installments ideally ended with an element of tension. Secondly, when an author has to tell his or her story in such small increments (2 tiers), certain kinds of narratives become difficult: for instance, working with atmosphere and slow rhythm or constructing over-complex narrative structures.

Though the American newspaper comic strips have been collected in book form since early twentieth century as well, the success of these book editions in the USA was relatively limited. Even worldwide there are few examples that can match the degree and the longevity of the Flemish model. Between 1945 and 1977, five top-selling series (*Suske en Wiske, Nero, Jommeke, De Rode Ridder, Kiekeboe*) were launched in this Flemish dual system, and except for one series, *Nero*, they are still being produced in Flanders, ranging in total from 140 to more than 250 titles. This means that one will find a few albums in almost every Flemish household, with many families possessing extensive collections. These comics may nowadays be destined primarily for children, but they are also enjoyed by many adults. It is important to note that the formula of this Flemish dual system has not stayed completely the same since 1945. Though the combination of daily and album publication still exists today, some elements have changed over the course of time. For instance, the use color in albums was only generalized in the 1980s, and the power balance between daily publication and album publication shifted from newspapers to books in the 1970s.

The Particularity of the Flemish Tradition

For a better understanding of the particularities of the mainstream Flemish comic strip in the 1950s, a comparison with two neighboring traditions within the Low Countries, Francophone production in Belgium and Dutch production in the Netherlands, is useful. Though Flemish comics share with comics from the Netherlands the same Dutch language and with Francophone comics from Belgium the same nationality, Flemish comics should be considered to a certain degree as a separate category of comics.

A first point of difference with most Dutch comic strips in the 1950s concerns the use of speech ballons. While various mainstream newspaper comics of the Netherlands (*Tom Poes, Panda, Eric de Noorman, Kapitein Rob*) kept separating texts and drawings, Flemish comics trips, like the Belgian Francophone comics, opted for speech balloons integrated within the drawing. Moreover, even within the same publication format (the daily comic), Flemish and Dutch newspaper strips differed from each other in tone and atmosphere. The Dutch comics specialists Evelyn and Kees Kousemaker acknowledged that Dutch newspaper comics were generally rather neat and bourgeois, while the Flemish were more loosely drawn and written and contained more popular language: "There is a nonchalance in the way these typical characters solve difficult situations, in which they are continually thrown. A certain atmosphere and spirit radiates from these Flemish humorous comics [...] by the expression of a distinctive sense of life" (1979: 80).[4]

In comparison with their French-language counterparts, the Flemish protagonists after the war displayed more negative characteristics. The main Flemish characters were more self-deprecating and farcical. They also looked more lower-class than the rather smooth bourgeois heroes of the French-language stories. While the characters in the weeklies *Tintin* (1929–1976) and *Spirou* (1938–) were still almost entirely boys and men, in the Flemish comics, women and girls (such as Wiske, Sidonie, Madam Pheip and Susan) were already playing a major role. And while the French-language comics in the first postwar decades flourished mainly in specialized weeklies such as *Spirou* and *Tintin*, the Flemish strip thrived foremost in the Flemish daily papers and their children's supplements. This difference in publication format had far-reaching consequences for the production, form, and content of the comics. Flemish comics artists working for a newspaper had to produce one or two strips a day without interruption. So they had to produce more, and more quickly, than the authors who worked for French comics weeklies like *Spirou* and *Tintin*. The poor quality of newsprint usually meant that the stylistic potential of the Flemish artists was restricted. Even for the books of Flemish comics, publishers often used mediocre paper and soft covers until the 1970s. This allowed them to keep the price down, and print runs of more than fifty thousand were, and still are, no exception—and this for a population of only six million Flemish people.

As I have already pointed out, the editing of a story also differs between a daily and a weekly installment. In newspapers, artists tried to insert an element of tension (a cliffhanger) into the end of every two strips (because they were published at that rate), while they usually employed

---

4   My translation from the Dutch: "De nonchalance waarmee deze typisch figuren de moeilijke situaties, waarin zij voortdurend terechtkomen, oplossen. Er straalt een bepaalde sfeer en geest uit Vlaamse humoristische beeldverhalen [...] door de uiting van een kenmerkend levensgevoel, een levensfilosofie en levenshumor."

such narrative devices at the end of an episode of one or more pages in the weeklies. Overly complex narrative structures were thus unfeasible in daily installments of just two strips. Furthermore, while French-language strip comics were soon oriented toward the larger market of France, the Flemish comics production enveloped itself in its own cocoon. Flemish comics sold extremely well on the home market. They had no trouble at all in establishing a position in the region because they were intended mainly for a Flemish readership (some 4.6 million people after the war). Many stories in *Suske en Wiske* and *Nero* are obviously set in Flanders, and the protagonists are clearly identified as Flemish. By contrast, the French-language authors limited the explicitness of their Belgian characters because they were focusing on a larger market abroad. They would rather not figure a Belgian hero but locate their protagonists in other countries—primarily France (Michel Vaillant, Ric Hochet, Gil Jourdan) and, to a lesser extent, the UK (Blake et Mortimer) or the USA (Buck Danny, Jerry Spring, Lucky Luke).

Moreover, Flemish strips sometimes explicitly capitalized on controversial political issues. Authors such as Marc Sleen, Bob De Moor, and Willy Vandersteen, for example, took the side of king Leopold III on the Royal Question that divided the country after the Liberation. Such explicit political stands were unthinkable in the postwar *Tintin* and *Spirou* stories because, for a small region like French-speaking Belgium, it was quite a challenge to get a foothold in France, which in 1949 was even trying to protect its own comics production by means of legislation, though under the pretext of protecting public morals.[5] Most French-speaking Belgian authors and publishers adapted to this situation, but they also captured a considerable share of the market in just a few decades. Unlike their French-speaking counterparts, the Flemish comics publishers exported hardly anything—a major exception were the more than 900 German *Bessy* books that the Studio Vandersteen produced for the German market between 1965 and 1985. While the majority of Flemish comics are read within the boundaries of their own region, French-language publishers like Dupuis, Lombard, and Casterman have for decades exported the bulk of their production. Yet thanks to this regional orientation, the Flemish authors who published in the newspapers could allow themselves a little more leeway in terms of content. In relation to the Dutch comics of the Netherlands and in relation to the Francophone comics in Belgium, Flemish comics occupied a particular place in the decades after WWII.

---

5   Cf. Martens 1988: 34; Morgan 2003: 145.

Popular Flemish Genres

The succesful postwar Flemish series were mostly built around a limited group of recurring protagonists that often gave their name to the title of the series. Various types of comics could be produced in the dual system. Except for some 'realistic' adventure series, like the western series *Bessy* (1952–1997) or the knight series *De Rode Ridder* (1959–), the most successful genre in Flanders was the crossover of adventure story and humoristic 'family' narrative drawn in a rather loose, comical style.[6] The direct inspiration for such an approach came from the popular French-language comic *Tintin*, which was, in turn, inspired by the French Alain Saint-Ogan's *Zig et Puce* (1925–1954). Examples of the Flemish humorous adventure comics are Willy Vandersteen's *Suske en Wiske* (1945–), Marc Sleen's *Nero* (1947–2002), Pom's *Piet Pienter en Bert Bibber* (1951–1995), Jef Nys's *Jommeke* (1955–), and Merho's *Kiekeboe* (1977–).

To varying degrees, all of these series cultivate a paradoxical stance toward adventure. In the *Encyclopedia of Adventure Fiction*, Don D'Ammassa defines adventure as

> an event or series of events that happens outside the course of the protagonist's ordinary life, usually accompanied by danger, often by physical action. Adventure stories almost always move quickly, and the pace of the plot is at least as important as characterization, setting and other elements of a creative work. (2008: vii–viii)

Adventure is undeniably a popular feature in various media (literature, film, television series, games, comics), but as an object of study, it has been mostly neglected by academics.[7] The adventure hero was, for instance, an important vector for the colonial and masculine values of the nineteenth century. This particular type of hero still thrived in the twentieth century; think of heroes such as Tarzan or Superman. The adventure story in itself can span various (sub)genres or take on the form of a crossover with other genres like comedy.[8]

Though every Flemish comics series has certain idiosyncratic aspects, they also share various features. For starters, they are all produced in a more or less similar way (first daily publication of two tiers in the newspapers, then collection in an album). In the 1950s, Flemish comics were still dominantly published in monochrome. The number of pages of each story was not completely fixed yet; page variation ranged from 40 to

---

6   Family has to be taken in a broad sense because it mainly concerns a group of more or less loosely related characters.
7   Exceptions are Bellet 1985; Burgess Green 1991; Letourneux 2010.
8   A forerunner of the crossover humoristic adventure story is Miguel de Cervantes's *Don Quixote*, which parodies the chivalric novels of the Middle Ages.

64. All these series were drawn in a round, slightly caricatured and vivid style. The main characters are clearly identified as Flemish and contemporary, though friends from other places or times can join the core team. Though male characters are dominant, female characters are also recurring and can play prominent roles. Examples are the girl Wiske and her aunt Sidonie in *Suske en Wiske*, the girl Petatje and her adoptive mother Madam Pheip in *Nero*, and the young woman Susan in *Piet Pienter en Bert Bibber*. Furthermore, the male characters are seldom heroes in the classical sense; many of them are not very bright and are quite impulsive. On top of that, a character like the big-bellied Nero is quite lazy and sometimes even very egotistical. Wiske is a rather clever and nosy, but also sanguineous and hot-tempered girl. Usually, these characters have a friend who counterbalances their personality. Van Zwam, Nero's friend, is a very clever detective; Suske is a courageous boy and emotionally more stable than Wiske, his adoptive sister.

As is usually the case in the adventure genre, the protagonists of these series often travel to other countries, fictive or not, using inventions such as the Gyronef (professor Barabas's jet helicopter) in *Suske en Wiske*, professor Adhemar's open cockpit rocket(s) in *Nero*, or professor Gobelijn's flying sphere in *Jommeke*. Suske and Wiske even travel in time thanks to professor Barabas's time machine, likely inspired by Vincent Trout Hamlin's newspaper comic strip *Alley Oop* (1933–). These voyages allow for compelling narrative variations and keep the stories moving forward, which is necessary because all of these series consist of many albums: more than 200 albums of *Nero* and of *Jommeke*, and more than 250 of *Suske en Wiske*.

Having drawn the main contours of these various Flemish series, I will now concentrate on one particularly rich example: the *Suske en Wiske* series of the 1950s and 1960s, when Vandersteen was the main author of the series. *Suske en Wiske* was the most lucrative series throughout the Low Countries for many decades. While it shares general similarities with other Flemish series, is it also different in ways that I shall discuss in the following.

The Paradoxical Adventure

The basic narrative structure of a *Suske en Wiske* story is quite similar to most adventure stories. The classical three-act structure underpins the comic (even if there are no explicit breaks between acts); the character's story is revealed in a straight line, time frame, or cycle. The three-act structure is a common device proposed in most scriptwriting handbooks.[9] The first act involves the set-up (who, what, where, when, why) and the inciting incident that will prompt the story and will define the challenge for the protagonists (their dramatic goal)—what Paul Wells calls the "premise" (2007: 99). In contrast to a one-shot, a series such as *Suske en Wiske* does not need to introduce the main recurring characters in every new segment. The reader is supposed to know the main characters from previous stories. Furthermore, in a humoristic adventure story, the characters are strongly typified, so that their basic traits are immediately apparent. But their stereotypical makeup is also their dramatic weakness: they are generally rather predictable. Vandersteen tries to obtain variation by introducing new, though still stereotypical, characters. Some of these new characters, like Lambik and Jerom, perform in almost every story and become part of the 'core family.' Other characters, like Arthur, Theofiel, or Krimson, only appear in some stories.

Additional features of the adventure genre's basic narrative structure can be found in *Suske en Wiske*. A recurring challenge for the protagonists is the securing of an important feature (an invention/a particular material/a magic formula) from abuse by the antagonist. While the opening sequence is usually located at home, the following scenes can bring the characters to the most different locations (foreign countries, fictive or not) and other time periods (thanks to professor Barabas's time machine). In the following sequences (the second act), the protagonists try to solve the (re)defined problem, but they are confronted with (expected and unexpected) complications and setbacks, which the antagonist provokes to varying degrees. Often, luck favors the protagonists, sometimes to a degree that is not very convincing, but we are clearly not in a completely realistic context anyway. In the last sequences (the third act), the final confrontation between protagonist and antagonist is played out, the remaining mysteries are revealed, the problem is solved, and the antagonist is disabled or converted—sometimes with the help of a deus ex machina.

However, particular stories of *Suske en Wiske* contain more than this general and conventional narrative development of the adventure story. Indeed, the action is often interrupted by funny situations or events that have little to do with the main storyline. Based on the space and the intensity that these humoristic digressions receive, it is evident that they are as important as the dramatic development itself. There is a continuous switch between the rather serious elements (linked to the adventure) and the funny, farcical elements. By and large, *Suske en Wiske* balances

---

9 Cf. Root 1979: 11; Dancyger 2001: 43; Field 2005: 89.

adventure and humor, which are almost like two sides of the same coin. Moreover, such genre-mixing is achieved through references to the external world. Especially at the end of a story, some kind of explicit ethicial position is sometimes presented in reference to the real world. Usually it is done in humorous fashion, but it can be deadly serious, as in *De dulle Griet (Mad Meg)*, where a well-known character from a Brueghel painting is brought to life to find out why people wage wars. The story ends on a sarcastic note with a crying Vietnamese girl under a barrage of bombs, followed by Wiske, who normally winks cheerfully at the reader, now hiding her face in her hands. This is not the classic happy ending to be expected in the series. The state of the world has become too serious, and there seem to be none of the simple kind of solutions a comic strip would normally provide.

Character Profiles

Regarding character profiles, the adventure genre favors particular types. Yet again, in a crossover series such as *Suske en Wiske*, transgressions from these types are crucial. Adventure stories are notorious for their 'masculine' heroes, even if they are of the female sex like Lara Croft.[10] The use of violence by the masculine protagonist is almost conventional, though the protagonist does not use violence offensively, but rather defensively. By contrast, the protagonists and title characters in *Suske en Wiske* are two children (of no precise age; their ages vary in the series between 7 and 14 years), and the adults around them are not typical masculine or femine types. Sidonie is a tall, skinny, flat-chested woman, and Lambik is a rather fat, lazy, impulsive, stupid character. Even Jerom, another friend with a well-defined body, does not look like the typical American (super)hero. In his first appearances, he is dressed in animal skin, can only speak in a very simplified language, and drinks buckets of beer. Moreover, this character shares a house with Lambik; two unrelated men living together was not exactly a common occurence in 1950s Flanders. Remarkably, adult men living together can be found in many comics of that time; think, for instance, of Tintin, Haddock, and Tournesol sharing the castle of Molinsart.

Both children, Suske and Wiske, are presented as aunt Sidonie's adopted kids. The reason for using these kinds of surrogate families is, of course, that real parents would never allow their children to become involved in such adventures and would rather emphasize their

---

10 See Jansz and Martis 2007.

performance in school. So Suske and Wiske are like mini-adults with childlike traits; they never have to go to school, and they drive a wide variety of vehicles without a driver's licence. But they sometimes behave in a genuinely childish way (e.g., Wiske's close bond with her doll). Characters may express emotions, but they do not behave like real people. Through the presence of some adults, such as aunt Sidonie and friend Lambik, the reader is made to forget that these adults are not the children's actual parents. In addition, the children themselves never think or talk about these actual parents.

Temporal Particularities

Within a comics series, separate stories can form an overarching unity in various ways. The *Suske en Wiske* series is a typical example of what Umberto Eco calls "loop series" (1990: 86): every new story marks a new beginning without much connection with stories before or after. The temporal particularities like those of the loop series are not specific to the *Suske en Wiske* series, but they form an important characteristic of many comics series. The structure of the loop series has many consequences for *Suske en Wiske*. Every new story can be considered a fresh start in a game. The range of possibilities of the characters are known and limited; only the situation (another conflict) seems different. The reset at the start of a new story also enables the characters to always remain the same age. It further involves some kind of memory loss because even after having experienced scores of examples of rather magical phenomena, they still meet new fantastic elements with disbelief. Furthermore, the characters seem to be disconnected from their environment: while everything (cars, furniture, etc.) is changing around them according to the evolution in the real world, they themselves do not age.[11] A normal childhood would be much too short to experience all these adventures. What is more, all of the characters seem quite indestructible, or they must have enormous quantities of good luck. An explosion tears only their cloths to tatters. They may swoon, but they always recuperate quickly and never suffer severe consequences. The humoristic context makes these improbalities acceptable for the reader.

The Italian narratologist Daniel Barbieri has proposed the concept of "interdiegetic time" (1992: 56) for the totality of all the stories combined in a series. In various comics, this interdiegetic time is paradoxical and inconsistent. While every separate story may be quite coherent in itself,

---

11 Cf. Fresnault-Deruelle 1977: 78.

taken together, all the stories do not form one coherent story arc. For Barbieri, the stronger every separate story in a series is, the weaker the interdiegetic bonds are between the stories of a series.[12] There is no planned development of the characters over many stories in *Suske en Wiske*. There are only weak relations or brief developments that carry from one story to another. For instance, in *De Stemmenrover*, Lambik receives a talisman that becomes very handy in two following stories, *Het Taterende Testament* en *De Zonnige Zageman*. Within the adventure genre, different types of serial stories are possible, of course. In *XIII* (Vance and Van Hamme, 1984–) or The *L'Incal* series (Moebius and Jodorowsky, 1981–1989), for example, we encounter a series that forms a much stronger interdiegetic unity than *Suske en Wiske*. In these series, every installment is part of an ongoing, coherent story.

Specific Narrative Strategies

As in most comics, the text boxes in *Suske en Wiske* are usually filled by an extradiegetic, heterodiegetic, and unidentified narratorial voice that collaborates with the visual storytelling.[13] For instance, when the narratorial voice speaks of a mysterious, unknown character, the face of the person is kept in the *hors champ* (by framing the face outside the panel border, by obscuring the face). As is often the case, the narratorial voice does not only deliver information about time and location but also builds bridges between two sequences, verbally compressing events that are less interesting to show visually. Furthermore, the text in the boxes can present story information of which both protagonists and readers are unaware because it is outside their field of vision: "Wiske is going upstairs, when somebody downstairs kills the light" (Vandersteen 1996: 46).[14] The narratorial voice sometimes also announces events that will happen in the near future in order to make a situation more dramatic: "Aunt Sidonie could not presume that the opportunity would soon arise in tragic circumstances" (Vandersteen 1996: 113).[15]

What is more, the information that the reader of *Suske en Wiske* receives from the narratorial voice is sometimes ambiguous (open to

---

12 Cf. Barbieri 1992: 68.
13 The narratorial voice only rarely identifies itself explicitly as that of Willy Vandersteen, the comics artist himself. On questions of narrative perspective and the functions of narrators in graphic narratives, see also Jan-Noël Thon's contribution in this volume.
14 My translation from the Dutch: "Wiske begeeft zich naar de bovenverdieping, als plots beneden iemand het licht uitknipt!"
15 My translation from the Dutch: "Tante Sidonie kon niet vermoeden dat de gelegenheid zich weldra onder tragische omstandigheden zou voordoen."

contrasting interpretations) or even deliberately misleading. For the sake of tension, it may leave important elements out, and, while usually quite omniscient, it also seems to be unaware of various story elements (like the identity of the mysterious character). Furthermore, it sometimes reacts to what a character has said in a previous panel—"But... That is not so easy!" (Vandersteen 1996: 42)—or raises doubts—"...if everything works out" (Vandersteen 1996: 27). As Mikkonen rightly concludes in another case study, "narrative agency in graphic storytelling is not only a composite of different semiotic sources or channels, but necessarily variable and morphic in its use of these sources" (2015: 12).

Given *Suske en Wiske*'s humoristic and often fantastic contexts, the reader may not approach the series with a set of realist expectations. This is important because in such narratives, impossible things can happen: a character may be running across the ceiling out of pure joy. If readers want to enjoy the comic, they will have to accept such illogical events as part of the make-believe game.[16] Moreover, in many stories, Vandersteen includes explicit self-reflexive or metaleptic elements for humoristic purposes.[17] In some cases, a character seems well aware of its fictional status as a drawing. For instance, Lambik erases his small stick with a piece of gum and draws himself a much bigger stick to fight with. Such autoreferential humor recurs in various stories. It is safe to say that such strategies are intended to raise the reader's awareness of the fictional status of what he or she is reading. Of course, the reader is reminded of the artifice of the narrative by additional elements as well, for instance, by the style of the images (simplified drawings) and the plot (fantastic events). Such explicit self-reflexive and autoreferential references are, however, atypical of the more 'serious' adventure genre.

Nevertheless, the (fictional) storyworld presented in *Suske en Wiske* still corresponds largely to the (actual) world we live in, as most physical laws remain valid. One character running across the ceiling does not necessarily mean that the law of gravity no longer exists in the diegetic world (after all, the other characters are still standing on the floor). The infringements of narrative plausibility are thus rather selective and short; they never risk undermining the overall credibility of the diegetic world. For Vandersteen, this mix of fantasy and realism is crucial. Without the grounding in realism, the comic's conscious ventures into fantasy would be much less visible and understandable, while a completely fantastical storyworld in which everything at every moment is unpredictable or unlikely would most likely have confused the regular readers of the series.

---

16 On mimesis as make-believe, see Walton 1990.
17 See also Groensteen 1990.

Conclusion

As I have argued previously, a publication format is not only defined by its material aspects (size, paper quality, etc.) but also by its temporal (daily, weekly, monthly, one-shot) and editorial parameters (length of an episode, regulations regarding content or the public).[18] Each publication format contains an aesthetic system with a set of norms that offers a bounded set of alternatives to the individual creator of comics. In Flanders, two different publication formats (daily and book series) became intertwined. Other countries have developed dual or multiple publication systems, and various interactions of publication formats are possible—a continuous soap such as *Les Autres Gens* (2010–2012) is first published daily on the Internet but afterwards collected in a typical French album series (2011–2013)—, but the Flemish dual tradition is an important example of a quite developed and successful system (especially within Flanders, because Flemish series were usually not widely distributed).

My case study of the crossover genre of humoristic adventure within the Flemish dual system has shown that although there is no strict narrative formula that determines every story of *Suske en Wiske* in the 1950s and 1960s, a number of recurring dominant techniques were nevertheless present. The publication format of the album series (of 220 tiers) together with the daily installments (of two tiers) in a newspaper influenced the total concept of the series. Every story had to be told in 220 tiers of the same format because every page in an album consisted of four equal tiers. Furthermore, a publication in short installments of only two tiers needed efficient use of that limited space: an efficient way of storytelling. The stories were told in quite a linear, chronological way, and they were interlaced with flashbacks only occasionally. The internal timing of the stories was generally independent of the external time, but occasionally references to the external time occur, most likely because publication on a daily basis offered the unique possibility of commenting on the news of the day. A quite omniscient narratorial voice helped to condense the information and led the reader from one scene to another, but this seemingly trustworthy narrator could also be ambiguous or misleading. Every short installment was destined to arouse the reader sufficiently, be it by humor, by suspense, or a combination of both. The *Suske en Wiske* series, then, can be understood as a prime example of the art of balancing the rather anarchaïc farce and the rigid makeup of the adventurous story. The crossover genre of the humoristic adventure lent itself extremely well to these story structures and publication formats.

---

18 See Lefèvre 2000.

Works Cited

Barbieri, Daniele (1992). *Tempo, immagine, ritmo e racconto: Per una semiotica della temporalità nel testo a fumetti*. Bologna: Università degli studi di Bologna. Print.
Bellet, Roger (1985). *L'Aventure dans la littérature populaire au XIXe siècle*. Lyon: PU de Lyon. Print.
Burgess Green, Martin (1991). *Seven Types of Adventure Tale: An Etiology of a Major Genre*. University Park: Pennsylvania State UP. Print.
D'Ammassa, Don (2008). *Encyclopedia of Adventure Fiction*. New York: Facts on File. Print.
Dancyger, Ken (2001). *Global Scriptwriting*. Boston: Focal. Print.
Eco, Umberto (1990). *The Limits of Interpretation*. Bloomington: Indiana UP. Print.
Field, Syd (2005). *Screenplay: The Foundations of Screenwriting*. New York: Delta. Print.
Fresnault-Deruelle, Pierre (1977). *Récits et discours par la bande: Essais sur les comics*. Paris: Hachette. Print.
Groensteen, Thierry (1990). "Bandes désignées (De la réflexivité dans les bandes dessinées)." *Contrebandes* 13–14: 132–65. Print.
Jansz, Jeroen, and Raynel G. Martis (2007). "The Lara Phenomenon: Powerful Female Characters in Video Games." *Sex Roles* 56.3–4: 141–48. Print.
Kousemaker, Evelyn, and Kees Kousemaker (1979). *Wordt Vervolgd, Stripleksikon der Lage Landen*. Utrecht: Spectrum. Print.
Lefèvre, Pascal (1995). "Fifty Years of Bob and Bobette." *The Low Countries 1995–96*. Rekkem: Stichting Ons Erfdeel. 46–52. Print.
— (2000). "The Importance of Being Published: A Comparative Study of Comics Formats." Anne Magnussen and Hans-Christian Christiansen (eds.). *Comics & Culture: Analytical and Theoretical Approaches to Comics*. Copenhagen: Museum Tusculanum P. 91–105. Print.
— (2003). *Willy Vandersteens* Suske en Wiske *in de krant (1945–1971): Een theoretisch kader voor een vormelijke analyse van strips*. Leuven: KU Leuven. Print.
— (2006). "The Battle Over the Balloon: The Conflictual Institutionalization of the Speech Balloon in Various Countries." *Image (&) Narrative* 14: n.p. Web.
— (2011). "Some Medium-Specific Qualities of Graphic Sequences." Jared Gardner and David Herman (eds.). *Graphic Narratives and Narrative Theory*. Special issue of *SubStance* 40.1: 14–33. Print.
Letourneux, Matthieu (2010). *Le roman d'aventures 1870–1930*. Limoges: PULIM. Print.

Martens, Thierry (1988). *Le journal de Spirou: 1938–1988, cinquante ans d'histoire(s)*. Charleroi: Dupuis. Print.

Mikkonen, Kai (2015). "Narrative Agency in Comics." Forthcoming. Manuscript kindly made available by the author. 1–26. Print.

Morgan, Harry (2003). "Répliques." *9e Art* 8: 140–45. Print.

Root, Wells (1979). *Writing the Script: A Practical Guide for Films and Television*. New York: Holt, Rinehart and Winston. Print.

Vandersteen, Willy (1996). *De avonturen van Suske en Wiske: De Straatridder*. Originally published in the daily *De Standaard* from July 2, 1955, to Nov. 14, 1955, and first published as an album in 1956 by Standaard Boekhandel. Antwerpen: Standaard Uitgeverij. Print.

Walton, Kendall L. (1990). *Mimesis as Make-Believe: On the Foundations of the Representational Arts*. Cambridge: Harvard UP. Print.

Wells, Paul (2007). *Basics Animation: Scriptwriting*. Lausanne: Ava. Print.

CHRISTINA MEYER
(Hannover)

Un/Taming the Beast, or Graphic Novels (Re)Considered

When I began to work on this chapter, I asked myself, what exactly are graphic novels (for I did not quite know what to do with this label)? And how do graphic novels, compared to 'non-graphic' and 'non-novelistic' texts, such as newspaper comic strips, comic books, or nonfictional graphic narratives, narrate and convey meaning?[1] While the first question points to taxonomic and terminological problems that have been raised by a number of scholars in comics studies and, on a larger scale, have kept literary and cultural theorists busy, the second question draws attention to an aspect that has not yet gained much attention: the *narrativity* of comics. As Henry John Pratt has recently pointed out: "[C]ommentators on comics assert that narrativity is one of the defining characteristics of the medium [..., and] I think it is plausible to assume that comics is a predominantly narrative medium" (2009a: 107). Hence, "[i]t is curious [...] that the topic of narrative in comics is so unexplored" (Pratt 2009a: 107).[2]

Taking seriously Pratt's claim about the narrativity of comics, this chapter investigates *principles of storytelling* in one particular branch of the comics medium: texts commonly labeled graphic novels. The aim is to give a (preliminary) answer to the question of how these texts narrate and generate meaning.[3] Mike Carey and Peter Gross's *The Unwritten*, published by the DC imprint Vertigo, will serve as a case study for this

---

1   The term 'comic book' is inaccurate. Comic books were not published in book format but were printed on 'raunchy' paper, their pages stapled together in tabloid-sized magazine form. They were sold at newsstands and drug stores, whereas graphic novels are typically sold in book stores and/or comic stores. Cf. Gravett 2005: 36; Hatfield 2005: 8; Wandtke 2012: 16–17.
2   In their introduction to the special issue of *SubStance*, Gardner and Herman note that the contributors were asked to bring into their reading of graphic novels theories and methodologies from narratology in order to "pose challenges to existing models of story" (2011: 3). Though none of the contributions in this collection deals directly with the issues I discuss here, they served as rewarding background readings for this chapter.
3   Cf. Pratt 2009a: 108.

investigation.[4] *The Unwritten* is especially suitable for narratological analysis because it plays off against each other different genre conventions and storytelling practices in order to reflect on its own status as an—unfinished—intertextual and intermedial narrative, on its graphic form, and on its comics-specific visual/verbal means of representation.

One purpose of this chapter is to examine the diverse *patterns of narrativity*—i.e., *The Unwritten*'s serial structure, its aesthetic complexity, its (interweaving) narrative strands, or story-layers, and its multiple levels of narration. In my analysis of these patterns, I draw particular attention to the ways in which *generic promptings* are inscribed in *The Unwritten*. This includes paratextual cues such as prefaces, acknowledgments, introductions, appendices; contextual cues such as publisher and artist(s) information; and formulaic, oftentimes clichéd, story and plot cues. The question is: what is the use of charting the varying functions and effects of such promptings, and in how far can a close reading of one text further our understanding of central storytelling principles in graphic novels? Generic promptings can, after all, be found in all kinds of texts. This chapter assumes that graphic novels are *forms* of storytelling that are particularly prone to speak about themselves and to themselves through generic promptings. What this chapter will argue, then, is that the production and interpretation of narrative in *The Unwritten* and, on a larger scale, in graphic novels, is not so much (or not only) dependent on the complex *interplay* of words and images, but rather on generic promptings *in* the text.

Research on the narrativity of comics in general, and on the narrativity of graphic novels in particular, has not paid sufficient attention to the functionality and dynamics of generic promptings. Therefore, the second purpose of this chapter is to bring forward an additional perspective on reading and understanding graphic novels. Spanning a complex web of generic promptings that activates *and* breaks reader expectations and, while doing so, develops its own theory about its generic status, history, and form, Carey and Gross's *The Unwritten* provides a particularly interesting case study. The enigmatic character named Mr. Pullman takes

---

4   British (script)writer Carey has worked on Marvel's *X-Men* and *Ultimate Fantastic Four*, as well as DC/Vertigo's *Hellblazer*. American artist Peter Gross has self-published a series titled *Empire Lanes* and created *The Books of Magic* (DC/Vertigo). For more information on Gross and Carey, see Allison 1987; Ekstrom 2009. Carey and Gross have also won praise for their co-authored series *Lucifer* (DC/Vertigo), a Neil Gaiman's *Sandman*-related spin-off. While Carey and Gross are the key artists responsible for script, story, and art, additional artists are involved in the production of this project, each of whom adds further visual styles to the graphic novel. One name that runs through the series is Yuko Shimizu, the Japanese artist who draws the cover art for *The Unwritten*. For more information on Shimizu's artwork and professional life, see her website *yukoart.com*.

on a special function, frustrating reading expectations based on clear-cut genre categories. At one point in *The Unwritten*, he serves to cut through or, onomatopoetically speaking, to "skutchhhhhh" (Carey and Gross 2010a: n.p.) genre conventions. To borrow from Karin Kukkonen's work on Vertigo's series *Fables*,[5] "self-reflexive of its textual traditions and conventions" (2010: 22) as *The Unwritten* is, it not only reflects back on itself as narrative but also on traditions of the comics medium (topoi, formulaic elements, iconic characters), the history of the American comics industry (especially the early days), and the ways in which the comics medium has been perceived and redefined throughout the years.[6]

Significantly, I do not consider graphic novels to be a genre but rather as *forms* of comics storytelling just as comic books are not a particular genre in the comics medium but rather constitute forms of storytelling printed in a specific format and delivered through a specific carrier medium. After all, graphic novels are not confined to one format, even though they usually follow the standard comic book size of 17 x 26 cm (6 ⅝ × 10 ¼ inches). Nor are they limited to one carrier medium. Whatever topic graphic novel artists may choose, and there are really no limits, they may use different modes of narrative, such as auto-/biography, satire, parody, pastiche, to name but a few, just as they may draw on recognizable genre traditions (from literature, film, comics, etc.) in order to either maintain or deconstruct them. Frequently, graphic novels are originally published as series of magazine issues, then collected in trade paperbacks, and sometimes later reprinted in so-called deluxe editions.[7] As such, graphic novels follow a logic of serial storytelling and serial publication similar to the serialized novels of the nineteenth century, which prior to book publication were printed serially in periodicals, newspapers, and magazines.[8] The material production of graphic novels can involve anything from "entirely digitally created art" to basic pencil drawings and from the use of simple ink as well as "collage and acrylic [...] to photography and Mac manipulation" (Round 2010: 16–17).

---

5   *Fables* is a Vertigo series that started in 2002. Zolkover 2008 offers a wonderful reading of Willingham's *Fables*. See also Kukkonen 2010.
6   Graphic novels owe this self-referential mode of representation to the early American newspaper comics of the late nineteenth century and the opening decades of the twentieth century, many of which self-consciously reflect on their own status as a narrative construct, their place within the Sunday colored supplement, and the artists' roles in making the respective comics (cf. Inge 1991: 2–4). This is not the place to elaborate on this issue, but I will do so in a larger work now in progress.
7   Throughout this chapter, I will also use the term 'text' to describe *The Unwritten*. My understanding of the concept of text is based on semiotics—hence: graphic novels are sign systems (in the vast arena of sign systems out there) that generate meaning by means of particular textual cues/signs inscribed in them.
8   See Lund 1993; Meyer and Bonk 2013.

The Unmaking of Graphic Novels

Definitions of graphic novels are not hard to come by, even though they tend to differ in tone and highlight different aspects.[9] In what follows, I will not simply list probable definitions of graphic novels in order to place *The Unwritten* into existing classifications. My discussion of varying definitional efforts is intended to demonstrate how comics criticism has participated in popularizing certain views of the graphic novel. I further argue that looking at contemporary graphic novels like *The Unwritten*, which develop their own theories about their generic status, will allow us to arrive at a better understanding of the aesthetics and discursive structures of contemporary graphic novels.

As Derek Parker Royal has recently asked, "Does this name [graphic novel] provide more gravitas to the medium, or is it merely a critical (and commercial) affectation? Is 'novel' a useful word to apply to long-form comics, or does the imposition of terminology from textual fiction delegitimize the unique project of comics as a medium?" (2011: 162). In other words: is the label a misnomer, or does it, as David Coughlan argues, "at least highlight comics' capacity for visual narration, for storytelling that partakes of both *mimesis* and *diegesis*, or showing and telling?" (2006: 834, original emphases).

Academics frequently ask such questions. A prominent example is Hillary Chute and Marianne DeKoven's (2006) introductory essay to their special issue of *Modern Fiction Studies*. Here, the authors propose the use of the broader term 'graphic narrative' instead of 'graphic novel' (warning of its potentially misleading connotation) in order to stress the—visual and verbal—"work of narration" (Chute and DeKoven 2006: 767) in the comics medium, a medium they consider to be literary more than anything else.[10] For Stephen Tabachnick, however, "[t]he graphic novel is an *extended* comic book, written *by adults for adults*" (2010: 3, emphases added). Tabachnick holds that this extended comic book "treats *important content* in a *serious artistic way* and makes use of high *quality paper* and production techniques not available to the creators of the Sunday comics and traditional comic books" (2010: 3, emphases added). While Tabachnick attempts to frame (the newness of) graphic novels by creating medial allegiances to previous forms of storytelling (comic book and newspaper comics), stressing the role of specific audiences, recognizing particular types of content, and noting their high production values, Charles Hatfield (2005: 5) grasps these forms of storytelling by 'unframing' them:

---

9   See Cohn 2005; Meskin 2007.
10 See also Chute 2008.

> Only recently (especially since 2000) have graphic novels [...] begun to reach bookstores more regularly. Despite this, the term 'graphic novel' has become common parlance—a curious thing, as few of the volumes so christened aspire to be anything like novels in terms of structure, breadth, or coherence. Indeed a graphic novel can be almost anything: a novel, a collection of interrelated or thematically similar stories, a memoir, a travelogue or journal, a history, a series of vignettes or lyrical observations, an episode from a longer work—you name it.

As Hatfield further suggests, it is "[p]erhaps this very *plasticity* [that] helps explain the currency of the term" (2005: 5, emphasis added).[11]

Quite obviously, the term 'graphic novel' encourages (a set of) expectations.[12] Whereas 'graphic' seems unproblematic, alluding to the huge variety of styles and modes of expression that artists use and combine (or play off against each other), the second half of the term, 'novel,' proves more difficult. According to Paul Gravett, "[t]he term novel can make people expect the sort of format, serious intent, and weighty heft of traditional literature, as if a graphic novel must be the visual equivalent of 'an extended, fictional work'" (2005: 8).

Considering the potential pre-history of the comics medium,[13] it seems safe to say that no matter *where* I start or from which perspective I look at graphic novels, and no matter *how* I begin to answer the question of *what*, narratologically speaking, graphic novels are (by establishing, for example, semiotic analogies to other media or alliances to other forms of narration within the comics medium), I will most likely fail to provide a satisfying definition.[14] While I do not shy away from saying what I think graphic novels may be—heterogeneous forms of visual-verbal storytelling in the comics medium with a (not necessarily sequentially, coherently arranged) mise-en-page and a (not necessarily cohesive) plot structure, published either digitally or in glossy print-form, and made of more than the 32 interior pages of comic books—I also think that such definitions do not take us far enough. Media scholar Jason Mittell, to whom I owe my approach to genre theory, asserts: there is a "tradition [in genre theory that] poses questions of definition, looking to identify the core elements that constitute a given genre by examining texts so as to delimit the formal mechanisms constituting the essence of that genre" (2001: 4–5).

11　Gravett states that "graphic novels are not limited to one genre category" (2005: 8). They "need not be in book form. They can exist as uncompiled part works, serials in magazines and papers, even in unpublished manuscripts" (Gravett 2005: 9).
12　Cf. also Hatfield 2005: 5.
13　Meneses links graphic novels to the newspaper comics of the late nineteenth and early twentieth centuries and regards these "as a direct predecessor of the graphic novel for reasons concerning format, code, scope, and popular response: political, social, and individual issues were discussed and satirized, usually in one-page format, in periodical editions such as *Punch* magazine" (2008: 598).
14　On this terminological controversy, cf. also Stein, Meyer, and Edlich 2011: 517.

As Hatfield warns us, however, to simply put such labels as 'comic book' and 'graphic novel' aside, as if they were non-existent or of no relevance, means to go through the (academic) world with blinders on, and to disregard the historicity of these terms.[15] Given the fact that the term 'graphic novel' has been in use now for more than fifty years, it might be useful to look into how the label has operated within and beyond a given text, and how its value and meaning has shifted.[16] If we take a look at *The Unwritten*, for example, the label 'graphic novel' is excluded from paratextual enunciations, such as cover pages, promotional praise, foreword, and introduction. This is both interesting and telling. The effacement of these two words from the cover and from the inside paratexts seems to result from a conscious strategy of avoiding any kind of expectations that the term might encourage. Such reluctance to employ the term is quite contrary to its appearance on the dust jackets, on inside title pages, and in introductions to texts like Joe Orlando and Len Wein's *The Sinister House of Secret Love* #2 (1972—a "Graphic Novel of Gothic Terror," as the cover page tells us), George Metzger's 48-page collection of serialized strips *Beyond Time and Again* (1976[17]; subtitled "A Graphic Novel" on the inside title page), Will Eisner's *A Contract with God and Other Tenement Stories* (1978), Jack Katz's *First Kingdom* (1974–1977, reissued by Century Comics in 2005), and Richard Corben's *Bloodstar* (1979).

This discrepancy indicates a shift of meaning and value of the term 'graphic novel.' If we look back to the 1960s and 1970s, its introduction and proliferation in magazines and fanzines and eventually on the works' covers themselves certainly helped to bring a fresh view into the field of comics, freeing them from the demonized status they had been given through the public as well as scholarly debates in the first half of the twentieth century. Once the label was placed on the cover of a comic or cropped up in blurbs and other promotional texts, that work was automatically elevated to a 'higher,' more literary, or novelistic, level and was thus ascribed particular cultural value. This, however, primarily tells us something about the discursive formation of the label through its repetitive use by diverse agents ranging from critics and fans to publishers and through its appearance within the comics themselves, in articles, or in promotions. It is also indicative of the specific socio-historical moment when the term 'graphic novel' was popularized by scholars, fans, and critics, rather than of the quality or nature of the form itself.

During the 1980s and 1990s, we saw a growth of publications labeled graphic novels: Art Spiegelman's highly acclaimed *Maus* (1986, 1991);

---

15 Cf. Hatfield 2005: 6.
16 On the 'origins' of the term, cf. Gravett 2005: 8.
17 Metzger's strips had previously been serialized in underground papers from 1967 to 1972.

Marvel's 1980s version of *Daredevil* (with Frank Miller's entrance to the production of the series); the multi-authored, long-lasting *The Saga of the Swamp Thing* series (1982–2004); Frank Miller's *Batman: The Dark Night Returns* (1986); and Alan Moore and Dave Gibbons's *Watchmen* series (1986–1987).[18] Moreover, the label had its first peak in public and scholarly discussions in the final decade of the twentieth century. There are reasons as to why these two developments occurred at approximately the same time. Jared Gardner observes that "the contemporary graphic novel came of age in the late 1980s and 1990s in America at precisely the same time as the rise of the personal computer" (2006: 802). According to Gardner, this was "no coincidence. Suddenly, the need to be able to read and navigate sequential text/image fields is more pressing (and less culturally devalued) than at any time in modern history" (2006: 802). Gardner emphasizes the relation between graphic novels and new media devices, and thus the relation between these forms of storytelling to new ways of perceiving and understanding the world around us. I would point to two further reasons: the previously analog fan cultures of the 1960s and 1970s went digital in the 1990s, and digitization helped to spread and intensify the discussions surrounding the graphic novel phenomenon. Furthermore, the advent of the direct sales system in the 1970s did not only change the distribution system and the infrastructure of the production, dissemination, and consumption of comics at large, but it also had an impact on the aesthetics of graphic novels: on the ways stories were told, arranged, and implicitly or explicitly interwoven with other stories from other graphic novel series.[19]

In this respect, it might be more useful to analyze the 'generic practices'[20] that have evolved around a given text in scholarly as well as in public debates (for instance, in the blogosphere). As Mittell points out in a different context, "genres are cultural categories that surpass the boundaries of media texts and operate within industry, audience, and cultural practices as well" (2001: 3). Yet as he succinctly puts it, there is "nothing intrinsic about [a] category itself" (2001: 5).[21] Instead of asking

---

18 Cf. Gravett 2005: 77; Weiner 2010: 6–7.
19 Cf. Kelleter and Stein 2012: 278–79. Weiner (2010: 4–6) discusses the influence of the underground comix on the rise of graphic novels. Uchmanowicz addresses the interest of academics in the term graphic novel: "That the graphic-logo's pivot into the new century appears incumbent upon understanding both its history and form warrants consideration in light of current debates in literary studies about the competing status of the two interpretive positions [i.e., new critics and new historicist] over the past 100 years" (2009: 364).
20 I borrow this term from Mittell 2001: 8.
21 On questions of serial genre development, cf. Kelleter and Stein 2012: 266. Furthermore, see Stein 2014, who discusses the superhero genre evolution and what he calls 'genre economy' in the context of popular seriality.

what graphic novels are, more useful examinations might include such questions as: how has the term 'graphic novel' become a meaningful and useful category, and who were/are the actors in the discourses surrounding this term? How does the label operate within and beyond a given text? What do graphic novels do in comparison to other forms of storytelling? I approach these questions by investigating the paratextual and textual cues inscribed in the respective texts and pinpointing the roles they play in meaning making processes.

Paratextual Cues I

At the center of *The Unwritten* is a character named Tom Taylor, who is the son of a well-known author of fantasy-mystery stories, Wilson Taylor. These stories are built around a boy named Tommy Taylor and his two friends Peter and Sue.[22] Basically, *The Unwritten* is about Tom's quest to find an answer to the question "Who are you?" He comes upon this question during a symposium on the Tommy Taylor stories and its filmic adaptations. In search of his identity, Tom navigates through cities like London and New York, visits different countries, and literally has to walk through literary and pop cultural history. As the story progresses, he becomes more and more entangled with the fictional characters of past centuries.

Carey and Gross began *The Unwritten* in 2009, with monthly magazine issues published by Vertigo, and the series is still ongoing. Six trade paperback volumes, each of which comprises 5–7 magazine issues, have been published up until now. Readers of *The Unwritten* may thus not only buy and read the text in the form of serialized magazine issues but also collect/consume the story as a multi-volume trade paperback. Furthermore, the *comiXology* website (launched in 2007) offers digitalized versions of the magazine issues to be purchased and then used via such devices as iOS, Android, or Fire, or to be read online via any kind of browser on your computer.[23] Such multiple publication complicates matters, for the online versions and the originally printed magazine issues differ from each other (mostly because the advertisements and teaser previews of other Vertigo series have been omitted in the online versions), just as the trade paperbacks are arranged slightly differently. These differences raise questions about (exponentially increasing) readerships,

---

22 I focus on the first trade paperback of *The Unwritten*. Its complete title reads: *The Unwritten: Tommy Taylor and the Bogus Identity*. Occasional remarks on other volumes and magazine issues will complement my analysis.

23 See http://blog.comixology.com/comixology_product_line/.

about means of production and dissemination, and about the aesthetics of *The Unwritten*.

That *The Unwritten* is published by Vertigo is hardly surprising, given the fact that this DC imprint offers greater freedom to comics artists than other—mainstream—publishers. When comics artist David Mack talks about the "niche" that Brian M. Bendis, Mike Oeming, and Mack himself "carve[d] out [...] at Marvel," he addresses an aspect that seems equally important for the collaborative work of Mike Carey and Peter Gross at DC's 'niche' venture Vertigo,[24] namely, that these imprints are "little compartment[s where at least some artists are] given complete autonomy in terms of what we do" (Jenkins 2011: 673). I was unable to ascertain the degree to which Carey and Gross were autonomous in their creation of *The Unwritten*. But by looking at the narrative and visual dynamics of their work, one may say that they certainly probe the limits of representation to an extent that might not have been possible with most other publishers. The implied target audience of *The Unwritten*, as I will show, is comprised of loyal Vertigo consumers, comics fans, literary studies scholars and critics, and any kind of "mature reader."[25]

The Unwritten is a testing ground for intertextual and intermedial citations and allusions, just as it is a postmodern playground for generic deconstructions. Narrative in *The Unwritten* is not simply established through its inter- and metatextuality but, more importantly, by means of a network of generic promptings. Through generic cues inscribed in the text (both verbally and visually), *The Unwritten* offers storytelling principles that other forms of graphic storytelling do not provide.

The functionality of generic cues can be traced on different levels. The cover page is the best place to begin because it represents the reader's first encounter with the comic and is thus the place where generic promptings start to operate. On the cover of the first trade paperback of *The Unwritten*, one finds the publisher's logo (printed on the lower-right side of the front page), a drawing, the artists' names, and, below the volume's complete title, three lines saying that comics artist Bill Willingham, the "Creator of FABLES," wrote the introduction to this volume of *The Unwritten*. Obviously, this name dropping (*Fables*/Willingham) serves as a marketing strategy and a cue to invite those readers who are familiar with (and maybe fans of) the narrative and aesthetics of the *Fables* series to look

---

24 According to DC Comics website, "Vertigo was created in 1993 as a venue for material of an edgier, more sophisticated nature. Many of today's most provocative writers and artists [...] have found a creative home at Vertigo"; cf. also Round 2010: 15–17. Furthermore, see Contino's article (Feb. 2001) on Vertigo's founding editor Karen Berger. Vertigo is now a creator-owned publishing place.

25 This is printed on all the copyright pages of *The Unwritten* and is the 'label' that Vertigo uses on its website.

into, and eventually buy, this new serialized graphic novel. This practice continues inside the first volume of *The Unwritten*.[26] The review quotations on the first two pages of the first trade paperback feature praise by comics artist Brian K. Vaughan, the "Eisner-winning writer of Y: THE LAST MAN," by "Hugo-nominated writer for BBC's Doctor Who" Paul Cornell, and by "Philip K. Dick Award-winning sci-fi novelist" Richard Morgan.[27] By labeling and highlighting the titles and status of selected comics celebrities, *The Unwritten* distinguishes itself from other works while simultaneously capitalizing on the cultural acclaim of previously successful texts.[28] Author names, series titles, and designations such as "Will Eisner award winner" and the like become currencies of their own—or cultural capital—and carve out a particular place for *The Unwritten* in the comics market. Furthermore, such labels simultaneously are cues for readers to classify the text and bring into the reading process acquired knowledge about stories, character constellations, and styles of other Vertigo series as well as other graphic novels. Such processes are prompted by the paratextual insertion on the cover page and the promotional praise inside *The Unwritten*, and they can be traced in fan blog entries as well. One anonymous fan reviewer writes in a piece title "The Unwritten (Comic Review)" (2011: n.p.):

> Ever since it was birthed by *Sandman*, the Vertigo comic line seems to have a fascination with stories about stories. From the modern hit *Fables* (in which fairy tale characters literally live in New York), to more obscure titles like *Testament* (with rebels in a near future dystopia who repeat the mythic cycles of traditional religions), to constant spin-offs of *Sandman* itself, like the current *House of Mystery* (which features a different character narrating a story-within-the-story every month), this is the closest Vertigo comes to a unifying theme. *The Unwritten* is the latest example of this, with a plot that literally explores the power of stories to control the world.[29]

---

26 This also shows that author/artist names and book titles have become bearers of (cultural) meaning. The commodification of names is not a new development and not confined to the comics medium. On "celebrity authors," cf. Okker 2003: 21–22; Round 2010: 27.

27 These quotations are taken from the first two unnumbered pages of the first paperback volume.

28 This marketing technique manifests itself likewise in the choice of advertisements and promotions included in the magazine issues of *The Unwritten*. The ads usually announce other Vertigo series or offer sneak previews of new episodes of a different story. Author and artist names can serve to "guarantee greater sales," Uricchio and Pearson state, and "[t]he emergence of the direct distribution system, which permitted more accurate tracking of individual title sales, further augmented comic-book auteurism by giving rise to a royalty system now used by both the major comic book companies, DC and Marvel" (1991: 189). With this distribution system, criteria of quality and marketability are combined within individual authorship. Kelleter and Stein (2012: 278–79) explain how this change in the distribution system has impacted the possibilities of serial storytelling in superhero comics.

29 On Vertigo's 'obsession' with stories about stories, cf. also Kukkonen 2010: 24.

In another online entry, a blogger compares *The Unwritten* to Alan Moore's *Watchmen* and states, "what Mike Carey is doing with the story of *The Unwritten* is much more complex than Moore's *Watchmen*. *Watchmen* was a visual feast. *The Unwritten* is a literary, mind stretching banquet" (Melissa 2012: n.p.).[30] Blogs such as these, by fans and professionals alike, are certainly, to borrow a phrase from Jason Mittell, only one part of all the "generic practices that circulate around" *The Unwritten* (2001: 8). But they are especially interesting because they show the ways in which their respective authors position themselves in the debates and competing claims about the social meaning, cultural value, and relevancy of the medium of comics (and, in this particular case, of *The Unwritten*). Thus, they show how fan bloggers and professional online reviewers participate in the proliferation—and consolidation—of (popular) culture knowledge and thereby also impact the development of generic awareness.[31]

Paratextual Cues II

Generic practices do not just evolve around *The Unwritten*; they actually run through the text itself—by means of captions, page numbers, subheadings, and so forth. The first trade paperback, titled *The Unwritten: Tommy Taylor and the Bogus Identity*, is given a (visual) structure by means of chapter headings and/or interim illustrations by Japanese artist Yuko Shimizu. The cover image of each magazine issue is reprinted in the respective trade paperback to indicate for the reader that there is a break in the story. In the first paperback volume, the magazine cover illustrations are not simply reprinted; they are endowed with headlines and caption numbers ("Tommy Taylor and the Bogus Identity Chapter One," "Tommy Taylor and the Bogus Identity Chapter Two," and so forth) that help readers navigate through the story. While the first paperback volume includes chapter headings, the other paperback volumes leave out these paratextual structuring principles. There, the only indicators of new chapters are the in-between illustrations by Shimizu.

The first three "Bogus Identity" chapters are followed by a new chapter titled "Tommy Taylor and the Bogus Identity Conclusion." The next and final chapter of the first trade paperback bears the caption "How the Whale Became," which opens up a playground for intertextual—as

---

30 Further reviews can be found on websites like *comixology.com*, *newsarama.com*, *comicbookresources.com*, or *comicsalliances.com*. On the latter, comics scholar Chris Murphy (2011) shares his views on *The Unwritten*. In addition to these online comments, one can also find video discussions of *The Unwritten* on YouTube.
31 On "Wertungskontexte," or contexts of evaluation, cf. also Kelleter and Stein 2012: 287.

well as intermedial—references. While the caption quite obviously alludes to Ted Hughes's children's book *How the Whale Became, and Other Stories* (1963), it also invites us to associate this part of *The Unwritten* with another set of background readings. For one, the caption prompts us to think of Joseph Rudyard Kipling and his writings, especially his short story "How the Whale Got His Throat" (this reference is also visually-verbally triggered in this chapter when the reader encounters a representation of the writer Kipling and stumbles across quotations from Kipling's writings). On the other hand, when continuing to read through the pages, the recurrent visual representation of a giant whale activates the reader's potential knowledge of Herman Melville's *Moby Dick* (a cue planted again in later chapters of *The Unwritten*—the most recent of which is the main character's encounter with the *Pequod* whaleship in magazine issue #42).

Before the actual story of *The Unwritten* begins, readers find a copy of the cover page illustration by Yuko Shimizu. Upon turning this page, they come across a pencil sketch of the artist, showing a man with a rope around his neck that is made up of the words "TEXT TEXT TEXT TEXT." This flip page (end result on the one side, pre-work on the other) and also the annotations at the end of the first volume invite readers to take part in the work in progress, allowing them to discover how the product they are holding in their hands has come into being. In the "Cover Sketch Gallery" section at the end of the first trade paperback, readers encounter the black-and-white ink sketches of the opening three pages of *The Unwritten*, and they can trace the changes that have been made (e.g., the frames or borders, and dimensional lines that have been erased) before the lettering and coloring and the actual printing of the pages. M. Thomas Inge's exploration of metacomics and the ways in which these metacomics self-consciously reflect on the usages of "pencils, ink, and paper [as well as] the borders or panels and the placement of dialogue in balloons" (1991: 6) are useful here. Inge did not specifically address the marginalia of *The Unwritten*, but what he says about the self-reflexivity of metacomics—that they show the processes of, and reflect on, the making of a comic—also holds true for the sketch gallery and the sample pages in "*The Unwritten* Miscellanea." The sketches collected in the miscellanea section endow the work with a kind of aura—giving readers an insight into "the original prose passage [and] the adaptation process" of *The Unwritten* ("*The Unwritten* Miscellanea," Carey and Gross 2010a: n.p.).

This is handmade, the pencil sketches and notes imply, and here are the original ideas put on paper. As Paul Cornell writes in the preface to the second trade paperback edition, the comic is not simply about the interconnected narrative strands, or 'narrated worlds,' of Tom/Tommy Taylor but about the whole process of how the work unfolds, develops, and refers back onto itself.[32] "There's no format," Cornell states, except for the borders of a given page and the number of pages in the respective magazine issue. Inside these physical borders, "the stories here all contribute to a bigger tale, but we're not waiting to see what our hero and his friends will get up to on their quest this issue. They might not be in it. Or they might be, but it might not be about them. [...] the digressions and notes in the margin are just as interesting" (Cornell 2010: n.p.).[33]

These marginalia are part of the making of *The Unwritten*. This meta-technique (the inclusion of manuscript notes and sketches by the artists) serves to sustain a sense of intimacy between producer and consumer, and it invites readers to witness and take part in the working process, to participate in the very creation/making of *The Unwritten*. This is similar to the metafictional "behind-the-scenes look at the creation of fiction" (Inge 1991: 1) that we find in many postmodern novels. Here, however, the inclusion of the creator's preliminary artwork also serves as a visual discourse of authenticity. Following Cornell's idea that the notes in the margins are as important as the main text, I consider the sample pages to be parts of the visual and verbal dynamics in the production and reception of *The Unwritten*.[34] The appendix, the cover page, the promotional praise, the introduction, all of the paratextual insertions are constitutive elements in the meaning making process.

---

[32] I borrow the term 'narrated world' from Herman 2011: 160; cf. also 167–68. On narrated worlds, or storyworlds, see also Ryan 1991; Herman 2007; Alber 2009.

[33] This includes the online "Annotations" to the first magazine issue of *The Unwritten* on the *mikeandpeter.com* website.

[34] In the hardcover "Deluxe Edition" of Gaiman and McKean's graphic novel *Black Orchid* (2012), one can find a similar strategy. Here, the appendix includes letter correspondence between artist and editor. For a reading of Gaiman's and McKean's *Black Orchid*, see Sheppeard 2009. Moore's *From Hell* (a series that ran from 1989 to 1996 and was reprinted as a graphic novel in 1999) does not confine itself to one appendix but offers two (cf. Gravett 2005: 164). On the function of such peritexts, cf. also Kelleter and Stein 2012: 287; for further paratextual analysis, see Daniel Stein's contribution in this volume. The strategy of reissuing and promoting a previously published text as single 'deluxe' issue tells us something about the 'product differentiation' and the cultural value that publishers inscribe to a given text. These products do not have *intrinsic* worth but are endowed with attributes to indicate prestige, such as permanent and expensive book binding, hardcover material, higher-quality paper, etc. On these issues, cf. Uricchio and Pearson 1991: 189–90; Round 2010: 15–17. Round discusses the 'highbrow status' invoked by such attributes. It seems that selling a product as meaningful, as worthy of buying and collecting, today is based on an idea of exclusiveness that shows in the price of these deluxe products.

Paratextual Clues III: Generic Promptings and Storytelling Devices

The Unwritten starts off in medias res with a boy (Peter) and a girl (Sue). These kids are placed in some kind of grayish underworld with piles of dead bodies of so-called Gossamoks—"half-ghost, half-devil" (Carey and Gross 2010a: n.p.) creatures, as the unnamed extradiegetic narrator explains—, and they are searching for another boy named Tommy. Further visual and verbal ingredients on the first three pages are: the prominence of the color red (to indicate blood), a representation of a golden trumpet, a few colored letters that denote some magic incantations, someone called "Count Ambrosio" who wants to "play the final lullaby" but is instead transformed into stone, and a "little winged cat" (Carey and Gross 2010a: n.p.) by the name of Mingus. All of these elements invite readers to activate knowledge about fantasy novels (especially those recently read) and bring into the reading process the accumulated clichés of fantasy stories.[35]

The third page of the first issue of *Unwritten* ends with the same narrative voice explaining, "Peter Price lifted the golden trumpet to his lips and blew the final, irrevocable note" (Carey and Gross 2010a: n.p.). When flipping this page over and turning to the next, readers see a caption that reads "Afterword"—the afterword to *Tommy Taylor and the Golden Trumpet*—as well as a hand signing the book with the name Tommy Taylor. They learn (*after the fact*) that the previous pages had actually represented the final pages of the most recent Tommy Taylor fantasy novel. This narrative structure of a frame story surrounding an embedded story, however, becomes more and more difficult to apply the further we read on.

While the opening three pages of *The Unwritten* establish parameters for a fantasy-adventure-saga, the fourth page abruptly ends this genre classification as a plausible reading strategy. This "Afterword" page functions as a kind of bridge to the 'real' storyworld of *The Unwritten* and as a link to Tom Taylor, who is at a London "Tommy Con" to sign autographs. The words and images on the pages convey that the name of Tommy Taylor is a trademark and commercially viable product, and a crowd of people lines up to get a hold on that product—a signature by

---

35 By planting explicit (and a few implicit) references to the *Harry Potter* cycle, *The Unwritten* deliberately plays with and pokes fun at the novels—and especially to the media hype surrounding them. In the first trade paperback, Tom Taylor says about the Tommy Taylor character: "Yes, people have seen similarities with *Harry Potter*. Books of magic. The worst witch" (Carey and Gross 2010a: n.p.). Insights from research in the 'emergent area of narrative inquiry'—i.e., cognitive narratology (cf. Herman 2007: 306; see also Boyd 2006; Stroud 2008)—as well as psychology (e.g., Collins 1991; Esrock 1994) are valuable in this regard and will surely bring about interesting projects in comics studies in the future.

Tom/my Taylor. As Tom/my explains in one of the speech balloons: "Tommy Taylor is so much bigger. Forty percent of people who can read have read at least one of my father's books. And that's not even counting the movies, the games, the comics…" (Carey and Gross 2010a: n.p.). The next few pages build up another set of story expectations, namely, to find a story about a world of fan conventions and communities as well as a world in which someone named Tom Taylor is some sort of celebrity. Here and on other occasions, *The Unwritten* visually and verbally engages with comics culture as a whole. In that sense, it ventures beyond the intra- and metadiegetic storyworlds of Tom/my Taylor by including the extra-textual, 'real' world of comics culture. The most obvious examples are those pages on which Carey and Gross print (fictive) fan pages (they even include the hyperlinks) and online discussion forums such as *Tommyology*, *Tommy's Truth*, or *The POSTnation*.

A previously constructed line between an intradiegetic Tom Taylor storyworld and a metadiegetic Tommy Taylor storyworld,[36] and thus the line between what we might consider fact/fiction, or reality/fantasy, begins to dissolve on the ninth page of the first volume, when a London-based "King's college" media student with the telling name of Lizzie Hexam asks the question: "who are you?" (Carey and Gross 2010a: n.p.). As a matter of fact, because of her position in the middle of a triptych of panels, staring directly at the readers, each consumer of *The Unwritten* is implicitly confronted with the same question.

From that moment on, the distinction the reader has been lured into making between Tom Taylor and Tommy Taylor becomes problematic; it seems more and more difficult to apply the further we continue reading. The first three chapters still allow us to consider Tom/my Taylor as a sort of lynchpin between *different* storyworlds, between layers of narration, between different spatial and temporal levels. With the fourth magazine issue, and thus the fourth chapter in the first trade paperback, the binary tension of here/there does not hold anymore. The reassuring deictics of a clearly delineated here, there, this, then, now, loses its referents and becomes useless, not only for the characters inside the story of *The Unwritten*, but for the readers of *The Unwritten* as well.

From issue to issue, key characters like Tom and Lizzie (and their alter-egos Tommy and Sue, who are joined a little later by someone named Richie) become more and more entangled in a web of other stories, words, and letters. At one point, it is suggested that Tom Taylor is fiction turned alive, or "the word made flesh" (Carey and Gross 2010a:

---

36 See also Silke Horstkotte's analysis of graphic storyworlds in this volume. Furthermore, see Jan Noël Thon's contribution, in which he proposes a dichotomy of 'first-order'/primary and 'second-order'/secondary. See also Ryan and Thon 2014.

n.p.).[37] Some of the figures from Tom's 'real' world are, metaphorically speaking, melting away; their physical bodies *transform* into (bluish) words and letters. This reverses the reading process of texts in which the reader, by means of the words presented to him or her, creates a mental image of a character.[38] In *The Unwritten*, characters 'sink' into literary history to become some kind of blueprint-letter version of their physical body images. Some of them reappear in later issues as new characters (or animals) in another storyworld. In the second paperback, a character named Pauly Bruckner, who was beaten unconscious by Tom/my's father Wilson Taylor, is 'reborn' as a foul-swearing white slayer-rabbit called Mr. Bun, who is trapped in a world full of animals with names like Nedward, Tig Hedgehog, Dogling, Wilfred Weasel, and Mrs. Matilda Mouse. Mr. Bun has to deal with a fierce-looking person named Miss Liza, who lives in a "Rose Tree Cottage" (Carey and Gross 2010a: n.p.) and is dressed in clothes that in many ways recall Walt Disney's animated film version of Alice in *Alice in Wonderland* (1951).[39] This character, rather than simply linking *The Unwritten* to a film, points to the Disney animated adaptation of a (canonized) literary text and thus evokes a classic of illustrated literature as well as a classic of American film animation.

Bruckner's/Bun's repetitive suicidal efforts are in vain; he cannot find a way out of the "hundred-acre **gulag**" (Carey and Gross 2010b: n.p., original emphasis) into which he seems to have fallen. Later, in magazine issue #24, this rabbit finally escapes from Miss Liza and from her Willowbank world (in reference to Faith Jacques's illustrated children's book, *Willowbank Wood*) only to fall deeper into another rabbit hole, a dark labyrinth of seemingly infinite staircases—a "fucking subbasement from **Hades**," as Bruckner/Bun calls it, with animals that "look like one of the ten **plagues** from the Bible. The plague of cute **vermin**" (Carey and Gross 2011a: n.p., original emphasis). With Bruckner/Bun still on his quest to find his way back to "the real world" (Carey and Gross 2011a: n.p.), the episode ends with the white rabbit vanishing inside a striped hat, evaporating into unknown areas only to reappear as a voiceless Pauly Bruckner, a human-looking puppet in the fifth paperback volume.

In the recent magazine issue #36 (reprinted in the seventh trade paperback in 2013), the Bruckner/Bun character reappears on the scene in yet another storyworld, where he encounters an aged, wrinkled, bald, mask-wearing superhero character called The Tinker. They both seem to

---

37 The citation can be found in the first chapter of the first paperback volume, on a double-page showing four lines of panels that represent so-called DNN news reports.
38 On the 'ontological status' of fictional characters, see, for example, Eder, Jannidis, and Schneider 2010.
39 Cf. Carey and Gross 2010b: n.p.

have 'descended' into the pop-culture-fiction-world full of comic figures, fairy-tale characters, and children's-book protagonists, wandering through an apocalyptic, orange-colored wasteland. This is an underworld made of representations of a number of well-known artifacts from American culture, such as Walt Disney's Tinker Bell; a band-aided Humpty-Dumpty; a long-nosed, elderly-looking Count von Count; the iconic, black-sunglasses-wearing man of the 1992 *Memoirs of an Invisible Man*; and a not-so-muscular/not-so-v-shaped version of Superman.

In the course of this narrative, the Mr. Bun rabbit suddenly becomes a 'human' figure/man again, happily announcing to The Tinker: "Opposable thumbs! No more fucking carrots" (Carey and Gross 2012c: n.p.). Trying to figure out a way to avoid the so-called wave, from which all the other inhabitants of this outland are fleeing, Pauly-once-rabbit-now-human-again and The Tinker end up in a white, blank space—literally. On the final page, the reader is left with four rectangular, yellow narrator boxes. An unspecified narrative voice notes that "the wave" was approaching, and "[i]t came on them in complete silence. The perfect whiteness of an unwritten page" (Carey and Gross 2012c: n.p.). The final words of rabbit-Bun/human-Bruckner in his accompanying speech balloon read: "Oh fuck" (Carey and Gross 2012c: n.p.). At the bottom of this page, one finds a white panel with orange frame-lines surrounding it, and two further narrator boxes inside of this panel, the last of which reads: "What happened to them next was a most fortuitous coincidence" (Carey and Gross 2012c: n.p.).

In this and the previous issues of *The Unwritten*, Mr. Bun is a highly entertaining character poking fun at all kinds of stock characters that have been created throughout literary history. The Mr. Bun parts are filled with visual and verbal cues that open up (parodistic) intertextual avenues to be discovered by the reader and thus serve as postmodern self-reflexive reminders for the reader to reconsider the thought system and reading habits brought to the interpretation of *The Unwritten*. One example appears at the beginning of the Willowbank episode, where an unknown narrator and the voice of Pauly Bruckner/Mr. Bun captured inside speech balloons interact (see figure 1). Their dialogue reads:

"In a hole in the side of a hill, there lived a rabbit. [...] His name was Mr. Bun."
"Pauly Bruckner."
"Mr. Bun."
"Pauly Bruckner! Pauly Bruckner! **Pauly Bruckner!**"
"And one day—I believe it was a Tuesday in late July—he set out for the edge of the wood." (Carey and Cross 2010b: n.p., original emphasis)

Figure 1: Mike Carey and Peter Gross, *The Unwritten: Inside Man* (2010).
© Mike Carey and Peter Gross. Used with permission of DC Comics.

Different levels of narration and sources and degrees of focalization merge on this particular page—though the font style of the unknown, unspecified narrative voice is different from that of Mr. Bun/Pauly Bruckner. And even though the speech balloons with the words of the rabbit stand out because of their inner whiteness, the interactions between the unidentified extradiegetic (first hetero-, then homodiegetic) narrator and that of the intradiegetic Pauly Bruckner/Mr. Bun are visually placed on the same level of narration.[40] What is interesting about this interaction between two different narrating agencies is that this metalepsis is situated in-between the Tommy and Tom storyworlds, in a kind of middle ground, or, to use the comics terminology, in the 'gutter' between two panel sequences.[41]

With this and other parts in *The Unwritten*, Carey and Gross ponder the typographic means of producing graphic texts in the comics medium (fonts, speech balloons, panel borders, etc.), while also challenging clear-cut distinctions of modes of speech presentation. As Inge has observed, there is a "general disposition among the artists to engage in self-parody of their profession and the artistic form in which they are working" (1991: 7) in order to explore the possibilities and limits of visual-verbal narration.

In a similar vein, Bun's/Bruckner's company in magazine issue #36 of *The Unwritten*, The Tinker, functions as a testing ground, but he is endowed with——especially visual (or iconographic)—cues to negotiate

---

[40] Against the background of questions about the representation of the mind in comics and other forms of graphic narratives, Mikkonen 2011 critically engages with transmedial narratology and the challenges posed by the comics medium. On 'postclassical narratology' and strategies to represent consciousness in graphic novels, cf. Herman 2011: 160-62.

[41] On the concept of metalepsis, see Kukkonen 2011.

the idea of the *origin* of the American superhero genre and make visible the *iconographic effect* of superhero characters.[42] Framed by the context of the American comics business of the 1930s and 1940s, The Tinker is a (fictional) comic superhero character created by a woman named Miriam Walzer, who publishes her *All-Crime Comics* stories under the pseudonym of Milton Jardine. His full name is Edward Tinker; he is an 'ordinary' man who, in times of crisis and crime, changes his clothes, puts on a mask, and fights evil. "The priceless treasures [a magic belt, an invisibility cloak, and seven-league boots] turn harmless Edward Tinker into something all criminals fear—an **avenger!**" (Carey and Gross 2012a: n.p., original emphasis) The Tinker is first introduced in magazine issue #27 as part of Tom/my's father's biography and his (conspirational) doings in the 1930s—under the name of William Tallis. Interested in finding ways to deliver a story to as many people as possible, Wilson Taylor/William Tallis stumbles across The Tinker comics.[43] He is convinced that "most [...] people don't read Forster and Fitzgerald. They read the pulps. Listen to Amos 'N' Andy. And buy comic books. It's this that's shaping their thoughts. Their definition of themselves" (Carey and Gross 2012a: n.p.). Wilson Taylor tries to get a hold on the Tinker character in order to "control the product" (Carey and Gross 2012a: n.p.) and the channels through which it is distributed to the (potential) consumers.[44]

The Tinker has manifold functions. His appearance in the *All-Crime Comics* parodies the American comics publishing industry (*All-Crime Comics* evokes the comic books of EC Comics from the 1950s) and the denigration that has long accompanied the medium, which is emphasized by statements such as "[n]ew kinds of story are incubating, and they're coming in fast," or "these stories are like bombs" (Carey and Gross 2012a: n.p.).[45] What is more, The Thinker character and the story of his evolution are a reflection on the notions of the comics creator and ownership. As Miriam Walzer explains, "it's me who writes and draws the Tinker. He's all mine" (Carey and Gross 2012a: n.p.).[46] Furthermore, with The Tinker,

---

42 On iconographic effects of superhero comics stories and characters, cf. Kelleter and Stein 2012: 278.
43 The Thinker plays a key role in issues #27 to #30—reprinted in vol. 5 of *The Unwritten* (see Carey and Gross 2012a).
44 Wilson Taylor's affair with Miriam Walzer, out of which a son named Milton Jardine was born who has "the Tinker's powers," relates to *The Unwritten*'s overall topic of double (or multiple) selves. The fictional superhero The Tinker is brought into existence through the pen and ink and through the hands of Miriam Walzer, who then gives birth to a Milton Jardine—a Tinker boy turned real.
45 Numerous references to the comics industry can be found in magazines #27 through #29 of *The Unwritten*, too numerous, in fact, to be discussed here in full detail.
46 On the comics creator and the value ascribed to creative individuality, cf. also Round 2010: 20–21.

Carey and Gross position their text against the background of the superhero comic book and the numerous reinventions that the superhero genre has seen especially since the 1980s.

In the course of the narrative developed in *The Unwritten*, this Milton/Tinker *grows old* and attempts to write himself out of the 'real' world. With a piece of chalk from Lake Avernus, Milton/Tinker draws a frame on the concrete in front of him, which opens as a door and steps leading downwards. Odysseus-like, Milton/Tinker decides to leave the real world and descends to Hades to rescue "his beloved" (Carey and Gross 2012a: n.p.). Endowed with the "Tinker's bag of tricks" (Carey and Gross 2012a: n.p.), Milton/Tinker takes the steps down until "[t]he steps were growing thin. As though their commitment to being steps was wavering" (Carey and Gross 2012c: n.p.). The next thing we know is that Milton/Tinker encounters Mr. Bun/Pauly Bruckner.

The Tinker is deliberately inscribed with what William Uricchio and Roberta Pearson call "generic affiliation[s]" (1991: 209): with Batman, because the Tinker is an 'ordinary' man with no superpowers, and with Robin, The Boy Wonder character from the *Batman* stories. The mask, pants, and cape recall the 1940 comic book version, and so does the posture of The Tinker on the cover of magazine issue #28. He also has generic affiliations with Will Eisner's The Spirit, which is indicated by the suit The Tinker wears before he changes his dress to become a crime-fighter as well as by the shape of the mask. In addition, Carey and Gross link Miriam Walzer's superhero to folklore protagonists such as Le Petit Poucet in Charles Perrault's *Histoires ou contes du temps passé* (1697), who steals magic boots from a sleeping giant.

Coming back to Uricchio and Pearson, one could argue that this reference to the seven-league boots, as well as The Tinker's superhero-costume/normal-guy-outfit, and the action and setting of The Tinker's stories "activate" manifold "intertextual frame[s]" (1991: 196) for the reader to discover. Yet it is far more interesting that The Tinker, being created (or put together) as an intertextual construct, parodies questions of origin and originality and thereby ponders the iconographic legacies of superhero characters such as Superman, Batman, Robin, or The Spirit. The Tinker "predates Superman by a good two years. Go figure," says one of Tom/my's friends-turned-vampire Richie, a kind of "proto-superhero" (Carey and Gross 2012a: n.p.). Yet, as he continues, this Tinker "is seriously freaking me out, by the way. I mean I don't mind a little Dark Knight Returns. A little Watchmen even. This guy fights crime with seven-league boots and a cloak of invisibility. Stuff out of fucking fairy stories" (Carey and Gross 2012a: n.p.). In magazine issue #27 (part of vol. 5 of *The Unwritten*), Carey and Gross deliberately create a picture of The

Tinker lifting up a car that invokes the cover of *Action Comics* #1 (June 1938) (see figure 2).

Figure 2: Mike Carey and Peter Gross, *The Unwritten: On to Genesis* (2012). © Mike Carey & Peter Gross. Used with permission of DC Comics.

This visual reference serves to demonstrate that the reading and understanding of *The Unwritten* depends on the reader's knowledge of popular culture. Carey and Gross do not only underline their own immersion in comics culture; they also make their readers, implied and real, part of this immersedness. Moreover, this image shows how one particular attribute, one particular pose, or one particular setting can be turned into an iconic sign by means of repetitive citation and thus perpetuation, and it indicates how this impacts the reading and understanding of graphic novels. In other words, graphic novels like *The Unwritten* construct serial universes that are endowed with a narrative memory.[47]

The last example that explains the functions of The Tinker is both a visual and verbal statement on the formulaic elements of the superhero genre. About to kill Tom/my Taylor with an inflamed sword in order to do 'justice' and avenge his mother's early death (of cancer), The Tinker is stopped by a graphically adapted version of Frankenstein's monster, who tells him: "You are... a **Hero**. This... is **not**... what heroes do" (Carey and Gross 2012a: n.p., original emphasis). To view this page as merely a gimmick would miss the point. Carey and Gross use this encounter among Tom/my, The Tinker, and Frankenstein's monster to position their text against a specific tradition in the superhero genre, namely,

---

47 Cf. Kelleter and Stein 2012: 266.

against comics that are "self-referential, morally ambiguous, [...] and populated with introspective and disenchanted characters" (Williams and Lyons 2010: xx) while simultaneously composing their text as an intertextually and intermedially highly complex narrative. This heightened degree of intertextuality and intermediality is also part of the practices of literary distinction: references to canonized and culturally esteemed literary precursors lend themselves to further research projects in the fields of literary and cultural studies.[48]

A Preliminary Conclusion

The Unwritten does not only probe limits of representation. To speak with Jan Alber, it also "widen[s] our mental universe beyond the actual and the familiar, and provide[s] playfields for interesting thought experiments" (2009: 93). *The Unwritten* echoes what Jared Gardner has called "our growing appetite for texts that choose *not* to choose" (2006: 802, original emphasis), at least when it comes to concepts such as identity or categories such as time and space. These become unstable in *The Unwritten*, and narrative telos and closure become obsolete. As *The Unwritten* begins to unfold, it weaves a web of narrative complexity, comprised of numerous literary references to epic stories and fables, to medieval romance, gothic fictions, realism, and to fantasy so as to intermix the Tom/my story with other stories that were told and written in past centuries.

The Unwritten does not simply tell a story about stories; it is a story about the ways stories are told and entangled in other stories and literary history. Steven Hall states in the introduction to the third trade paperback that it is an "ambitious labyrinth of forking paths, and a thoughtful exploration of the very nature of stories both on the page and in the wider world" (2011: n.p.). In the end, *The Unwritten* is a text not just about how to make a story but also about how to *make sense of the world*.[49]

Trying to make sense of what is happening around them, the key characters of *The Unwritten* (as well as the reader) ride through a veritable pop-culture-literary-history-galaxy. I use this compound term on purpose. In the second trade paperback volume (magazine issue #11), a Harry-Potter-lookalike Tom/my Taylor—after being killed by what is called an

---

[48] The references to world literature, film adaptations of literary texts, and other visual media are too many to be analyzed here in their entirety.

[49] This manifests itself most obviously in magazine issue #17, where the reader is confronted with a "Pick-A-Story®" (cf. Carey and Gross 2011b: n.p.). This spin-off story is discussed in Meyer and Bonk 2013.

"echo" of Joseph Goebbels—finds himself in a comic version of planet Vogsphere from the filmic adaptation (2005) of Douglas Adams's sci-fi radio comedy *The Hitchhiker's Guide to the Galaxy* (1978), forced to fill out a "buff colored form"—and a "BF33(z)" as well as a "BF33(k)" document, respectively (Carey and Gross 2010b: n.p.).

In that sense, *The Unwritten* lends itself to intermedia storytelling analyses such as those conducted by the contributors to Marina Grishakova and Marie-Laure Ryan's essay volume *Intermediality and Storytelling* (2010), which may lead to a better understanding of the aesthetics of graphic novels. On the other hand, because of the 'interpretive frames' that *The Unwritten* sets free, one might gain further insight into the dynamics of storytelling in graphic novels as creative acts. As Frank Kelleter and Daniel Stein have observed, "serial narratives set free a great number of creative practices on the part of their addressees" (2012: 261; my translation from the German: "Serielle Erzählungen [...] setzen in großer Zahl kreative Handlungen auf Seiten ihrer Adressanten frei"). In many ways, *The Unwritten* plants cues that invite the reader to take part in a serial, intertextually highly complex game. This, again, leads to an ever-expanding "Serienwissen" (series knowledge) which is not only comprised of the reading of one particular installment (and the generic promptings inscribed therein) but of the reading of an episode in the context of older episodes and of episodes of other graphic novel series.[50] In a similar vein, albeit in a different context, David Herman speaks of 'scripts' that are stored in our memory and help us read, understand, and evaluate situations and that are mobilized by means of particular cues in a text. We "make predictions," to borrow Herman's expression here, "about emergent situations and sequences of events on the basis of prior, stereotypical situations and sequences stored in the memory as knowledge of representations" (1999: 21). The 'scripts' that *The Unwritten* triggers through its various cues and generic promptings are fascinating and thus worth looking into in greater detail for two reasons: first, because Carey and Gross inscribe into their graphic novel what might be called *comics*

---

50 Cf. Kelleter and Stein 2012: 279. In addition to all the paratextual and textual cues discussed in this chapter, one would also need to take a closer look at how, plot-wise, *The Unwritten* plants conspiracy theory cues. The most obvious of these cues is the insertion of an agency, a mysterious cabal, which, since ancient times, has tried to rule the world by controlling the stories that are being told and printed and the ways in which these stories are distributed and consumed. Carey and Gross humorously suggest that Kipling was involved in this agency; in another issue, the newspaper comics artist Homer Davenport, who had worked for William Randolph Hearst and published political cartoons in Hearst's *New York Journal* during the final decade of the nineteenth century, is depicted as a person who finds out about the agency but then decides—for the sake of his family—to destroy any kind of evidence (cf. Carey and Gross 2012b). This context of conspiracy literature that *The Unwritten* draws on deserves detailed analysis in future research projects.

culture scripts, meaning scripts that draw on images, stereotypical situations, and formulas from previous comics sources and other forms of graphic narrative. Second, *The Unwritten* does not only offer numerous intertextual and intermedial references to other texts but also engages (both verbally and visually) with the 'actual' world. In that sense, *The Unwritten* does not only pose narratological but also ontological and epistemological difficulties and challenges for fan-readers and academics alike.

Thus, *The Unwritten* and graphic novels in general are, I would say, valuable research projects for scholars from a variety of the domains, including narrative theory, cognitive science, psychology, language acquisition, and communication theory as well as (inter)-media studies, art history, literary criticism, and comics studies. And because this is a preliminary conclusion, meant to open doors for further research, I will end here with three wishes: First, may Mike Carey and Peter Gross continue to write and draw the series and add further details to the comics culture scripts and to Tom/Tommy's quest for (him)self. Second, may there be future studies on *The Unwritten* and other graphic novels that help us to rethink and redefine "prior accounts of narrativity" (Herman 2011: 158). Third, may there be more cross-fertilizations and "points of convergence" (Herman 2007: 326) among research fields and academic disciplines. In other words, I look forward to future scholarship that will broaden our understanding of how the "medium-specific properties"[51] of graphic novels and other forms of graphic narrative can enlighten the study of narrative discourse and how theories of storytelling are negotiated and deconstructed in the medium of comics.

Works Cited

Alber, Jan (2009). "Impossible Storyworlds and What to Do with Them." *Storyworlds: A Journal of Narrative Studies* 1: 79–96. Print.

Allison, Bob (1987). "Artist Adopts Love of Comics." *Kentucky New Era*, Sept. 16. "Lifestyles" section, page 6B. Print.

Boyd, Brian (2006). "Fiction and Theory of Mind." *Philosophy and Literature* 30.2: 590–600. Print.

Carey, Mike, and Peter Gross (2010a). *The Unwritten: Tommy Taylor and the Bogus Identity*. Vol. 1. Colors by Chris Chuckry and Jeanne McGee. Original Series Covers by Yuko Shimizu. Lettered by Todd Klein. Originally published in single magazine form as *The Unwritten* #1–5, 2009. New York: DC Comics. Print.

---

51 Cf. Herman 2011: 158; see also Pratt 2009b.

— (2010b). *The Unwritten: Inside Man*. Vol. 2. Colors by Chris Chuckry, Jeanne McGee, Kurt Huggins, and Zelda Devon. Original Series Covers by Yuko Shimizu. Lettered by Todd Klein. Originally published in single magazine form as *The Unwritten* #6–12, 2009–2010. New York: DC Comics. Print.

— (2011a). *The Unwritten* #24. Colors by Chris Chuckry. Lettered by Todd Klein. Cover by Yuko Shimizu. New York: DC Comics. Print.

— (2011b). *The Unwritten: Dead Man's Knock*. Vol. 3. Colors by Chris Chuckry and Jeanne McGee. Lettered by Todd Klein. Original Series Covers by Yuko Shimizu. Finishes of "The Many Lives of Lizzie Hexam" by Ryan Kelly. Originally published in single magazine form as *The Unwritten* #13–18, 2010. New York: DC Comics. Print.

— (2012a). *The Unwritten: On to Genesis*. Vol. 5. Colors by Chris Chuckry. Original Series Covers by Yuko Shimizu. Lettered by Todd Klein. Originally published in single magazine form as *The Unwritten* #25–30, 2011. New York: DC Comics. Print.

— (2012b). *The Unwritten: Tommy Taylor and the War of Words*. Vol. 6. Colors by Chris Chuckry, Fiona Stephenson, and Lee Loughrige. Original Series Covers by Yuko Shimizu. Lettered by Todd Klein. Originally published in single magazine form as *The Unwritten* #31–35 and #31.5–35.5, 2012. New York: DC Comics. Print.

— (2012c). *The Unwritten* #36. Colors by Chris Chuckry. Cover by Yuko Shimizu. Lettered by Todd Klein. New York: DC Comics. Print.

— (2012d). "Annotations." *Mikeandpeter.com*. Web.

Chute, Hillary (2008). "Comics as Literature? Reading Graphic Narrative." *PMLA* 123.2: 452–65. Print.

Chute, Hillary, and Marianne DeKoven (2006). "Introduction: Graphic Narrative." Hillary Chute and Marianne DeKoven (eds.). *Graphic Narrative*. Special issue of *Modern Fiction Studies* 52.4: 767–82. Print.

Cohn, Neil (2005). "Un-Defining 'Comics': Separating the Cultural from the Structural in Comics." *International Journal of Comic Art* 7.2: 236–48. Print.

Collins, Christopher (1991). *The Poetics of the Mind's Eye: Literature and the Psychology of Imagination*. Philadelphia: U of Pennsylvania P. Print.

Contino, Jennifer M (2001). "A Touch of Vertigo—Karen Berger." *Sequential Tart*, Feb. Web.

Corben, Richard (1979). *Bloodstar*. New York: Ariel Books. Print.

Cornell, Paul (2010). "Introduction." Mike Carey and Peter Gross. *The Unwritten: Inside Man*. Vol. 2. New York: DC Comics. N.p. Print.

Coughlan, David (2006). "Paul Auster's *City of Glass*: The Graphic Novel." Hillary Chute and Marianne DeKoven (eds.). *Graphic Narrative*. Special issue of *Modern Fiction Studies* 52.4: 832–54. Print.

Eder, Jens, Fotis Jannidis, and Ralf Schneider (2010). "Characters in Fictional Worlds: An Introduction." Jens Eder, Fotis Jannidis, and Ralf Schneider (eds.). *Characters in Fictional Worlds: Understanding Imaginary Beings in Literature, Film, and Other Media*. Berlin: De Gruyter. 3–64. Print.

Eisner, Will (1978). *A Contract with God and Other Tenement Stories*. New York: Baronet. Print.

Ekstrom, Steve (2009). "Life as Fiction? Mike Carey on Vertigo's *The Unwritten*." Interview with Mike Carey. *Newsarama.com*, Mar. 26. Web.

Esrock, Ellen J. (1994). *The Reader's Eye: Visual Imaging as Reader Response*. Baltimore: Johns Hopkins UP. Print.

Gaiman, Neil (2012). *Black Orchid*. Illustrations by Dave McKean. New York: DC Comics. Print.

Gardner, Jared (2006). "Archives, Collectors, and the New Media Work of Comics." Hillary Chute and Marianne DeKoven (eds.). *Graphic Narrative*. Special issue of *Modern Fiction Studies* 52.4: 787–806. Print.

Gardner, Jared, and David Herman (2011). "Graphic Narratives and Narrative Theory: Introduction." Jared Gardner and David Herman (eds.). *Graphic Narratives and Narrative Theory*. Special issue of *SubStance* 40.1: 3–13. Print.

Gravett, Paul (2005). *Graphic Novels: Everything You Need to Know*. New York: Collins Design. Print.

Grishakova, Marina, and Marie-Laure Ryan (eds.) (2010). *Intermediality and Storytelling*. Berlin: De Gruyter. Print.

Hall, Steven (2011). "Introduction." Mike Carey and Peter Gross. *The Unwritten: Dead Man's Knock*. Vol. 3. New York: DC Comics. N.p. Print.

Hatfield, Charles (2005). *Alternative Comics: An Emerging Literature*. Jackson: UP of Mississippi. Print.

Herman, David (1999). "Parables of Narrative Imagining." Review of Mark Turner, *The Literary Mind* (Oxford: Oxford UP, 1996). *Diacritics* 29.1: 20–36. Print.

— (2007). "Storytelling and Sciences of Mind: Cognitive Narratology, Discursive Psychology, and Narratives in Face-to-Face Interaction." *Narrative* 15.3: 306–34. Print.

— (2011). "Storyworld/Umwelt: Nonhuman Experiences in Graphic Narratives." Jared Gardner and David Herman (eds.). *Graphic Narratives and Narrative Theory*. Special issue of *SubStance* 40.1: 156–181. Print.

Inge, M. Thomas (1991). "Form and Function in Metacomics: Self-Reflexivity in the Comic Strips." *Studies in Popular Culture* 13.2: 1–10. Print.

Jenkins, Henry (2011). "Comics as Poetry: An Interview with David Mack." Daniel Stein, Christina Meyer, and Micha Edlich (eds.). *American Comic Books and Graphic Novels*. Special issue of *Amerikastudien/American Studies* 56.4. 671–97. Print.

Kelleter, Frank, and Daniel Stein (2012). "Autorisierungspraktiken seriellen Erzählens: Zur Gattungsentwicklung von Superheldencomics." Frank Kelleter (ed.). *Populäre Serialität: Narration—Evolution—Distinktion. Zum seriellen Erzählen seit dem 19. Jahrhundert*. Bielefeld: transcript. 259–90. Print.

Kukkonen, Karin (2010). *Storytelling Beyond Postmodernism: Fables and the Fairy Tale*. Tampere: Tampere UP. Print.

— (2011). "Metalepsis in Comics and Graphic Novels." Karin Kukkonen and Sonja Klimek (eds.). *Metalepsis in Popular Culture*. Berlin: De Gruyter. 213–231.

Lund, Michael (1993). *America's Continuing Story: An Introduction to Serial Fiction, 1850-1900*. Detroit: Wayne State UP. Print.

Melissa (2012). "Graphic Novel Review—*The Unwritten* Volumes 2, 3 & 4 by Mike Carey and Peter Gross." *Swampofboredom.com*. Web.

Meneses, Juan (2008). "A Bakhtinian Approach to Two Graphic Novels: The Individual in Art Spiegelman's *Maus* and Chester Brown's *Louis Riel*." *International Journal of Comic Art* 10.2: 598–606. Print.

Meskin, Aaron (2007). "Defining Comics?" *Journal of Aesthetics and Art Criticism* 65.4: 369–79. Print.

Metzger, George (1976). *Beyond Time and Again*. Huntington Beach: Kyle & Wheary Indica. Print.

Meyer, Christina, and Jens Bonk (2013). "Serializing 'Gravitational Distortions': Techniques of Refutation, Digression and Interruption in *The Unwritten*." *International Journal of Comic Art* 15.2: 682–701. Print.

Mikkonen, Kai (2011). "Graphic Narratives as a Challenge to Transmedial Narratology: The Question of Focalization." Daniel Stein, Christina Meyer, and Micha Edlich (eds.). *American Comic Books and Graphic Novels*. Special issue of *Amerikastudien/American Studies* 56.4: 639–53. Print.

Mittell, Jason (2001). "A Cultural Approach to Television Genre Theory." *Cinema Journal* 40.3: 3–24. Print.

Murphy, Chris (2011). "*The Unwritten*: The Grown-Up Boy Wizard Comic Begins a Twice-Monthly 'War of Words.'" *Comicsalliance.com*, Nov. 29. Web.

Okker, Patricia (2003). *Social Stories: The Magazine Novel in Nineteenth-Century America*. Charlottesville: U of Virginia P. Print.

Orlando, Joe, and Len Wein (1972). *The Sinister House of Secret Love* #2. "To Wed the Devil." Art by Jerome Podwil and Tony DeZuniga. New York: DC Comics. Print.

Pratt, Henry J. (2009a). "Narrative in Comics." *Journal of Aesthetics and Art Criticism* 67: 107–17. Print.

— (2009b). "Medium Specificity and the Ethics of Narrative in Comics." *Storyworlds: A Journal of Narrative Studies* 1: 97–113. Print.

Round, Julia (2010). "'Is this a book?' DC Vertigo and the Redefinition of Comics in the 1990s." Paul Williams and James Lyons (eds.). *The Rise of the American Comics Artist: Creators and Contexts*. Jackson: UP of Mississippi. 14–30. Print.

Royal, Derek P. (2011). "Sequential Sketches of Ethnic Identity: Will Eisner's *A Contract with God* as Graphic Cycle." *College Literature* 38.3: 150–67. Print.

Ryan, Marie-Laure (1991). *Possible Worlds, Artificial Intelligence, and Narrative Theory*. Bloomington: U of Indiana P. Print.

Ryan, Marie-Laure, and Jan-Noël Thon (eds.) (2014). *Storyworlds across Media: Toward a Media-Conscious Narratology*. Lincoln: U of Nebraska P. Print.

Sheppeard, Sallye (2009). "Entering the Green: Imaginal Space in Black Orchid." Angela Ndalianis (ed.). *The Contemporary Comic Book Superhero*. New York: Routledge. 205–15. Print.

Spiegelman, Art (1986). *Maus: A Survivor's Tale*. I: *My Father Bleeds History*. New York: Pantheon. Print.

— (1991). *Maus: A Survivor's Tale*. II: *And Here My Troubles Began*. New York: Pantheon. Print.

Stein, Daniel (2014). "Popular Seriality, Authorship, Superhero Comics: On the Evolution of a Transnational Genre Economy." Marcel Hartwig, Evelyne Keitel, and Gunter Süß (eds.). *Media Economies: Perspectives on American Cultural Practices*. Trier: Wissenschaftlicher Verlag Trier. 133–57. Print.

Stein, Daniel, Christina Meyer, and Micha Edlich (2011). "Introduction: American Comic Books and Graphic Novels." Daniel Stein, Christina Meyer, and Micha Edlich (eds.). *American Comic Books and Graphic Novels*. Special issue of *Amerikastudien/American Studies* 56.4: 501–29. Print.

Stroud, Scott R. (2008). "Simulation, Subjective Knowledge, and the Cognitive Value of Literary Narrative." *Journal of Aesthetic Education* 42.3: 19–41. Print.

Tabachnick, Stephen E. (2010). "The Graphic Novel and the Age of Transition: A Survey and Analysis." *English Literature in Transition, 1880–1920* 53.1: 3–28. Print.

"The Unwritten (Comic Review)" (2011). *Cult of the New*, Apr. 24. Web.

Uchmanowicz, Pauline (2009). "Graphic Novel Decoded: Towards a Poetics of Comics." *International Journal of Comic Art* 11.1: 363–85. Print.

Uricchio, William, and Roberta E. Pearson (1991). "'I'm Not Fooled by That Cheap Disguise.'" Roberta E. Pearson and William Uricchio (eds.). *The Many Lives of the Batman: Critical Approaches to a Superhero and His Media*. New York: Routledge. 182–213. Print.

Wandtke, Terrence R. (2012). *The Meaning of Superhero Comic Books*. Jefferson: McFarland. Print.

Weiner, Stephen (2010). "How the Graphic Novel Changed American Comics." Paul Williams and James Lyons (eds.). *The Rise of the American Comics Artist: Creators and Contexts*. Jackson: UP of Mississippi. 3–13. Print.

Williams, Paul, and James Lyons (2010). "Introduction." Paul Williams and James Lyons (eds.). *The Rise of the American Comics Artist: Creators and Contexts*. Jackson: UP of Mississippi. xi–xxiv. Print.

Zolkover, Adam (2008). "Corporealizing Fairy Tales: The Body, the Bawdy, and the Carnivalesque in the Comic Book Fables." *Marvels & Tales* 22.1: 38–51. Print.

HENRY JENKINS

(Los Angeles)

Archival, Ephemeral, and Residual: The Functions of Early Comics in Art Spiegelman's *In the Shadow of No Towers*

> What will last? What is ephemeral? What is timeless? What is passing? (Spiegelman in Heller 2004: n.p.)
>
> [Dust] is not about rubbish, not about the discarded; it is not about a surplus, left over from something else; it is not about waste. Indeed, Dust is the opposite thing to Waste, or at least, the opposite principle to Waste. It is about circularity, the impossibility of things disappearing, or going away, or being gone. Nothing can be destroyed. (Steedman 2002: 166)

Contemporary culture is awash with 'stuff.' Since the Industrial Revolution, shifts in mass production and consumption have dramatically increased the amount of material goods that enter our lives. This 'stuff' is often discussed in terms of its 'disposability' in a world where, we are often told, nothing is 'made to last.' Yet there has also been a sentimentalization of everyday life, which results in people holding onto things that have outlived their usefulness because these materials remind us of other times ('the good ol' days'), other people ('the dearly departed'), or other aspects of ourselves. Collecting, once an elite hobby, has been democratized: almost everyone collects something, often items others throw away. Consequently, we cannot easily separate our belongings from our sense of belonging.

A growing body of work in cultural studies explores how we ascribe meaning and value to 'stuff.' Some of this work is framed around the archival, which tends to stress values of tradition and legacy, or perhaps the ways that contemporary authors build upon what has come before.[1] Other work concerns the ephemeral, referring to uncertainty about which materials survive or are lost.[2] And still other writers speak about the residual, describing how works that may seem to have lost their currency exert a strong influence (perhaps most powerfully in the kinds of nostalgic narratives we construct).[3]

---

1 See Taylor 2003; Derecho 2006.
2 See Grainge 2011.
3 See Acland 2007.

In this chapter, I am interested in the ways old icons transmit old values into the present, representing the locus of conflicting claims and bids on legacy and tradition (archive), offering vehicles for expressing autobiographical and collective memories (ephemera), and embodying old ideologies which still exert a claim on our current thinking (the residual).

New media platforms, such as eBay and YouTube, make the exchange of old media and old artifacts more central to our lived experience. On the one hand, as William Uricchio (2011) notes, the instability of digital platforms puts the very notion of a stable archive into crisis. On the other hand, as Will Straw suggests (2007: 4), the Internet becomes the site where we collectively construct and exchange stories around older stuff:

> The Internet [...] provides the terrain on which sentimental attachments, vernacular knowledge, and a multitude of other relationships to the material culture of the past are magnified and given coherence [...]. On the Internet, the past is produced as a field of ever greater coherence, through the gathering together of disparate artifacts into sets or collections and through the commentary and annotation that cluster around such agglomerations, made possible in part by high-capacity storage mechanisms.

There is a strong connection between old stuff and stories: stuff encapsulates our personal and collective narratives, and we also often construct narratives to explain our relationship to stuff. Every object, it seems, has a story, and part of how we connect with the past is to insert ourselves into these continuing narratives about the production and circulation of stuff. In many cases, these stories assert value claims for objects that might otherwise be discarded as 'junk' or 'trash.'

When we write about earlier forms of cultural production—early comics, say—as trash, we comment on the duration of their meaningfulness and about the value placed on their content. Often, high art is defined as that which cannot be disposed of without a significant cultural loss. Comics that once seemed perishable—old strips rotting away on yellowing newsprint or perhaps discarded and replaced by microfilm—are now being reassembled and republished for posterity. Such processes cannot be separated from debates about the artistic merits of the comics medium or from the formation of canons of comics worth passing to the next generation. Thus, we negotiate about the cultural value of comics, but comics also are a vehicle through which the culture speaks to itself about its relationship to old stuff. As stories told with pictures, comics represent a privileged space for constructing stories about our relationship with stuff. A prose novel can ignore its mise-en-scène in ways a graphic novel cannot.

Art critic John Berger argues that paintings were a central means by which early modern Europe expressed new relationships to possessions as the rise of capitalism was creating a new class structure and fostering materialist values. As Berger explains: "Oil paintings often depict things. Things which in reality are buyable. To have a thing painted and put on a canvas is not unlike buying it and putting it in your house. If you buy a painting you buy also the look of the thing it represents" (1972: 83). The early capitalists, Berger suggests, used paintings to display things they owned (or hoped to own). Creating a painting was a form of conspicuous consumption, whereas looking at a painting was aspirational consumption. The spiritual value of art, Berger suggests, was frequently overwhelmed by its exchange value.

Today, comics are giving especially vivid expression to a culture preoccupied with the processes of circulation and appraisal, not simply accumulation and possession. Comics certainly may have moments of display (often, splash pages heavy in visual details), but they also trace the trajectories through which stuff travels: characters want stuff, and stories put stuff into motion. Philipp Blom has emphasized the relationship of collections to narrative: "Every collection is a theatre of memories, a dramatization and a mise-en-scène of personal and collective parts, of a remembered childhood and of remembrance after death" (2002: 191). Blom's reliance on narrative metaphors to describe collections is no accident: collections and stories are both ways of managing memory.

Comics offer us a way of (re)performing this memory work, not simply cataloging our collections, but also sharing the memories they evoke. Hillary Chute describes how Alison Bechdel's *Fun Home* (2006) functions as a kind of scrapbook, where the artist painstakingly reconstructed everything from old photographs and letters to news clippings in her effort to communicate her family's troubled history: "She re-created absolutely everything in the book, re-inhabiting the elements of her past to re-present them—and to preserve them, to publically re-archive them" (Chute 2010: 183). Bechdel raids her family archives in search of the graphic elements through which she can depict intergenerational conflict. Bechdel's focus on family archives reflects an important strand of feminist autobiography and domestic melodrama, especially focused around parent-daughter relations, which runs through contemporary graphic novels, such as C. Tyler's *You'll Never Know* (2009), Mary and Bryan Talbot's *Dotter of Her Father's Eyes* (2012), and Joyce Farmer's *Special Exits* (2010).

Such projects represent, however, only one of a range of approaches which contemporary comics artists are taking toward our relationships with stuff. In *Projections* (2012), Jared Gardner identifies an archival impulse shaping works by Ben Katchor, Kim Deitch, and Chris Ware. Their protagonists are often "the compulsive combers of archives, warehouses, and dumpsters" (Gardner 2012: 150), and these narratives are motivated by the artists' own fascinations as collectors. These artists raid not "the ordered collections of the academic library" but rather "archives in the loosest, messiest sense of the word—archives of the forgotten artifacts and ephemera of American popular culture, items that were never meant to be collected" (Gardner 2012: 150). Gardner further speaks, somewhat romantically, of the "perverse pleasures" of those who "fetishize" older stuff, turning it into something more meaningful than "the random gleanings of the packrat or hoarder" (2012: 150). Consider what Art Spiegelman says about his collecting passions in the introduction to *The Wild Party*: "I get the same pleasure from used bookstores that an alcoholic finds in bars. Both places, though public, make room for feverish solitude and both allow unhealthy cravings to be filled to excess" (1999: v).

As with the other authors Gardner identifies, Spiegelman's relationship to early comics and other printed matter has always been more contradictory than this tongue-in-cheek description might suggest. As a critic, editor, and curator, he has been instrumental in shaping the emerging canon of his medium. As J. Hoberman writes, "Encyclopedic in his comic book knowledge, Spiegelman has, in effect, (re)created a number of his precursors. The abstract sensationalist Chester Gould (*Dick Tracy*), the Bronx expressionist Will Eisner (*The Spirit*), and the vulgar modernist Harvey Kurtzman (*MAD* Magazine) all look different today through the Spiegelman prism" (1998: 5). As an artist, Spiegelman often uses early comics for inspiration, as in "The Malpractice Suite," which deconstructs and recontextualizes some panels from a *Rex Morgan* newspaper strip (Spiegelman 2005); his opera with jazz composer Phillip Johnston, *Drawn to Death! An Opera in Three Panels* (n.d.), which depicts the early history of comics publishing; or his 2010 collaboration with Pilobolus, *Hapless Hooligan in 'Still Moving,'* which translates the language of early comics into a dance performance. Spiegelman's best known work, *Maus* (1996), originally published in two volumes in 1986 and 1991, retells the story of his parents' experiences in a Nazi concentration camp through the genre vocabulary of funny animal comics. Spiegelman's interest in early comics has often been formal (framing, juxtaposition, movement, image-text relationships, reflexivity) and metaphorical (associations, especially of race and ethnicity, but also class, which are encoded into classic character types). But insofar as he inserts characters from one narrative context into another, these acts of creative recycling raise important narratological issues.

Against the background of these observations, this chapter focuses primarily on Spiegelman's *In the Shadow of No Towers* (2004), which recontextualizes early comic strips in order to deconstruct dominant narratives about the terrorist attacks on New York City on September 11, 2001. *No Towers* consists of twenty pages of comics, each printed tabloid size on heavy cardboard stock: ten of the pages were produced by Spiegelman in the twelve months after 9/11, while the other ten constitute an archive of early twentieth-century comics. 9/11 hit Spiegelman like "a ton of bricks" (2004: n.p.). A long-time Manhattan resident, a father whose children went to school at the World Trade Center's base, Spiegelman had spent the previous few years working as a cover artist and art editor for *The New Yorker*. His often controversial images sometimes spoke to, sometimes spoke at, sometimes outraged his fellow New Yorkers (and the magazine's diasporic readership). 9/11 provoked old anxieties for the son of concentration camp survivors. After 9/11, Spiegelman was drawn back to comics as a vehicle for narrating these traumatic memories.

In the following, I want to explore three different ways we could think about the cultural work performed by early comics in *No Towers*. The first would read the featured comics as an archive, serving Spiegelman's larger curatorial mission to map his medium's formal evolution. A second framing might be suggested by the title of Spiegelman's September 10, 2004, lecture at New York's Cooper Union, "Ephemera vs. the Apocalypse." Here, Spiegelman finds "poignancy" in the persistence of early newsprint across time, even as once monumental structures (such as skyscrapers) or myths (such as American invulnerability) perish. And third, I will consider early comics as constituting the residual, with iconic comics characters functioning as 'ghosts' of older ideologies as America falls back on the same old scripts to employ disruptive new experiences. Too often, Spiegelman suggests, dominant narratives overwrite disturbing memories to rally the public behind consumerist and militarist ideologies. Spiegelman, by contrast, refuses to reduce what happened to a simple, linear narrative, falling back, instead, on fragmented, contradictory images.

Comics as Archive

> Like Carl Barks's Uncle Scrooge cavorting in his money bin, kids loved to dive around in them [old comics] like porpoises, and burrow through them like gophers, and toss them up and let the comics hit them on the head. The adult world saw comics as junk culture—toxic, or at best, harmless. But, today, in hipster clothing and Clark Kent glasses, the once disreputable comic book confidently strides into bookstores, museums, and universities cleverly disguised as the upwardly mobile "graphic novel." (Spiegelman and Mouly 2009: 9)

In "Portrait of the Artist as a Young %@#*!," an autobiographical graphic essay produced to introduce the 2005 reprint of *Breakdowns*, Spiegelman recounts how his father influenced his taste in comics. Disdainful about how young Art "waste[s]" (2005: n.p.) his time and money, Art's father had bragged that he could buy many more comics for the same money. Dad finally brings home old EC horror and crime comics, being dumped on the market in the wake of Fredric Wertham's senate testimony. As Spiegelman notes, "I had never seen comics like these before! [...] I fell head over heels into a dangerous adult world of violent, sexually charged imagery" (2005: n.p.). We might understand this story as an origin myth for Spiegelman's work as a curator, critic, and educator who has helped to define which comics get passed along to the next generation, a process Spiegelman and Mouly described in 2009 as "out of the trash and into the treasury" (2009: 9).

While in earlier times, collectors sought to possess objects that were assumed to already contain great value and prestige, more contemporary collectors often ignore questions of exchange or use value, forming their collections from "the cast-offs of society, overtaken by technological advance, used and disposable, outmoded, disregarded, unfashionable" (Blom 2002: 165). These objects are often selected according to idiosyncratic criteria, though choices may also be subcultural, as niche communities form around shared interests. The objects in a collection, Blom argues, "mean something, stand for something, carry associations that make them valuable in the eye of the collector" (2002: 166). We might, thus, distinguish the collection from the archive, which, as Diana Taylor holds, has institutionalized status: "the archival, from the beginning, sustains power" (2003: 19). The contents of an archive are "enduring materials" to be preserved and protected, "supposedly resistant to change" (Taylor 2003: 19). As Taylor notes further, "What makes an object archival is the process whereby it is selected, classified, and presented for analysis" (2003: 19). This process requires a mobilization of cultural capital by either the institution or the individual curator: their judgment certifies an artifact's value for preservation.

Within the realm of comics, few exercise the amount of cultural capital Spiegelman commands, and thus, few have his capacity to transform yesterday's 'trash' into the contents of a 'treasury,' archive, or canon. As Jeet Heer notes, comics creators, like all other artists, seek instruction and inspiration from their own tradition. Whereas elite artists may track down exemplars in museums and libraries, comics creators were forced to "educate themselves in the history of comics by scrounging through used book stores" (Heer 2010: 4). The comics tradition, until recently, was preserved within personal collections, whereas Chris Ware

(Heer's focus), Spiegelman, and others helped to construct the archive for future generations and thus to shape the metanarrative—what Heer describes as "a pedigree and lineage" (2010: 4)—through which we will understand the medium's history.

Too often, the comics Spiegelman and Ware produce are defined by what they are not: underground comics are *not* mainstream, alternative comics are *not* dominant, and both are understood as *sui genre* within a space where one or two genres—superheroes, and perhaps, depending on the period, funny animals or crime comics—determine the general public's understanding of the comics medium. Spiegelman, Ware, and others feel compelled to construct another metanarrative to situate their work within comic's historical trajectory. Here, for example, is how Spiegelman connects 1930s sex comics with the 1960s underground boom: "The Tijuana Bibles weren't a direct inspiration for many of us; they were a precondition. That is, the comics that galvanized my generation—the early *MAD*, the horror and science fiction comics of the Fifties—were mostly done by guys who had been in turn warped by those little books" (1998 [1997]: 97). He traces a chain of influence—from Tijuana Bibles to the vulgar modernists to the underground comics and then, beyond, to his contributors at *Raw* (Spiegelman and Mouly's comics anthology published from 1980 to 1991) and today's graphic novelists.

Across many essays, not to mention public lectures and classes taught to his students at the San Francisco Academy of Art and later New York's School of Visual Arts, Spiegelman has introduced what he calls "Comics 101." Much like the auteurist critics who shaped film studies in the 1960s, Spiegelman and his contemporaries are involved in a process of rescuing works from undeserved neglect. Consider, for example, what he says about EC horror comics creator Bernard Krigstein (1998b [1990]: 90):

> Over its 150-or-so-year-old history, a handful of innovators have added to the basic vocabulary of the form. Few have added more than Bernard Krigstein. [...] He was an explorer, a discoverer, a pioneer, a visionary. [...] He didn't condescend; he offered his best (and that was as good as anything gets) to a mostly uncaring audience in a medium that was almost universally despised. Much of his work still remains undiscovered and unexplored in moldering old newsprint.

The first generation of collectors turned curators—represented in Heer's (2010) account by Bill Blackbeard—relished the work of 'realist illustrators,' such as Hal Foster, Milton Caniff, Alex Raymond, and Jack Kirby, mostly associated with adventure comics. Ware, as Heer notes, has been especially associated with comics artists who depict everyday life, such as Frank King and Guyas Williams. Spiegelman, like Ware, is drawn toward formal experimentation. Spiegelman's writings focus primarily on two moments—the emergence of the comic strip in the early twentieth century (Winsor McCay, Lyonel Feininger, George Herriman) and the period immediately following the Second World War (Will Eisner, Harvey Kurtzman, Jack Cole, Basil Wolverton, and Bernard Krigstein). The first, he understands as a period when the conventions of modern comics were still taking shape: "The first decade of comics was the medium's Year Zero, the moment of open-ended possibility and giddy disorientation that inevitably gave way to the constraints that came as the form defined itself" (Spiegelman 2004: n.p.). The second was a period in which comics experimented with more mature themes and a more self-conscious relationship to mass culture—especially targeting an older readership of G.I.s returning from World War II. More recently, Spiegelman and Mouly (2009) have proposed a third core group (Sheldon Mayer, Walt Kelly, John Stanley, and Carl Barks), artists who created children's comics in this postwar period and thus shaped many of his generation's earliest encounters with the medium.

Spiegelman's tastes have helped to define the priorities of publishers such as Fantagraphics or Sunday Comics Press, which are reprinting classic comic strips; his metanarrative has shaped how comics enthusiasts read these archival editions. That said, Spiegelman has embraced this curatorial role with some ambivalence. He worries that the canonization of *Maus* in the college classroom may cut his work off from its popular roots, turning his graphic novel into "a kind of official culture that may not be allowed to live and breathe" (Jacobowitz 2007: 158). Spiegelman puts it bluntly in an essay reviewing *The Smithsonian Collection of Newspaper Comics*: "the comic strip doesn't need a pedigree" (1998 [1978]: 82). He often celebrates how comics operate outside official culture, calling them the "hunchback half-witted bastard dwarf step-child of the graphic arts" (1998 [1988]: 74), the "art that doesn't know its name" (1998 [1978]: 82), or the "art that crawls past our cultural radar" (1998 [1997]: 97). But in this same 1978 review, he speaks of the need to rescue early comics from "the uncritical and self-congratulatory nostalgia that surrounds the subject," refusing "the kind of intellectual slumming that condescendingly celebrates them because they are vulgar" (1998 [1978]: 82). Spiegelman fears what happens to objects in archives: they gather dust; they no longer circulate; they become sacred relics, but they do not necessarily provoke new creative responses.

Instead of simply constructing archives to preserve and protect the founding funnies, Spiegelman's editorial decisions juxtapose early comics with the work of contemporary artists. Spiegelman and Mouly's magazine *Raw* has been credited with introducing American readers to European comics artists, such as Jacques Tardi or Joost Swarte, of suggesting a way forward from the dead end that the underground comics had become by the late 1970s, and of coalescing a generation of new creators who helped shape the next few decades of graphic novels. But *Raw* also increased awareness of earlier comics auteurs, featuring a reprint from Winsor McCay's *Dreams of the Rarebit Fiend* (1904–1911) in the very first issue. Spiegelman and Mouly's *Little Lit* (2000, 2001, 2003) series similarly mixed classic works by Basil Wolverton, Walt Kelly, Jules Feiffer, and Crockett Johnson alongside works by contemporary alternative comics creators and children's book illustrators. While it is hard to define a unifying style or theme in *Raw*, the effort to deconstruct and redeploy archival images, especially classic comics, was one important throughline. For example, the first number of *Raw*'s second volume (1989) included not only an installment of Spiegelman's own *Maus* and a Basil Wolverton "Powerhouse Pepper" reprint, but also Charles Burns's "Teen Plague"— the blueprint for his later *Black Hole* (1995–2005) graphic novel—, which uses iconography from 1950s horror comics to explore adolescent sexual panic; Kim Deitch's "Kala in Kommieland," which rereads the politics of the McCarthy era through the imagebank of early television cartoons; and Ben Katchor's "The Smell of Exterior Street," which continues his ongoing fascination with 'forgotten New York.'

Spiegelman's decision to reprint a selection of early comic strips alongside his *No Towers* pages can be seen as a continuation of this same commitment to explore links between historic and contemporary comics art.[4] His specific selections emphasize the ways post-9/11 concerns were prefigured a century earlier. For example, some pages celebrate the Manhattan cityscape (as when Winsor McCay demonstrates his fascination with architectural detail). Other pages deal with destruction and catastrophe (as when the Katzenjammer Kids join forces with Hans and Fritz to wreak havoc on a 4th of July celebration). And still others perpetuate stereotypes about the Islamic world (as when Happy Hooligan passes himself off as "Abdullah, the Arab Chief" and tangles with a camel). The selected pages are not simply illustrative; they are also exemplary. The artists featured here (including Winsor McCay, Richard Felton Outcault, Rudolph Dirks, Frederick Burr Opper, George McManus, Lyonel Feininger, Gustave Verbeck, and George Herriman) represent the canon Spiegelman had promoted over the previous decades. Spiegelman spoke in interviews about the basic "comics literacy" (Witek 2007: 297) he assumed from his readers, but if he can take such knowledge for granted, it is primarily because he has taught a generation of readers which early comics mattered and how to read them.

---

4   For other explanations, see Smith 2008.

Furthermore, Spiegelman does not simply bracket off these earlier comics from his own creative contributions to this book. Continuing in the *Raw* tradition, he uses fragments, snippets, isolated images, removed from their original context and layered over very contemporary experiences, as the basic building blocks of *No Tower*'s own narrative. Spiegelman rejects the monumentalism that too often surrounds the archive and instead embraces an approach that explores the partial, incomplete nature of the ephemeral and the active influence of the residual.

Comics as Ephemera

> Poetry readings seemed to be as frequent as the sound of police sirens in the wake of September 11—New Yorkers needed poetry to give voice to their pain, culture to reaffirm faith in a wounded civilization. [...] The only cultural artifacts that could get past my defenses to flood my eyes and brain with something other than images of burning towers were old comic strips; vital, unpretentious ephemera from the optimistic dawn of the 20th century. That they were made with so much skill and verve but never intended to last past the day they appeared in the newspaper gave them poignancy; they were just right for an end-of-the-world moment. (Spiegelman 2004: n.p.)

If discussions of the archival often emphasize the processes of selection and curation, the concept of the ephemeral emphasizes the disposability and perishability of everyday forms of culture. 1940s era collector John Johnson defined the ephemeral as "everything that would normally go into the waste paper basket after use" (Grainge 2011: 2), while Mary Desjardins talks about "throwaways not thrown away" (2006: 40). Uricchio links the current interest in the ephemeral back to a growing uncertainty about which current media will survive: "Our media, as physical objects subject to wear, tear, reformatting and ultimately decay, are fleeting in ways that we are only now beginning to realise" (2011: 25). If there is often something monumental about archives (and especially about the buildings that house them), the ephemeral is here today and gone tomorrow.

Spiegelman evokes these associations when he tells us that *No Towers* wanted to juxtapose "these monumental buildings that become ephemeral, and this ephemera [comic strips] that became monumental" (Heller 2004: n.p.) or describes the World Trade Center as being "as transient and ephemeral as, say, old newspapers" (Dreifus and Spiegelman 2004: n.p.). Spiegelman positions comics in contrast to a range of other representational media: "I was taking my cultural sustenance from the old Sunday comics, because I couldn't stand listening to music—it was too beautiful, I couldn't follow poetry—I couldn't keep the concentration level high enough to follow it, and, if I turned on a TV, it would immediately go to a news report" (Heller 2004: n.p.). Poetry readings, he suggests, allowed intellectuals to "reaffirm faith in a wounded civilization"; art was designed as part of a common heritage, whereas comics were "never intended to last past the day they appeared in the newspaper" (Heller 2004: n.p.). He then contrasts "poets, authors, and painters" who thought of themselves as "living inside a history" with "the working stiffs at newspapers" (Heller 2004: n.p.) who had no thought beyond the day's deadline. Spiegelman finally characterizes himself as much closer to the newspaper cartoonists: "I did acknowledge that the work had urgency without thinking of the work as making any bid for posterity" (Heller 2004: n.p.).

Spiegelman drew *No Towers*'s first pages with no clear sense of when or where they would be published. What he produced was so raw, intimate, and out of sync with dominant media representations that the artist struggled to find an American publisher. Spiegelman ended up forging his own "coalition of the willing" (Heller 2004: n.p.), publishing the evolving work through various outlets, such as *The Jewish Forward* in America, *Die Zeit* in Germany, and *The Independent* in Great Britain. *No Towers* was only published more widely, as a book by Random House, in 2004.

Spiegelman had long cited the slow speed and long-term commitment required to produce a graphic novel as the primary reason he did not move immediately from *Maus* into another large scale project: "one has to assume that one will live forever to make them" (Spiegelman 2004: n.p.). In this case, he has said that he was not sure the world would last long enough for him to finish what he had started: "Considering that it takes him at least a month to complete each page, he should've started the 'weekly' series in September 1999 to get it all told by judgment day" (Spiegelman 2004: n.p.). Spiegelman thought of his pages as having a limited shelf life; he did not have "the Olympian privilege" of looking at these events as "a closed book of some kind," but rather the pages were "a report from the epicenter" (Heller 2004: n.p.).

No Towers, then, is a book composed of fragments, single pages (whether Spiegelman's own or the earlier comics he reproduced), often small clusters of images within each page, which sometimes cohere into micro-narratives but never constitute a coherent whole. Spiegelman's critics, such as the *New York Time*s's Michiko Kakutani (2004: n.p.), argued *No Towers* was "a fragmentary, unfinished piece: brilliant at times, but scattershot, incomplete and bizarrely truncated." For those of us who admire *No Towers*—I am, for instance, thinking of Kristiaan Versluys

(2006), Martha Kuhlman (2007), Hillary Chute (2007), and Christina Meyer (2010)—the false starts, half-finished thoughts, contradictions, and irresolution convey a largely unprocessed response to 9/11. Spiegelman refuses closure (whether understood in emotional, ideological, or narratological terms). Fragmentation was at the heart of his earliest work as a cartoonist, and so was a desire to capture and convey his own frayed emotional relationship to the world, a set of formal practices and themes which comes together especially memorably in "Prisoner on the Hell Planet" (1973), his account of his mother's suicide and his own nervous breakdown. With *Maus*, Spiegelman had moved toward a more classically constructed, though still highly reflexive, story, whereas his agitated state after 9/11 pushed him back toward a more fragmented structure.

Spiegelman's fascination with the fragility of comics needs to be read in relation to *No Tower*'s focus on the precariousness of memory; Spiegelman used early comics to assert control over his own emotions—control not in the sense of 'grooming' and 'packaging' them, but rather in the sense of maintaining ownership over them, preventing them from being transformed into something that can be sold or mobilized toward someone else's ends. In the book's introduction, he tells us about a "pivotal image" from that morning, "one that didn't get photographed or videotaped into the public memory but still remains burned onto the inside of my eyelids several years later"—the image of the glowing framework of the North Tower "just before it was vaporized" (2004: n.p.). Spiegelman discusses the "humiliating results" of his various attempts to draw or paint this memory; he "eventually came close to capturing" it digitally on his computer, but even then, only partially: "I managed to place some sequences of my most vivid memories around the central image but never got to draw others" (2004: n.p.).

From the start, Spiegelman identifies *No Towers* with a certain kind of failure, with his inability to communicate intersubjectively, to represent visually, something that he can also not erase from his memory. On the first page, he asserts the priority of his own lived experiences over the nation's shared cultural memories that were primarily a composite of the images most often televised: "Those crumbling towers burned their way into every brain but I lived on the outskirts of Ground Zero and first saw it all live—unmediated" (Spiegelman 2004: 1). For a second time, he writes about "memory" as something imposed upon us against our will, as "burned" onto our eyelids, a metaphor closely linked to the burning of the towers themselves (Spiegelman 2004: n.p.). By the second page, we get a sense of how little he actually saw and how much less he recalls:

He *didn't actually see* the first plane smash into the tower a few blocks south of his Soho home. They *heard* the crash behind them while heading North. He *did see* the face of a woman heading south [...]. So he and his wife, blasé New Yorkers, deigned to *turn around*. [...] He ran back home to phone the school, so he *only saw the second plane smash into the tower on TV*, though he *heard* the deafening crash *right outside his window*. He *saw* the burning towers as he and his wife ran to Canal Street, toward the school, but *his view was obstructed* as he ran up the next block. He *could only see* smoke billowing *behind a giant billboard* [...]. It was for some dopey new Schwarzenegger movie about terrorism. (Spiegelman 2004: 2, emphases added)

Spiegelman cannot find a stable vantage point on the events. This instability of perspective is suggested by his shifting pronouns—from the first-person "I" on the first page to the third-person "he" on the second, and then, ultimately, to the shared experience of the husband and wife expressed through the third-person plural "they." These shifts in subjectivity are accompanied by fluctuations between representational modes—cartoons depicting Spiegelman and his wife, a photograph of the smoke pouring from the Towers, images from *Katzenjammer Kids* (1897–) comic strips, a billboard for *Collateral Damage* (2002, Andrew Davis), and finally, the digitally reconstructed image of the glowing buildings. If *Maus* found a stable visual vocabulary, more or less, for representing its parallel father-son stories, Spiegelman relentlessly looks for new images to express these contradictory and evolving feelings, but all fail him.

His 'eyewitness' account is mostly characterized by what he did not see or did see directly: he didn't turn around, he wasn't at the right place at the right time, a billboard blocked his view, smoke obscured what was happening. Our media fail us, much like the school computer which freezes just as the moment the worried parents access Nadja's class schedule; media are inadequate to capture the experiences of our senses, much as Spiegelman, repeating his father's description of the concentration camps, finds the smell of smoke as "indescribable" (2004: 3); media do not allow us to process and make sense of what is happening, much as the school principal's intercom announcements are hopelessly out of sync with conditions on the ground. Our memories are not our own—they are produced and reproduced by media, and they are distributed collectively across the population without regard to individual perspectives. On page 4, Spiegelman asserts confidently, "he saw the falling bodies on TV much later [...] but what he actually saw got seared into his skull forever" (2004: 4). But by page 5, "I've gotta shut my eyes and concentrate to still see the glowing bones of those towers" (2004: 5). And by page 6, we learn "he is haunted now by the images he didn't witness" (2004: 6). By the final page of the book, Spiegelman (2004: 10) describes his own experiences being interviewed for television, unable to step outside the script the reporter wants to put around his memories.

In *No Tower*'s introduction, Spiegelman refers to the early comic strips as "vital, unpretentious ephemera from the optimistic dawn of the 20th century" (2004: n.p.). And that phrasing seems to have stuck in the heads of many who have discussed the work. *New York Times* critic David Hajdu maintains, "[Spiegelman] lost himself in nostalgia for an irretrievable era in his art—the Old World of comics—much as his aging father longed for the Europe that had existed before the war" (2004: n.p.). Susan Stewart (1993) has written about nostalgia as a form of utopian imagination: we hope for a return to a world that never really existed, a world simplified beyond recognition and stripped of the conflicts which characterize the present. Yet this literal interpretation of his statements does not do justice to the complex ways Spiegelman has used the ephemeral nature of comics to discuss his own feelings of impotence and inadequacy or to express his concerns about the ways that more powerful media systems (especially television) might override his own memories. And it does not acknowledge Spiegelman's recognition that these comics represent anything other than a simpler, more innocent, or more optimistic era.

Comics as Residual

> Figures from the past [...] creep up to remind us of their existence and of the influence they wield in the present. For an era such as ours that puts a premium on advancement and change above all else, declarations of the presence of the past can be confusing or alarming. (Acland 2007: xiii)

Early in *No Towers*, Spiegelman depicts himself in his *Maus* persona, having fallen asleep over his drawing board, a Sunday funny paper and a lit cigarette clutched in his hands. The sleeping artist is visited by iconic early comics characters, such as Ignatz, Happy Hooligan, and the Yellow Kid. Is this a dream or a nightmare? The ambiguity is especially clear if we read this panel alongside his 1990 lithograph, *Lead Pipe Sunday* (as reprinted in Spiegelman 1998). The earlier work shows a similar (but more expansive) set of characters, holding "a sunday outing" over the crumpled bodies of their murdered parents—a man and a woman he identifies as "art and commerce." We even see Dick Tracy holding a smoking gun, linking him directly to the acts of violence that gave birth to the medium. In a 1993 interview, Spiegelman recounts another such nightmare. Having fallen asleep in the basement of a fellow comics collector, Spiegelman dreamed that he was trapped inside the body of Happy Hooligan. After a series of misadventures seeking to pry the character's tin pan hat from his head, a sobbing Spiegelman is told, "Don't worry, Buddy Boy, it's just the style you're drawn in" (Epel 2007: 146–47).

In keeping with these earlier, more troubling representations, Spiegelman describes the iconic comics characters who appear throughout *No Towers* as 'ghosts' who have been 'disinterred' by the blasts and are coming back to 'haunt' him with messages from the past. Historically, icons have been images that encapsulate stories (especially sacred stories). In this case, iconic characters from comics bring with them a whole universe of narrative associations for those of us who know how to read them. In that sense, they are very much like ghosts, disembodied voices from the past that force us to confront unresolved conflicts or dredge up memories that should not be forgotten. Angels sometimes comfort us, but ghosts disturb and unsettle us.

Spiegelman's archival interest in comics rests on an appreciation of their aesthetic merit, their timeless appeal. His fascination with comics as ephemeral rests on their materiality, as old newsprint yellows and crumbles into dust. Yet, Spiegelman also reads early comics characters as residual. Raymond Williams wrote about some elements as "the residue [...] of some previous cultural formation" (quoted in Acland 2007: xx). Whereas the archaic might refer to materials or practices that are no longer culturally relevant, the residual refers to aspects of the culture "formed in the past" but still "an effective element of the present" (quoted in Acland 2007: xxi). The residual is that part of the past we have not put behind us.

Spiegelman suggests that the "distorted reporting" of early twentieth-century newspapers would have "made Fox News proud" and compares the decision to erase the German heritage of popular cartoon characters during the First World War with "the more recent American experiment in vindictive euphemism that brought us 'Freedom Fries'" (2004: n.p.). His depiction of Hearst and Pulitzer links their use of cartoons as a tool in a circulation war (and their subsequent taming of the more vulgar or disruptive elements of early comics) with the ways those same papers functioned to force assimilation on the immigrant population or to "inflame" the public behind a series of unnecessary military incursions (Spiegelman 2004: n.p.). Spiegelman tells us late in the book that "the killer apes" have "learned nothing" from previous horrors, such as Auschwitz and Hiroshima, and thus are doomed to repeat "the same old deadly business as usual" (2004: n.p.). All of these claims appeal to our understanding of these early comics as residual culture.

Spiegelman's best-known work, *Maus*, was similarly inspired by his discomfort with the residue of noxious ideologies that cling to beloved cartoon characters.[5] Spiegelman attended a lecture where his mentor Ken

---

5   See Spiegelman 2012.

Jacobs connected early animated characters, such as Mickey Mouse or Felix the Cat, with the minstrel show tradition. Jacobs described how subsequent generations of animators had simplified and sanitized these characters, but these figures still bear traces of earlier representations of blacks as "subhuman, monkey-like creatures with giant minstrel lips" (Spiegelman 2011: 112). Around this same time, Spiegelman was asked to contribute to an underground comics anthology, *Funny Aminals*. Other underground cartoonists had unleashed their repressed sexuality through pastiches of classic Disney characters.[6] Spiegelman similarly wanted to use pastiche to call attention to this history of racist stereotypes, proposing a story where "Ku Klux Kats" performing atrocities on black-faced mice. Ultimately, Spiegelman turned his attention to something closer at hand— his own family's struggles during the Jewish Holocaust, calling attention to the ways Hitler's ideologies were embodied in cartoon representations of Jews as vermin.

When Spiegelman, in *No Towers*, describes his struggles to retain his own memories in the face of pervasive media coverage, he depicts a clash between the North Tower's glowing embers and one of the Katzenjammer Kids whose devilish face gradually displaces it. A few pages earlier, Spiegelman uses Mama Katzenjammer to represent a terrified woman fleeing the catastrophe. Throughout *No Towers*, he returns to the image of the two boys (with burning towers atop their heads) and to their red-faced father seeking to punish them for their reckless actions. For example, he shows an enraged Uncle Sam pouring gas on the fire and setting the boys ablaze in a futile effort to battle a hornet's nest, resulting in even more vicious attacks.

As the book progresses, early comics figures often embody ideologies Spiegelman seeks to dispel. George W. Bush is depicted as leading a "backward march" (2004: 7) in an upside down world inspired by Gustave Verbeck. *Krazy Kat*'s Officer Pup in Herriman's strip (1913–1944) is linked to the repressive responses of the New York City Police to any signs of social unrest (2004: 8). Two pages conclude with panels inspired by McCay's *Little Nemo* (1905–1914). At the end of each strip, McCay shows Nemo as he is waking up in or falling out of his own bed and is comforted by his mother. This convention is often read as reassuring, but Spiegelman's use of this same device is unsettling. In one, the mother, now wearing a gas mask, downplays the boy's anxieties about John Ashcroft (2004: 6). By the second, the final panel is upside down, Nemo has turned into Spiegelman's *Maus* persona, the mother is now an American Eagle who threatens him: "now hush before mama liberates

---

6   See, for example, the notorious Air Pirates case, as documented in Levin 2003.

you" (2004: 7). Spiegelman depicts himself, at various points in *No Towers*, as the father from *Bringing Up Father* (1913–2000), so rattled by Internet conspiracy theories that he confuses his wife for a terrorist, and as the hapless Happy Hooligan. Moving beyond early comics, Spiegelman uses a 1950s *Mars Attacks* bubble gum card to represent the attack on the Pentagon, suggesting several layers of displacement, as we understand current politics through historic science fiction images (which displaced earlier Cold War anxieties).

Spiegelman writes in *No Towers* about "weapons of mass displacement," suggesting that the Bush administration had sought to distract Americans from seeking a deeper understanding of the root causes of terrorism or responding to inequalities of wealth and power within their own country: "we demolished Iraq instead of Al-Qaeda" (2004: 9), and we punished Martha Stewart rather than investigating Halliburton or Enron. In some cases, he deploys his early comics icons to demonstrate this process at work: the mother in *Little Nemo* offers false assurances, explaining away legitimate fears; the Katzenjammer Kids become whipping boys for the nation's misdirected rage; the mother in *Bringing Up Father* is the subject of mistaken identity, a white bath towel wrapped around her head confused for a turban. Spiegelman as Happy Hooligan becomes one more poster child for a national agenda that refuses to deal with human costs.

Photography critic Susan Lurie (2006) has explored the ways that certain disturbing and unsettling images—especially those of people leaping or falling from the Towers—were included in the event's initial raw coverage but displaced from subsequent representations in the name of constructing a safer, more secure spectatorial position. In some cases, she suggests, older representations of the nation under attack, such as those surrounding Pearl Harbor and America's entry into the Second World War, offered a more predictable, even reassuring narrative. Yet Lurie is also interested in how "images of falling people" have functioned as "icons of dissent" as activists and artists rejected attempts to sanitize popular memory (2006: 60). Lurie describes various projects that have reproduced those images photographically, drawn them, or even performed them, in order to force people to think more deeply about what is being removed from dominant representations of 9/11.

Spiegelman uses early comics similarly throughout *No Towers*. The book's front cover layers the images of various cartoon characters hurling through space on top of the emblematic black on black representation of the two towers Spiegelman had originally created for *The New Yorker*. These falling figures remind us of the people who leaped from the towers, even if Spiegelman also offers a more playful explanation—showing them kicked by a goat. On the back cover, he depicts the falling figures in a similar black-on-black technique. And inside the book, he writes about how disturbed he was by images of the people who fell from the skies, an account he illustrates with the down-and-out Happy Hooligan tumblesaulting through space. Rather than seeing displacement, then, simply as a tool for evasion or distraction, these examples suggest how displacement may also be used, in the Freudian sense, to work past (or even call attention to) acts of censorship. Here, again, we see the residual at work not to comfort but to discomfort the reader, to confront us with aspects of our past we would prefer to forget, rather than those which are the source of nostalgia for a simpler time.

Final Thoughts

On the final page he created for *No Towers*, Spiegelman complains about the "bombardment of kitsch" (2004: 10) on 9/11's one-year anniversary. He illustrates the notion of kitsch with a gaudy commemorative clock that eventually blows up in his face. In deciphering this image, one understands that kitsch represents an abstraction from the immediacy of lived experience; kitsch translates our personal memories into commodities that can be bought and sold; kitsch reduces something earth-shattering into something trivial. There cannot be a greater contrast to the *memento mori* that Spiegelman references in this same passage. *Memento mori* were artworks produced in the ancient world to remind their owners of our own mortality. By the nineteenth century, *memento mori* had come to refer to photographs taken of the deceased, often images of dead babies or children so that they could be remembered more vividly by their heartbroken parents. Kitsch anesthetizes with its sentimentality, whereas *memento mori* provokes raw, human emotion. Spiegelman saw 9/11 as a wake-up call, a reminder of his own mortality, especially since he feared that the rhetoric and festivities surrounding the tragedy's anniversary would lull everyone back to sleep.

Nostalgia, as is often noted, can be a deeply conservative force in contemporary culture. But as Svetlana Boym has suggested, it does not have to result in complacency. Boym distinguishes two prevailing forms of nostalgia—one, which she calls restorative, offers a "transhistorical reconstruction of the lost home" (2001: xviii), while the other, which she calls reflective, uses the past to express uncertainties and discomforts about the present. She writes: "Restorative nostalgia does not think of itself as nostalgia, but rather as truth and tradition. Reflective nostalgia dwells on the ambivalences of human longing and belonging and does not shy away from the contradictions of modernity. Restorative nostalgia protects the absolute truth, while reflective nostalgia calls it into doubt" (Boym 2001: xviii). Restorative nostalgia drives many fundamentalist movements—the desire to construct a simple narrative about setting right what has once gone wrong ('restoring America') and putting things ('the Vietnam Syndrome') to rest, once and for all. Reflexive nostalgia, on the other hand, "does not follow a single plot but explores ways of inhabiting many places at once and imagines different time zones"; reflexive nostalgia, Boym suggests, "loves details, not symbols" (Boym 2001: xviii).

Boym's distinction gives us a productive vocabulary for thinking about the different narrative stakes in nostalgia. Spiegelman's *No Towers* represents reflexive nostalgia at work. Contrary to the author's own statements, *No Towers* returns to early comics not as a source of comfort or as a celebration of the power of civilization to overcome threats, but rather because early comics offer him a language through which to voice his own uncertainties about the future and his own distaste with the ways that history keeps repeating itself. What emerges is an incomplete, incoherent, even incompetent narrative, lacking "a single plot." *No Towers* refuses to accept an "Olympian vantage point" because Spiegelman cannot yet process what he has seen with his own eyes. Spiegelman does not trust an authentic self to emerge; he is seduced by conspiracy theories and suffers from "news poisoning"; he consumes endless television replays trying to come to grips with what has happened, but never finds the answers he seeks. As Jared Gardner writes, "[t]o be an ephemeralist is to accept history (including the history of the self) as itself ephemeral" (2012: 175). Spiegelman distrusts the motives of those who would construct a simple, linear path forward from the 'apocalypse.' Rather, he wants his readers to struggle with the contradictions and uncertainties for a bit longer. Stuff of the past—in this case, early comics—surfaces here as a form of aesthetic validation (the archival), as a symbol of the fragility of cultural memory (the ephemeral), and as an embodiment of the ways that old ideologies tend to reassert themselves in new forms (the residual).

No Towers offers us only one example of the ways that contemporary graphic novels construct narratives around our complex relationships with stuff. Gardner is right to see comics creators and consumers as using the medium to confront the persistence of older materials in our everyday life, yet we should be attentive to the very different roles which the historical imagination plays in the work of different artists or even within the work of the same artist at different moments in time. Accordingly, one useful approach may be to read these artists as participating in an ongoing conversation about the place of the archival, the ephemeral, and the residual in contemporary culture.

Works Cited

Acland, Charles R. (2007). *Residual Media*. Minneapolis: U of Minnesota P. Print.
Bechdel, Alison (2006). *Fun Home: A Family Tragicomic*. Boston: Houghton Mifflin. Print.
Berger, John (1972). *Ways of Seeing*. London: Penguin. Print.
Blom, Philipp (2002). *To Have and to Hold: An Intimate History of Collectors and Collecting*. Woodstock: Overlook. Print.
Boym, Svetlana (2001). *The Future of Nostalgia*. New York: Basic. Print.
Chute, Hillary (2007). "Temporality and Seriality in Art Spiegelman's *In the Shadow of No Towers*." *American Periodicals* 17.2: 228–44. Print.
— (2010). *Graphic Women: Life Narrative and Contemporary Comics*. New York: Columbia UP. Print.
Derecho, Abigail (2006). "Archonic Literature: A Definition, a History, and Several Theories of Fan Fiction." Karen Hellekson and Kristina Busse (eds.). *Fan Fiction and Fan Communities in the Age of the Internet*. Jefferson: McFarland. 61–78. Print.
Desjardins, Mary (2006). "Ephemeral Culture/eBay Culture: Film Collectibles and Fan Investments." Ken Hillis, Michael Petit, and Nathan Epley (eds.). *Everyday eBay: Culture, Collecting, and Desire*. New York: Routledge. 31–44. Print.
Dreifus, Claudia, and Art Spiegelman (2004). "A Comic Book Response to 9/11 and Its Aftermath." *New York Times*, Aug. 7. Web.
Epel, Naomi (2007). "Art Spiegelman." Joseph Witek (ed.). *Art Spiegelman: Conversations*. Jackson: UP of Mississippi. 143–51. Print.
Farmer, Joyce (2010). *Special Exits*. Seattle: Fantagraphics. Print.
Gardner, Jared (2012). *Projections: Comics and the History of Twenty-First-Century Storytelling*. Stanford: Stanford UP. Print.
Grainge, Paul (2011). "Introduction: Ephemeral Media." Paul Grainge (ed.). *Ephemeral Media: Transitory Screen Culture from Television to YouTube*. London: British Film Institute. 1–19. Print.
Hajdu, David (2004). "Homeland Insecurity." *New York Times*, Sept. 12. Web.
Heer, Jeet (2010). "Inventing Cartooning Ancestors: Ware and the Comics Canon." David M. Ball and Martha B. Kuhlman (eds.). *The Comics of Chris Ware: Drawing Is a Way of Thinking*. Jackson: UP of Mississippi. 3–13. Print.
Heller, Steven (2004). "Art Spiegelman: The Sky is Falling!" *American Institute of Graphic Arts*, Oct. 1. Web.
Hoberman, J. (1998). "Introduction." Art Spiegelman. *Art Spiegelman, Comix, Essays, Graphics, and Scraps*. Rome: Sellerio Editore. 5. Print.

Jacobowitz, Susan (2007). "'Words and Pictures Together': An Interview with Art Spiegelman." Joseph Witek (ed.). *Art Spiegelman: Conversations*. Jackson: UP of Mississippi. 152–62. Print.
Kakutani, Michiko (2004). "Portraying 9/11 as Katzenjammer Catastrophe." *New York Times*, Aug. 31. Web.
Kuhlman, Martha (2007). "The Traumatic Temporality of Art Spiegelman's *In the Shadow of No Towers*." *Journal of Popular Culture* 40.5: 849–66. Print.
Levin, Bob (2003). *The Mouse and the Pirates: Disney's War against the Counterculture*. Seattle: Fantagraphics. Print.
Lurie, Susan (2006). "Falling Persons and National Embodiment: The Reconstruction of Safe Spectatorship in the Photographic Record of 9/11." Daniel J. Sherman and Terry Nardin (eds.). *Terror, Culture, Politics: Rethinking 9/11*. Bloomington: Indiana UP. 69–102. Print.
Meyer, Christina (2010). "'Putting it into boxes': Framing Art Spiegelman's *In the Shadow of No Towers*." MaryAnn Snyder-Körber and Andrew Gross (eds.). *Trauma's Continuum: September 11th Re-Considered*. Special issue of *Amerikastudien/American Studies* 55.3: 479–94. Print.
Smith, Jordan Rendell (2008). "9/11 TragiComix: Allegories of National Trauma in Art Spiegelman's *In the Shadow of No Towers*." *Shift: Queen's Journal of Visual and Material Culture* 1: 1–22. Print.
Spiegelman, Art (1973). "Prisoner on the Hell Planet—A Case History." *Short Order Comix* #1. Print.
— (1996). *The Complete Maus*. Originally published as *Maus*, Vol. I, 1986 and *Maus*, Vol. II, 1991. New York: Pantheon. Print.
— (1998). *Art Spiegelman: Comix, Essays, Graphics, and Scraps*. Rome: Sellerio Editore. Print.
— (1998 [1978]). "The Art That Doesn't Know Its Name." *Soho Review of Books*, Dec. 25. Reprinted in *Art Spiegelman: Comix, Essays, Graphics, and Scraps*. Rome: Sellerio Editore. 82. Print.
— (1998 [1988]). "Comix: An Idiosyncratic Historical and Aesthetic Overview." Nov.–Dec. Reprinted in *Art Spiegelman: Comix, Essays, Graphics, and Scraps*. Rome: Sellerio Editore. 74–81. Print.
— (1998a [1990]). *Lead Pipe Sunday*. Reprinted in *Art Spiegelman: Comix, Essays, Graphics, and Scraps*. Rome: Sellerio Editore. 65–72. Print.
— (1998b [1990]). "Obituary for Krigstein." *The Comics Journal* 134. Reprinted in *Art Spiegelman: Comix, Essays, Graphics, and Scraps*. Rome: Sellerio Editore. 90. Print.
— (1998 [1997]). "Those Dirty Little Comics." Bob Adelman (ed.). *Tijuana Bibles: Art and Wit in America's Forbidden Funnies 1930s–1950s*. New York: Simon and Schuster. Reprinted in *Art Spiegelman, Comix, Essays, Graphics, and Scraps*. Rome: Sellerio Editore. 97–100. Print.

— (1999). *The Wild Party: The Lost Classic of Joseph Moncure March*. New York: Pantheon. Print.
— (2004). *In the Shadow of No Towers*. New York: Pantheon. Print.
— (2005). *Breakdowns*. New York: Pantheon. Print.
— (2011). *MetaMaus*. New York: Pantheon. Print.
Spiegelman, Art, and Phillip Johnston (n.d.). *Drawn to Death! An Opera in Three Panels*. Opera.
Spiegelman, Art, and Françoise Mouly (eds.) (1989). *Open Wounds from the Cutting Edge of Commix*. Raw 2.1. New York: Penguin.
— (eds.) (2009). *The TOON Treasury of Classic Children's Comics*. New York: Abrams ComicArts. Print.
Spiegelman, Art, and Pilobolus (2010). *Hapless Hooligan in 'Still Moving.'* Dance theater piece.
Steedman, Carolyn (2002). *Dust: The Archive and Cultural History*. New Brunswick: Rutgers UP. Print.
Stewart, Susan (1993). *On Longing: Narratives of the Miniature, the Gigantic, the Souvenir, the Collection*. Durham: Duke UP. Print.
Straw, Will (2007). "Embedded Memories." Charles R. Acland (ed.). *Residual Media*. Minneapolis: U of Minnesota P. 3–15. Print.
Talbot, Mary M., and Bryan Talbot (2012). *Dotter of Her Father's Eyes*. Seattle: Dark Horse Comics. Print.
Taylor, Diana (2003). *The Archive and the Repertoire: Performing Cultural Memory in the Americas*. Durham: Duke UP. Print.
Tyler, C. (2009). *You'll Never Know: A Good and Decent Man*. Seattle: Fantagraphics. Print.
Uricchio, William (2011). "The Recurrent, the Recombinatory and the Ephemeral." Paul Grainge (ed.). *Ephemeral Media: Transitory Screen Culture from Television to YouTube*. London: British Film Institute. 23–35. Print.
Versluys, Kristiaan (2006). "Art Spiegelman's *In the Shadow of No Towers*: 9/11 and the Representation of Trauma." Hillary Chute and Marianne DeKoven (eds.). *Graphic Narrative*. Special issue of *Modern Fiction Studies* 52.4: 980–1003. Print.
Witek, Joseph (2007). "Interview with Art Spiegelman." Joseph Witek (ed.). *Art Spiegelman: Conversations*. Jackson: UP of Mississippi. 267–300. Print.

Part IV

Graphic Narrative across Cultures

JULIA ROUND

(Bournemouth)

Anglo-American Graphic Narrative

American Dreams in British Accents

Today, the British and American comics industries seem frequently joined in the minds of the world.[1] Given their history, this is unsurprising. Each country has a comics industry that grew from newspapers and strips into anthologies and serials around the turn of the twentieth century. Golden Ages then produced children's entertainment from archetypal superheroes to cartoon menaces. A shared war and serviceman readers made adult audiences dominant, leading to sexualization and melodrama alongside crime, horror, and humor. Imports and exports meant that comics were subject to moral panic and censorship in both countries, and responses to this reception included the rise of an anarchic underground publishing industry and new distribution system as well as gritty science fiction adventures and tempered superheroes in the mainstream. Most recently, the rebooting of these has been a shared activity, with mutual social commentary revamping the superhero into today's dark knights, who have invaded bookstores to now appear in graphic novels owned by the world's biggest entertainment corporations.

It would be impossible to cover all of the historical influences exchanged between British and American comics while still providing any degree of depth.[2] Instead, this chapter will summarize key convergences, actions, and reactions that have occurred over the last century. These include strategies such as metafiction and postmodernism; layered and problematized forms of narration and address; and the construction and conscious use of alterities, which will be discussed alongside the ideas of narratologists such as Mark Currie, Gérard Genette, and Charles Hatfield. I will situate these developments with reference to the basic narrative strategies found in the comics medium more generally: the depiction of

---

1   See, for example, recent critical collections such as Goggin and Hassler-Forest 2010; Williams and Lyons 2010; Jakaitis and Wurtz 2012.
2   For further information, see Barker 1984; Sabin 1993, 2001; Gordon 1998; Nyberg 1998; Savage 1998; Chapman 2011; Murray 2011; and many other fine historical and cultural studies that have been written on the histories of comics in both countries.

time as space, the reliance upon an active reader, and the creation of the hyperreal.³ To discuss these developments, this chapter focuses on two historical periods. First, I will give a snapshot of the current mainstream American comics industry. I will argue that the current graphic novel rebranding and move to (g)literacy have both grown from a collaboration of American extroversion and British introspection that became prevalent in the 1980s due to the political climates of both countries. Thematic precursors to these approaches can be seen in the American underground and British science fiction comics of the 1970s and 1980s, and these genres, styles, and themes will be analyzed within the context of the public criticism and censorship of comics in both countries in the 1950s.

The "Lit Invasion"⁴

In American comics today, the Big Two (DC and Marvel) draw their creators from around the world. A 'top comics writers' survey online finds British names such as Alan Moore, Grant Morrison, Neil Gaiman, and Warren Ellis listed alongside Americans Stan Lee, Frank Miller, Brian M. Bendis, and Ed Brubaker. Many of the top-rated runs on mainstream titles are collaborations between authors and artists from these two nations, such as Neil Gaiman's *Sandman*, Chris Claremont and John Byrne's *X-Men*, Alan Moore's *Swamp Thing*, Garth Ennis and Steve Dillon's *Preacher*, and Grant Morrison's *New X-Men*.⁵ Ever since Alan Moore redefined DC's ailing *Saga of the Swamp Thing* #21 back in 1984, American superheroes have frequently been rearticulated in British accents. Moore also created 'blue collar warlock'⁶ and all-round badboy John Constantine for this series (introduced in *Swamp Thing* #37), who would go on to star in *Hellblazer*.

Chris Murray identifies a first and second wave of British writers who, spearheaded by Alan Moore, have brought a literary sensibility to American comics through their reinterpretations of superhero titles over the last thirty years. Of course, British writers had previously worked on American titles (such as Chris Claremont's *X-Men* run), but this work tended to follow rather than challenge generic expectations. Murray argues that, by contrast, these creators "saw themselves as writers in a long

---

3   See also Silke Horstkotte's contribution in this volume.
4   See Murray for a full discussion of what he calls the "Lit Invasion" (2010: 44). On the influence of British comics writers and artists in the superhero genre, see also Kukkonen and Wood 2010; Little 2010; Ecke 2013.
5   See Cronin 2010.
6   See Christensen 2003.

tradition of subversive imaginative production" (2010: 44). They used this self-identification, along with their critical distance from American superheroes, to redefine the genre, using metaphor, realism, and social commentary. First-wave creators such as Neil Gaiman, Grant Morrison, and Peter Milligan were instrumental in launching DC's Vertigo imprint at the start of the 1990s with the revisionist titles *Sandman* (Gaiman et al. 1989-1996), *Animal Man* (Morrison et al. 1988-90, #1–26), *Doom Patrol* (Morrison et al. 1989-1993, #19–63), and *Shade the Changing Man* (Peter Milligan and Chris Bachalo 1990–1996). A second wave of writers such as Garth Ennis, Warren Ellis, and Mark Millar soon followed, adding *Preacher* (Ennis and Dillon 1995-2000), *Hellblazer* (Ennis et al. 1991–1999, #41–83, #129–133), *Transmetropolitan* (Warren Ellis and Darick Robertson 1997–2002), and *Lucifer* (a *Sandman* spin-off, Mike Carey et al. 2000–2006) to the mix.

Gathering these titles under the Vertigo imprint was the work of DC editor Karen Berger (personal interview, Round 2008: n.p.), who describes her vision for the Vertigo imprint as being

> led by the ideas, by the writers really wanting to do something different in comic books, really wanting to shake up the status quo, really wanting to take the form and, you know, again, stretch it, stretch the boundaries of what you could do. When we first started Vertigo, the pre-Vertigo titles, they were characters that either were DC supernatural or horror characters, but they were either reinvented or updated for the times. And again, used as a backdrop to tell stories about the real world, the politics, the social issues, you know, relationships, just looking at the world in an odd perspective, and I guess it caught on. But what's really interesting is that the writers on those books became so popular, and the books that they did, Neil and Grant, really changed, ended up changing how superhero comics were done, and if you look at now, twenty years later, superhero comics are pretty much writer-driven.

The notion behind Vertigo was one of redefinition. Rather than 'rebooting' (completely discarding all previous history, as in Christopher Nolan's *Batman* films) these titles absorbed and subsumed their previous incarnations. For example, Neil Gaiman's *Sandman* encompassed previous titles such as *Sandman Mystery Theatre* (upon which it was based) by explaining that the capture of Gaiman's Lord of Dreams had left a void that Wesley Dodds, star of the previous title, attempted to fill:

> *Wesley Dodd's* nightmares have *stopped* since he started going out at night.
>
> He puts evil people to *sleep* with gas, then sprinkles *sand* on them, leaves them for the *police* to find in the *morning*...
>
> The idea came to him in his *sleep*.
>
> He doesn't dream about the *man* in the strange *helmet* any more. *No more* burning eyes. Everything's all *right*. (*Sandman* #1, 1989, original emphases)

Other famous DC titles such as *House of Mystery* and *House of Secrets* were also incorporated, for example, by including host characters Cain and Abel in Gaiman's fictional land of The Dreaming (where the Sandman resides). They are named as keepers of mysteries and secrets, respectively, and Gaiman creates a backstory (told by Abel) whereby the Sandman approached him after his (biblical) death and invited him and his brother to live in The Dreaming and tell stories. Gaiman thereby implies that the 1970s *House of...* comics were being told by these characters from within *his* comic; he writes the comics industry into his text, providing a history for *Sandman*. This type of absorption is a form of retconning (retroactive continuity, whereby a character's parameters are retroactively redefined to create a single coherent history) rather than rebooting. It sustains previous events but reframes them, also serving a commercial function as it allows for sustained self-promotion and reinforcement of the surrounding comics market.

Along with this self-conscious acknowledgement of their own publication history came an exploitation of the techniques of comics storytelling. This exploitation included the depiction of time-as-space, the creation of the hyperreal through an excess of perspectives, and the active involvement of the reader between panels. As critics such as Scott McCloud and Will Eisner point out, time in comics is depicted spatially. McCloud states: "In learning to read comics we all learned to perceive time spatially, for in the world of comics, time and space are one and the same" (1993: 100). McCloud cites panels containing conversation, where remarks and replies are portrayed in speech bubbles reading from left to right/top to bottom and which therefore portray a period of time. Even non-dialogic panels can indicate the passing of time through familiar content (a pause in a conversation, for example, will be perceived as a few seconds) or other means. Similarly, Eisner notes that "[t]here is an almost geometric relationship between the duration of dialogue and the endurance of the posture from which it emanates" (1996: 60), and the implications of this comment can surely be extended to non-dialogic panels: the pose a character holds will directly affect the length of time the panel is perceived to last. However, these basic narrative strategies are increasingly exploited and modified in recent Anglo-American comics: for example, in Neil Gaiman and Dave McKean's *Signal to Noise* (1992), which presents a panoramic series of pictures masquerading as sequential ones (see figure 1). Furthermore, it is worth noting that (as in this instance) this technique may also reference the fictional status of what is being told on this page.

Figure 1: Neil Gaiman and Dave McKean, *Signal to Noise* (1992).
© Victor Gollanz. All rights reserved.

The hyperreal is created by an excess of perspective—in comics, the reader's visual point of view moves extensively. One minute we may be granted the perceptual point of view of a character in the story, but the very next panel may then cut to a wide angled view of the scene as a whole. Similarly, the information given by word and picture together may be supportive (they clarify each other) or subversive (they contradict each other for effect). For instance, a character may claim in his or her narration to have been unafraid ("Hell no") while a flashback image belies this (see figure 2). Grant Morrison's reinterpretation of *Animal Man* interrogates comics' use of the hyperreal by allowing Buddy Baker (Animal Man) to become aware of his own status as a comics character and to step out of the panel to confront his own creator, asking, "Am I real or what?" (#19, 1990). These British writers exploit and reflect upon the medium within which they work, bringing a literary self-consciousness to bear in their revaluation of titles.[7]

Sandman and *Doom Patrol* also confront the role of the reader in comics through their use of visual and verbal perspective. In *Doom Patrol,* Cliff Steele breaks the fourth wall, looking directly out of the panel at the reader as he asks, "Yeah, but is this a *book* or is it *real?*" (#21, 1989). This comment fits within the conversation he is having, but the choice of panel perspective gives it metafictional significance. A similar occurrence takes place within *Sandman* as Dream of the Endless often addresses his remarks to actual readers and diegetic characters alike, asking, for example: "But you have seen very little, mortal dreamer. Would you like to stay longer?" ("The Castle," Prologue, *The Kindly Ones,* 1996). Here, Dream directly faces the reader, even extending a hand toward him or her, and again this choice of perspective puts the reader in the position of the character being addressed, adding another layer of meaning to the narrative.

---

7   For a more detailed discussion, see Murray 2010; Ecke 2013.

Figure 2: Garth Ennis and Steve Dillon, *Preacher: Gone to Texas* (1996).
© DC Comics. All rights reserved.

This strategy can also be used within the verbal strand of the panel. At the end of *Sandman* #72 (1997) (the final words of the concluding story arc, as the final three issues were one-shot specials), the reader is fully immersed in the story, addressed through the panels in a variety of ways (see figure 3). Initially, the text is intradiegetic dialogue, as Morpheus says, "They are awake. All but one..." Morpheus is referring to the reader, ostensibly experiencing the comic's events as a dream. However, this slips seamlessly into extradiegetic narration addressed directly to the reader by the narrator/Gaiman: "and then, fighting to stay asleep, wishing it would go on for ever, sure that once the dream was over, it would never come back ... you woke up."

Figure 3: Neil Gaiman, Michael Zulli, Daniel Vozzo, and Todd Klein, *The Sandman* #72 (1997). © DC Comics. All rights reserved.

The mobility of narrative techniques available to comics makes these sorts of changes of linguistic point of view not only possible, but discreet. They can also be combined with a supportive (or subversive) use of the visual strand. To borrow from Genette's (1980) literary terminology: the visual strand in figure 3 is intradiegetic (that is, it gives us Daniel's perceptual point of view; we can see his hand pushing open the door), while the verbal strand leaves the diegetic realm completely and becomes not just extradiegetic (belonging to an omnipotent narrator) but also addresses the reader directly ("you woke up"). This combination of perspectives alerts us to the need for a narrative theory that acknowledges and incorporates the interplay between word and picture, something that Charles Hatfield (2005) calls code-to-code tension. This is typical of the literary sensibility apparent in these Anglo-American comics, and it complicates the relationship between writer, reader, and character.[8]

To call these comics literary is not, of course, to say that all these writers are verbose. Garth Ennis habitually uses a minimum of narration in his comics. The main storyline of *Preacher*, for example, is almost entirely dialogue-driven with the exception of the briefest of narrative boxes to orient us: "Six months later" and "Six months earlier" (#43, 1998; #45, 1999), "Now" (#14, 1996b), and (a personal favorite) "Couple years back, 'fore they was dead" (*Preacher Special: The Good Old Boys*, 1997). The playfulness apparent in this last caption is significant—these creators are aware of the ongoing serialized narrative within which they are working and are able to comment upon it.

Intradiegetic narration (from one of the characters) occurs a little more often in *Preacher*, where it is used to emphasize an interesting literary condition that Mark Currie calls "fictional truth," also known as "ironic authentication" (1998: 118).[9] This type of narration draws attention to itself and also foregrounds its subjectivity, making it clear to us that what we are reading is fiction, after all. A good example can be seen in figure 2, where, as noted, Tulip's narration is belied by the flashback scene to which it refers. Stressing the contrast between actual events and her telling of them removes any doubts we may have about the truth of what we are *seeing*, as it is so clearly more accurate than the subjective version we are being told. *Preacher* uses the condition of fictional truth in intradiegetic

---

[8] See Round 2007 for a fuller discussion of the possible effects of this type of interplay. See also Jan-Noël Thon's contribution in this volume.

[9] I use the term here in its postmodern and literary sense, i.e., the narrative strategy of drawing attention to the false and constructed nature of what is being told in order to paradoxically demonstrate a commitment to 'truth.' This is slightly different from analytic philosophy's use of the term as referring to what is true in the world of a fictional narrative (as argued by David Lewis, Kendall Walton, and Gregory Currie, among others).

narrative to detract attention from the fact that all fiction lives in this condition, making its story as a whole more convincing.

These strategies complicate the presentation of a single authoritative narrative voice and, accordingly, could be linked to the type of decentralization often found in postmodernism. Over the last three decades or so, comics have increasingly become self-conscious and aware of their own potential for narrative play and excess. The reader is given a multiplicity of points of view both visually and verbally, which contrast with our strong sense of our own identities. Jean-François Lyotard's (1984) theory of the formation of the social bond through language games implies an incorporation of the formation of personal identity, but it is Mark Currie's postmodern narratology that focuses primarily on the significance of proliferating points of view. Currie posits that narrative founds identity in that we construe our identities against those of others, via difference, and externalize our conception of them by using narrative methods: by telling our own stories (1998: 17). However, he also raises the question of view, of vision, commenting on the "tension between seeing and writing [...] in contemporary narratology" (1998: 127) since seeing overrules the authority of verbal narrative. In these comics, the literal pictorial view assigned by the panel (which is often a diegetic character's perceptual point of view) and the narrative input granted to the reader are set against the strongly contrasting notion of our own identities as observers, as controlling devices (such as an extradiegetic narrative voice or constant shifts in visual perspective) within the text remind us.

Of course, comics' use of overtly stylized art subverts this idea still further, as there is no truth or realism inherent in the mode (drawing) or style (which is generally non-realistic), and as seeing in comics is therefore elevated to the same fictional status as writing within this medium. If "postmodern art is not so much ambiguous as it is doubled and contradictory" (Hutcheon 1995: 87), then comic book art is postmodern in the extreme as it often denies notions of realism in both style and content (for example, the extraordinary feats and bright colors of superhero comics). Contemporary Anglo-American comics further illustrate a postmodern notion of art in the age of mechanical reproduction (Walter Benjamin). Although original comics art is available, comics themselves exist in no original state. From the written script to the final penciled/colored pages that exist in various stages (or perhaps just digitally) there is no 'original' entire comic book to be manually copied and distributed.

Currie links the condition of fictional truth to that of narrative identity: "When I tell my own story, I must deny that I am inventing myself in the process in order to believe that I am discovering myself"

(1998: 131). All these variations on postmodernism and narratology place comics and their readers in an interesting position. Narrative knowledge is intrinsic to our formation of identity, which is why a critic like Michael Bamberg (1997) identifies the continual 'testing out' and performance of identities in the manner short stories repeatedly surface within conversation. Like Currie's observations, Bamberg's model allows the exploration of the self "at the level of the talked-about *and* at the level of tellership" (2012: n.p., original emphasis).

However, comics can subvert this knowledge by playing with the narrative conditions of fictional truth and the restrictions of seeing-versus-writing in ways that most other literary forms cannot. Meanwhile, other characteristics of the medium (such as its hybrid signifiers, use of stylized art, and the gutter) continue to allow repetition of identity-affirming reader involvement. Essentially, the level of reader involvement (and, hence, the consequences for narrative identity) becomes postmodern due to this multiplicity. In this way, and by evoking the Lyotardian notion of fluctuating speaker and addressee, comics' narratology is capable of sustaining these elements of postmodernism.

The Legacy of Alan Moore

In acknowledging the narrative strategies of the comics medium and exploiting its tenets, many writers follow Alan Moore, who is a central figure in any discussion of the British influence on comics. After his work for *2000AD* and other British underground titles, Moore's rewriting of *Swamp Thing* would set the tone for British and American comics of the 1980s, and it popularized a new notion of comics authorship. As Karen Berger explains (quoted in Round 2008: n.p.):

> [I]t was really Alan Moore who changed the perception of writers in comics. He just turned the whole thing around, I mean he brought a respectability to the form, you know, by his sheer genius and talent and storytelling abilities. And [he is] such an intelligent and passionate human writer and he really showed that you could do comics that were, you know, literary, but modern and popular, and could really stand next to a great work of fiction, of prose fiction, and that really changed everything. There was really no going back after Alan did *Swamp Thing*.

Far from going back, Moore would offer other treatises on the superhero: *V for Vendetta* (1982–1989), *Miracleman* (1982), *Watchmen* (1986–1987), and *Batman: The Killing Joke* (1988). *The Killing Joke* sits alongside Frank Miller's *Batman: The Dark Knight Returns* (1986) as the two great revisionist Batman stories of the 1980s, and it is no coincidence each wrote the introduction for the other's book. But whereas Moore's comic explores the psychological similarities between hero and villain (or, to put it another way, the internal concerns of the superhero), for example, through its reiterations of the phrase "There were these two guys in a lunatic asylum," Miller's comic considers the tensions between the superhero and society (his external concerns).

V for Vendetta, first published (though unfinished) in *Warrior* magazine (1982–1985), offers a similar type of social critique by exploring visions of the superhero-as-terrorist in a dystopian London. *Watchmen* literalizes the metaphorical impact of the 1954 Comics Code on superhero characters, making this the basis of its plot. Here, the Comics Code becomes the Keene Act (based on the senate hearings that led to the censorship of horror comics in America in the 1950s), which makes it illegal for superheroes to maintain their secret identities and continue fighting crime. This type of reflective metaphor is characteristic of contemporary Anglo-American comics.

Miracleman (originally published as "Marvelman" in *Warrior*) prefigures the type of fictional framing Gaiman would later use in *Sandman*, as Moore writes his series *around* those series that had been published previously: revealing that the character's Silver Age adventures were actually simulations to keep him and Young Miracleman in a Matrix-style limbo, using stories and villains taken from comic books, while the two actually languished in a laboratory as part of a military research project that was trying to improve the human body using alien technology. The project was terminated when the scientists realized their enhanced brains were trying to reject the simulations and got scared they would break free, but Moran survived the 'real' mission and explosion that dispatched Kid Miracleman. Moore's story begins by introducing us to a middle-aged Moran suffering from migraines, dreams of flying, and haunted by dreams of his 'magic word,' which he is unable to remember. But even when he is restored to his super-identity, he struggles with being Miracleman, hating his alter ego at times. Miracleman is even able to give his wife Liz a baby, while the infertile Moran cannot. Moore's run ended with Miracleman, having traded the last vestiges of Moran (his humanity) in order to remake the world as a 'utopia,' wondering about the darker side of his creation (#16, 1989). Neil Gaiman would later pick up the reins and continue the series, again reflecting on the Golden and Silver Ages.

Moore's and Miller's comics use the superhero to explore issues such as censorship, oppression, and fascism. Although their creators stand on different sides of the political center—Moore is famously left-wing and an advocate of free speech, whereas Miller has been accused of misogynistic characterization and a right-wing political agenda—their critiques of power and government in their respective Batman titles show many of the same influences.[10] As Chris Murray (2010) argues, the social context in both countries is relevant here. The superhero was a problematic figure in the 1980s, when both countries had a conservative agenda and right-wing leadership. In the UK, Margaret Thatcher's Conservative Party was destroying trade unions, closing down factories and coal mines, putting millions out of work, levying standard taxes (the Poll Tax) at all regardless of income, and crippling the benefits system. Thatcher claimed that "[t]here is no such thing as society" (quoted in Keay 1987: n.p.) and that the party stood for rampant individualism: the survival of the fittest. In the United States, Ronald Reagan's presidency initially brought wide tax cuts, but his Reagonomics model also reduced federal spending and assistance to local governments, froze the minimum wage, and cut the budgets of non-military initiatives such as Medicaid, food stamps, and education programs. Many citizens felt that this type of trickle-down economics primarily benefitted the wealthy and that the needs of the everyman and everywoman were being trampled by the higher classes.

The omnipotent superhero was obviously a problematic figure in these contexts. Though Jerry Siegel and Joe Shuster had originally conceived of Superman as the ultimate immigrant, representative of their American Dream, back in the 1930s, the notion of a superior race and being had been tainted by the Nazi propaganda of World War 2 and become potentially fascist by the 1980s. Perhaps because of the massive impact of Thatcherism in the UK, British SF comics like *2000AD* were already exploring the fascist overtones of the superhero, for example, in titles such as *Judge Dredd* (1977–). British writers like Moore displayed a cynicism and distance that allowed them to push these relevant concerns to the foreground in their treatment of superheroes, and this critique sold.

In recent years, then, the mainstream of British and American comics have been characterized by a critical distance from their superhero subjects and a self-aware and metafictional streak that challenges easy conceptions of authorship and readership and makes use of the tensions of comics narratology.[11] A focus on literariness and authorship brought by British writers, along with emergence of the graphic novel format, the increasing presence of comics in bookstores, higher production values, and abstract covers that make use of a multitude of artistic styles, have helped to redefine comics as complex pieces of artful storytelling, rather than throwaway budget entertainment. This chapter will now look to the censorship battles of the 1950s in both the UK and USA to trace some of the cross-cultural roots of these changes.

---

10   Miller's politics are criticized in Comics Grid 2011; Flood 2011.
11   See Hatfield 2005.

Censorship, the Underground, and the Comics *Auteur*

Both British and American comics struggled with public outrage and censorship during the 1950s, resulting in the dumbing down of mainstream titles and the rise of an anarchic underground industry in both countries. The type of strong, cynical authorial voice that Moore pioneered and that remained dominant in the Vertigo titles arguably has its roots in the British and American underground, and this concluding section will consider the evolution of this movement. In comics, the 1950s were dominated by censorship and negative press in both countries as the authorities struggled to put in place a workable system that would protect young readers from what was considered inappropriate content. These actions would completely change the face of comics publishing by redefining the medium as childish entertainment in the public mind, neutering the superhero and other action-based genres, and producing vibrant underground publishing cultures based on grassroots production and anarchic aims. It is this emasculation of the superhero that led to a strong subversive streak in underground comics publishing as creators sought to re-expand the narrative capabilities of the medium.

The American Comics Code was conceived in 1948 after public outrage aimed primarily at crime and horror comics had brought the issue of violent and unsuitable content to national attention.[12] The attacks on comic books were initially financially motivated; in 1940, literary critic Sterling North published the first 'anti-comics' article bemoaning that over $1 million per month was being spent by children on comic books. But in the following years, the level of violence and the subjects of the stories featured in the new-style crime and horror comics began a storm of public debate that was amplified by reports of growing numbers of juvenile delinquency arrests. Comics' artistic styles and appearances also came under attack: the large-breasted female figure that became a stereotype of comic book art was probably introduced initially for the servicemen and soldiers who became part of the readership during World War II.[13] Once initiated, however, this exaggerated drawing style remained, and its sexual (and sexist) dimensions probably aggravated public perception of crime and horror comics so that much of their content was perceived as not simply violent but sadistically and sexually violent.

---

12 For a full discussion of this fascinating history, see Nyberg 1998.
13 Cf. Savage 1998: 12.

In 1948, the comics industry adopted a six-point code of self-censorship that prohibited allegedly indecent drawings, scenes of sadistic torture, vulgar language, glamorous or alluring representations of criminal activity or divorce, and ridicule of any religious or racial group. However, most publishers ignored the Code in their pursuit of profits. Further failed attempts at outside legislation culminated in a Senate hearing, where the threat of censorship finally forced the industry to commit to self-regulation. Thus, the 1954 Comics Code was born. Expanded from the 1948 version, the new Code forbade presentation of specific details and methods of crime, any representations of kidnapping, use of the words "horror" or "terror" in titles, depictions of torture, vampires, ghouls, as well as cannibalism and werewolfism. It further restricted advertising to acceptable products. Revised and expanded again in 1971, it eventually included dictates such as, "[i]n every instance good shall triumph over evil and the criminal punished [*sic*] for his misdeeds," and the catch-all, "[a]ll elements or techniques not specifically mentioned herein, but which are contrary to the spirit and intent of the Code, and are considered violations of good taste or decency, shall be prohibited" (quoted in Nyberg 1998: 166, 167).

Exportation of American comics meant that these concerns were shared in the United Kingdom, where guides for worried parents such as George Pumphrey's *Children's Comics: A Guide for Parents and Teachers* (1955) were produced, warning of "comics' evil communications" (1955: 61). It was not long before this "literature that glorifies the brute [...] [and] encourage[s] sadism" came to political attention and was criticized in the House of Commons (Mr. M. Edelman, Labour Party, 17 July 1952). In 1955, the UK Children and Young Persons (Harmful Publications) Act was passed. It prohibited the printing, publishing, or selling of any work consisting wholly or mainly of stories told in pictures that was likely to fall into the hands of children which portrayed "(a) the commission of crimes; or (b) acts of violence or cruelty; or (c) incidents of a repulsive or horrible nature; in such a way that the work as a whole would tend to corrupt a child or young person into whose hands it might fall" (British Government 1955: n.p.). Both countries now had in place a network (whether from outside legislation or a self-patrolled censorship) with which to limit the production of comic books to those deemed appropriate for all ages. Both may be viewed as a response to mass media and changes in the social climate that included an emergent teenage culture, a greater emphasis on popular culture, and an increase in consumerism that focused on these concerns.

Whether comics were responsible for juvenile delinquency, and indeed whether there was a significant increase in crime, is immaterial to this discussion, although there seems little doubt that the majority of the crime and horror comics published were entirely unsuitable for children. The real import of this issue is that it defined all comics in Britain and America as children's literature despite their wide readership. Couching the 'clean up' demands in terms of child protection rather than censorship was necessary for their success, but it also meant that when the Code was finally implemented, it took no account of any adult readership, unlike modern-day film certificates. The consequences were years of bland, formulaic comics and the derision of the genre. It is widely held that the 1954 Comics Code was responsible for the collapse of the American industry, and it is true that many companies shut down as a result of its restrictions, including EC Comics. The negative publicity certainly had an adverse effect on sales, as did the advent of television. There were other factors, though. One antitrust suit forced America's leading comics distributor to pull out of national distribution in 1955 (*United States* v. *American News*), which severely affected the comics industry's economy. However, the majority of publishers survived, although the extent of the Code's impact on their creativity is less clear.

But the American industry's priority has always been one of production, not creativity. The legal battles that feature from the very beginning of comics publishing evidence this, as does the prominent advertising that glutted the pages of early comics.[14] As Ian Gordon notes: 'Superman was not so much a character who helped sell comic books as a product that comic books sold" (1998: 134), and both the authors and the publishing company cashed in on associated products and merchandising. After the Code's introduction, publishers were also reluctant to experiment, and so the profitable formula of superheroes was endlessly reworked. Characters became licenses, and comedy and morality became the backbone of the vast majority of titles possessing the Code's "Seal of Approval."

For example, the Batman story "The Valley of Giant Bees" (#84, Jun. 1954) is a campy tale in which Batman, rather than using science or deduction, defeats the horde of giant bees with a balloon shaped like a giant spider. This use of childish humor and slapstick formed the basis of an era that also introduced Ace the Bathound and Bat-Mite (an elf-like creature) as well as harmless fantasy, magic, science fiction, and alien themes. Practices of recycling and exaggerated humor formed the basis of

---

14 On the narrative impact of legal decisions and considerations concerning American superhero comics, see Gaines 1991: ch.7.

the Silver Age of comics, commonly understood as beginning in 1956 with DC's *Showcase* #4, starring a revamped version of their Golden Age superhero the Flash. Marvel had attempted to bring back three of their superheroes in *Young Men* #24 (1953) without much success, but the popularity of the DC *Showcase* comic led to The Flash being given his own title. In 1961, Marvel put out its first new superhero title and, spearheaded by Stan Lee and Jack Kirby, the Marvel Age followed: introducing the Fantastic Four, the Incredible Hulk, Spider-Man, the X-Men, and others. The notion of superhero team-ups further prefigured the creation of the separate DC and Marvel universes. DC would later introduce the concept of parallel worlds by having both the Golden and Silver Age Flash characters appear together in *Flash* #123 (1962). Like the original superhero, these concepts would come to dominate the mainstream comics industry and allow for its eventual maturation through crossover titles and Elseworlds stories.

In 1971, the Code was revised and relaxed, although it still took no account of an adult readership. However, with the rise of underground comics (or comix) in the late 1960s, a largely subversive literature dealing with subjects such as sex and drugs, comics were again being written for an older audience. Comix and their increasing fan market led to a rise of specialty stores that changed the distribution system, moving the product out of newsstands and drugstores and into headshops and dedicated stores.

As Jean-Paul Gabilliet (2010) argues, the institutional and infrastructural changes of the 1960s and 1970s created strong auteurs in the American underground: writer-artists like R. Crumb who produced anarchic comics aimed at a countercultural audience. They were heavily inspired by drugs and music, as Crumb recalled: "People have no idea of the sources for my work. I didn't invent anything; it's all there in the culture; it's not a big mystery. I just combine my personal experience with classic cartoon stereotypes" (Crumb and Poplaski 2005: 260). These comics were about evading censorship—*all* censorship, including the 'inner censor'—and some of Crumb's most famous characters (Mr. Natural, Flaky Foont, Angelfood McSpade, Eggs Ackley) appeared in 1966, after a bad acid trip, during a period which he called "the most un-self-conscious period of my life" (Crumb and Poplaski 2005: 132). In Britain, too, auteur creators such as Bryan Talbot were producing acid-trip stories like "The Adventures of Luther Arkwright" (serialized in *Near Myths*, 1978), a psychedelic science fiction story set in parallel universes, between which the titular protagonist is able to move.

Science fiction came to dominate the British market from the mid-1970s, originally following the cinematic trend, but with titles like *2000AD* (whose flagship strip was *Judge Dredd*) venturing beyond the narrative and generic parameters of science fiction film. Published in-house, there was tight control on the level of violence, a contentious issue at the time as the war comic *Action* was under attack for its depictions of graphic (and often gratuitous) violence, football hooliganism, and so forth.[15] Artists such as Kevin O'Neill commented that "*Action* being taken off the stands influenced *2000AD* for the better. It made us concentrate on the science-fiction and fantasy aspect, build up a kind of mythos for the comic" (quoted in Chapman 2011: 146).

Although *2000AD* would still come under attack, James Chapman notes that it was responsible for introducing visual innovations to British comics, such as the tendency to include asymmetric panels or action spilling from one frame into the next (2011: 148). It also had a strong tendency toward dystopia and social satire, for example, in *Judge Dredd*, where the television shows of Mega-City One include *You Bet Your Life* (where contestants literally risk life and limb for cash prizes) and *Sob Story* (where viewers decide whether to send money or abuse after hearing the contestants' sad life stories). If *2000AD* was inspired by the (American) science fiction cinema that had broken through into the mainstream—such as *Rollerball* (1975, Norman Jewison), *Death Race 2000* (1975, Paul Bartel), and *Logan's Run* (1976, Michael Anderson)—it fed these elements back into American comics. This type of reciprocity finds a parallel in today's transmedia comics franchises: the revisionist Batman texts of the 1980s feed into the Christopher Nolan franchise in terms of subject matter, tone, and scope.[16]

In 1989, the American Comics Code was again revised—with the important amendment that instead of being compulsory, the stamp of Code approval would now act only as a guarantee that the comic was suitable for children. Sidestepping the Code in this way was the first move toward reasserting that comics were suitable for *all* ages, and the new wave of adult comics was signaled, in part, by the rise of the graphic novel format and an influx of British talent. The *2000AD* stable opened its doors and writers well-versed in gritty, realistic science fiction were let loose on a variety of superhero titles.

---

15 See Chapman 2011 for a full discussion.
16 Nolan's franchise is discussed at length in Brooker 2012; on *2000AD*, see Little 2010. For further analysis of transmedia storytelling and other recent developments in superhero comics, see Ndalianis 2009.

Anglo-American comics today put forward exceptional ideals that now contain within themselves reflection on their own consequences and impact (whether it is the psychological effects of being a savior or the consumerist culture within which they exist). On film, America today still gives us glittering celebrity-embodied superheroes that dominate the globe (Batman, Superman, Spider-Man), alongside movies based on British writers' revaluations of these fables, such as *Watchmen* (2009, Zack Snyder), *V for Vendetta* (2005, James McTeigue), *Kick Ass* (2010, Matthew Vaughn). Many of the comics discussed in this chapter seem to be based on American archetypes that have been rearticulated in a British accent. While this accent may be over-reliant on national stereotypes, the comics it produces seem to combine American confidence and idealism with British doubt and cynicism. Here, the pioneer spirit meets pragmatism, and it seems that both industries have been shaped by their cultural history but, most of all, have also been inspired by what the other has to offer.

Works Cited

Bamberg, Michael (1997). "Positioning between Structure and Performance." *Journal of Narrative and Life History* 7: 335–42. Print.
— (2012). "Identity and Narration." Peter Hühn, J. Christoph Meister, John Pier, and Wolf Schmid (eds.). *living handbook of narratology*. Hamburg: Hamburg UP. N.p. Web.
Barker, Martin (1984). *A Haunt of Fears: The Strange History of the British Horror Comics Campaign*. London: Pluto. Print.
British Government (1955). *Children and Young Persons (Harmful Publications) Act*. London: House of Lords. Print.
Brooker, Will (2012). *Hunting the Dark Knight: Twenty-First Century Batman*. London: I.B. Tauris. Print.
Chapman, James (2011). *British Comics: A Cultural History*. London: Reaktion. Print.
Christensen, William A. (1993). "The Unexplored Medium." *Wizard Magazine: The Sting Connection*, Nov. Web.
Comics Grid (2011). Banner by Frank Miller. *Comics Grid*, Nov. Web.
Cronin, Brian (2010). "Top 125 Comic Book Writers Master List." *Comic Book Resources*, Dec. 7. Web.
Crumb, Robert, and Peter Poplaski (2005). *The R. Crumb Handbook*. London: MQ Publications. Print.
Currie, Mark (1998). *Postmodern Narrative Theory*. Basingstoke: Macmillan. Print.

Ecke, Jochen (2013). "Warren Ellis: Performing the Transnational Author in the American Comics Mainstream." Shane Denson, Christina Meyer, and Daniel Stein (eds.). *Transnational Perspectives on Graphic Narratives: Comics at the Crossroads*. London: Bloomsbury. 163-79. Print.

Eisner, Will (1996). *Graphic Storytelling and Visual Narrative*. Tamarac: Poorhouse. Print.

Ennis, Garth (1996a). *Preacher: Gone to Texas*. Vol. 1. Art by Steve Dillon. Colors by Matt Hollingsworth. Lettered by Clem Robins. Cover by Glenn Fabry. Originally published in single magazine form as *Preacher* #1-7, 1995. New York: DC Comics. Print.

— (1996b). *Preacher* #14. Art by Steve Dillon. Colors by Matt Hollingsworth. Lettered by Clem Robins. Cover by Glenn Fabry. New York: DC Comics. Print.

— (1997). *Preacher Special #1: The Good Old Boys*. Art by Steve Dillon. Colors by Matt Hollingsworth. Lettered by Clem Robins. Cover by Glenn Fabry. New York: DC Comics. Print.

— (1998). *Preacher* #43. Art by Steve Dillon. Colors by Matt Hollingsworth. Lettered by Clem Robins. Cover by Glenn Fabry. New York: DC Comics. Print.

— (1999). *Preacher* #45. Art by Steve Dillon. Colors by Matt Hollingsworth. Lettered by Clem Robins. Cover by Glenn Fabry. New York: DC Comics. Print.

Flood, Alison (2011). "Alan Moore Attacks Frank Miller in Comic Book War of Words." *The Guardian*, Dec. 6. Web.

Gabilliet, Jean-Paul (2010). *Of Comics and Men: A Cultural History of American Comic Books*. Trans. Bart Beaty and Nick Nguyen. Jackson: UP of Mississippi. Print.

Gaiman, Neil (1989). *The Sandman* #1. Art by Sam Kieth and Mike Dringenberg. Colors by Robbie Busch. Lettered by Todd Klein. Cover by Dave McKean. New York: DC Comics. Print.

— (1992). *Signal to Noise*. Art by Dave McKean. London: Victor Gollanz. Print.

— (1996). *The Sandman: The Kindly Ones*. Vol. 9. Art by Richard Case, Glyn Dillon, Marc Hempel, D'Israeli, Kevin Nowlan, Dean Ornston, and Teddy Kristiansen. Colors by Daniel Vozzo. Lettered by Todd Klein and Kevin Nowlan. Cover by Dave McKean. Originally published in single magazine form as *The Sandman* #57-69, 1993-1995. New York: DC Comics. Print.

— (1997). *The Sandman: The Wake*. Vol. 10. Art by Michael Zulli, Charles Vess, Bryan Talbot, John Ridgeway, Jon J. Muth, and Daniel Vozzo. Colors by Daniel Vozzo and John J. Muth. Lettered by Todd Klein.

Cover by Dave McKean. Originally published in single magazine form as *The Sandman* #70–75, 1995-1996. New York: DC Comics. Print.

Gaines, Jane M. (1991). *Contested Culture: The Image, the Voice, and the Law.* Chapel Hill: U of North Carolina P. Print.

Genette, Gérard (1980). *Narrative Discourse.* Trans. Jane E. Lewin. Ithaca: Cornell UP. Print.

Goggin, Joyce, and Dan Hassler-Forest (eds.) (2010). *The Rise and Reason of Comics and Graphic Literature: Critical Essays on the Form.* Jefferson: McFarland. Print.

Gordon, Ian (1998). *Comic Strips and Consumer Culture 1890–1945.* London: Smithsonian Institution P. Print.

Hatfield, Charles (2005). *Alternative Comics: An Emerging Literature.* Jackson: UP of Mississippi. Print.

Hutcheon, Linda (1995). "Historiographic Metafiction." Mark Currie (ed.). *Metafiction.* London: Longman. 71–91. Print.

Jakaitis, Jake, and James F. Wurtz (eds.) (2012). *Crossing Boundaries in Graphic Narrative: Essays on Forms, Series and Genres.* Jefferson: McFarland. Print.

Keay, Douglas (1987). "An Interview with Margaret Thatcher." *Woman's Own*, Sept. 23. Web.

Kukkonen, Karin, and Anja Müller-Wood (2010). "What Happened to All the Heroes? British Perspectives on Superheroes." Mark Berninger, Jochen Ecke, and Gideon Haberkorn (eds.). *Comics as a Nexus of Cultures: Essays on the Interplay of Media, Disciplines and International Perspectives.* Jefferson: McFarland. 153–63. Print.

Little, Ben (2010). "*2000AD*: Understanding the 'British Invasion' of American Comics." Mark Berninger, Jochen Ecke, and Gideon Haberkorn (eds.). *Comics as a Nexus of Cultures: Essays on the Interplay of Media, Disciplines and International Perspectives.* Jefferson: McFarland. 140–52. Print.

Lyotard, Jean-François (1984). *The Postmodern Condition: A Report on Knowledge.* Manchester: Manchester UP. Print.

McCloud, Scott (1993). *Understanding Comics.* New York: Paradox Press. Print.

Moore, Alan (1988). *Batman: The Killing Joke.* Art by Brian Bolland. Colors by John Higgins. Lettered by Richard Starkings. Cover by Brian Bolland. New York: DC Comics. Print.

— (1989). *Miracleman* #16. Art by John Totleben. Forestville: Eclipse. Print.

Morrison, Grant (1989). *Doom Patrol* #21. Art by Richard Case, Doug Braithwaite, Scott Hanna, Carlos Garzon, John Nyberg, and Brian Bolland. Colors by Daniel Vozzo and Michele Wolfman. Lettered by John Workman. New York: DC Comics. Print.

— (1990). *Animal Man* #19. Art by Chas Truog, Tom Grummett, and Doug Hazlewood. Colors by Tatjana Wood. Lettered by John Costanza. Cover by Brian Bolland. New York: DC Comics. Print.

Murray, Chris (2010). "Signals from Airstrip One: The British Invasion of Mainstream American Comics." Paul Williams and James Lyons (eds). *The Rise of the American Comics Artist: Creators and Contexts.* Jackson: UP of Mississippi. 31–45. Print.

Murray, Christopher (2011). *Champions of the Oppressed? Superhero Comics, Popular Culture, and Propaganda in America During World War II.* New York: Hampton. Print.

Ndalianis, Angela (ed.) (2009). *The Contemporary Comic Book Superhero.* New York: Routledge. Print.

North, Sterling (1940). "A National Disgrace." *The Chicago Daily News*, May 8. Print.

Nyberg, Amy K. (1998). *Seal of Approval: The History of the Comics Code.* Jackson: UP of Mississippi. Print.

Pumphrey, George (1955). *Children's Comics: A Guide for Parents and Teachers.* London: Epworth. Print.

Round, Julia (2007). "Visual Perspective and Narrative Voice in Comics: Redefining Literary Terminology." *International Journal of Comic Art* 9.2: 316–29. Print.

— (2008). "An Interview with Karen Berger." *Comics and Literature—julia round dot com*, May 8. Web.

Sabin, Roger (1993). *Adult Comics: An Introduction.* London: Routledge. Print.

— (2001). *Comics, Comix and Graphic Novels: A History of Comic Art.* London: Phaidon. Print.

Savage, William W., Jr. (1998). *Commies, Cowboys, and Jungle Queens: Comic Books and America, 1945–1954.* Hanover: Wesleyan UP. Print.

Williams, Paul, and James Lyons (eds.) (2010). *The Rise of the American Comics Artist: Creators and Contexts.* Jackson: UP of Mississippi. Print.

JAN BAETENS[1] AND STEVEN SURDIACOURT[2]
(Leuven)

European Graphic Narratives:
Toward a Cultural and Mediological History

In the past, discussions of European graphic narratives have primarily focused on the specificity of these narratives and on the differences with other, non-European practices. The issue has thus largely been understood in dichotomous terms, as if the field of the European graphic narrative could only be defined in contrast to its American (and later Japanese) counterpart. This contrastive approach has also resulted in a certain negligence of the internal complexity of the field, since it often reduced the European tradition to the Franco-Belgian *bande dessinée* while considering other (European) forms as more or less imperfect variations of that idealized model.

Especially in the decade between the first academic, heavily semiotic engagements with the 'language of comics' in the 1970s and 1980s[3] and the recent embrace of scholarship inspired by the cultural studies paradigm (approximately since the turn of the century), the debate was dominated by such comparative reflections. Two questions in particular were frequently raised: (1) the question of primacy, i.e., the question whether or not the European graphic narrative production should be considered a belated imitation or, in a more optimistic reading, a reappropriation of the American newspaper comics; and (2) the question concerning the conceptualization and evaluation of differences between both traditions. The answers to both questions crystallized mostly around definitional issues, and more specifically around the problem of determining the central features of the modern comics form. The celebration of *The Yellow Kid*'s centennial in 1995, for instance, initiated a series of sometimes heated discussions on the nature (and status) of

---

[1] This research has been supported by a grant of BELSPO, in the framework of its IAP program 2012–2017 (IAP 7/01: "Literature and Medium Innovation"). Jan Baetens is affiliated with KU Leuven.
[2] Steven Surdiacourt is affiliated with KU Leuven/FWO-Flanders.
[3] See Fresnault-Deruelle 1973; Groensteen 1988; Peeters 2007; for a recent study, see Beaty 2007.

Rodolphe Töpffer's graphic narratives. His *histoires en estampes* (engraved stories) do indeed seem to lack some of the more striking features of the form. First, Töpffer uses captions in his stories instead of speech balloons. Secondly, Töpffer's 'little books,' as he used to call them, were printed as autonomous texts in small print runs. And, third, his stories were not really directed toward a popular audience.[4]

Our current view of the history of graphic narration has rendered obsolete most of the sketched discussions. Since scholars have learned to appreciate the multiple beginnings, multiple forms, and multiple histories of graphic storytelling, the question of primacy (who came first, and who invented what?) has lost much of its urgency.[5] Moreover, and more importantly, we realize today that questions of specificity should not be studied in a strict geographical perspective. Questions such as "where did it all start?" and "how did national traditions develop?" are interesting but not decisive. Finally, our understanding of medium specificity itself has evolved. The modernist preoccupation with defining what graphic storytelling is in contrast to all it is not (photo novellas or picture books, to mention two examples often associated with the comics field) has given way to a less essentialist approach. This approach focuses on the ways in which particular works are exploring, questioning, and modifying common practices within a given field. Medium specificity is then understood less as an essence than as an ongoing process of negotiation with what is considered typical of a certain medium at a particular moment in time.[6]

This chapter presents a history of the European graphic narrative that is in tune with the recent cultural and 'mediological' turn in comics scholarship.[7] Contemporary narratology has indeed integrated many insights from cultural studies (hence the opening to the historical context and the social stakes of storytelling) as well as from 'mediology,' a term coined by the French scholar Régis Debray (1991), whose historical communication studies tend to analyze processes of meaning production and reception in reference to media structures and transformations. Our historical overview will highlight the correlation between the evolution of visual storytelling and a wide range of technological and communicational innovations that have reshaped the media landscapes of their time. Graphic narratives, in other words, will not be treated as isolated and independent genres or media, but as parts of continually reconfigured

---

4   See Groensteen and Peeters 1994.
5   See Gaudreault 2008; Smolderen 2009; Boillat 2012.
6   See Costello 2008.
7   See Gardner 2012; Hatfield 2012.

media networks or dynamic cultural series.[8] For obvious reasons, our account will be far from complete. We will have to restrict ourselves to some key moments in the history of (mostly Francophone) graphic storytelling. And instead of exploring the full complexity of the various cultural series, we will focus on some fundamental aspects of the ongoing dialogue between graphic narratives and other media, techniques, and devices. This will help, we hope, to map the shifting power relations between media, which are always both influencing other media and being influenced by them.

A New Way of Telling: Töpffer's 'Engraved Stories'

Graphic storytelling was not invented by the Swiss teacher, part-time artist, and writer Rodolphe Töpffer (1799–1846), who published seven visual novels between 1831 and 1846. These novels have nevertheless generally been acknowledged as foundational examples of the practice of storytelling by means of the combination of image and text in sequentially arranged panels. Admired by cultural icons such as Goethe and read by many others during the nineteenth century, Töpffer's *histoires en estampes* are much more than simple forerunners of the contemporary graphic novel. Rather, Töpffer's stories represent a key moment in the larger shift from caricature drawing (which could have a strong sequential and narrative dimension, as William Hogarth's series of engravings show) to forms of drawing that accord a central function to the story (while preserving a strong comical side, both in style and in content).

Töpffer's pictorial revolution, on which the artist himself has extensively written (he was also a teacher, after all), should not be restricted to purely graphic innovations. There is no doubt that the combination of words and images, the sequential arrangement of images (and words), and the exploration of the narrative and expressive possibilities of images beyond their traditional illustrative function are central aspects of Töpffer's artistic renewal. But it is at least as important to take into consideration his relation to a wide array of technological and mediological transformations that were reshaping the world of printing and communication in the 1820s and 1830s.

Two technological innovations particularly influenced Töpffer's artistic practice: the autolithographic technique and the daguerreotype. Autolithography, a new engraving process in which the artist could make his or her drawings directly on the printing surface, enabled the

---

8   See Gaudreault 2008.

production of more spontaneous etchings. The use of this technique, which was not always adopted by more traditional artists since it forced them to use a simpler drawing style, influenced Töpffer's work in two distinct ways. First of all, it helped him to infuse each of his images with a particular rhythm. In Töpffer's engraved stories, a sequence is thus no longer a series of static illustrations held together by the sense of an encompassing action, but a dynamic string of lively images. The rhythmic composition of the drawings themselves creates a form of narrative tension within each image and also between the various juxtaposed panels. Second, autolithography allowed Töpffer to expand the expressive (and also the comical and cartoonesque) potential of drawings. The technique required the use of a simplified version of the more naturalistic style that was characteristic for engravings at the beginning of the nineteenth century. These 'simplified' images were well suited to the satirical aims Töpffer was pursuing in his work and can now be read as a visual critique of bourgeois rationalism and an embrace of Romantic creativity.[9]

The seemingly 'childish' style of Töpffer's little books, a necessary precondition for his rhythmic and cartoonesque treatment of the story, is also in accordance with the author's ideas on the nature of both photography and drawing. These media are characterized, he thought, by two distinct modes of representation: identity and resemblance. While the principle of identity leads to mechanical, almost naturalistic reproductions of the referent (perfectly exemplified by the then newly invented daguerreotype), the principle of resemblance is oriented toward the representation of the essence of a person or an object (best realized through the drawing's unparalleled capacity to reduce a referent to its essential form).

Töpffer's attitude toward the innovations of the printing business at the beginning of the nineteenth century showed some more reluctance. His choices concerning the publication and circulation of his books ran counter to some of the major tendencies of the era. These tendencies were specifically the massive use of illustrations in print literature—Romanticism paved the way for the golden age of illustration in the Victorian era—and the expansion of literature beyond the classic domain of the printed book or the specialized magazine—the early nineteenth century saw the advent of what Sainte-Beuve (1839) called 'industrial literature,' a literature oriented toward broader audiences and published mainly in the popular press. In this context, Töpffer's choice to circulate his work as self-published booklets, printed in small runs, appears as a notable (but complex) anachronism. Töpffer does indeed seem to opt for

---

9   See Smolderen 2009.

an older and more elite form of literary circulation, which is far from obvious given the apparent lightness of his work. (This is paradoxically illustrated by the popularity of the illegal reprints and imitations of Töpffer's stories.) At the same time, Töpffer's preference for the book prefigures contemporary attempts to 'upgrade' the often despised comics.

The choice of the book as publishing format was (just like the choice of the autolithographic technique), of course, not a neutral decision, but one that significantly shaped Töpffer's engraved stories. Both the oblong format of the book and the (ensuing) reproduction of a single strip per page proved to be ideal instruments for the realization of the kind of dynamism and narrative effect Töpffer was seeking.

The Gag Strip as Cultural Form

Although they were printed in book form and offered, under their satirical veneer, an impressive overview of the zeitgeist of the early nineteenth century (addressing, for instance, the already mentioned conflict between fantasy and rationality), Töpffer's engraved novels were not yet considered literature. And the increasing association of the practice of visual storytelling with low- and middle-brow publications throughout the century further strengthened the cultural marginalization of his work. In the second half of the nineteenth century, European magazines (the situation of the newspapers is quite different) did indeed start including all kinds of short graphic narratives. Most of the featured narratives were one-page gags, whose burlesque humor gave the Töpfferian model a new twist. In the following, we will describe the gag strip not as a mere technique, but as a full-fledged "cultural form," a concept introduced by Raymond Williams (1974) to highlight the systematic interaction between form and content, medium and audience, art and technology, production and cultural context.

One of the most notable cartoon artists of the second half of the nineteenth century was undoubtedly the German caricaturist, painter, and poet Wilhelm Busch (1832–1908). Busch mainly earned his fame with his longer stories, such as *Max und Moritz* (1865), *Die fromme Helene* (1872), and *Maler Klecksel* (1884), which would strongly influence the early American production (Meier 1992). The most striking feature of Busch's stories is their modularity, i.e., a technique of composing based on the relative independence of each panel, which offered a great liberty at the moment of deciding the final layout.[10] Unlike Töpffer's drawings, which are held

---

10 Cf. Smolderen 2009: 95.

together by his idiosyncratic use of the line and by a strong narrative drive, most of Busch's images are enclosed on themselves. This modularity is a direct effect of the xylographic technique (rediscovered and improved in the 1830s[11]), in which each image was composed and executed as a separate woodcut. As Hans Ries notes, the main advantage of this technique is that the comic strips could easily be adapted to a range of different publication formats mostly by the same publisher (Braun and Schneider) and oriented toward distinct audiences: from the quarto page (laid out in two columns) of *Fliegende Blätter*, and the horizontal form of the pictorial broadsheet (*Münchener Bilderbogen*) containing 12 to 15 images per page, to the oblong octavo format of the *Münchener Bilderbücher* presenting one or two hand-colored images on the *belle page* only.[12] Even the captions could be adapted (or left out altogether) to meet the requirements of a specific publication format. Since the artist rarely knew in advance in which format(s) his work would be published, he delivered the draft for his strips "as loose individual drawings, for which the sequence was determined, but not the spatial arrangement" (Ries 1998: 118). The result of this method of reproduction was a strongly segmented text, particularly suited for the depiction of gags (with their sustained rhythm) but less so for the representation of longer narrative threads.

Like Busch's work, most of the captioned gag strips focused less on storytelling than on the exploration of comic effects. This emphasis on gag and slapstick seems to signal a significant departure from the literary project. The visual and thematic transformations of graphic narratives (the gag is a kind of minimal narrative, after all) in the second half of the nineteenth century can, however, only be considered anti-literary as long as we use the concept in the narrow sense of canonized, high literature. In reality, there was an intensive process of formal and thematic exchange between the comic strip and other (popular) forms of storytelling and representation. The recurrence of certain jokes (the classical 'sprinkler sprinkled,' for example) and themes in different media is telling in this regard. As Thierry Smolderen (2009) convincingly demonstrates in his landmark study on the history (or, rather, histories) of the comic strip, the evolution of graphic storytelling in the nineteenth century cannot be understood without taking into account its dialogue with other media, such as photography or the emergent cinema. The influence of Eadweard Muybridge's chronophotography, for instance, helped to establish the classic form of graphic storytelling. Its grid-like page layout and its sharp separation of foreground (where the action takes place) from background

---

11 See Held 1936; Lauster 2007.
12 Cf. Ries 1998: 117–18.

(a stable backdrop) became central features of the comics medium between the end of the nineteenth century and the advent of the graphic novel in the last decade of the twentieth century (an amazingly long period when compared with the rapid succession of innovations in cinema). In another notable chapter of his book, Smolderen focuses on the connection between the renewal of the speech balloon and the invention of the phonograph. This new medium prepared the way for the inclusion of the missing voice in fixed and moving images.

The exploration and description of the process of formal and thematic exchange between various media clearly reveals the cultural relevance of the graphic narrative, which ceases to be a mere divertimento and becomes a hub, a node in the mediological fabric of an era. In addition, it discloses one of the possibilities that are now being explored as part of a progressive broadening of what is meant by the basic notions of story and storytelling. At the same time, however, it suggests that the shift from a text-based approach of narratology to a multimedial or intermedial approach of storytelling does not force the researcher to drop issues of medium specificity.

The *Ligne Claire* Aesthetics:
A Matter of Telling no Less Than a Matter of Showing

In 1929, with the publication of the first installment of what would become his first album (*Tintin au pays des Soviets*), Hergé started building a graphic universe that would fundamentally alter the practice of visual storytelling. The originality of his work is easily underestimated if we describe it in purely aesthetic terms. Like other cartoonists, Hergé amply borrowed from pre-existing models. He acknowledged the influence of, among others, *Bécassine* (a French comic series by Jacqueline Rivière and Joseph Pinchon with a female protagonist of the same name, launched in 1905) and *Bringing Up Father* (the famous family strip by George McManus, started in 1913). His use of rounded forms, his elegant and economic ways of drawing, and even the physiognomy of his leading character clearly echo the drawing style of these and other models. The actual impact of Hergé's work can only be grasped by taking into account the complex relations between storytelling and visual style as well as the cultural and mediological context of Tintin's adventures.

Hergé's *ligne claire* style is usually described as a drawing technique characterized by a clear and uniform line; the absence of shading, cross-hatching, and chromatic variation within the contour line; and (at least in the first half of Hergé's career) an equally detailed execution of fore- and background. Although this definition in purely visual terms is not incorrect, it neglects an important dimension of Hergé's style: the organic relation between style and narration. For Hergé, who needed some time to fully master it, the *ligne claire* was less a way of drawing (and of showing) than a way of telling. The *ligne claire* style is thus in first instance a narrative device, invented to sustain a smooth and efficient storytelling. The strong stylization of the drawings enables the easy identification of characters and their environment by the reader and the creation of dynamic images. It also reinforces the dynamic orientation of each story segment, leading the reader from one panel to the next.

Character recognition, internal movement, and sequential dynamism were, as we have noted earlier, already important concerns to Töpffer. But in Hergé's work, these structuring principles acquire new functions since they are deployed in an entirely different context: the context of modern mass communication with its characteristic problems and complexities. One of the difficulties that the *ligne claire* helped to overcome was that of the heterogeneous audience. Although *The Adventures of Tintin* were initially oriented toward a juvenile audience (Hergé's work was published in a weekly newspaper supplement for children), the actual reading audience was much broader and diverse from the very beginning. It was certainly not a coincidence that the subtitle for the magazine *Tintin* (first published in September 1946) would run: "The Journal for the Youth from 7 to 77." The advantage of the *ligne claire* style was that it could (and still does) appeal to both younger and more educated readers. The *ligne claire* versatility also contributed to the global popularity of the series, which was further reinforced by the gradual omission of geographic, linguistic, and cultural markers (too) strongly associated with Belgium.

The *ligne claire* was also an efficient answer to the problems raised by the publication in installments. This publication format became dominant in the 1920s, when the newer comics abandoned the serial logic of the daily or weekly strip and started to offer continuous stories (probably as a belated reaction to the movie serials of the 1910s).[13] In this publication model, the *ligne claire* style facilitated the recognition of characters and narrative situations introduced in previous installments. It also, and more importantly, sustained the narrative arch of the entire story, spanning the (temporal) gaps between the installments. The *ligne claire*, as we have seen, helps to strengthen the narrative drive and pace of the story and hence its forward orientation. Instead of having to rely on quickly worn-down cliffhanger mechanisms (*Tintin* readers know that Hergé uses cliffhangers in a rather unobtrusive way, despite the heavily serialized character of his

---

13 See Jared Gardner's contribution in this volume as well as Gardner 2012.

work), an author making use of the *ligne claire* aesthetic can depend on the narrative drive of each page or strip to arouse the reader's desire to discover what follows in the story.[14]

Adult Graphic Narratives and the Magazine Culture

It is difficult to describe the history of European graphic narratives without discussing the magazine as a specific host medium. An influential publication format in the European context, situated somewhere in-between newspapers, comic books, and actual books (the three major American forms of publication), the comics magazine developed rapidly after the Second World War. The magazine format (with its weekly or monthly presentation of serialized material) was certainly not entirely new, nor exclusively European. One of the important forerunners in France, the magazine *Le Journal de Mickey*, for instance, was established in 1934 by the American publisher Paul Winkler, founder of the Opera Mundi syndicate and copyright holder of the Disney comics in France. But it played an important role in the renewal of postwar graphic storytelling. More specifically the 'magazine era,' spanning the years between the creation of *Pilote* (1959–1989) and the cessation of *(A Suivre)* (1978–1997), saw the emergence of an entirely new reading culture characterized by the segmentation of the readerly audience and the evolution toward more traditional forms of book publishing.[15]

As noted before, the actual audience of comics was not exclusively composed of juvenile readers, even if the medium was considered a form of youth literature (or, rather, youth entertainment). Newspaper comics often contained dissimulated or manifest political subtexts, and, in general, parents did not remain indifferent to the visual stories created for their children. Furthermore, the gradual introduction of new genres, from the 1920s onwards, such as the adventure strip, the jungle strip, the detective strip, the science fiction strip, the aviator strip, and so forth, was a clear attempt to broaden the readerly audience. Yet during the heydays of magazine culture in Europe, two new and interrelated phenomena reconfigured the existing situation.

The first major change was the advent of graphic narratives oriented toward a predominantly adult audience. These 'adult' narratives appeared first as reshaped versions of existing genres and formats, such as the

---

14 See Fresnault-Deruelle 2002, 2006 for recent scholarship on the multi-layered nature of this minimalist style.
15 On the impact of different publication formats on narrative forms, see Pascal Lefèvre's contribution in this volume.

Western (*Lucky Luke*) or the historical comic (*Astérix*). The renewed genres continued to appeal to a juvenile audience but offered the adult readership a second layer of allusions and implicit meanings. On the levels of story content and plot structure, however, these narratives were less innovative than they seemed at the time. A more fundamental change was brought about by a second wave of adult narratives, which enriched the renewed genres with a more serious tone (turning rapidly into political and social satire, as in the post-1968 *Rubrique-à-brac* series by Gottlib), a more complex narrative organization (paving the way for a 'literary' approach of the medium, as seen in the work by Régis Franc, an author who also plays with the mediological possibilities of his publication format: magazines, daily newspapers, books), and more risqué material (sex and violence, in short, yet with a clearly marked preference for the former; Jean-Claude Forest's *Barbarella*, serialized in 1962 and published in 1966, has been key in this regard). In this case, the reorientation of the stories toward an adult readership went hand in hand with a fundamental renewal of the medium itself: other kinds of stories were told in new and different ways.

Thanks to these structural changes, European comics could become one of the main channels of youth protest in the second half of the 1960s, even if they did not really (contrary to the American situation) represent an underground culture. Despite recurrent problems with censorship, adult comics were in general not banned from newsstands or bookshops in Europe. This provided a solid ground for the institutionalization of the field, which was the second major development of the 'magazine era.' Of course, the institutionalization of the medium implied more than the mere possibility of legally selling it. The establishment of a viable economic structure for the publication of graphic narratives was at least as important. At the same time, the comics business gradually diversified, as a result of the systematic republication of magazine serials in album format and the progressive penetration of these albums in institutions that had never before been open to comic book culture: the bookshop, the library, the school. The availability of adult comics in book format (i.e., the hardcover A4 album) contributed to the slow, timid, but incontestable acceptance of graphic narratives in traditional literary culture.[16]

Of the endeavors to bridge the divide between visual and verbal culture, *(A Suivre)* was certainly one of the most remarkable. The magazine claimed to only publish graphic narratives that could offer the reader an experience similar to reading 'real' literature. For *(A Suivre)*, which was a breeding ground for a number of exceptional new authors and remarkable works (Tardi, Peeters and Schuiten, Pratt, Muñoz, Sampayo), this meant a

---

16 See Morgan 2003; Baetens and Van Gelder 2007.

reorientation from series to novels. The notion of the 'graphic novel' still had to gain currency, but the stories published by *(A Suivre)* came close to our current understanding of the term: the one-shot publication that was no longer part of a series and whose material, thematic, and stylistic properties were no longer defined by the preexisting constraints of a publication format (number of pages, thematic restrictions of an imposed genre, or the obligation to use the visual style of a studio, etc.). The author of an *(A Suivre)* story was, in short, supposed to have the same creative freedom as a literary writer. In addition, the double remuneration offered by *(A Suivre)* (for the magazine installments and for the publication as an album) guaranteed the financial independence of many young artists and enabled them to devote themselves to their work professionally.

Initiatives such as *(A Suivre)* were clearly indebted to the cultural context in which they appeared. From a literary point of view, the late 1970s and early 1980s represent a kind of intermezzo between the heydays of Modernism (the legitimacy of Modernist and Avantgarde practices was definitely in decline) and the rise of Postmodernism (the symptoms of which were not yet clearly visible). This intermezzo was characterized by the massive return of formerly despised notions such as story, character, psychology, suspense, linearity, and simplicity (if not plain and simple entertainment) in literary discourse.[17] The literary ambitions of *(A Suivre)* were perfectly well adapted to these changes in literary taste. As the readers grew tired of the allegedly esoteric experiments in highbrow literature and started to look for alternatives in other traditions (Latin-American magical realism, for instance) and media, graphic narratives appeared as excellent 'antidotes' to the excesses of 'good' literature. The literary models adopted by the *(A Suivre)* authors were, moreover, rather traditional (the primary model was the adventure novel à la Robert Louis Stevenson). Even if the resulting graphic narratives were regularly more experimental than their literary examples, the ideal of the adventure novel and of the literary experience it offers (excitement, suspense, immersion, empathy) was never abandoned.

Graphic narratives have greatly contributed to the narrative turn in contemporary writing. And, contrary to the academic stereotype of the 1960s and 1970s that narrativity and modernity are antagonistic forces, the graphic narratives of the 'magazine era' were stepping stones toward their future reunion, as the title of Thierry Groensteen's (1987) influential conference already suggested: *Bande dessinée, récit et modernité* (Comics: Storytelling and Modernity).

---

17 Abbott 2008 gives a good overview of the current position of narratological studies; Hatfield 2005 has been crucial in the renewed foregrounding of narrative rather than pictorial or semiotic aspects in comics studies.

Fiction versus Nonfiction: An Outdated Model?

By the beginning of the 1990s, the production of comics had developed into a thriving culture industry, determining both the modes of production and the form of the published narratives. Taking advantage of the financial crisis that hit the mainstream production in the late 1980s, a number of small press editors emerged and started to contest the established (and largely mercantile) practices of the field. The most influential of these editors was undoubtedly L'Association, created in 1990 as an artist-run publishing cooperative guided by a DIY ('do-it-yourself') philosophy. Today, L'Association has itself become one of the major publishing houses on the French book market, while some of its most innovative practices have been adopted by the mainstream industry.

The publishing cooperative contributed to the evolution of the graphic narrative (and its acceptance as literature) throughout Europe with the introduction of new publication formats inspired by the model of the novel, the liberation of graphic style, and the broadening and renewal of the existing genre spectrum. First, L'Association, following the example of *(A Suivre)*, focused on the publication of separate (one-shot) narratives. The small press publisher also rejected the standardized publication format used by the mainstream industry: the hardcover, full color, forty-eight page, A4 album (baptized 48cc by Jean-Christophe Menu, one of the co-founders). Instead, L'Association opted for a production process in which the publication format was adapted to the published content (rather than the other way around). The consequent application of this principle led to the creation of a diversified catalogue, containing both very small and rather large books. Second, the books published by L'Association stood out by a particular use of graphic style, even if there were striking differences between the various books and authors. The authors wielded expressive and (predominantly) black-and-white styles that set their works apart from the mainstream production with its colored, realistic imagery. Typical examples in this regard are the works by Jean-Christophe Menu, who places strong emphasis on the very act of drawing and tries to keep the directness of the first, unedited sketch in the printed book. This particular use of style did, of course, not merely serve the purposes of cultural positioning. It also sustained the narrative development of the (mostly quite elaborate) stories, as it allowed for a kind of "picture-writing" (Spiegelman 2011: 168, 193, 201). In its search of different stories, thirdly, L'Association encouraged its authors to experiment with new modes of storytelling. With the publication of, among others, Dupuy and Berberian's *Journal d'un album* (1994), Menu's *Livret de phamille* (1995), and David B.'s *L'Ascension du Haut Mal* (1996–2003), the publisher contributed both to the introduction and the development of the autobiographical mode in European graphic narratives. But the catalogue of L'Association also contained graphic narratives that explored the boundaries between fictional and nonfictional modes of storytelling.[18] One of the best examples of this kind of semi-fictional storytelling is *La Guerre d'Alan* (2000–2008) by Emmanuel Guibert. In this story, the author reconstructs the experiences of an American soldier, Alan Cope, during the Second World War based on conversations with the retired Cope.

While its contestation of accepted, largely mercantile practices and their aesthetic and narrative renewal was certainly driven by an avantgarde spirit, L'Association aimed primarily at expanding the existing field. Other artists, however, have started to challenge in a more radical manner the existing forms and traditions of graphic storytelling.

Graphic Narrative after the Book

The ongoing debates about the graphic novel, a term now widely accepted to designate what are deemed serious, adult graphic narratives, should not stay fixed on old-fashioned comparisons between American and European models, authors, and works. An obstinate analysis of these contemporary forms in relation to the issue of autobiography and semi-autobiography will probably prove to be equally fruitless in the long run, in spite of the importance of these modes of storytelling in the most successful graphic narratives of the past decades—Spiegelman's *The Complete Maus* (1996), Satrapi's *Persepolis* (2007), and Bechdel's *Fun Home* (2006) come to mind. The same holds true for the recurrent (but quite superfluous) question whether graphic narratives belong to the literary field or not (they obviously do, even if they are entirely wordless or abstract). But more fundamental changes seem to be taking place today, changes that will concern not only subject matter but media structures and cultural practices, as well. One could think here of webcomics and the changes they may produce in both the making and the reading of comics.

Contemporary graphic narratives in Europe are exploring practices that could reshape the field in far-reaching ways. Two major tendencies can be discerned. First, recent technological innovations allow for the reconfiguration of the traditional drawing and printing process. In this linear process, each of the phases (sketching, penciling, inking, coloring, and mechanically reproducing) both repeats and completes the previous

---

18   Cf. Menu 2011: 47–99. See also Nancy Pedri's contribution in this volume, in which she discusses the blurring of boundaries between fact and fiction.

one. Thanks to the technological evolution of the production and reproduction of graphic narratives, it is now possible to combine various phases and to abandon the strict linearity of the traditional process. Secondly, a new DIY spirit is appearing in the more progressive sectors of the field. Authors work collectively and begin to publish their own work outside the classic commercial circuits (which seem no longer interested in cutting-edge material). The books they publish do no longer have the standardized and streamlined forms that used to characterize comics mainstream production and graphic novel production. Following the philosophy of L'Association of adapting a publication's format to its specific content (and not the other way around), several independent publishers have experimented with book designs that challenge the status of the book as a host medium. Instead of being a mere container, the book then becomes a part of the work itself. The catalog of the artist collective FRMK (aka Fréon, later Frémok) offers numerous examples of this practice. Olivier Deprez, one of the members of the said collective, tries, for instance, to reinvent graphic storytelling by turning the act of drawing (in his case, woodcutting) and printing (of the woodcuts and of the book) into the act of storytelling itself, independently of the book's specific content. The story told by Deprez is as much the story represented in the book (if there is a story, which is no longer always the case) as the story of the manufacturing of the images and the book, including the book's storage, circulation, handling, and destruction.

In this kind of artistic practice, the book or the album increasingly ceases to be the ultimate form of the work. Having started out in the basement of print culture and gradually acquired the cultural recognition and status associated with the book, today's graphic narratives have turned away from the book as their ultimate ideal. Books remain, of course, highly significant, although more as visual art objects than as objects to be read (in the traditional sense of the word), and as part of a larger medial space. Graphic narratives continue to be published, but they are also converted into installations, performed by live artists, or combined with other types of creations made by other types of artists. The Belgian avantgarde comic artist Vincent Fortemps, for example, 'performs' comics on stage: in a creative dialogue with a rock band and a D-jay, he produces a visual narrative that is projected on screen in real time, each new drawing replacing, and destroying the previous one, in a sequence that is filmic rather than cartoonesque. Some of his books, among them *Chantier-Musil* (2004), manage to give a flavor of this kind of experience.

Graphic literature has started its long outbound journey, away from its traditional venues, its well-known word and image interactions, its customary subjects, themes, and plots. This journey is open-ended, and it may even bring the graphic narrative into fields that have no longer a connection to literature. But it is a passionate journey whose outcome will also prove of great importance for the future of storytelling.

Works Cited

Abbott, H. Porter (2008). *The Cambridge Introduction to Narrative*. New York: Cambridge UP. Print.
Baetens, Jan, and Hilde Van Gelder (2007). "Permanences de la Ligne Claire: Pour une esthétique des trois unités dans *L'Ascension du Haut-Mal* de David B." *MEI* 26: 183–93. Print.
Beaty, Bart (2007). *Unpopular Culture: Transforming the European Comic Book in the 1990s*. Toronto: U of Toronto P. Print.
Bechdel, Alison (2006). *Fun Home: A Family Tragicomic*. Boston: Houghton Mifflin. Print.
Boillat, Alain (2012). "Le récit minimal en bande dessinée: L'histoire constamment réitérée d'un éternuement dans la série Little Sammy Sneeze de Winsor McCay." Sandrine Bedrane, Françoise Revaz, and Michel Viegnes (eds.). *Le récit minimal*. Paris: Presses Sorbonne Nouvelle. 103–17. Print.
Costello, Diarmuid (2008). "On the Very Idea of a 'Specific' Medium: Michael Fried and Stanley Cavell on Painting and Photography as Arts." *Critical Inquiry* 34.2: 274–312. Print.
Debray, Régis (1991). *Cours de médiologie générale*. Paris: Gallimard. Print.
Dupuy and Berberian (1994). *Journal d'un album*. Paris: L'Association. Print.
Forest, Jean-Claude (1966). *Barbarella*. Paris: Losfeld. Print.
Fortemps, Vincent (2004). *Chantier-Musil*. Brussels: Frémok. Print.
Fresnault-Deruelle, Pierre (1973). *La Bande dessinée: Essai d'analyse sémiotique*. Paris: Hachette. Print.
— (2002). *Hergé ou la profondeur des images plates*. Brussels: Moulinsart. Print.
— (2006). *Les mystères du Lotus bleu*. Brussels: Moulinsart. Print.
Gardner, Jared (2012). *Projections: Comics and the History of Twenty-First-Century Storytelling*. Stanford: Stanford UP. Print.
Gaudreault, André (2008). *Cinéma et Attraction: Pour une nouvelle histoire du cinématographe*. Paris: CRNS. Print.
Gottlib (2002). *Rubrique-à-brac (l'intégrale)*. Paris: Dargaud. Print.
Groensteen, Thierry (ed.) (1988). *Bande dessinée: Récit et modernité*. Paris: Futuropolis/CNBDI. Print.
Groensteen, Thierry, and Benoît Peeters (1994). *Töpffer: L'invention de la bande dessinée*. Paris: Hermann. Print.

Hatfield, Charles (2005). *Alternative Comics: An Emerging Literature*. Jackson: UP of Mississippi. Print.
— (2012). *Hand of Fire: The Comics Art of Jack Kirby*. Jackson: UP of Mississippi. Print.
Held, Julius S. (1936). "The Illustrations of the 'Fliegende Blätter.'" *Germanic Museum Bulletin* 1.3: 20–21. Print.
Lauster, Martina (2007). *Sketches of the Nineteenth Century: European Journalism and its Physiologies 1830–50*. Basingstoke: Palgrave Macmillan. Print.
Meier, Werner (ed.) (1992). *Das Max und Moritz Buch: The Original Verse and Drawings of Wilhelm Busch with Language Notes (Language–German)*. German and English Edition. New York: McGraw-Hill. Print.
Menu, Jean-Christophe (1995). *Livret de phamille*. Paris: L'Association. Print.
— (2011). *La bande dessinée et son double*. Paris: L'Association. Print.
Morgan, Harry (2003). *Principes des littératures dessinées*. Angoulême: Éditions de l'an 2. Print.
Peeters, Benoît (2007). *Lire Tintin: Les Bijoux ravis*. Rev. edition. Brussels: Les Impressions Nouvelles. Print.
Ries, Hans (1998). "Comic Strips in the Work of Wilhelm Busch." Charles Dierick and Pascal Lefèvre (eds.). *Forging a New Medium: The Comic Strip in the Nineteenth Century*. Brussels: VUB UP. 115–28. Print.
Sainte-Beuve (1839). "La littérature industrielle." *Revue des deux mondes* 19: 675–91. Print.
Satrapi, Marjane (2007). *Persepolis*. Originally published as *Persepolis* 1–4, 2000–2003. Paris: L'Association. Print.
Smolderen, Thierry (2009). *Naissances de la bande dessinée: De William Hogarth à Winsor McCay*. Bruxelles: Les Impressions Nouvelles. Print.
Spiegelman, Art (1996). *The Complete Maus*. Originally published as *Maus*, Vol. I, 1986 and *Maus*, Vol. II, 1991. New York: Pantheon. Print.
— (2011). *MetaMaus*. New York: Pantheon. Print.
Williams, Raymond (1974). *Television: Technology and Cultural Form*. Fontana: London. Print.

JAQUELINE BERNDT
(Kyoto)

Ghostly: 'Asian Graphic Narratives,' *Nonnonba*, and Manga

On 'Asian Graphic Narratives'

Graphic narratives from Asia enjoy an increasing critical attention.[1] However, a common 'Asian' culture can hardly be determined. Works as diverse as Marjane Satrapi's *Persepolis* (2000–2003), Kishimoto Masashi's long-running series "Naruto" (1999–),[2] Tatsumi Yoshihiro's *gekiga* short stories of the early 1970s,[3] Doha's webcomic *The Great Catsby* (2005–), Kaoru's *Maid Maiden* (2009–),[4] and *Liquid City*, the second volume of which was nominated for the Eisner Awards (Best Anthology) in 2011,[5] share mainly two things: their creators' descent, and the most basic formal properties of comics. At the same time, they differ significantly in terms of readership, publication format, genre, cultural status, and the broader mediascape in which they are located.[6] Including the historically changing influx of American comics, Franco-Belgian *bande dessinée*, and Japanese

---

1   See Lent 1999, 2001, 2004, 2010; as well as the contributions in Berndt 2010, 2011, 2012; Berndt and Kümmerling-Meibauer 2013; Berndt and Richter 2006; or Lent's *International Journal of Comic Art*, such as Ogi, Lim, and Berndt 2012. One of the earliest accounts from an insider's perspective was Wong 2002. Noteworthy is also the *City Tales* comic-blog (Goethe Institut Jakarta, since 2011), which conjoins artists from Jakarta, Hanoi, Bangkok, Kuala Lumpur, Singapore, and Melbourne working in a variety of styles and genres.
2   Titles of manga that started out as magazine series are given in quotation marks in order to distinguish them from their publication site, that is, the magazine the title of which is italicized. Japanese (Chinese, Korean, and other Asian) names are given in their domestic order, surnames preceding given names (except in the works cited and in citations to authors' works published in Western languages, where they appear in the English order).
3   On gekiga (lit. dramatic picture), see Brophy 2010; Holmberg 2011; as well as the second and third sections of this chapter; one example of Tatsumi's works in translation is Tomine 2005. The Romanization of Japanese words in this chapter follows the modified Hepburn system (http://en.wikipedia.org/wiki/Hepburn_romanization). Japanese words are written without "s" in their plural form. For technical reasons, this chapter refrains from marking long vowels, either by means of macrons or spelling (such us 'shounen').
4   Kaoru is an original non-Japanese shojo manga artist of Chinese descent located in Kuala Lumpur who publishes in the Malay language prior to Chinese and English. See Gan 2011.
5   See Liew and Lim 2011.
6   Tojirakarn 2011, for example, highlights the importance of domestic popular novels by female writers for the establishment of original manga-style girls' comics in Thailand. Wong 2010b introduces an example of girls' comics uninfluenced by shojo manga.

manga, these conditions affect what kind of stories are told and how, often to an extent which outweighs fundamental aesthetic similarities.

In view of both the diversity of graphic narratives and Asia's geopolitical, religious, and linguistic diversity (which applies to other continents as well), any attempt to generalize 'Asian' comics reveals itself to be a projection, a ghost haunting contemporary criticism in the wake of Western orientalism. In turn, against the backdrop of occidentalism and self-orientalization in Asia, 'European comics' become subject to homogenization, for example, in the name of *bande dessinée*.[7] While this mutual desire to generalize deserves to be acknowledged and not just to be deconstructed, it also calls for contextualization, albeit not at any cost and not only applied to the Other. If a notion like 'Asian graphic narratives' is to make sense, then as a tool that helps to raise critical awareness of allegedly universal presumptions underlying the study of graphic narratives. The fact that the majority of theoretically ambitious publications still exhibits an astonishing inclination to address their topic in general while actually relying on a rather limited body of works gives rise to methodological blind spots that make themselves felt once cultural borders are crossed.

Thierry Groensteen's *The System of Comics* (2007) may serve as an example in this regard. Although available in Japanese, its application within manga studies is hampered not only by the discussion of works unavailable to manga readers but also by assumptions derived from a fundamentally different comics culture. *The System of Comics* suggests, for example, that contemporary artists can choose from a pool of aesthetic devices that have been increasing continuously since the late nineteenth century. This, however, is not an option for manga artists. Manga are typically rooted in weekly and monthly magazines that have formed the backbone of the world's largest comics industry since the 1950s. As such, they are prone to fashions. Both editors and consumers discriminate stylistic devices fastidiously. These devices range from the specific quality of lines (brushstrokes are a present no-go) to the rendering of flashbacks (indicated today mainly by blackened gutters). Outside of Japan, both manga translations and manga-style productions—original as well as derivative ones—are not part of an established mainstream but rather a new kind of alternative comics; yet, even though non-Japanese artists do not have to meet industrial standards, unless aiming at the Japanese market, they too observe the above-mentioned up-to-dateness, first and foremost, in favor of the taste communities to which they belong.

---

7   See Miyake 2012. For a non-homogenizing view on European graphic narratives, see Jan Baetens and Steven Surdiacourt's contribution in this volume.

Another difference pertains to assumptions of authorship. Due to the predominance of serialization, contemporary manga artists, as distinct from many of the Japanese pioneers, are only rarely well-planned with respect to the overall story arc and aesthetic intent, but very methodical in regard to the single installment's storyboard.[8] What recurs in recent Western publications on graphic narratives is, furthermore, the idea that the hand-drawn graphic line "brings us back to the embodied author" (Gardner 2011: 66). In Japanese works, as distinct from most non-Japanese manga productions, hand-drawing is still prior to CGI, but, in comparison to Western comics, it plays a different role. For one thing, the contrast between calligraphic onomatopoeia and consequently mechanical typefaces for almost any sort of script is striking. Like other aspects, this relates to a basic characteristic, namely, the fact that in manga the agency of the reader often counts more than that of the creator as 'author.' Manga artists may employ assistants who mimic the line of the master, and a specific line work that astonishes readers at first may become 'naturalized' due to familiarization in the course of a series. This is not to say that Japanese manga criticism ignores the narrative workings of the graphic line. On the contrary, it has pursued them since the mid-1990s, but on the understanding that the hand-drawn line in manga is put in the service of a highly conventionalized 'visual language.'[9]

In view of the fact that graphic narratives do not possess a universal grammar or preexistent lexicon, systematic discussions have denied them the status of language, and with good reason. Yet, both a different body of texts and different ways of relating to these texts may change the picture. Graphic narratives characterized by a high degree of codification as well as reader literacy easily evoke the impression of a 'visual language.' The persisting prominence of this notion among manga critics and readers indicates less a paucity of theoretical expertise than the reference to a cultural practice that cherishes sharing and mediality.[10] Naming manga a 'visual language' points beyond the issue of decoding sweat beads or nose bleeds. It refers, above all, to the existence of specific communities that value less a single work's aesthetic or ideological qualities than its facilitating relationships and support of reader participation,[11] from empathy and immersion to fan art/fiction and CosPlay.

---

8   Consisting of a rough panel layout, character faces, placement of speech balloons, lexias and sound words (cf. Ito 2005: 158; Jap. *name*).
9   Inoue 1995 as well as Natsume 1997 set out from analyzing the graphic line, but not related to 'authors.' See LaMarre 2010 for a non-auteurist discussion of the 'power of the plastic line' in manga.
10 Cf. Cohn 2010; Petersen 2011: 185.
11 Cf. McCloud 2006: 217.

Closely related, 'visual language' signifies a mode of expression that can and has to be memorized in order to be reproducable.[12] The majority of artists and readers treat manga's pictorial elements like script. Famously, Tezuka Osamu (1928–1989), the pioneer of graphic narratives in postwar Japan, defined his drawing style as hieroglyphic (1979: 43):

> You know, just recently I realized that I am not aiming at drawing pictures. This isn't my profession anyway, right? I've never done sketching, my drawing is completely self-taught. That's why, as an instrument of expression, as a tool for telling stories, I draw something like pictures, but as I really came to think recently, these aren't pictures to me. [...] They are something like hieroglyphs.

Takekuma Kentaro—who is, together with Natsume Fusanosuke, one of the central authors of *Manga no yomikata* (*How to Read Manga*), the first systematic attempt to explore the grammar of narrative manga[13]— suggests that we understand manga not in terms of pictorial art, but as script (*sho*). After all, manga do not visualize observations but thoughts, and their creators draw upon the reservoir of patterns and cyphers in their head that they have acquired through copying the style of their favorite manga artist as if doing writing exercises.[14] Similarly, the majority of premodern Chinese (and Japanese) art prioritized neither faithful mimetic reproduction nor artistic originality but rather the variation of standardized components, as Sinologist Lothar Ledderose (2000) has illuminated. According to him, both Chinese script and traditional painting, notwithstanding sculpture, are to be understood in terms of a modular system, escaping a notion of the pictorial that settles beyond conventionality and dependence on specific 'language' communities.

For these reasons, manga has tacitly come to represent 'Asian graphic narrative.' In fact, manga may even be regarded the stronghold of graphic narratives as such. After all, book-length comics with developmental storylines, aging characters, and explorations of the inner self—so-called *story manga*—started their triumph in Japan already around 1950, and they crossed cultural borders within East Asia long before the more recent wave of globalization.[15] But as much as there is to be said for manga as representatively Asian, as much can be held against it. First, graphic narratives from Japan do not necessarily exhibit a universal compatibility. Apart from postcolonially informed separations between 'Japan' and 'Asia' that are still prevalent in Japanese-language discourse, the verticality of Japanese script and its progression from right to left form obstacles for

---

12 For a discussion of copying as the bedrock of creation in manga, see Takemiya 2003.
13 See Inoue 1995; see also Natsume 1997, 2008, 2010.
14 Cf. Takekuma and Yamamura 2006: 9–10.
15 See Choo 2010; Leem 2012; Yamanaka 2013 for the Republic of Korea; Wong 2010a for Hong Kong; Chew and Chen 2010 for the People's Republic of China.

intercultural transfer, and the magazine as the major publication format has not taken roots anywhere outside of Japan, not even in Korea.[16] Secondly, non-Japanese artists and editors of manga-style graphic narratives facilitate the separation of 'Japan' from 'Asia' when they cater more or less exclusively to the first instead of other markets in the same region. This tendency surfaces, for example, in Taiwan, where manga publishers rarely engage in developing ties within the Chinese-language realm including Hong Kong, Singapore, the Philippines, and Malaysia. Thirdly, the Korean case deserves attention. On the one hand, the historical influx of Japanese manga—among other things, via piracy—is repudiated, while, on the other hand, both government and publishers try to carve out a commercial fortune for Korean manhwa overseas by simultaneously distancing themselves from manga and capitalizing on its reputation.[17] Finally, it is manga's proliferation among younger people worldwide that should prevent critics from limiting these graphic narratives to Asia alone; for its advocates, manga is a kind of world comics.

It goes without saying that such assertions are contextual and fluid in themselves, dependent on what 'manga' is set against. Contrapositioning manga against other kinds of graphic narratives tends to neglect the internal differentiation that, in the case of comics, applies to both their historic and their generic diversity. The real challenge, however, is to equilibrate apparent universals and particularities. 'Manga' exists without existing, like one of Mizuki Shigeru's ghosts, upon which I shall touch in the next section of this chapter. It is a highly segmented culture—suffice it to mention the genres of boys' (shonen), youth (seinen), and girls' (shojo) manga—, but across all subdivisions, it can be taken as a participatory variant of graphic narratives not limited to manga style that, in its ghostly ambiguity, calls for revisiting evaluative criteria based on modern notions of authorship, work, and aesthetic sophistication.

The Ghost Stories of *Nonnonba*

In January 2007, Mizuki Shigeru's manga *Nonnonba*[18] was, in its French translation, awarded the Grand Prix for Best Album at the International Comics Festival in Angoulême. Whereas Japanese critics were delighted, Bart Beaty, an expert on Franco-Belgian alternative comics, published a

---

16 See Yoo 2012 for a stylistic comparison of contemporary Korean and Japanese girls' comics with respect to translated editions.
17 See Yamanaka 2006, 2013.
18 This chapter uses the title of the English edition.

review on his website that culminated in the verdict that *Nonnonba* is "one of the dullest comic books I have ever read" (2007: n.p.). In all probability, Beaty's critical focus was less on the book itself than on the festival's jury and, in a broader sense, the reception of Japanese comics in France at that time. CJ Suzuki, for example, traces the honoring back to the fact that "Mizuki's manga evoke a profound impression of the 'authentic' image of traditional Japan or Japaneseness, which would satisfy the Western, Japanophile expectation" (2011: 234–35). Instead of pursuing this line of argumentation, that is, the 'orientalizing' of Japanese comics, I will question the practicability of allegedly universal evaluative criteria through a close reading of one episode of *Nonnonba*, in due consideration of specifically mangaesque aspects.

Granted, *Nonnonba* is unlikely to pass as 'manga proper,' neither among contemporary fans nor Japanese critics. As distinct from the majority of long-running series, *Nonnonba* consists of almost self-contained episodes, 26 to be precise, each of which is between 8 and 22 pages long. Although Mizuki had published several 40-page episodes under the heading of "Nonnnonba" in the boys'-manga magazine *Weekly Shonen Champion*,[19] the two Japanese *tankobon* volumes[20] of *Nonnonba to ore* (1991–1992) were largely based on his novel of the same title (1977) and published in tandem with the short TV series produced by NHK, namely, its local station in Tottori, Mizuki's native region.[21]

In *Nonnonba to ore* (Nonnonba and I), as the Japanese title reads, Mura Shigeru (b. 1922)—better known by his pen name Mizuki Shigeru—depicts the 9-year-old Muraki Shige and his daily life in a remote village in Tottori prefecture in the 1930s. The title's 'I' suggests a personal, if not autobiographical stance, while its first noun points to the old woman (*ba*) from whose stories the 'I' learns about *yokai*, "a word variously understood as monster, spirit, goblin, ghost, demon, phantom, specter, supernatural creature, lower-order deity, or more amorphously as any unexplainable experience or numinous occurrence" (Foster 2008: 8). The old woman is not only a substitute grandmother to Shige but also a *nonnon*, as both *kannon*, the Buddhist god/dess of mercy, and shamans are called in his home dialect. Although she is one of the protagonists, she does not

---

19 Beginning in issues #49 (Dec. 1, 1975: 107–46) and #1 (Jan. 1, 1976: 219–58), where they appeared next to installments of Tezuka Osamu's "Black Jack," Yamakami Tatsuhiko's "Gakideka," Azuma Hideo's "Futari to 5-nin," and other series that have entered the canon of boys' manga since then.
20 *Tankobon* is the Japanese name for bounded book editions of manga that has entered Western languages signifying a distinct publication format of comics, next to the American 'comic book' and the Franco-Belgian 'album.'
21 In 1991 and 1992, five episodes each.

appear in all book chapters. In "Bean Counter" (*Azuki-Hakari*),[22] for example, she is completely absent, which does, however, not diminish the suitability of this 10-page episode to represent Mizuki's storytelling.

"Bean Counter" opens with the panorama view of a bay, framed by trees in the foreground and accompanied by the laconic verbal insert, "The Muraki home." Zooming in while crossing the gutter to the next tier-wide panel, the reader witnesses a conversation between Shige's parents. His father, a dilettante and epicurean, has just quit his job at the local bank and now considers writing film scripts, while his mother moans about the family's income. On the first three pages alone, the parents appear eleven times each, mostly in medium close-ups, with the mother leaning toward the left and the father toward the right. The conversation comes to an end with a balloon conveying speechlessness ("...") on part of the mother, who faces the right, that is, the 'past' of Japanese script. Remarkably, Drawn & Quarterly maintained the Japanese right-to-left reading direction. This promotes the book as a manga,[23] while adhering to the initial layout that guides the reader's gaze mainly by intra-panel components, above all, character faces and bodies pointing forwards or backwards.[24]

Through a turn to the left, supported by the almost diagonal placement of the stairs in which the mother is standing, her and the reader's gaze arrive at Shige. He has just returned from a performance of "The Haunted House," a play mentioned incidentally at the episode's beginning. On the next one and a half pages, Shige tells his brother that he has been looking for inspiration to depict a scary yokai, the so-called *Azuki-Hakari*, or bean counter, whom he wants to feature in the picture book he is working on. All he knows about this creature is that it makes horrific noise on the ceiling by throwing beans. The brothers' talk is punctuated by two panels occupying the entire tier, on the bottom of the fifth page and on the top of the sixth, respectively. In a change of perspective, both convey a similar outside view of roofs, trees, and pylons; by means of vertical lines and onomatopoeia they indicate rain and the

---

22 For the Japanese edition, cf. Mizuki 2007: 129–38; for the English edition, cf. Mizuki 2012: 133–42.
23 In contradistinction, the Tatsumi anthologies also published by Drawn & Quarterly and edited by comics artist Adrian Tomine were reformatted to accomodate the Western reading direction: "if a comic book (or 'graphic novel') is to reach as wide an audience as possible, the last thing it needs is another obstacle for new readers to surmount" (Tomine 2005: n.p.).
24 On the centrality that 'manga proper' gives to guiding the reader's gaze, see Inoue 1995 and Kanno 2004.

elapsing of time.²⁵ The whole family is already asleep, and only Shige is still sitting over his drawings when he is suddenly roused by a voice represented in a strangely waved balloon with an organic-looking gooseneck tail. Over the entire seventh page, Shige responds to the (still invisible) Azuki-Hakari, who spouts hackneyed phrases such as, "I exist without existing" (Mizuki 2012: 139). Preceded by a lightning-shaped zigzag line traversing the first panel of the eighth page diagonally from top right to bottom left, the yokai makes its appearance before Shige's (and the reader's) eyes, only to proclaim that destiny predetermines into what family you are born and what you will do in life. When Shige wants the Azuki-Hakari to stay a little longer (on top of the tenth and last page), the ghost refuses with the remark that "more time does not necessarily lead to a deeper understanding" (Mizuki 2012: 142) and vanishes on another zigzag line, this time running from top left to bottom right. The ghost's exit is underlined by a sound word at the tail of another wavy line placed in the first panel of the next tier, that is, right below the last close-up of Azuki-Hakari. The episode ends with sweat drops and another speechless balloon, but it does not offer any punch line or specific moral (which can hardly be gained from the previous platitudes either). The very last panel, an almost exact copy of the outside view on top of the sixth page that had opened Shige's encounter with the yokai, closes the circle. It is still raining, and nothing has really changed.

Beaty gives mainly three reasons for his dislike of Mizuki's book. First, he points to the fact that *Nonnonba* is a "slow-paced or plot-absent comic" that is not "driven by unique visual sensibilities and expansions of the comics form [...;] the art does absolutely nothing to hold the attention" of the reader; second, he finds that "none of the characters is well developed or interesting, and the book relies on sentimental stereotypes at almost every turn"; third, he disapproves of the obvious discrepancy between the manga's alleged autobiographical realism and "an element of the fantastic," which to him results in the simplistic message, "hey, youth is a magical time of imagination" (Beaty 2007: n.p.).

Nonnonba's panel layout, to begin with, is indeed sedate, basically breaking the page into four tiers with two panels each. Although sizes slightly alter and certain instances are emphasized through blow-ups, none of the panels ever stretches over the entire double spread, drawing attention to a larger frame, neither literally nor figuratively. The reader is supposed to 'scan' the panels, more or less one by one, and page after page from top right to bottom left. The effect of transparency induced by

---

25 Unfortunately, the English edition replaces the initially hand-drawn sound words by edged printed letters that do not blend in visually.

the moderate layout is undermined by the caricatured character design, especially that of the boys. But meticulously depicted hand-hatched backgrounds and the rendering of characters' outlines with the G-pen, which allows for mutable stroke width, lend a realist weight to bodies and scenes, characteristic not only of Mizuki's particular style but also gekiga. Pioneered around 1960 by Tatsumi Yoshihiro, Saito Takao, and Mizuki himself, among others, these adult-oriented comics showed a strong inclination to employ medium close-ups like those in the episode introduced above, as well as small eyes.[26] Before returning to these stylistic issues in the next section, I will examine *Nonnonba*'s narrative.

A Ghostly Mode of Storytelling

Nonnonba's supposed shortcomings include its vacillating between narrative progression and undramatic episodes, the personal and the conventional, the realist and the fantastic. Some critics have appreciated *Nonnonba* as a "modest autobiography (no imposing first-person discourse, but a story that reveals itself little by little)" (Guilbert 2008),[27] and readers interested less in autobiography than in modern Japan have acknowledged its historical depth.[28] Indeed, the manga contains many allusions to Japanese militarism, the gap between the still traditional periphery and the modern center Tokyo, as well as gender hierarchies such as those condensed in the selling of Shige's friend Miwa to a brothel. However, at the center of delving into the personal and collective past are the yokai, topically as well as aesthetically, and not merely as a means of nostalgia.[29] At a first glance, these ghosts belong to a realm beyond modern anthropocentrism, a world where natural and social predeterminations prevail like in the rural parts of prewar Japan. In such a world, mortal diseases are part of daily life. Concordantly, the death of Shige's cousin Chigusa is not laden with tragic meaning.[30]

---

26 Cf. Ito 2005: 214.
27 See also the thorough discussion by Lefèvre 2007.
28 See Suzuki 2011, based on Foster 2008.
29 Due to his representation-centered approach, Suzuki assumes that Mizuki's yokai manga (not only *Nonnonba*) foster nostalgia for a lost nativist past (cf. 2011: 232), but he misses the implications of the yokai's fundamental ambiguity that undermine binarisms, for example, between tradition and modernity, allegedly Japanese spatialized narratives and 'Western' developmental plots (cf. 2011: 235).
30 Besides her equation with a ghost upon her first appearance, by means of vertical lines on the upper half of her face (Mizuki 2012: 95), it is noteworthy that she is the only character with big dark eyes, which can be traced back to the girls' manga Mizuki created in the late 1950s for rental gekiga. On a side note, Chigusa as well as Miwa do not feature in Mizuki's novel (1977).

Besides historical background, it is *Nonnonba*'s commitment to slowness, its withdrawal from straightforward storytelling, and its abstention from psychologizing that makes the appearance of the yokai plausible. Mizuki's ghosts, however, are endowed with an astonishing presence and visual determinacy. Supposed to oscillate between the visible and the invisible, to finally escape modern rationalization and stay indefinite, they look modernized if taken as isolated images and short-circuited with general discourses of modernization.[31] As a matter of fact, the initially oral folklore saw its first visualizations in late eighteenth century, taking the form of printed matter circulating in urban areas. Although Mizuki draws heavily on the style of those early-modern pictures, it should not be overlooked that his figures, in all similarity, appear in modern manga, where they are contextualized by factors such as comics aesthetics, generic markers, industrially fostered readership segmentation, and the medium's cultural positioning. Not visualization in general, but specifically visualization in manga—as a historically distinct imaginary and discursive space—confirms the yokai's status as inhabitants of a vague intermediary realm.

This can be deduced from a comparison with the literary predecessor of *Nonnonba*. Its protagonist carries Mizuki's real name Mura Shigeru and thus suggests the narrative to be more authentic than the manga. Most importantly, the novel exhibits a striking restraint to give precise accounts of the yokai, whereas the manga depicts them in detail. Considering that manga in general is expected to provide not necessarily authentic but verisimilar fictional worlds (and that Mizuki does not directly claim an autobiographical voice in *Nonnonba*), it becomes obvious how a manga-specific ambiguity of what to take for real and the in/determinacy of yokai can go hand in hand. The unpacking of such potential, however, depends on the reader. What may still appear as a lack of consistency to literary critics has been embraced by younger non-Japanese readers since the late 1990s: the seemingly incompatible, the appropriation of elements from different cultural backgrounds and media, or the generic blend that complicates, among other things, the categorization of erotica (*hentai*) as serious pornography. In short, not refined purity, but spectacular, and sometimes uncanny, hybridity is one of the crucial contemporary attractions of manga on a global scale.

With this in view, manga's representational penchant to feature the co-existence of ostensible opposites like the super/natural or fluid boundaries between humans and nonhumans cannot easily be ascribed to Japanese (or even 'Asian') traditions. Rather than placing contemporary

---

31 Cf. Kinoshita 1993: 56.

popular narratives directly in continuous cultural or religious traditions, theater specialist Fukushima Yoshiko foregrounds not traditions as such but their mediation when she proposes, "Japanese theater, especially *shogekijo*, consciously re-encountered traditional Japanese theater and literary arts through story-comics" (2003: 15).[32] In her analysis of stage adaptations of specific manga,[33] Fukushima refers to 'manga discourse' as "a rule-oriented, codified discourse appealing especially to the visual and aural senses" (2003: 76). Such a broad notion of what otherwise could be called the 'mangaesque' allows her to clarify the aesthetic accomplishments of allegedly apolitical, spectacularly superficial, and speedy productions: the distance toward illusionism, the prevalence of non-psychologized characters whose emotions are rather expressed through rapid movements than dialogue, and the 'decorative' rather than representation-oriented use of words. Fukushima also turns to *monogatari*, an archetype of narrative that traces back to the Japanese Middle Ages.[34] Initially intertwining myth and novel, oral and written tales, escape from, and resistance to, social reality, this narrative model has been, on her account, revived by manga artists since the 1950s.[35] Noteworthy in this regard is that she mentions Mizuki as well as Tezuka.

Already in his *Manga daigaku* (*Cartoon College*, 1950[36]), Tezuka explained how narratives should be structured and maintained *ki-sho-ten-ketsu* to be the foundation of both comic strips—in postwar Japan usually composed of four vertical panels—and story manga.[37] In contradistinction to the European three-act structure with its succession of set-up, confrontation, and resolution, the rhetorical structure of *ki-sho-ten-ketsu* consists of four steps in accordance with the four-line compositions of Chinese poetry from which it was derived.[38] First, something happens (*ki*). Then, this occurence is elaborated on, taken in (*sho*), or made acceptable, by considering several aspects in a way closer to spatial juxtaposition than linear succession. A plot-oriented reader may get the impression not of two different steps, but of an excessively long introduction. Even Saso Akira, manga artist and professor, combines the first two steps when he

---

32 Shogekijo literally means 'small theater' and, since the late 1970s, refers to troupes that set themselves apart from modern script-based theater, the underground of the late 1960s, and traditional forms of play such as Kabuki.
33 By Noda Hideki and his troupe Yume no yuminsha (Idlers Playing and Sleeping in a Dream, 1976–1992).
34 See, for example, Murasaki Shikibu's *Genji Monogatari* (*The Tale of Prince Genji*, early eleventh century), which is often called the world's first novel.
35 Cf. Fukushima 2003: 58.
36 Title translation according to Tezuka 1977 [1948]: 4.
37 Cf. Tezuka 1977 [1948]: 110–11.
38 For a Communication Studies approach, see Maynard 1997: 158–162.

offers the following formula: "(A1+A2) + B = C. That is to say, A1: at the *ki* stage, you raise a problem; A2: at the *sho* stage, the problem deepens, it seethes; B: *ten* happens due to the entrance of a different element, whereby the problem gets solved, or a new aspect of the problem becomes visible (C: *ketsu*)" (Saso 2009: 118). For manga readers, the second phase serves as a process of relationship building with the text, which may be enjoyed for its own sake (as the journey being the destination) or taken as a preparation for the shift. The twist (*ten*) often appears protracted, and it does not bring the narrative to a close. A kind of epilogue follows, wrapping up the story without providing any moral (*ketsu*). In many cases, this looks like an open ending to those unfamiliar with fictions other than classic representations leading to resolution or dialectic sublation. But the East Asian tradition of *ki-sho-ten-ketsu* did resonate with international modernism, as Kurosawa Akira's prize-winning film *Rashomon* (1950) exemplifies. Its narrative revolving around the truth instead of addressing the core issue directly received credit as an alternative to Western traditions of representation.

Against the backdrop of *ki-sho-ten-ketsu*, the Azuki-Hakari episode turns out not to be 'plot-absent,' but compliant with a different sort of plot. To begin with the latter half, the twist (*ten*) clearly sets in with the ghost's voice on the bottom of the sixth page, that is, after about two thirds of the episode. Then, it stretches over three and a half pages before reaching the end (*ketsu*), which consists merely of the last two tiers presenting the ghost's trace, the drawing protagonist, and the outside view. Although difficult to subdivide, the very fact that the first two phases of *ki* and *sho*—or A1 and A2—clearly occupy almost six out of ten pages would meet the approval of manga artist Takemiya Keiko. According to her, the dullest thing to do is an even segmentation,[39] for example, four times two and a half pages in *Nonnonba*'s case.

Rhetorical structures such as *ki-sho-ten-ketsu* set priority onto the reader's affective participation, often at the expense of linear argumentation. This participatory potential made *ki-sho-ten-ketsu* an attractive model for structuring manga narratives to be serialized in special weekly or monthly magazines, which, in the Japanese comics market, began to become standard around 1960.[40] Manga are not Japanese 'comic books' but, in principle, graphic narratives first serialized in magazines

---

39   Cf. Takemiya 2010: 127–28.
40   Related to serialization, it should also be noted that the link between the elitist tradition of *ki-sho-ten-ketsu* in Chinese poems written by Japanese and modern story manga is to be found in the serial novels published in Japanese newspapers of the pre-war era, for example, Yoshikawa Eiji's *Musashi* (1935, in *Asahi Shimbun*), on which Inoue Takehiko based his manga "Vagabond" (1998-, in *Weekly Morning*).

where installments of different series interact with each other in the eye of the reader. Precisely the magazines have helped to keep *ki-sho-ten-ketsu* alive, applying it to both micro and macro levels, that is, single installments and entire series. Prolongations of popular manga such as "Dragon Ball" (1984–1995) and "Naruto" (1999–) are highly reminiscent of the second phase (*sho*). But modern consumers cannot be hooked in the long run without drama. As is well known, the Japanese mainstream sets itself apart from the American one insofar as such manga are basically not open-ended narratives[41]: Despite all extensions due to commercial conditions, they eventually reach closure. Since 1948, manga characters have died, causing irreversible effects for the narrative.

As mentioned above, the second phase seems to privilege spatial juxtaposition over temporal progression. Thus, it does not come as a surprise that Scott McCloud quotes a manga by Mizuki when introducing his "aspect-to-aspect" (1994: 87) type of panel transition. He also equates Mizuki with Tezuka in this regard and runs the risk of being dismissed as 'universalizing,' especially from a manga studies angle that views Tezuka's work as too human-centered and too West-oriented, his line work too clear, and his framing too 'cinematic' to be discussed on a par with Mizuki's.[42] Nonethless, differences are a matter of perspective. Not only from McCloud's perspective in the early 1990s, but also from that of 1970s shojo manga or recent shonen manga shaped by gamification, Tezuka and Mizuki have a lot in common. In addition to their commitment to manga as a 'visual language,' they share the attention to *ki-sho-ten-ketsu* as a model that allows for contextual ambiguity in regard to straightforward storytelling. And as the next section demonstrates, even Mizuki's manga exhibit a 'cinematic' approach toward panel and page, albeit not necessarily in the sense of dynamic action.

The Ghostliness of Manga: Post/Cinematic Devices

In his ground-breaking monograph *Tezuka Is Dead* (Jap., 2005), Ito Go introduces the notion of 'manga ghost'[43] in order to highlight the aesthetic ambiguity crucial to graphic narratives. But he does not revisit the interrelation between pictorial and scriptural signs, temporality and spatiality, or sequenciality and simultaneity, as may be expected from a

---

41 Carrier ties the posthistoricality of comics on the micro level to "extended, essentially open-ended narratives" (2005: 56).
42 Cf. the summary given by Suzuki 2011: 230–35.
43 Jap. *manga no obake*. Being well aware of the differences between *obake* and *yokai*, I use the same translation for the sake of my discussion of ambiguity.

European academic point of view. Targeting the modernist dichotomy of 'fantasy vs. realism' that is as much prevalent in the cultural reception of manga[44] as in cinema-oriented manga criticism,[45] he focuses on indeterminacy concerning character and frame. With respect to the first, Ito sets out from Tezuka's early graphic narrative *The Mysterious Underground Man* (*Chiteikoku no kaijin*, 1948),[46] which features a rabbit who behaves like a man, wearing trousers, walking around on two legs, and speaking the human language. To Ito, this Mimio (literally, ear man) is an archetype of the manga- or comics-specific ghost, above all, because he intertwines two seemingly irreconcilable sides.[47] Mimio is a protocharacter (*kyara*),[48] a drawn image not rooted in real life. As such, he can only pretend to have a body and an inner self. Yet, under certain conditions, this spurious creature morphs into a realist novel-like character (*kyarakuta*).[49] In fact, as Tezuka's narrative evolves, Mimio's ears become invisible, pictorially as well as metaphorically, until they recur when he dies after saving the earth. Asked for a last word, he wants his humanhood to be confirmed by his fellow characters.

Historically, Mimio stands at a crossroads. His ambiguity still testifies to the fact that manga in general is "a hybrid of the fantastic as epitomized by character icons' large decorative eyes [or ears in Mimio's case; JB], and 'naturalist realism' in regard to depictions of the everyday" (Ito 2012: 440), but he also heralded the four prime decades of story manga during which the two sides were more or less neatly separated and the latter predominated, last but not least within emerging manga criticism. Since around 1990, manga culture has seen a major shift back toward the first, that is, the pole of fantasy, fabrication, and figurativeness. As a result, 'inconsistency' is now more often embraced than deprecated.

Ito's discussion of proto-characters, which as such applies to comics across cultures, has enjoyed vivid attention outside Japan less in relation to comics research than media convergence and fandom studies. But regarding manga-specific ways of storytelling, it is actually his second issue—the indeterminacy of the frame, or field of vision (*fureimu no*

---

44 Outside of Japan, manga has been received mainly as a fantastic fictional realm inhabited by cute doe-eyed and cat-eared creatures, a fact that serves Ito as his point of departure for elaborating on *Tezuka Is Dead* (cf. 2012: 440). See also Brenner (2007: 77–79), who titles one section "East Meets West: Fantasy vs. Realism."
45 Between the 1960s and the 1990s, the truism that Tezuka's postwar story manga was innovative due to the employment of 'cinematic' devices prevailed in Japanese manga discourse. A typical example is Takeuchi 2005.
46 For the translation of the title, cf. Onoda Power 2009: 46.
47 Cf. Ito 2005: 139.
48 See Ito 2007 for an extract in English translation.
49 Cf. Ito 2005: 273.

fukakuteisei)—that calls for attention. Ito sets out from the fact that, in contrast to cinema, printed graphic narratives involve an unsettling of the reader who incessantly has to decide whether to privilege the single panel or the entire page, if not the double spread. The page may, for example, push itself to the fore of the reader's attention when characters grasp panel borders (as in Tezuka's pre-gekiga manga), or body-length images of girls posing like fashion dolls are superimposed vertically over horizontal tiers of panels (as in shojo manga).[50] Then again, the page may go unnoticed in cases like the *Nonnnonba* episode introduced above, where characters stay within borders and appear as if filmed by a hidden camera.

In light of this, it is notable that Pascal Lefèvre chooses "Lone Wolf and Cub"[51] in order "[t]o demonstrate that formal analysis can be used for all kinds of comics" (2012: 71). Foregoing caricatured deformations of its characters and presenting their duels by means of "a film-like technique of shot/reverse-shot" (Lefèvre 2012: 77), this series' mise-en-scène and framing is not representative of manga in general but particularly gekiga and with it the majority of productions in the male genres of shonen and seinen manga during the 1970s and 1980s. What appears 'film-like' in the comparatively unspectacular *Nonnonba* is the montage of single panels that, by their unequivocal content, resemble discrete pieces of reality, 'shots' or frozen moments to be visually scanned in sequence. In tandem with gekiga's inclination to seclude the storyworld (from intrusions by the artist entering the scene as a character, or other extradiegetic gags), the characters do not only stay embedded within the panels but also maintain their visual identity therein. Even when multiplying, they remain recognizable.

This applies, for example, to the shonen manga "Naruto." At the beginning, it seems to comply with clear identities, favoring the alternation between seeing and being seen with respect to the confrontation between antagonists as well as between 'me' and 'I.' The reader's gaze proceeds mainly from bordered panel to bordered panel, facilitated in the English translation now and again by small arrows in the top-right corner of some double spreads saying, "Read this way." Tapered frames are reserved for especially fierce duels.[52] In some cases, large panels that stretch over the entire width of the double spread and occupy its upper half suggest that the opponents actually act on common ground, as do heavily hatched motion images within panels. But none of these elements draws attention

---

50 Groensteen observes that "certain mangas are signaled by a massive use of panels that are superfluous from a strictly narrative point of view [...]. More than the panel, it is therefore the page or the sequence that [...] constitutes a pertinent unit" (2009: 116).
51 *Kozure okami*, by Koike Kazuo and Kojima Goseki, 1970–1976 in *Weekly Manga Action*.
52 Cf. Kishimoto 2003a: 172–73.

to the page as a frame or field of vision. In line with this, the protagonist stays recognizable as himself, even if his eyes narrow to slits occasionally, or his body shrinks to *chibi*[53] size in order to suggest certain affective states. He always sets himself apart visually from the people who may appear with him in the same panel as inner images.[54] Although half human, half fox demon, Naruto does not give the impression of a 'ghost,' not even when he applies the doppelganger technique that allows him to assume the form of multiple clones. But as these clones suggest from the start, the apparently clear, or 'cinematic,' panel layout is deceptive, the visible not to be trusted.[55] This contrasts with *Nonnonba*'s invitation to accept the realness of yokai. In addition, "Naruto" deviates from the gekiga-induced tradition of 'cinematic' realism in its visualization of characters' 'inner selves.'

Several panels contain two views of the same character, an external and an internal one. "Naruto" applies this post-cinematic device, which has come to prominence since the 1990s, mainly to the female character Sakura, who literally stands beside herself, showing a smile to the outside world while actually being grim-faced inside (the English translation marks the latter as "Inner Sakura"; Kishimoto 2003a: 90, 100 186). Sometimes she also distorts her face to such an extent that she would not be recognizable anymore in an isolated image (for example, when she witnesses the accidental kiss between Naruto and Sasuke, rejecting it as gay or, self-reflexively, an allusion to Boys' Love manga).[56] While such 'out-of-body shots'[57] are reserved solely for female characters and thus help to confirm the gender-conservative bias of "Naruto" in terms of its representational approach,[58] the inner voice of boys is likewise presented in a post-cinematic way when lexias of inner monologue are spread over numerous panels and related to the character only by means of his huge eyes, which attract the reader's attention and entice him or her to stitch the parts of the page together in a more ambiguous, imaginative way less predetermined by characters' gazes and what they see.[59] Ito traces this back to shojo manga. Outsiders understand its infamous saucer eyes

---

[53] Literally meaning 'diminutive person,' this word has become a technical term in global manga fandom.
[54] Cf. Kishimoto 2003b: 59.
[55] Cf. Ito 2011b: 11.
[56] Cf. Kishimoto 2003a: 92. In order to stress that character icons are not necessarily an integral part of panels as 'shots,' Ito (2012: 478) also discusses the chimera-like intertwining of highly stylized heads or faces with realistically depicted bodies for one and the same character, and the interlocking of different perspectives within the same panel (for example, half-profile and frontal views).
[57] Cf. Izumi 2008: 39–44; Ito 2012: 471.
[58] See Fujimoto 2013.
[59] Cf. Ito 2011:12.

usually in a representational way, conceiving them as exaggerated 'mirrors of the soul' or manifestations of an 'Asian' inferiority complex against Caucasians, but their perceptional and technical function does often go unnoticed. In its emphasis on feelings and atmosphere, shojo manga favored collage-like multi-layered page designs with borderless panels to support its narratives, which approximated literary rather than 'cinematic' realism. But male genres came to present the standard of manga. Ito questions their alleged universality when he asserts, "we should not lose sight of the fact that 'cinematic' realism was given rise by a twofold repression of the 'mangaesque'" (2005: 219), that is to say, the repression of the proto-character and that of the page as the crucial frame for manga.

With its unusual amount of inner monologue as such and, relatedly, also its alternate leaning on huge eyes and gazes mediated by small eyes, "Naruto" attests to the fact that typical manga today intertwine what was previously separated. Acknowledging the indeterminacy of the frame, series like "Naruto" stand by manga's ghostliness, and they raise an awareness for it in retrospect as well. Thus, contemporary readers may approach older works like *Nonnonba* in a different way, as well. Manga's ghostliness has regained momentum at a time when due to digitalization, virtualization, and an increased extent of aesthetic interactivity, the role and constitution of the modern narrative is subject to fundamental change. Whether story manga will further on be read as narrative representations or whether they will serve mainly as vehicles for game-like motions is not necessarily rooted in the narrative itself, but, in the end, rather a matter of perspective and context. As a highly intertextual 'system,' manga provides both kinds of pleasure.[60]

Works Cited

Beaty, Bart (2007). "Bart Beaty's Conversational Euro-Comics: NonNonBa, Shigeru Mizuki." *The Comicsreporter*, Apr. 5. Web.

Berndt, Jaqueline (ed.) (2010). *Comics Worlds and the World of Comics: Towards Scholarship on a Global Scale*. Kyoto: imrc. Print.

— (ed.) (2011). *Intercultural Crossovers, Transcultural Flows: Manga/Comics*. Kyoto: imrc. Print.

— (ed.) (2012). *Manhwa, Manga, Manhua: East Asian Comics Studies*. Leipzig: Leipzig UP. Print.

Berndt, Jaqueline, and Bettina Kümmerling-Meibauer (eds.) (2013). *Manga's Cultural Crossroads*. New York: Routledge. Print.

---

60 Cf. Ito 2011a: 75.

Berndt, Jaqueline, and Steffi Richter (eds.) (2006). *Reading Manga: Local and Global Perceptions of Japanese Comics*. Leipzig: Leipzig UP. Print.

Brenner, Robin (2007). *Understanding Manga and Anime*. Westport: Libraries Unlimited. Print.

Brophy, Philip (2010). "Osamu Tezuka's *Gekiga*: Behind the Mask of Manga." Toni Johnson-Woods (ed.). *Manga: An Anthology of Global and Cultural Perspectives*. New York: Continuum. 128–36. Print.

Carrier, David (2000). *The Aesthetics of Comics*. University Park: Pennsylvania State UP. Print.

Chew, Matthew M., and Lu Chen (2010). "Media Institutional Contexts of the Emergence and Development of *Xinmanhua* in China." *International Journal of Comic Art* 12.2: 171–91. Print.

Choo, Kukhee (2010). "Consuming Japan: Early Korean Girls Comic Book Artists' Resistance and Empowerment." Daniel Black, Stephen Epstein, and Alison Tokita (eds.). *Complicated Currents: Media Flows, Soft Power and East Asia*. Clayton: Monash Univ. ePress. 6.1–6.16. Web.

Cohn, Neil (2010). "Japanese Visual Language: The Structure of Manga." Toni Johnson-Woods (ed.). *Manga: An Anthology of Global and Cultural Perspectives*. New York: Continuum. 187–203. Print.

Foster, Michael Dylan (2008). "The Otherworlds of Mizuki Shigeru." *Mechademia* 3: 8–28. Print.

Fujimoto, Yukari (2013). "Women in 'Naruto,' Women Reading 'Naruto.'" Jaqueline Berndt and Bettina Kümmerling-Meibauer (eds.). *Manga's Cultural Crossroads*. New York: Routledge. 172–91. Print.

Fukushima, Yoshiko (2003). *Manga Discourse in Japanese Theater: The Location of Noda Hideki's Yume no Yuminsha*. London: Kegan Paul. Print.

Gan, Sheuo H. (2011). "Manga in Malaysia: An Approach to Its Current Hybridity through the Career of the Shojo Mangaka Kaoru." *International Journal of Comic Art* 13.2: 164–78. Print.

Gardner, Jared (2011). "Storylines." Jared Gardner and David Herman (eds.). *Graphic Narratives and Narrative Theory*. Special issue of *SubStance* 40.1: 53–69. Print.

Groensteen, Thierry (2007). *The System of Comics*. Trans. Bart Beaty and Nick Nguyen. Jackson: UP of Mississippi. Print.

— (2009). *Manga no shisutemu: koma wa naze monogatari ni naru no ka*. Trans. Noda Kensuke. Tokyo: Seidosha. Print.

Guilbert, Xavier (2008). Review *NONNONBÂ*. Dec. 2006. English trans. Mar. 2007. *du9: l'autre bande dessinée*. Web.

Holmberg, Ryan (2011). "An Introduction to Gekiga, 6970 A.D." *The Comics Journal*, Mar. 24. Web.

Inoue, Manabu (ed.) (1995). *Manga no yomikata*. Tokyo: Takarajimasha. Print.

Ito, Go (2005). *Tezuka izu deddo: Hirakareta manga hyogenron e*. Tokyo: NTT. Print.
— (2007). "Manga History Viewed through Proto-Characteristics." Philip Brophy (ed.). *Tezuka: The Marvel of Manga*. Melbourne: National Gallery of Victoria. 107–13. Print.
— (2011a). "Tezuka Is Dead: Manga in Transformation and Its Dysfunctional Discourse." Trans. and introd. Miri Nakamura. *Mechademia* 6: 69–83. Print.
— (2011b). "Particularities of Boys' Manga in the Early 21st Century: How *NARUTO* Differs from *DRAGON BALL*." Jaqueline Berndt (ed.) *Intercultural Crossovers, Transcultural Flows: Manga/Comics*. Kyoto: imrc. 9–16. Print.
— (2012). "Manga no futatsu no kao." Hiroki Azuma (ed.). *Nihon 2.0: Shiso chizu β*. Vol. 3. Tokyo: Genron. 236–483. Print.
Izumi, Nobuyuki (2008). *Manga o meguru boken 1*. N.p.: Piano Fire. Print.
Kanno, Hiroshi (2004). *Manga no sukima*. Tokyo: Bijutsu shuppansha. Print.
Kinoshita, Naoyuki (1993). "Mizuki Shigeru to iu kataribe." *Mizuki Shigeru to nihon no yokai*. Tokyo: NHK. 54–56. Print.
Kishimoto, Masashi (2003a). *Naruto*. Vol. 1. San Francisco: VIZ Media. Print.
— (2003b). *Naruto*. Vol. 2. San Francisco: VIZ Media. Print.
LaMarre, Thomas (2010). "Manga Bomb: Between the Lines of Barefoot Gen." Jaqueline Berndt (eds.). *Comics Worlds and the World of Comics: Towards Scholarship on a Global Scale*. Kyoto: imrc. 262–307. Print.
Ledderose, Lothar (2000). *Ten Thousand Things: Module and Mass Production in Chinese Art*. Princeton: Princeton UP. Print.
Leem, Hye-Jeong (2012). "Koo Woo-Young's 'Lim Kok-Jeong' (1972–73), a Dramatic Graphic Narrative (geukhwa) Serialized in a Newspaper." Jaqueline Berndt (ed.). *Manhwa, Manga, Manhua: East Asian Comics Studies*. Leipzig: Leipzig UP. 11–41. Print.
Lefèvre, Pascal (2007). "Seduction of the European Critic: A Case Study of Shigeru Mizuki's *NonNonBâ*." Paper delivered at the conference *La globalisation culturelle et le rôle de l'Asie*, Maison de la Culture du Japon. Paris, Mar. 16.
— (2012). "Mise en scène and Framing: Visual Storytelling in *Lone Wolf and Cub*." Randy Duncan and Matthew J. Smith (eds.). *Critical Approaches to Comics: Theories and Methods*. New York: Routledge. 71–83. Print.
Lent, John A. (ed.) (1999). *Themes and Issues in Asian Cartooning: Cute, Cheap, Mad, and Sexy*. Bowling Green: Bowling Green State U Popular P. Print.

— (ed.) (2001). *Illustrating Asia: Comics, Humor Magazines, and Picture Books.* Honolulu: U of Hawai'i P. Print.
— (ed.) (2004). *Comic Art in Africa, Asia, Australia, and Latin America through 2000: An International Bibliography.* Westport: Praeger. Print.
— (2010). "Manga in East Asia." Toni Johnson-Woods (ed.). *Manga: An Anthology of Global and Cultural Perspectives.* New York: Continuum. 297-314. Print.
Liew, Sonny, and Cheng T. Lim (eds.) (2011). *Liquid City Volume 2.* Berkeley: Image Comics. Print.
Maynard, Senko K. (1997). *Japanese Communication: Language and Thought in Context.* Honolulu: U of Hawai'i P. Print.
McCloud, Scott (1994). *Understanding Comics: The Invisible Art.* New York: Harper Perennial. Print.
— (2006). *Making Comics: Storytelling Secrets of Comics, Manga, and Graphic Novels.* New York: HarperCollins. Print.
Miyake, Toshio (2012). "Italy Made in Japan: Occidentalism, Orientalism and Self-Orientalism in Contemporary Japan." Graziella Parati (ed.). *New Perspectives in Italian Cultural Studies: Definition, Theory, and Accented Practices.* Madison: Fairleigh Dickinson UP. 195–214. Print.
Mizuki, Shigeru (1977). *NonNonBa to ore* [novel]. Tokyo: Chikuma. Print.
— (1991–92). *NonNonBa to ore* [manga]. Vol. 1–2. Tokyo: Chikuma. Print.
— (2006). *NonNonBâ.* Trans. Jean-Louis Capron, Patrick Honnoré, and Yukari Maeda. Paris: Editions Cornelius. Print.
— (2007). *NonNonBa to ore* [manga]. Tokyo: Kodansha 2007. Print.
— (2012). *Nonnonba.* Trans. Jocelyne Allen. Montreal: Drawn & Quarterly. Print.
Natsume, Fusanosuke (1997). *Manga wa naze omoshiroi no ka?* Tokyo: NHK. Print.
— (2008). "Manga: *Komatopia.*" Trans. Margherita Long. Introd. Hajime Nakatani. *Mechademia* 3: 65–74. Print.
— (2010). "Pictotext and Panels: Commonalities and Differences in Manga, Comics and BD." Jaqueline Berndt (ed.). *Comics Worlds and the World of Comics: Towards Scholarship on a Global Scale.* Kyoto: imrc. 37–52. Print.
Ogi, Fusami, Cheng T. Lim, and Jaqueline Berndt (eds.) (2011). "Women's Manga beyond Japan: Contemporary Comics as Cultural Crossroads in Asia." Special issue of the *International Journal of Comic Art* 13.2: 3–199. Print.
Onoda Power, Natsu (2009). *God of Comics: Osamu Tezuka and the Creation of Post-World War II Manga.* Jackson: UP of Mississippi. Print.
Petersen, Robert S. (2011). *Comics, Manga, and Graphic Novels: A History of Graphic Narratives.* Santa Barbara: ABC-CLIO. Print.

Saso, Akira (2009). *Saso noto*. Kyoto: Kyoto Seika University, Manga Dept., Story Course [textbook for internal use, not for sale]. Print.
Satrapi, Marjane (2005). *Persepolis*. Vol. 1–2. Jap. trans. Sonoda Keiko. Tokyo: Basiliko. Print.
Suzuki, CJ (2011). "Learning from Monsters: Mizuki Shigeru's Yokai and War Manga." *Image & Narrative* 12.1: 229–44. Web.
Takekuma, Kentaro, and Koji Yamamura (2006). "Animeishon no sozoryoku: Terebi anime kara ato animeishon made." *Wochikochi* [The Japan Foundation's Monthly] 13: 8–17. Print.
Takemiya, Keiko (2003). "Moho ga sodateru sozo no dojo." Shoji Yamada (ed.). *Moho to sozo no dainamizumu*. Tokyo: Bensei shuppan. 17–48. Print.
— (2010). *Manga no kyakuhon gairon*. Tokyo: Kadokawa Gakugei Shuppan. Print.
Takeuchi, Osamu (2005). *Manga hyogengaku nyumon*. Tokyo: Chikuma. Print.
Tezuka, Osamu (1977). *Manga daigaku*. Tokyo: Kodansha. Print.
— (1979). "Kohi to kocha to shinya made..." Interview by Kazuki Chiseko. *Pafu*. 5.9: 34–73. Print.
— (1982 [1948]). *Chiteikoku no kaijin*. Tokyo: Kodansha. Print.
Tojirakarn, Mashima (2011). "Why Thai Girls' Manga Are Not 'Shojo Manga': Japanese Discourse and the Reality of Globalization." *International Journal of Comic Art* 13.2: 143–63. Print.
Tomine, Adrian (2005). "Introduction." Yoshihiro Tatsumi. *The Push Man and Other Stories*. Ed. Adrian Tomine. Montreal: Drawn & Quarterly. N.p. Print.
Yamanaka, Chie (2006). "Domesticating Manga? National Identity in Korean Comics Culture." Jaqueline Berndt and Steffi Richter (eds.). *Reading Manga: Local and Global Perceptions of Japanese Comics*. Leipzig: Leipzig UP. 191–202. Print.
— (2013). "'Manhwa' in Korea: (Re-)Nationalizing Comics Culture." Jaqueline Berndt and Bettina Kümmerling-Meibauer (eds.). *Manga's Cultural Crossroads*. New York: Routledge. 85–171. Print.
Yoo, Soo-Kyung (2012). "On Differences between Japanese and Korean Comics for Female Readers: Comparing 'Boys Over Flowers' to 'Goong.'" Jaqueline Berndt (ed.). *Manhwa, Manga, Manhua: East Asian Comics Studies*. Leipzig: Leipzig UP. 43–78. Print.
Wong, Wendy (2002). *Hong Kong Comics*. New York: Princeton Architectural P. Print.
— (2010a). "Globalizing Manga: From Japan to Hong Kong and Beyond." Toni Johnson-Woods (ed.). *Manga: An Anthology of Global and Cultural Perspectives*. New York: Continuum. 332–50. Print.

— (2010b). "Drawing the Ideal Modern Woman: Ms. Lee Wai-Chung and Her *Ms. 13-Dot*." Jaqueline Berndt (ed.). *Comics Worlds and the World of Comics: Towards Scholarship on a Global Scale*. Kyoto: imrc. Print. 177–84. Print.

MONIKA SCHMITZ-EMANS
(Bochum)

Graphic Narrative as World Literature

Graphic Narrative as a Genre of Literature:
The Construction of Comic Art in Analogy with Verbal Storytelling

Today, comics studies are integrated into many university programs of world literature studies, and handbooks defining the genres of literature include articles about comics, manga, and the graphic novel.[1] Obviously, the concept of 'literature' has been modified in order to integrate graphic narratives. Several reasons for this recent development can be named.

The past decades have seen various attempts to define the art of comics with regard to media aesthetics as well as to comics' cultural uses and functions. According to the most influential approach, comics represent an art of *storytelling* that is rooted in a basic and transcultural human inclination to give a narrative form to experiences and imaginations. In the course of human history, this inclination has manifested itself in changing medial forms and languages. Narratological approaches reflect about comics as 'graphic narratives' and especially about the structure and poetics of the 'graphic novel' by implicitly or even explicitly comparing them with verbal storytelling.[2] Theorists comment on formal and functional analogies as well as on distinctions concerning the use of image sequences as a narrative device. Altogether, advanced comics theory owes much to structuralism and semiotics, especially to the structural analysis of narratives as it was developed in order to describe and compare popular as well as literary narratives, folktales, and novels. Constructed from a viewing point defined by this methodological approach, comics are interpreted as an art that structurally and functionally should be compared with the works of literary writers.

Influential comics artists themselves have explicitly conceptualized their works in accordance with structuralist and semiological theories. In his groundbreaking autoreflexive *Understanding Comics*, Scott McCloud points out that any definition of the comic must necessarily refer to the

---

1   See Packard 2009.
2   Cf. Campbell 2007: 13. See also Schüwer 2008; Gardner and Herman 2011; Schmitz-Emans 2012.

level of form instead of content.³ Proposing to define comics as an autonomous art of *storytelling*, McCloud highlights comics' sequential structure. According to this notion, one single picture does not yet tell a story. While this opinion might be viewed critically, it does exemplify the strong focus McCloud places on the narrative dimension of comics.

Another famous artist who has reflected on comics as a *narrative medium* through an autoreflexive approach is Will Eisner, who defines comics as 'sequential art.' His metacomic books, *Comics and Sequential Art* (2004) and *Graphic Storytelling and Visual Narrative* (2001) offer an introduction to the art of comics as well as to the history of storytelling in a broad and fundamental sense. According to Eisner, comics derive from a long tradition of telling stories through images in different media, such as cave paintings, tapestries, illuminated manuscripts and books, sequential drawings and paintings, films, and even theater as a storytelling art that uses visual means of expression. Like McCloud, Eisner calls to mind earlier artists who created image sequences in order to tell stories. (Thus, he points to Frans Masereel and Otto Nückel; McCloud even refers to ancient Egyptian, Greek, and Roman as well as to medieval and modern examples of image sequences.) Regarding comics as *graphic* narrative, Eisner maintains that the visual components of a piece of art must be subordinated to the story that is told. Conventional reading, in that sense, also means to 'imagine' in a literal sense: to transform written signs into mental images and image sequences. Compared with verbal narratives, comics facilitate this kind of reception process, as the visual images that are combined with the words catalyze the image sequences within the reader's mind that emerge from storytelling. From Eisner's perspective, images are functionally analogous to verbal expressions and can thus be regarded as the elements of a language. Eisner subsumes all kinds of artistic representation from dancing performances, drawing, and theater to various print media, film, electronic media, and finally the comic book under the term 'storytelling.'⁴ Viewed from his perspective, art as such primarily dedicates itself to the creation or retelling of stories, and these stories resemble each other at all times and in all cultures. Comics artists, as Eisner eventually suggests, use "universally understood images" (2004: 1).

If "universally" is supposed to mean 'by nature,' this opinion surely provokes critical response. If, however, it is used as a synonym to

---

3   Cf. McCloud 1993: 5–6.
4   See also the work of early narratologists such as Barthes 1977 [1966] and Chatman 1978 or the more recent attempts at a 'transmedial narratology' by Ryan 2006; Herman 2009; Thon 2014.

'globally,' it is at least close to truth.[5] Of course, the different 'languages' (in the sense of: 'representational styles') used in comic art are shaped by highly different cultural codes and traditions. Among the readers of comics, however, there is a strong inclination to transgress cultural borders and to get acquainted with culturally different codes. The manga industry, for instance, by now produces 'globally understood images,' (although Japanese readers may often still 'understand' more than Western readers do) based on Western graphic artists' and readers' intense studies of the manga codes. In general, however, the pictorial codes of comics are usually not prohibitive to readers from different cultural and linguistic spaces. Whether or not one agrees with Eisner's and McCloud's concepts of comics as sequential art and whether or not one defines them as a species of 'graphic storytelling,' both examples of metacomic art exemplify that dealing with comics implies dealing with theoretical issues that are discussed in literary theory as well: 'language,' 'signs,' 'codes,' 'grammar,' 'meanings,' 'communication,' 'storytelling,' 'narrative structures,' and their effects. Comics theory and literary criticism strongly converge in the field of narratology.[6]

Both Western and Eastern comic art appear as extremely multi-faceted from a stylistic point of view. General comics theories, however, have to develop a global perspective, as McCloud explicitly stresses. By taking cultural and personal styles of storytelling into account, *Understanding Comics* presents itself as an introduction not only to the basic characteristics of comic art but to a new kind of world literature as well: a literary genre that invents itself as using a global language in regionally different dialects. Theoretical discourses about comics, one might also point out, have added new aspects and arguments to an already existing 'world literature' discourse.

'World Literature' ('Weltliteratur'): Concepts and Discourses

The term 'world literature' seems to be close at hand as far as the recent history of graphic storytelling is concerned. However, the ambiguity of this term should be taken into account. The expression 'world literature,' usually connotated positively, can be interpreted in different ways, and it is thus related to different conceptualizations of literature itself.[7] Discourses

---

5   For a detailed discussion of pictures as 'signs close to perception,' see Sachs-Hombach 2003.
6   For an early narratological approach, see Abbott 1986; for more recent work, see Schüwer 2008; Gardner and Herman 2011.
7   See Koppen 1984.

of 'world literature,' one should note, do not always make a clear distinction between fictional and nonfictional texts; scientific and philosophical works, essays, reports and sermons could, at least in nineteenth-century discourse, be subsumed under the term of 'world literature.'

(1) First, the term can be used in order to characterize *'world class' literature*. In this qualitative sense, it refers to canonization processes and to implicit or explicit criteria of aesthetic value. Describing graphic novels as pieces of 'world literature' in this sense implies aesthetic judgement and evaluation, and it suggests that an artwork of lasting value has been created that is worth remembering by future generations—either for its content or for its refined or innovative strategies of representation.

(2) Secondly, 'world literature' can summarily mean *'all the literature of the world'* or at least 'literature from all over the world,' and in this case it suggests that 'literature' should be regarded as a transnational and transcultural phenomenon, process, or art form. Related to the art of the graphic novel, the term 'world literature' might thus highlight the fact that artists from various countries and different cultures create generically similar works of graphic storytelling, and that the process of establishing a new literary genre has a global dimension.

(3) In a third sense, the term 'world literature' is related to the idea of a *mutual literary influence between different countries and cultures*, an exchange of ideas and strategies of representation that, at the same time, illustrates and fosters complex processes of cultural and economic transfer and interaction. (When Goethe used and eventually popularized the expression 'Weltliteratur,' it was exactly in this sense, and he postulated with regard to modernization processes that his time was the era of world literature.[8]) Viewed as 'world literature' from this perspective, contemporary examples of graphic storytelling present themselves as shaped by multicultural influences, sometimes as culturally hybrid phenomena.[9] It is especially the intense reception of the manga style in the Western world that has recently been of formative influence on contemporary comics artists from countries outside of Japan. The USA, however, have always been and still are the globally most influential source of inspiration to other countries, and as a consequence, in Europe as well as in Japan, comics were identified for a long time as an 'American' import, be it in an affirmative or a critical sense.

---

8   See Birus 1995.
9   Sabin already spoke of the emergence of "worldcomics" (1993: 183–209) two decades ago. For recent transnational approaches to graphic narrative, see Denson, Meyer, and Stein 2013.

All three concepts (or 'semantics') of 'world literature' can become relevant in discourses about graphic narratives: as a keyword, the term highlights either aesthetic achievements, broad distribution and reception, or multi-faceted stylistic influences from culturally different sources.

The Graphic Novel as a New Paradigm of 'World Literature'

Discourses about the 'graphic novel' as well as the (relatively short) history of this format itself illustrate the impact that concepts of literature and literary genres have had on the art of visual storytelling. In his introduction to a volume presenting *500 Essential Graphic Novels*, subtitled *The Ultimate Guide*, Gene Kannenberg Jr. (2008) gives a brief outline of the history of the graphic novel that is presented with regard to outstanding examples. He brings to mind Will Eisner, who popularized the term 'graphic novel' (after Richard Kyle had already used it in 1964[10]) when he published his comic book *A Contract with God* (1978). Eisner insists that graphic novels (in the sense he attributed to this neologism) should be regarded and judged from an aesthetic perspective and thus according their qualities as artworks. Actually, Eisner's paratextual information claims that *A Contract with God* represents a new genre of *literature* and thus implicitly invites the reader to compare such works with other literary works of art, especially with novels. Looking back to what he and others regard as his very invention of a new literary art form, Eisner stated in 2004 that the graphic novel could by then be regarded as an established literary genre. Several kinds of development substantiate this claim: the interest that contemporary publishers of literature take in graphic novels, the intense and aesthetically sensitive responses of readers and critics, and, of course, the fact that graphic artists obviously regard themselves as producers of graphic literature, as 'novelists.' Eisner, as he says, took the risk of creating a new form of 'comic literature,' and in his preface to a new edition of *A Contract with God*, he expresses his contentment to see the new genre flourish from the aspect of production as well as reception.

Thus, critical discourse about the decline or even the 'death' of conventional literary genres stimulated both theoretical and practical interest in new genres, especially the graphic novel, as an innovative art form. The novelist John Updike, who, as a youth, had intended to start a career as a cartoonist, proclaimed the 'death of the novel' in a speech to

---

10 Kyle employed the term 'graphic novel' in the Comic Amateur Press Alliance's newsletter *CAPA-ALPHA* #2 (Nov. 1964) as well as in his own magazine *Fantasy Illustrated* #5 (Spring 1966).

the Bristol Literary Society in 1969, pointing out that for innovative artists there might be a broad field of creativity opened up by experimenting with graphic storytelling. As he asserted, comic strip novels might become masterpieces of a new kind of literature.[11] Especially among representatives of experimental literature in the 1960s and 1970s, who explored new kinds of writing, of composing texts and images, and of using visual forms as media of expression, there was remarkable interest in the comic and its codes. Rolf Dieter Brinkmann, Gerhard Rühm, Helmut Heißenbüttel, and other German avantgarde writers integrated comic elements into their works, wrote texts in 'comic language,' and even created visual texts inspired by comics.[12] Dino Buzzati, with his comic poem (*Poema a fumetti*, 1969) telling the story of Orpheus as a pop singer strolling through a contemporary underworld, undertakes a rather singular enterprise: he composes his entire book as a sequence of comic panels in which his poem is integrated. While experiments like avantgardist art usually addressed a smaller public, the graphic novel as a genre of entertaining literature successively reached not only an expanding but also a more ambitious readership in the 1960s, 1970s, and 1980s.

Kannenberg not only affirms that the graphic novel was extremely successful in the decades after Eisner's *A Contract with God*, but he also relates this success to the growing importance of the book format within comic art. Rather than being viewed as "chunks of something larger," graphic narratives within books are read as "self-contained stories" (Kannenberg 2008: 7). Therefore, they can efficiently compete with other storytelling media, such as cinema and television films. One might argue that it was not so much the production of comic books but rather the act of calling them 'graphic novels' that created a new genre of literature. After all, it is the term itself that suggests that these books should be read as examples of literary storytelling. And, of course, there is another indication to the establishing process of this new art form, namely, the fact that a list of canonized works exists that are more or less consensually regarded as canonical by readers from different countries and cultures, even though there is a strong dominance of examples from just a few countries, especially the USA. Among the prize-winning comics and graphic novels, the bulk is represented by U.S. productions in English, such as Chris Ware's *Jimmy Corrigan: The Smartest Kid on Earth* (2000), which won the *Guardian*'s First Book Award in 2001; Alison Bechdel's autobiographical *Fun Home: A Family Tragicomic* (2006), selected as the best book of 2006 by *Time Magazine*. Yet other countries have established their

---

11 See Gravett 2005 for a discussion of Updike's speech.
12 See, for instance: Rühm 1972, 1975; Heißenbüttel 1974; Jandl 1979.

own award systems as well, and while indigeneous productions usually dominate these systems, translations of successful works allow for an increasing exchange between the different language cultures.

According to Kannenberg's retrospective remarks, the year 1986 has been of outstanding importance within the history of the graphic novel, as it was the publishing year of three groundbreaking works: Frank Miller's *The Dark Knight Returns* (1997) revitalized the popular character of Batman and combined social satire with new forms of graphic representation. Alan Moore and Dave Gibbons's *Watchmen* (2005) also took up the heritage of the superhero comic but combined it with an innovative form of speculative fiction, at the same time referring to a number of texts from the literary canon and even quoting from them. Moreover, Art Spiegelman's Pulitzer awarded *Maus* (1986, 1991) combined the ambitious attempt to represent Holocaust experiences with autobiographical elements dedicated to the artist's problematic relationship with his parents. All three examples are characterized by an autoreferential and media-reflexive dimension, *Maus* probably in the most obvious way. Due to the high artistic quality of many recent graphic novels, there is a remarkable tendency to create and confirm a canon—a process that might be compared at least tentatively to the post-colonial canonization process of non-Western 'literatures' after their having been ignored in the past—or to engage in processes of canonization concerning marginalized forms of literary writing (such as women's literature).

Stemming from pulp magazines that were regarded as artistically inferior products of mass culture and as a kind of fast food for readers, the graphic novel is now broadly accepted in the circle of 'respected' literary art forms. As a consequence, graphic novels and other comic books are now collected by libraries, having been rejected in former times as a consumer item that did not require preservation and long-term distribution. The interest of public media in new releases (that are regularly reviewed) as well as in bestsellers and lasting favorites in the meantime reflects and fosters this process of canonizing graphic novels. Newspaper feuilletons feature reviews of graphic literature, comic artists win prizes, comic books are openly claimed to be 'favorite books,' and they are intensely discussed on Internet platforms.[13] Kannenberg's observations concerning the U.S.-American scene are paralleled by analogous developments on the European bookmarket and its medial echoes. Thus, canonized 'classics,' for instance, are released as special series, and newspaper feuilletons dedicate special pages to examples of

---

13 For analysis of the graphic novel reception in German feuilletons, see Ditschke 2009; Schmitz-Emans 2012.

graphic storytelling as well as to critical reviews of new releases. Kannenberg's canon of 500 works, an explicitly open canon, is structured according to different genres: adventure, nonfiction, crime and mystery, fantasy, general fiction, horror, humor, science fiction, superheroes, war. The categories appear as slightly incompatible from a systematic point of view, as they refer to subjects (crime, war), to ontological concepts (fiction, nonfiction), and to sentiments and attitudes (horror, humor). Yet they actually represent the classification system that is commonly used in libraries and bookstores.

With regard to 'world literature' concepts and discourses, it should be stressed that the canons that are represented (and thus constructed) by Kannenberg and others are in principle understood as transnational and transcultural despite the fact that Kannenberg's selection criteria from his own guidebook only present examples in English language: either English originals or translations from other languages into English. Even though it is not addressed explicitly, this restriction to English texts brings to mind practical restrictions and compromises when Western scholars establish world literature canon lists and teach world literature in accordance with such lists. Restricted knowledge of foreign languages and cultures leads to 'transnational canons' that are filtered by national interests and competences, mainly by English language competence.[14] In concrete practical contexts, views of world literature from foreign countries are usually based on indirect knowledge (as, for instance, mediated by translation or by preceding descriptions). Concerning guides to 'graphic world literature' as well as to 'verbal world literature' it should, however, be acknowledged that at least the ideas of internationalism and transculturality are implied in theoretical reflections about genre aesthetics and genre history.

Genres of 'Graphic World Literature'

The implicit labeling of graphic novels as examples of a new genre of world literature implies comparison with more established forms of literature. Quite a number of 'graphic narratives' (or, more specifically, 'graphic novels') interpret themselves and are interpreted from external observation points by means of explicit and implicit comparison with non-graphic literature, especially with novel fiction. Several subgenres of the traditonal novel have been adapted by graphic novelists and adapted

---

14 Many scholars as well as their students read works from foreign languages in translations, and, as critics of recent world literature curricula have noted, even in academic world literature teaching, translations often replace the neglected originals (see Figueira 2008).

to this new medial form. Sometimes, single graphic novels have been compared with examples of traditional literary genres. So Chris Ware's *Jimmy Corrigan* is compared to a *Bildungsroman* that depicts a century of American history "via the personal history of its protagonist" (Bell and Sinclair 2005: 7). Such comparisons may appear somewhat provocative, but they highlight thematic and structural affinities and illustrate the flexibility of established genre concepts.

Even though the category of 'nonfiction' is frequently used in discourses about graphic narratives as well as about conventional literature, there is no clear borderline between the plots categorized by either term or by the verbal and visual strategies employed in order to represent either 'facts' or 'fictions.'[15] In constructivist theories of knowledge representation, the distinction between fiction and nonfiction has been questioned thoroughly—a process which has proven to be extremely influential and inspiring to both literary and graphic storytelling. Graphic storytelling offers many options to level out the difference between historical and fictitious stories. Thus, in recent graphic novels as well as in recent novels, many examples of 'history fiction' reacted creatively to the idea of regarding history itself as constructed. In both genres of 'literature,' the issue of 'realism' is therefore not related to suggestions of empirical facts that are represented as absolute 'truths,' but rather to ways of experiencing the world from an often rather subjective point of view.

'Realistic' genres: Autobiographies, biographies, historiographic writing, reports. The autobiographical as well as the heterobiographical genre has been successfully transferred into graphic storytelling, often connected with representations of historical situations and events. Art Spiegelman combines those genres in his groundbreaking *Maus*, which is not only *A Survivor's Tale* about his parents who experienced the Holocaust and thus a 'historical graphic novel,' but also an autobiographical story on two different levels: *Maus* represents the autobiographical memories of Art Spiegelman's father, Vladek, and this report itself is integrated into the autobiography of Art himself, who connects the representation of his own story with the retelling of Vladek's story.[16] *In the Shadow of No Towers* (2004), Spiegelman's more recent comic about the 9/11 events, again combines elements of autobiographical and historiographic narrative; again, the artist presents himself in changing roles and observes the realities he experiences from different points of view.[17]

---

15 See Herman 2009; Ryan 2010; Zipfel 2014.
16 For a more detailed narratological analysis of *Maus*, see Thon 2014.
17 For narratological analyses of *In the Shadow of No Towers*, see Chute 2006; Meyer 2008, 2010. See also Henry Jenkins's contribution in this volume.

In past decades, comics authors have presented several most original autobiographical novels, transforming themselves into comics characters and acting in the double role of the protagonist and the narrator. Marjane Satrapi's autobiography of her childhood and youth, *Persepolis* (2007), tells a story not only about the private experiences of a girl from Iran who experiences a clash of cultures. But as a personal story, it also documents aspects of political history in the Middle East. Further apart from political history, Alison Bechdel's autobiographical *Fun Home* depicts a family's private life and the private catastrophes shaping it.[18]

Critical reports and travelogues. Graphic narratives become an important form to tell stories from foreign countries, to report about political structures and crises, about wars and other catastrophes, about totalitarism, political suppression and the suffering of entire peoples as well as of individuals. They often explicitly thematize pictures, image programs, forms and strategies of visual representation as well as the limits of what can be represented. Joe Sacco, in his report about *Palestine* (2001), tries to highlight aspects of the Palestine world that are, according to him, usually overlooked by Western media. *Safe Area Goražde* (2000) depicts Sacco's experiences in the Bosnian war. Like *Palestine*, it combines personal impressions with historical and political background information. In a similar vein, graphic designer Guy Delisle's travel diary *Pyongyang* (2003) tells the story of a two months' stay in the North Korean capital.[19] Commenting on the image programs typical of the totalitarian regime, Delisle focusses on the political dimension of visual languages and on their possible abuse. Reporting about the work of a humanitarian organization of medical doctors in Afghanistan, titled *The Photographer* (2003–2006), Emmanuel Guibert, Didier Lefèvre, and Frederic Lemercier combine drawings and photographs with their narrative, the photographs offering realistic impressions from the war-shattered country, the drawings, however, picturing even subjects that had been invisible to the photographer or are beyond visibility in general.

Historical novels. Many subjects have been adapted by graphic novelists in a way that brings to mind historical novels that are based on past events but shape them according to different literary intentions. Thus, Peer Meter and Barbara Yelin (2010) received public acclaim for their retelling of the story of Gesche Gottfried, a woman who poisoned a number of people in the nineteenth century. Biographical narratives about historical characters tend to connect historical elements with elements of fictitious narrative. As a consequence, a clear distinction between the historical graphic novel

---

18 *Fun Home* is discussed further in Chute 2010.
19 The intricate connections among personal perspective, political reportage, and comics storytelling that shape the work of these artists are discussed in Banita 2013; Bartley 2013.

and (auto)biographical storytelling cannot be made. Chester Brown's *Louis Riel: A Comic Strip Biography* (2003), for example, illustrates a tendency to create historical narratives by integrating their heroes' life stories into broader socio-political contexts. Will Eisner's famous *The Plot: The Secret Story of the Protocols of the Elders of Zion* (2005) is dedicated to the presentation of meticulously reported historical facts and events; but as conjectures and narrative elements, especially concerning the involved characters' lives, are combined with the reconstruction of the history of the faked 'protocols,' *The Plot* may also be read as a historical novel. Eisner's works in general show the cartoonist's interest in this narrative genre. It is no coincidence, then, that Eisner's *Fagin the Jew* (2003), a graphic novel related to Charles Dickens's serial bestseller *Oliver Twist* (1837–1839), frames the socio-historical context of the story in a way that is similar to Dickens's work, although the attitute toward the narrator of Oliver Twist is altogether critical with regard to the way Fagin is characterized. The stories collected in Eisner's *The Contract with God Trilogy: The Life on Dropsie Avenue* (2006) evoke yet another historical moment: early to mid-twentieth-century immigrant life in New York.

Similar to traditional literature, graphic historical novels are often dedicated to the protagonists of famous historical events. But as Eisner shows exemplarily on different occasions, the protagonists of historical novels are not necessarily outstanding and famous characters. And they do not even have to be humans. In *Laika* (2007), Nick Abazdis reminds his readers of the puppy that became famous as world's first space traveler in the 1950s. Osamu Tezuka's eight-volume graphic story about the life of *Buddha* (1972–1983) can also be regarded as a historical novel, although elements of myths and legends are integrated into the narrative about Buddha's lifetime. Cities and other places may also be used as the 'protagonists' of graphic novels that take up representation strategies and thematic interests of history novels. Jason Lutes's *Berlin: City of Stones* (2000) and *Berlin: City of Smoke* (2008) are dedicated to Berlin in the final years of Weimar Republic when the rise of fascism already overshadows public and individual life. In Ben Katchor's *The Jew of New York* (1998), the characters' life stories form a picture of historical New York in the 1830s. Like its non-graphic literary counterpart, the genre of the historical graphic narrative dedicates itself to mediating between different thematic interests that are linked in a complex way, sometimes even shaped by strong tensions: the interest in large historical panels, on the one hand, and in individual and intimate life stories on the other; in broader historical developments and big events, on the one hand, and in personal experiences and feelings, on the other. Especially narratives about catatrophes, wars, and similarly precarious experiences offer opportunities to mediate between both interests, as narratives as diverse as Keiji Nakazawa's 'historiographic' manga story, *Barefoot Gen: A Cartoon of Hiroshima* (1973–1985), and Pat Mills's *Charley's War: 2 June–1 August 1916* (2005) indicate.

'Fantastic genres': Fantasy, gothic literature, tales, science fiction. As counterparts to narratives referring to actual historical and personal experiences within the broad field of the graphic novel there also exists a wide range of fantastic stories, science fiction, gothic fiction, and even (para)mythical fiction. Comics and graphic novels are used as important mythopoetic devices in contemporary cultural contexts; heroes and gods are created within comic books, and graphic novels tell model stories about the conflict between antagonistic powers. Neil Gaiman's *The Sandman* series (1989–1996) may have been the most successful comic series of the 1990s. Gaiman mixes elements of the fable, folktale, fairy tale, and other traditional genres, creating what has been characterized as 'modern myths,' partially in historical settings. This kind of mixture was globally sucessful. It also appeals to more ambitious readers, as it reflects upon imagination, creativity, and the arts. Thus, volume 3 of *The Sandman* contains the story of William Shakespeare performing *A Midsummer Night's Dream* in the presence of inhabitants of his own fantastic dream world. As Rocco Versaci puts it, "Gaiman appropriates the most sacrosanct figure in English literature to serve the needs of his comic book" (2007: 203). Thus, Gaiman uses his *Sandman* comics to reflect on storytelling and its functions not only with regard to graphic storytelling, but explicitly with references to the horizon of world literature.

In gothic fiction, the dark side of an imagined world is explored in continuation of gothic novels and stories as they emerged in European literature by the end of the eighteenth century and strongly influenced the history of the modern novel. Science fiction universes as well are represented by 'classical' SF novels as well as by graphic storytelling; like gothic literature, SF is a transgeneric category.

For different reasons, examples of 'realistic' as well as of 'fantastic' graphic storytelling are related to concepts of 'world literature.' The first group professes a leading interest in 'global' or at least in inter- and transnational processes (politics, historical developments, social structures) on the level of content. Regarding contents more distant from global realities, the second group presents characters and plots of partially 'mythic' ambition: superheroes and other projection surfaces for personal and collective identification, models of conflicts and conflict solving, visualizations of collective fears and personal obsessions. In spite of cultural differences on the level of codes, the stories from different countries resemble each other and indicate 'global' expectations within the readers' world community.

Refined autoreferential graphic narratives such as Alan Moore and Dave Gibbons's *Watchmen* or Moore and Kevin O'Neill's *The League of Extraordinary Gentlemen* (2002, 2004) present themselves as metacomics that reflect on the genesis and functions of different types of comics heroes and villains and, at the same time, build upon the strong historical connection between traditional literature and graphic narrative. The superheros and anti-heroes, as they are depicted here, had formative impact on the history of graphic storytelling, but they can also be seen as typical and representative 'literary' heroes. Especially the members of the League of Extraordinary Gentlemen are evidently quoted from well-known works of world literature, and thus this graphic novel indicates its intricate conceptual indebtedness to the specifically literary library.

Graphic Narratives Based on 'World Literature'

The history of graphic narratives and the history of concepts of 'world literature' are closely connected, and they have given rise to an important and multi-faceted tradition of adapting texts from the canon of world literature to the medium of comics. Comics adaptations of literary texts are closely linked to canonization processes. Serial graphic narratives about 'world literature classics' as well as single graphic novel releases adapting literary texts prefer canonized works as their starting platforms. In a way, comic adaptations prove the status of a text as a canonized work and, at the same time, confirm this status.

Adaptations, parodies, spin-offs, pastiches, portraits of literary authors: World literature reflected in graphic storytelling. Following a concept developed by Albert Kanter in 1941, the publishing house Gilberton Company started publishing graphic narratives based on the plots of literary works. They were at first called "Classic Comics" and then rechristened "Classics Illustrated" (CI) in 1947. They presented to their readers adaptations of 'world literature' in the sense of canonical works of literature that were evidently based on a Western canon. English literature was more widely represented than other literatures, but altogether the series aimed at retelling 'classics' from many national literatures. 160 titles were released, many of which were also translated into other languages. According to paratextual notes, the intention was to introduce especially young readers to the world of great literature, and so even the term 'comic' was used reluctantly. The CI paratexts underscore the idea that the volumes were not meant to be read as substitutes for the originals but as instructive vehicles preparing for future reading. Although the Gilberton Company employed famous comic artists such as Louis Zansky and Jack Kirby, CI designers were not usually eager to explore individual drawing styles. So CI's mostly rather conventional graphic language, shaped by a 'realistic' style, prevented the format from a more autonomous development as it was later on achieved by newer and more original adaptations of literary works. Other publishers adapted Gilbertson's CI concept; in 1976, the "Marvel Classic Comics" series started, initially with new editions of already released volumes, later on with adaptations of other canonized texts. In the 36 numbers that were released, the artists partially explored new drawing styles, although the series in general remained uniform.[20] In 1982, 1983, and 1984, the Publisher Oval Projects produced three Shakespeare comics in the CI format (*Macbeth*, *Othello*, *King Lear*). In 1990, Berkley/First Publishing started a new CI series, releasing 29 issues. Now the graphic styles employed tended to differ from the formerly homogeneous CI style, probably due to the influence of the graphic novel format since the 1980s. The different graphic artists' personal styles were regarded as contributing to the aesthetic qualities of the graphic novels. Famous artists such as Bill Sienkiewicz und Peter Kuper were engaged in the production. Yet even in Sienkiewicz's visually most original *Moby Dick* adaptation (1990), the opening paratext emphasizes the fact that the graphic novel depends on a literary classic and is mainly intended to affirm the established canon of world literature: "Classics Illustrated are adaptations of the world's greatest works of literature [...]. Each lavishly illustrated volume is an accurate representation of the original work—distinctive, fresh and innovative, yet faithful of the book and true to the intentions of the author" (1990: n.p.). Moreover, the paratextual comment offers no less than a kind of definition of what a literary 'classic' is, at the same time confirming the graphic narrative's self-understanding as a 'faithful' medium of adaptation (Sienkiewicz 1990: n.p.):

> There are reasons why the original works are classics: Each is unique, each has weathered the test of time, and each continues to reflect and address the underlying spirit of humanity in today's world. Classics Illustrated reflect those individual styles that made the original works great—not just the stories, but the nuances as well. These adaptations naturally are abridged, but care has been taken to maintain the narrative sweep and as much of the original dialogue and narration as possible.

---

[20] Versacci argues: "the style of artwork from issue to issue is unnervingly consistent, again creating a false sense of stylistic consistency among the source material writers. So, while the Marvel Classic Comics embrace their 'comic bookness' more so than the Classics Illustrated, they still fail to fully explore the medium's potential to create art" (2007: 193).

Obviously, common 'world literature' discourses are echoed by the framework of the CI narratives, and thus the series contributes to affirm the (mostly Western) world literature canon. Like the superhero comic, the western and the science fiction comic, the CI series stimulated a broad reception of comics as an autonomous publishing format. And the conception of the 'graphic novel' as a larger and autonomous form of graphic storytelling was of formative influence on comic adaptations of literature. Due to their extent, graphic novels offered the chance to retell already existing stories in complex and often rather refined ways.

Recently, numerous examples of ambitious graphic novels adapting literary texts have been released, sometimes as parts of a series ("Puffin Graphics," for instance, is famous for aesthetically ambitious and stylistically original adaptations of literature), sometimes as autonomous projects like Stéphane Heuet's adaptation of Marcel Proust's novel *A la recherche du temps perdu*, starting in 1998 and still a work-in-progress. Paul Karasik and David Mazzucchelli's adaptation of Paul Auster's novel *City of Glass* (1994) has achieved the status of a 'classic adaptation,' as have Bob Callahan and Scott Gillis's adaptation of Barry Gifford's *Perdita Durango* (1995) and various adaptations Franz Kafka's texts by Peter Kuper (2003), David Zane Mairowitz and Robert Crumb (1993), Daniel Casanave and Robert Cara (2006, 2007), and Chantal Montellier and David Zane Mairowitz (2008). Yet another set of examples that show creative graphic storytelling treading in the footsteps of literary authors are ambitious adaptations of the *Faust* legend, such as Falk Nordman's *Faust* (1996) and David Vandermeulen and Ambre's *Faust* (2006).

Next to these types of adaptations, which essentially retell a story from literature in order to inform readers about or remind them of the plot, we can also identify parodist works that connect such retellings with humoristic or satirical commentary. Of course, in a more general sense, all adaptations of literary works by graphic artists might be characterized as 'parodies.' But some works appear specifically 'mocking,' playing their game with canonized 'classics' as well as with 'high culture' as such. Some graphic artists also play with the elements of 'canonized classics' by creating 'modernized' versions of the old plots, as, for instance, Posy Simmonds with her graphic novel *Gemma Bovary* (1999), a self-referential parody on Flaubert's novel *Madame Bovary*. Not always clearly distinguished from parodies, spin-offs in graphic narratives often take up the stories that were already told in literary texts and offer the reader continuations, pre-histories, or 'alternative' stories. Will Eisner, in *Fagin the Jew* (2003), presents to the reader an alternative version of a part of Dickens's novel *Oliver Twist*, pointing to the anti-semitic traits of Dickens's text and giving the Jewish character Fagin an own voice that is opposed to the English novelist; Eisner's Fagin even meets Dickens and accuses him of being unjust. Many other graphic novelists create their stories by combining elements from different literary sources, as, for instance, in Moore and O'Neill's *League of Extraordinary Gentlemen*.

Presenting and affirming the canon: Poets' portraits and 'world literature collections.' Comics and graphic novels are not only created in order to retell literary plots and to 'quote' literary characters. References to literature are also constitutive for graphic narratives dedicated to literary authors. The single volumes of the popular series *...for Beginners*, paralleled by the series *Introducing...*, are dedicated to important scientists, philosophers, and authors, and among the literary writers portrayed here there are representatives of earlier as well as of twentieth-century literature. The volumes usually combine biographical information with remarks concerning the main works of their protagonists. Sometimes they suggest a close connection between biography and fiction, and sometimes they even include short adaptations of major works or quotations from them. The drawings are sometimes based on photos or other historical documents, and the graphic narrative is thus characterized by quotations on the level of images as well as on the level of language. Framing adaptations of literary texts by the life story of their authors suggests an autobiographical approach to the works cited. Sometimes the mixture of biographical facts and fiction appears as at least slightly parodic. In general, however, in spite of parodic and other ludic elements, the *Introducing...* and *...for Beginners* series are conceived as books that can be consulted in order to gain 'real' and useful information.

A playful attitude toward the concept of a literary canon characterizes a specific subgenre of graphic narratives that has become rather popular in the last decade: series and collections of very short comics, often only filling one single page, that refer to a selection of canonized 'classics,' compressing and condensing them extremely in the process of adaptation. Often, these pocket-size comics classics are almost wordless, except for their titles that quote the titles of literary works. At any rate, there is not much space for text elements, and the panels are necessarily laconic. Already due to the small-sized format, the pocket comic classics (as one might call them) appear as parodies; their humoristic or satirical energy, however, does not mainly aim at the respective text itself but at the process of canonization as a consolidation of 'high cultural' values, in the belief in canonized knowledge, and in the superficiality of its uses. In order to understand the pocket-size 'classic,' the reader should already know the texts referred to—or at least connect some ideas with them. However, the anthologies present themselves as useful means of 'instruction' that can be consulted quickly and without spending too much time on the acquisition of socially valued knowledge. Regarded as the successors of *Classics Illustrated*, these anthologies of 'world literature classics' appear as self-referential graphic narratives. They not only parody literary texts and their characters but also the idea of functionalizing comics as media of information and 'education.'²¹ Humorist graphic artists like Robert Sikoryak (1990) specialize in parodies of *Classics Illustrated*, presenting extremely short and distorted versions of literary classics such as Kafka's *Metamorphosis*.

In recent literary theory, defenders of the 'world literature' concept have especially stressed the necessity to integrate concepts of globalization into discussions about 'world literature.' If it were necessary at all, graphic narratives, especially adaptations of literature, might illustrate and confirm this claim. In an even more obvious way than most literary texts, examples of world literature comics present themselves as culturally hybrid aesthetic phenomena. Thus, the Puffin Graphics' *Macbeth* was retold by employing the graphic style of Japanese manga; recent new graphic stories have taken up this concept.²² Osamu Tezuka, pioneer of Japanese manga, transferred a large collection of dramatic plays from Western and Eastern literature into the world of manga; his manga series *Nanairo Inko* was originally published in the *Weekly Shonen Champion* in 1981 and 1982. Already in earlier decades, Tezuka had adapted European classics (plays, novels,

---

21 See Moga Mobo 2001; Mahrer-Stich 1993; Alber and Wolf 2003; Vandermeulen 2004; Lange 2008.
22 See e.g., Sexton, Grandt, and Chow 2008. In the same series, other Shakespeare tragedies have been adapted in the manga style. The author of the series' preface, Adam Sexton, argues in favor of the manga, stressing—somehow naively but with great emphasis—that unlike other art forms, manga can show even the invisible: "Like his tragedies, comedies, histories, and romances, [...] manga are of course visual. In fact, a manga is potentially more visual than a stage production of one of the plays of Shakespeare. Unbound by the physical realities of the theater, the graphic novel can depict any situation, no matter how fantastical or violent, that its creators are able to pencil, ink, and shade. At the same time, manga are potentially no less verbal than Shakespeare's spectacularly wordy plays, with this crucial difference: in a production of none of the plays onstage or onscreen, we can hear the words but can't see them. Though Shakespeare is never easy, reading helps. And that is precisely what manga adaptations of the plays allow. Perusing a Shakespeare manga, the reader can linger over speeches, rereading them in part or altogether. Especially in the long and intricate soliloquies typical of Shakespearian tragedy, this allows for an appreciation of the playwright's craft that is difficult if not impossible as those soliloquies move past us during a performance. [...] Take Romeo and Juliet's famous Queen Mab speech. Even the most creative stage director cannot faithfully present the minuscule fairy described by Mercutio. Manga artists can. The same is true of the drowning of Ophelia in Hamlet. It is precisely because these vignettes are unstageable that Shakespeare has his characters describe Queen Mab and the death of Ophelia in such great detail—they must help us imagine them. In its unlimited ability to dramatize, the graphic novel more closely resembles a contemporary film with a colossal special-effects budget than anything produced onstage in the Elizabethan era or since" (Saxton, Grandt, and Chow 2008: 2–3).

narratives) to manga style, often combining plot elements from the Western texts with Japanese elements and developing a personal drawing style that was influenced by Japanese traditions as well as by a globally understandable 'Disney' style.

Stylistic experiments like these are in a way correlated with the meaning that Goethe attributed to the term 'Weltliteratur.' Transgressing cultural borders, adapting elements of foreign cultures, and connecting them with one's proper cultural heritage, world's literatures develop in a process of mutual influence; new genres arise as well as new languages. And even more: transferred into the languages of foreign cultures, one's own cultural and literary heritages appear as renewed and open to innovative interpretation and continuation.

Works Cited

Abazdis, Nick (2007). *Laika*. New York: First Second. Print.

Abbott, Lawrence L. (1986). "Comic Art: Characteristics and Potentialities of a Narrative Art Medium." *Journal of Popular Culture* 19: 155–76. Print.

Alber, Wolfgang, and Heinz Wolf (2003). *50—Literatur gezeichnet*. Wien: Edition Comic Forum. Print.

Banita, Georgiana (2013). "Cosmopolitan Suspicion: Comics Journalism and Graphic Silence." Shane Denson, Christina Meyer, and Daniel Stein (eds.). *Transnational Perspectives on Graphic Narratives: Comics at the Crossroads*. London: Bloomsbury. 49–65. Print.

Barthes, Roland (1977 [1966]). "Introduction to the Structural Analysis of Narrative." *Image—Music—Text*. Ed. and trans. Stephen Heath. New York: Hill and Wang. 79–124. Print.

Bartley, Aryn (2013). "Staging Cosmopolitanism: The Transnational Encounter in Joe Sacco's *Footnoes in Gaza*." Shane Denson, Christina Meyer, and Daniel Stein (eds.). *Transnational Perspectives on Graphic Narratives: Comics at the Crossroads*. London: Bloomsbury. 67–82. Print.

Bechdel, Alison (2006). *Fun Home: A Family Tragicomic*. Boston: Houghton Mifflin. Print.

Bell, Roanne, and Mark Sinclair (2005). *Pictures and Words: New Comic Art and Narrative Illustration*. New Haven: Yale UP. Print.

Birus, Hendrik (1995). "Goethes Idee der Weltliteratur: Eine historische Vergegenwärtigung." Manfred Schmeling (ed.). *Weltliteratur heute: Konzepte und Perspektiven*. Würzburg: Königshausen & Neumann. 5–28. Print.

Brown, Chester (2006). *Louis Riel: A Comic-Strip Biography*. Montreal: Drawn & Quarterly. Print.
Buzzati, Dino (1969). *Poema a fumetti*. Milan: Arnoldo Mondadori Editore. Print.
Callahan, Bob, and Scott Gillis (1995). *Barry Gifford's Perdita Durango: A Graphic Thriller*. New York: Avon. Print.
Campbell, Eddie (2007). "What Is a Graphic Novel?" *World Literature Today: Graphic Literature* Mar.–Apr. 13. Print.
Casanave, Daniel, and Robert Cara (2006). *L'Amérique*. I: *Une villa aux environs de New-York*. Paris: 6 pieds sous terre. Print.
— (2007). *L'Amérique*. II: *Sur la route de Ramsès*. Paris: 6 pieds sous terre. Print.
Chatman, Seymour (1978). *Story and Discourse: Narrative Structure in Fiction and Film*. Ithaca: Cornell UP. Print.
Chute, Hillary (2006). "'The Shadow of a Past Time': History and Graphic Representation in *Maus*." *Twentieth-Century Literature* 52.2: 199–230. Print.
— (2010). *Graphic Women: Life Narrative and Contemporary Comics*. New York: Columbia UP. Print.
Delisle, Guy (2003). *Pyongyang*. Paris: L'Association. Print.
Denson, Shane, Christina Meyer, and Daniel Stein (eds.) (2013). *Transnational Perspectives on Graphic Narratives: Comics at the Crossroads*. London: Bloomsbury. Print.
Ditschke, Stephan (2009). "Comics als Literatur: Zur Etablierung des Comics im deutschsprachigen Feuilleton seit 2003." Stephan Ditschke, Katerina Kroucheva, and Daniel Stein (eds.). *Comics: Zur Geschichte und Theorie eines populärkulturellen Mediums*. Bielefeld: transcript. 265–80. Print.
Eisner, Will (2001). *Comics and Sequential Art*. Tamarac: Poorhouse. Print.
— (2003). *Fagin the Jew*. New York: Doubleday. Print.
— (2004). *Graphic Storytelling and Visual Narrative*. Tamarac: Poorhouse. Print.
— (2006). *The Contract With God Trilogy: Life on Dropsie Avenue*. New York: Norton. Print.
— (2005). *The Plot: The Secret Story of the Protocols of the Elders of Zion*. New York: Norton. Print.
Figueira, Dorothy (2008). *Otherwise Occupied: Pedagogies of Alterity and the Brahminization of Theory*. Albany: State U of New York P. Print.
Gaiman, Neil (2010). *The Sandman: Dream Country*. Vol. 3. Art by Colleen Doran, Kelley Jones, Malcolm Jones III, Charles Vess. Colors by Steve Oliff. Originally published in single magazine form as *The Sandman* #17–20, 1990. New York: DC Comics. Print.

Gardner, Jared, and David Herman (eds.) (2011). *Graphic Narratives and Narrative Theory.* Special issue of *SubStance* 40.1. Print.
Gravett, Paul (2005). *Graphic Novels: Stories to Change Your Life.* London: Aurum. Print.
Heißenbüttel, Helmut (1974). "KrazykatzBremenwodu: Lehrgedicht über Kommunikation." *Das Durchhauen des Kohlhaupts: Dreizehn Lehrgedichte. Projekt Nr. 2.* Darmstadt/Neuwied: Luchterhand. 71–96. Print.
Herman, David (2009). *Basic Elements of Narrative.* Chichester: Wiley-Blackwell. Print.
Jandl, Ernst (1979). *Sprechblasen.* Stuttgart: Reclam. Print.
Kannenberg, Gene, Jr. (2008). "Introduction." *500 Essential Graphic Novels: The Ultimate Guide.* New York: Harper Design. 6–10. Print.
Karasik, Paul, and David Mazzucchelli (1994). *Paul Auster's City of Glass.* New York: Avon. Print.
Katchor, Ben (1998). *The Jew of New York.* New York: Pantheon. Print.
Koppen, Erwin (1984). "Weltliteratur." Klaus Kanzog and Achim Masser (eds.). *Reallexikon der deutschen Literaturgeschichte.* Vol. 4. 2nd edition. Berlin: De Gruyter. 815–27. Print.
Kuper, Peter (2003). *The Metamorphosis.* New York: Crown. Print.
Lange, Henrik (2008). *90 Classic Books for People in a Hurry.* Stockholm: Nicotext. Print.
Lutes, Jason (2000). *Berlin: City of Stones.* Montreal: Drawn & Quartely. Print.
— (2008). *Berlin: City of Smoke.* Montreal: Drawn & Quartely. Print.
Mahrer-Stich, Irene (1993). *Alice im Comicland: Comiczeichner präsentieren Werke der Weltliteratur.* Zürich: Edition Moderne. Print.
Mairowitz, David Z., and Robert Crumb (1993). *Introducing Kafka.* New York: Totem. Print.
McCloud, Scott (1993). *Understanding Comics: The Invisible Art.* New York: Harper Perennial. Print.
Meter, Peer, and Barbara Yelin (2010). *Gift.* Berlin: Reprodukt. Print.
Meyer, Christina (2008). "'After all, disaster is my muse': Art Spiegelman's *In the Shadow of No Towers.*" Frank Kelleter and Daniel Stein (eds.). *American Studies as Media Studies.* Heidelberg: Winter. 107–17. Print.
— (2010). "'Putting it into boxes': Framing Art Spiegelman's *In the Shadow of No Towers.*" MaryAnn Snyder-Körber and Andrew Gross (eds.). *Trauma's Continuum: September 11th Re-Considered.* Special issue of *Amerikastudien/American Studies* 55.3: 479–94. Print.
Miller, Frank (1997). *Batman: The Dark Knight Returns.* Inks by Klaus Janson. Colors by Lynn Varley. Lettered by John Costanza. Originally published in single magazine form as *Batman: The Dark Knight Returns* #1–4, 1986. New York: DC Comics. Print.

Mills, Pat (2005). *Charley's War: 2 June–1 August 1916*. London: Titan. Print.
Moga Mobo (2001). *Moga Mobos 100 Meisterwerke der Weltliteratur*. Berlin: Ehapa. Print.
Montellier, Chantal, and David Zane Mairowitz (2008). *The Trial*. New York: Sterling. Print.
Moore, Alan (2002). *The League of Extraordinary Gentlemen: Vol. One*. Art by Kevin O'Neill. Colors by Ben Dimagmaliw. Lettered by Bill Oakley. Originally published in single magazine form as *The League of Extraordinary Gentlemen*, Vol. 1, #1–6, 1999–2000. London: Titan. Print.
— (2004). *The League of Extraordinary Gentlemen: Vol. Two*. Art by Kevin O'Neill. Colors by Ben Dimagmaliw. Lettered by Bill Oakley. Originally published in single magazine form as *The League of Extraordinary Gentlemen*, Vol. 2, #1–6, 2002–2003. London: Titan. Print.
— (2005). *Watchmen*. Illustrated and lettered by Dave Gibbons. Colors by John Higgins. Originally published in single magazine form as *Watchmen* #1–12, 1986–1987. London: Titan. Print.
Nordmann, Falk (1996). *Faust: Der Tragödie erster Teil*. Hamburg: Edition B & K. Print.
Packard, Stephan (2009). "Comic." Dieter Lamping (ed.). *Handbuch der literarischen Gattungen*. Stuttgart: Kröner. 113–20. Print.
Rühm, Gerhard (1972). "mickydrama." *Ophelia und die Wörter*. Darmstadt/Neuwied: Luchterhand. 149–59. Print.
— (1975). *Comic*. Linz: Edition Neue Texte. Print.
Ryan, Marie-Laure (2006). *Avatars of Story*. Minneapolis: U of Minnesota P. Print.
— (2010). "Fiction, Cognition, and Non-Verbal Media." Marina Grishakova and Marie-Laure Ryan (eds.). *Intermediality and Storytelling*. Berlin: De Gruyter. 8–26. Print.
Sabin, Roger (1993). *Adult Comics: An Introduction*. London: Routledge. Print.
Sacco, Joe (2000). *Safe Area Goražde*. Seattle: Fantagraphics. Print.
— (2001). *Palestine*. Originally published in single magazine form as *Palestine* #1–9, 1993–1995. Seattle: Fantagraphics. Print.
Sachs-Hombach, Klaus (2003). *Das Bild als kommunikatives Medium: Elemente einer allgemeinen Bildwissenschaft*. Köln: von Halem. Print.
Satrapi, Marjane (2007). *Persepolis*. Originally published as *Persepolis* Vol. 1–4, 2000–2003. Paris: L'Association. Print.
Schmeling, Manfred (1995). *Weltliteratur heute: Konzepte und Perspektiven*. Würzburg: Königshausen & Neumann. Print.

Schmitz-Emans, Monika, in cooperation with Christian A. Bachmann (2012). *Literatur-Comics: Adaptationen und Transformationen der Weltliteratur*. Berlin: De Gruyter. Print.

Schüwer, Martin (2008). *Wie Comics erzählen: Grundriss einer intermedialen Erzähltheorie der grafischen Literatur*. Trier: Wissenschaftlicher Verlag Trier. Print.

Sexton, Adam, Eve Grandt, and Candice Chow (2008). *Shakespeare's Macbeth*. Hoboken: Wiley. Print.

Sienkiewicz, Bill (1990). *Herman Melville: Moby Dick*. Classics Illustrated #4. Berkley: First Publishing. Print.

Sikoryak, Robert (1990). "Good Ol' Gregor Samsa." *Raw* 2.2. Print.

Simmonds, Posy (1999). *Gemma Bovery*. London: Cape. Print.

Spiegelman, Art (1986). *Maus: A Survivor's Tale*. I: *My Father Bleeds History*. New York: Pantheon. Print.

— (1991). *Maus: A Survivor's Tale*. II: *And Here My Troubles Began*. New York: Pantheon. Print.

— (2004). *In the Shadow of No Towers*. New York: Pantheon. Print.

Thon, Jan-Noël (2014). "Toward a Transmedial Narratology: On Narrators in Contemporary Graphic Novels, Feature Films, and Computer Games." Jan Alber and Per Krogh Hansen (eds.). *Beyond Classical Narration: Transmedial and Unnatural Challenges*. Berlin: De Gruyter. 25–56. Print.

Vandermeulen, David (2004). *Littérature pour tous*. 2nd edition. Montpellier: 6 pieds sous terre. Print.

Vandermeulen, David, and Ambre (2006). *Faust*. Montpellier: 6 pieds sous terre. Print.

Versaci, Rocco (2007). *This Book Contains Graphic Language: Comics as Literature*. New York: Continuum. Print.

Ware, Chris (2000). *Jimmy Corrigan: The Smartest Kid on Earth*. New York: Pantheon. Print.

Zipfel, Frank (2014). "Fictionality across Media." Marie-Laure Ryan and Jan-Noël Thon (eds). *Storyworlds across Media: Toward a Media-Conscious Narratology*. Lincoln: U of Nebraska P. 103–25. Print.

Index (Persons)

Abazdis, Nick   395
Acland, Charles R.   314
Aczel, Richard   68–70
Adams, Douglas   293
Alber, Jan   292
Altan, Francesco Tullio   10, 103–04
Ambre   399
Anderson, Carl   210
Anderson, Michael   341
Ashcroft, John   316
Auster, Paul   399
Azoulay, Ariella   137

B., David   10, 145–47, 147 (fig.), 207 (fig.), 358
Bachalo, Chris   327
Baetens, Jan   14, 89
Bagge, Peter   207
Bahr, Johann   241
Bails, Jerry   182–83
Bal, Mieke   221
Bamberg, Michael   334
Barbieri, Daniel   265
Barks, Carl   305, 308
Barry, Lynda   127
Barsalou, Lawrence   60
Bartel, Paul   341
Batiuk, Tom   251
Bauman, Zygmunt   61
Bazin, André   219, 225, 227
Beaty, Bart   137, 367–68, 370
Bechdel, Allison   10–11, 129–33, 131 (fig.), 132 (fig.), 206, 206 (fig.), 211, 303, 359, 390, 394
Bell, Roanne   393
Bendis, Brian   279, 326
Benjamin, Walter   219, 233, 333
Berbérian, Charles   358
Berger, John   303
Berger, Karen   327, 334
Berndt, Jaqueline   15
Blackbeard, Bill   307
Blom, Philipp   303, 306
Böger, Astrid   127
Bolter, Jay David   191, 199–201, 228

Bonhomme, Matthieu   10, 107
Bordwell, David   87, 111
Boym, Svetlana   318–19
Branigan, Edward   91, 93
Bridwell, Nelson   170
Briggs, Clare   244–45
Brinkmann, Rolf Dieter   390
Broome, John   169–70, 173, 175 (fig.)
Brown, Chester   395
Brubaker, Ed   326
Brueghel   263
Bukatman, Scott   225, 243
Burns, Charles   9, 39, 40 (fig.), 42 (fig.), 309
Busch, Wilhelm   14, 241, 351
Bush, George W.   316
Bushmiller, Ernie   247
Butts, Bob   177
Buzzati, Dino   390
Byrne, John   326

Callahan, Bob   399
Caniff, Milton   247, 250, 307
Cara, Robert   399
Carey, Mike   13, 208, 271–73, 278–79, 281–82, 284–94, 288 (fig.), 291 (fig.), 327
Casanave, Daniel   399
Cham, Jorge   251
Chaney, Michael A.   145–46
Chapman, James   341
Christiansen, Hans-Christian
Chute, Hillary   4, 6–7, 129, 136, 145, 274, 303, 312
Claremont, Chris   326
Cole, Jack   308
Collodi, Carlo   10, 112
Constantine, John   326
Coovadia, Imraan   148
Corben, Richard   276
Correll, Charles   249
Cornell, Paul   280, 282–83
Cosey   209
Coughlan, David   274
Couser, Thomas G.   127
Crabapple, Molly   207
Crane, Roy   247

Crary, Jonathan   223
Crumb, Robert   340, 399
Cupples and Leon   250
Currie, Gregory   89, 127
Currie, Mark   325, 332–34

D'Ache, Caran   241
Damasio, Antonio   58
D'Ammassa, Don   260
Darrow, Geof   211
Davies, David   127–28, 133
Davis, Andrew   313
Davis, Vanessa   208
Debray, Régis   348
Deitch, Kim   304, 309
DeKoven, Marianne   4, 274
Deleuze, Gilles   219, 232–33
Delisle, Guy   394
De Moor, Rob   259
Deprez, Olivier   360
Desjardins, Mary   310
Dickens, Charles   395, 399–400
Dillon, Steve   326–27, 330 (fig.)
Dirks, Rudolph   309
Disney   286–87, 316, 355, 402
Doane, Mary Ann   219
Doha   363
Drake, Arnold   170
Drechsler, Debbie   208
Du Maurier, George   49, 51
Dupuy, Philippe   358

Eco, Umberto   157–58, 162, 171, 184, 264
Edelman, Mr. M.   338
Eder, Jens   87
Edwards, Natalie   137
Eisner, Will   27, 34, 38–39, 127, 197, 207–08, 276, 290, 304, 308, 328, 386–87, 389–90, 395, 399–400
Ellis, Warren   14, 61, 62 (fig.), 326–27
Ennis, Garth   326–27, 330 (fig.), 332
Etter, Lukas   11, 205, 205 (fig.)
Ewert, Jeanne C.   204

Fagan, Tom   174, 177–78, 181–82
Farmer, Joyce   303
Feiffer, Jules   309
Feininger, Lyonel   308–09
Fies, Brian   143–44, 143 (fig.)
Finger, Bill   170, 181–83

Fisher, Bud   244–45
Flaubert, Gustave   399
Fludernik, Monika   202
Forest, Jean-Claude   356
Forster, E. M.   58
Fortemps, Vincent   360
Foster, Hal   307
Foster, Michael Dylan   368
Foucault, Michel   157–59, 167
Fowler, Roger   114
Fox, Gardner   170, 174, 176 (fig.)
Frahm, Ole   36
Franc, Régis   356
Fred   113–14, 208, 209 (fig.)
Friedberg, Anne   219
Friedrich, Mike   169–71
FRMK (Fréon, Frémok)   360
Fukushima, Yoshiko   373

Gabilliet, Jean-Paul   340
Gaiman, Neil   9–10, 14, 27–28, 31 (fig.), 35 (fig.), 37 (fig.), 74, 75 (fig.), 79–82, 80 (fig.), 81 (fig.), 90–91, 191, 326–30, 329 (fig.), 331 (fig.), 335, 396
Gallagher, Shaun   52
Gance, Abel   226
Gardner, Jared   2–4, 12, 133, 159, 177, 220, 232–33, 277, 292, 303–04, 319, 365
Genette, Gérard   10, 68, 72, 85, 104, 160, 164, 325, 332
Gerrig, Richard   55
Gibbons, Dave   9, 29 (fig.), 44 (fig.), 85, 191, 277, 391, 397
Gifford, Barry   399
Gillis, Scott   399
Gilmore, Leigh   134
Goblet, Dominique   112
Goebbels, Joseph   293
Goethe, Johann Wolfgang von   15, 349, 388, 402
Gordon, Ian   339
Gosden, Freeman   249
Gottlib   356
Gould, Chester   304
Graff, Larry   168
Grainge, Paul   310
Gravett, Paul   275
Gray, Harold   247
Greene, Sid   173
Grierson, John   144

Grishakova, Marina   293
Groensteen, Thierry   41, 54, 110–12, 144, 357, 364
Gross, Peter   13, 208, 271–73, 278–79, 282, 284–94, 288 (fig.), 291 (fig.)
Gross, Sabine   38
Grusin, Richard   191, 199–201, 228
Guibert, Emmanuel   359, 394
Guilbert, Xavier   371
Gunning, Tom   243

Hajdu, David   314
Hamilton, Edmond   170
Hamlin, Vincent Trout   261
Harrell, Stephen   180
Harvey, Robert C.   111, 194, 204–05
Hatfield, Charles   73, 274–76, 325, 332
Hayward, Jennifer   177
Hearst, William Randolph   242, 245, 315
Heer, Jeet   306–07
Heißenbüttel, Helmut   390
Hergé   14, 207, 353–54
Herman, David   2–4, 55–56, 293–94
Herriman, George   230, 245, 308–09
Herron, Ed   170
Heuet, Stéphane   399
Hirsch, Marianne   137–38
Hoberman, J.   304
Hodl, Ken   170
Hogarth, William   27, 241, 349
Holkins, Jerry   251
Hoppeler, Stephanie   205, 205 (fig.)
Horstkotte, Silke   9, 106–07, 120
Howarth, F. M.   241
Hughes, Ted   282
Hutcheon, Linda   134, 198, 333

Infantino, Carmine   172–73, 175 (fig.), 176 (fig.)
Inge, M. Thomas   282–83, 288
Ito, Go   375–79

Jacobs, Ken   315–16
Jacques, Faith   286
Jannidis, Fotis   70
Jenkins, Henry   13–14, 279
Jewison, Norman   341
Jodorowsky, Alejandro   265
Johnson, Crockett   309
Johnson, Mark   53

Johnston, Lynn   251
Johnston, Phillip   304
Jost, François   10, 104–06, 108, 110

Kafka, Franz   399, 401
Kakutani, Michiko   311
Kane, Bob   161–67, 163 (fig.), 165 (fig.), 169–70, 173, 181–84
Kanigher, Robert   170
Kannenberg, Gene   389–92
Kanter, Albert   397
Kaoru   363
Karasik, Paul   208, 399
Katchor, Ben   304, 309, 395
Katz, Jack   276
Kelleter, Frank   172, 293
Kelly, Walt   308–09
Kentaro, Takekuma   366
Kern, Stephen   219
Kindt, Tom   89–90
King, Frank   230, 245, 247, 307
Kipling, Joseph Rudyard   282
Kirby, Jack   307, 340, 398
Kishimoto, Masashi   363, 378
Klein, Todd   331 (fig.)
Kochalka, James   212 (fig.)
Krahulik, Mike   251
Krauss, Rosanlind   137
Kress, Gunther   220
Krigstein, Bernard   307–08
Kubert, Joe   170
Kuhlman, Martha   312
Kukkonen, Karin   1, 9, 273
Kuper, Peter   398–99
Kurosawa, Akira   374
Kurtzman, Harvey   304, 308
Kyle, Richard   389

Larcenet, Manu   116–18, 116 (fig.), 117 (fig.)
Latour, Bruno   156–57
Ledderose, Lothar   366
Lee, Stan   326, 340
Leech, Geoffrey B.   114
Lefèvre, Didier   394
Lefèvre, Pascal   13, 33, 377
Lemercier, Frédéric   394
Lent, John A.   8
Lessing, Gotthold Ephraim   54–55, 193, 197
Livingston, Paisley   91
Lloyd, David   11, 198

Lurie, Susan 317
Lutes, Jason 199, 199 (fig.), 395
Lyons, James 292

Mack, David 279
Mahler, Nicolas 207
Mairowitz, David Zane–399
Marchetto, Marisa Acocella 10, 140–42, 141 (fig.), 142 (fig.)
Marey, Étienne-Jules 108, 225
Marion, Philippe 41, 71, 89, 111–13, 117, 137
Maserell, Frans 386
Masolino da Panicale 224
Mathieu, Marc-Antoine 118
Mayer, Sheldon 308
Mazzucchelli, David 115, 208, 399
McCay, Winsor 9, 49, 50 (fig.), 52, 59–61, 63–64, 67, 113, 211, 225, 243–44, 308–09, 316
McCloud, Scott 27, 54, 56–57, 205, 208, 211, 232, 328, 375, 385–87
McKean, Dave 191, 328, 329 (fig.)
McLuhan, Marshall 32
McManus, George 245, 309, 353
McTeigue, James 198, 342
Meesters, Gert 112
Meister, J. Christoph 1
Melville, Herman 282
Menu, Jean-Christophe 358
Merho 260
Meskin, Aaron 5–6
Meter, Peer 394
Metz, Christian 36
Metzger, George 276
Meyer, Christina 13, 312
Michotte, Albert 52
Mikkonen, Kai 1, 10, 41, 88, 142, 266
Millar, Mark 327
Miller, Ann 139, 144
Miller, Frank 191, 277, 326, 334–35, 391
Milligan, Peter 327
Mills, Pat 396
Mitchell, W. J. T. 137
Mittell, Jason 158, 275–77, 281
Mizuki, Shigeru 15, 367–73, 375
Moebius 211, 265
Montellier, Chantal 399
Moore, Alan 9–11, 14, 27, 29 (fig.), 44 (fig.), 74, 74 (fig.), 83 (fig.), 85, 90–92, 191, 198, 277, 281, 326, 334–37, 391, 397
Moore, Stephen 198
Mordden, Ethan 139
Morgan, Richard 280
Morrison, Grant 14, 326–27, 329
Mortimer, Win 166
Mouly, Françoise 305–09
Müller, Hans-Harald 89–90
Muñoz, José Antonio 356
Murray, Chris 326, 336
Musturi, Tommi 10, 108, 109 (fig.), 113, 118, 119 (fig.)
Muybridge, Eadweard 225, 352

Nakazawa, Keiji 396
Natsume, Fusanosuke 366
Nizon, Paul 209
Noë, Alva 51, 54–55
Nolan, Christopher 327
Nordman, Falk 399
North, Sterling 337
Nückel, Otto 386
Nünning, Ansgar 69
Nys, Jef 260
Nylso 209, 210 (fig.)

Oeming, Mike 279
Olson, Greta 202
O'Neil, Dennis 162
O'Neil, Kevin 10, 74, 74 (fig.), 83 (fig.), 85, 90–92, 341, 397, 400
O'Neill, Patrick 129
Opper, Frederick Burr 242, 309
Orlando, Joe 276
Outcault, Richard Felton 5, 243, 309

Pacinda, George 180–81
Palmer, Alan 114
Patterson, Joseph Medill 245–46
Payne, Virginia 249
Pearson, Roberta E. 184, 290
Pedri, Nancy 10–11, 106–07, 120
Peeters, Benoît 197, 356
Perrault, Charles 290
Pilobolus 304
Pinchon, Joseph 353
Pom 260
Poplaski, Peter 340
Porter, Edwin S. 243
Pratt, Henry John 192, 271

Pratt, Hugo 356
Pratt, Murray 144
Prohías, Antonio 210
Proust, Marcel 399
Pulitzer, Joseph 315
Pumphrey, George 338

Rajewsky, Irina O. 195–99, 201
Raney, Vanessa 39
Raymond, Alex 231, 247, 307
Reagan, Ronald 336
Reizenstein, Ben 147
Reynolds, James 198
Rickenbacher, Kati 208
Ries, Hans 352
Rippl, Gabriele 11, 205, 205 (fig.)
Rivière, Jacqueline 353
Rizzolatti, Giacomo 51
Robertson, Darick 327
Round, Julia 14, 273
Royal, Derek Parker 274
Rühm, Gerhard 390
Ryan, Bill 180
Ryan, Marie-Laure 33, 55, 63, 72, 128, 192–94, 201, 203, 213, 293

Sacco, Joe 92–93, 394
Saint-Beuve 350
Saint-Ogan, Alain 260
Sampayo, Carlos 356
Saso, Akira 373–74
Satrapi, Marjane 10, 103, 359, 363, 394
Schmid, Wolf 68–69, 89
Schmitz-Emans, Monika 15
Schrauwen, Oliver 112
Schreiber, Nathan 199–200, 200 (fig.)
Schüwer, Martin 1, 7, 63–64, 196–97, 204, 211
Schuiten, François 356
Schulz, Charles 250
Schwartz, Julius 172, 177–78, 181
Shakespeare, William 396
Shimizu, Yuko 281–82
Short, Mick 114
Shuster, Joe 336
Siegel, Jerry 336
Sienkiewicz, Bill 398
Sikoryak, Robert 401
Simmonds, Posy 399
Sinclair, Mark 393

Sinigaglia, Corrado 51
Sleen, Marc 259–60
Smith, Greg M. 12
Smith, Jeff 85
Smith, Sidney 245–48
Smolderen, Thierry 352–53
Snyder, Zack 342
Spiegelman, Art 10, 13, 27, 92–93, 134–35, 135 (fig.), 138–39, 138 (fig.), 140 (fig.), 191, 276, 301, 304–19, 358–59, 391, 393
Stanley, John 308
Steedman, Carolyn 301
Stein, Daniel 11, 172, 293
Sterrett, Cliff 245
Stewart, Martha 317
Stewart, Susan 314
Straw, Will 302
Surdiacourt, Steven 14, 71
Suzuki, CJ 368
Swarte, Joost 308

Tabachnick, Stephen E. 146, 274
Takao, Saito 371
Takemiya, Keiko 374
Talbot, Bryan 191, 303, 340
Talbot, Mary 303
Tan, Shaun 86, 86 (fig.)
Tardi, Jacques 308, 356
Tatsumi, Yoshihiro 363, 371
Taylor, Diana 306
Tezuka, Osamu 366, 373, 375–77, 395, 401
Thatcher, Margaret 336
Thompson, Craig 10, 76, 77 (fig.), 78 (fig.), 84 (fig.), 88, 90–91
Thon, Jan-Noël 9–10
Töpffer, Rodolphe 5, 14, 67, 348–51, 354
Trondheim, Lewis 10, 107
Trudeau, Garry 251
Tyler, C. 303

Updike, John 389–90
Uricchio, William 184, 290, 302, 310

Vance, William 265
Vandermeulen, David 399
Vandersteen, Willy 259–62, 266
Van Hamme, Jean 265
Van Leeuwen, Theo 220
Vaughan, Brian K. 280

Vaughn, Matthew   342
Verbeck, Gustave   309, 316
Versaci, Rocco   127, 145, 396
Versluys, Kristiaan   311–12
Vozzo, Daniel   331 (fig.)

Walker, Brian   245
Walsh, Richard   68–70
Walton, Kendall L.   127–28, 138
Ware, Chris   191, 211, 248, 304, 306–07, 390, 393
Watson, Julia   136
Wein, Len   276
Wertham, Fredric   306
White, Biljo   174, 177–80, 179 (fig.), 183
Williams, Guyas   307
Williams, Ian   128–29
Williams, J. H. III   61, 62 (fig.)

Williams, Paul   292
Williams, Raymond   315, 351
Willingham, Bill   279
Winkler, Paul   355
Winshluss   112
Witek, Joseph   309
Wolf, Werner   193, 195–96, 199, 201–03, 205–06, 213
Wolk, Douglas   129, 145–47
Wolverton, Basil   308–09
Woo, Benjamin   137

Yagoda, Ben   128
Yelin, Barbara   394

Zansky, Louis   398
Zulli, Michael   331 (fig.)

Index (Works)

2000AD   334, 336, 341

Action   341
Action Comics   249, 291
Ada   10, 103–04
"Adventures of Luther Arkwright, The"   340
A la recherche du temps perdu   399
Alice in Wonderland   286
Alley Oop   261
Amazing Heroes   170
Amos 'n' Andy   248
Animal Man   327, 329
A. Piker Clerk   245
Are You My Mother?   11, 206, 206 (fig.)
Arrival, The   86, 86 (fig.)
Asterios Polyp   115
Astérix   356
(A Suivre)   355–58
Autres Gens, Les   267

Barbarella   356
Barefoot Gen: A Cartoon of Hiroshima   396
Batman (comics)   11, 161–64, 163 (fig.), 166–74, 178, 180–81, 290, 335, 339
Batman (films)   327, 341
Batman: The Dark Knight Returns   277, 334, 391
Batman: The Killing Joke   334
Batmania   172, 174, 177–83, 179 (fig.), 180–83
"Batmania Philosophy, The"   178
"Bean Counter" (*Azuki Hakari*)   369
Bécassine   353
Berlin: City of Smoke   199, 199 (fig.), 395
Berlin: City of Stones   395
Bessy   259–60
Beyond Time and Again   276
Black Hole   9, 39–42, 40 (fig.), 42 (fig.), 309
Black Paths   207 (fig.)
Blast   116–18, 116 (fig.), 117 (fig.)
Bloodstar   276
Bone   85
Brave and the Bold, The   172
Breakdowns   306

Bringing Up Father   245, 317, 353
Buck Rogers   247, 249
Buddha   395
Buster Brown   243

Cancer Vixen   10, 140–43, 141 (fig.), 142 (fig.)
Capa-alpha   182
Captain Easy   249
Chantier-Musil   360
Charley's War: 2 June–1 August 1916   396
Children's Comics: A Guide for Parents and Teachers   338
City of Glass   208, 399
Classics Illustrated   397–99, 401
Collateral Damage   313
Comics Journal, The   170
"Con-Cave Coming"   181
Contract with God, A   276, 389–90, 395

Daredevil   277
Death Race   341
Desolation Jones   61–63, 62 (fig.)
Detective Comics   161, 172, 175 (fig.), 176 (fig.)
Dick Tracy   245, 248, 304
Doom Patrol   327, 329
Doonesbury   251
Dotter of Her Father's Eyes   303
"Dragon Ball"   375
Drawn to Death! An Opera in Three Panels   304
Dreams of the Rarebit Fiend   9, 49–51, 50 (fig.), 53–61, 309
Dykes to Watch Out For   211

Epileptic   10, 145–47, 147 (fig.)
Eric de Noorman   257

Fables   273, 279–80
Fagin the Jew   395, 399–400
Family Upstairs, The   245
Faust   399
Funky Winkerbean   251
First Kingdom   276
Flash   340
Flash Gordon   247, 249

Index (Works)

Fliegende Blätter 352
... for beginners 400
For Better or For Worse 251
Fromme Helene, Die 351
Fun Home: A Family Tragicomic 10, 129–33, 131 (fig.), 132 (fig.), 303, 359, 390, 394
Funny Aminals 316

Gasoline Alley 230, 245–46, 251
Gemma Bovary 399
Gift 394
Great Catsby, The 363
Great Train Robbery, The 243
Guerre, d'Alan, La 359
Gumps, The 245, 248–50

Habibi 10, 76–79, 77 (fig.), 78 (fig.), 82, 84 (fig.), 85–86, 88, 90–91
Hapless Hooligan in 'Still Moving' 304
Happy Hooligan 242–44, 248, 250
Hellblazer 326
Henry 210
Histoires ou contes du temps passé 290
Hitchhiker's Guide to the Galaxy 293
Hogan's Alley 230
House of Mystery 280, 328
House of Secrets 328
How the Whale Became and Other Stories 282
"How the Whale Got His Throat" 281

"If the Truth Be Known or 'A Finger in Every Plot'" 182
In the Shadow of No Towers 305, 309–19, 393
International Journal of Comic Art 8
Introducing... 400

Jérôme et le lièvre 209, 210 (fig.)
Jew of New York, The 395
Jimmy Corrigan: The Smartest Kid on Earth 390, 393
Jommeke 257, 260–61
Jonathan 209
Journal de Mickey, Le 355
Journal d'un album 358
Judge Dredd 336, 341
Justice League of America 172

"Kala in Kommieland" 309
Kapitein Rob 257
Katzenjammer Kids 207, 313

Kick Ass 342
Kiekeboe 257, 260
King Lear 398
Krazy Kat 230–31, 245, 247, 316

Laika 395
La Qu... 118
L'Ascension du Haut Mal 358
Lead Pipe Sunday 314
League of Extraordinary Gentlemen, The 10, 74, 74 (fig.), 76, 82, 83 (fig.), 85–86, 90–92, 397, 400
L'île noire (Tintin) 109
L'Incal 265
Liquid City 363
Little Lit 309
Little Nemo in Slumberland 61, 113, 211, 225, 243–44, 316–17
Little Orphan Annie 245–48, 250
Little Sammy Sneeze 231
Livret de phamille 358
Logan's Run 341
"Lone Wolf and Cub" 377
Louis Riel: A Comic Strip Biography 395
Lucifer 327
Lucky Luke 356

Macbeth 398, 401
Madame Bovary 399
MAD Magazine 304, 307
Maid Maiden 363
Maler Klecksel 351
"Malpractice Suite, The" 304
Manga daigaku (Cartoon College) 373
Manga no yomikata (How to Read Manga) 366
Mars Attacks 317
Marvel Classic Comics 398
Maus 10, 92, 134–36, 135 (fig.), 138 (fig.), 140 (fig.), 276, 304, 308–09, 311–16, 359, 391, 393
Max und Moritz 351
Memoirs of an Invisible Man 287
Metamorphosis 401
Midsummer Night's Dream, A 396
"Million Dollar Debut of Batgirl, The" 172–73
Miracleman 334
Moby Dick 382, 398
Mom's Cancer 143–44, 143 (fig.)
Münchener Bilderbogen 352

Münchener Bilderbücher 352
Mutt and Jeff 244–46, 250–51
Mysterious Underground Man, The (Chiteikoku no kaijin) 376

Nanairo Inko 401
Nancy 247
Napoleon 226
"Naruto" 363, 375–79
Near Myths 340
Nero 257, 259–60
New X-Men 326
Nonnonba 15, 367–74, 377–79

Oliver Twist 395, 399
Omni-visibilis 10, 107–08
"Open Letter to All 'Batmanians' Everywhere" 182–83
"Open Letter to Editor Jack Schiff" 178
"Open Letter to Julius Schwartz" 178
Othello 398

Palestine 92–93, 394
Panda 257
Peanuts 250
Penny Arcade 251–52
Perdita Durango 399
"Perfect Crime—Slightly Imperfect, The" 173
Persepolis 10, 103, 359, 363, 394
Philémon 113, 208, 209 (fig.)
Photographer, The 394
Piet Pienter en Bert Bibber 260–61
Piled Higher and Deeper 251
Pilote 355
Pinocchio 10, 112
Plot: The Secret Story of the Protocols of the Elders of Zion, The 395
Poema a fumetti 390
Polly and Her Pals 245
"Portrait of the Artist as a Young %@#*!" 306
"Powerhouse Pepper" 309
Power Out 199–200, 200 (fig.)
Preacher 326–27, 330 (fig.), 332–33
"Prisoner on the Hell Planet" 138–39, 312
Puck 242
Pyongyang 394

Rashomon 374

Raw 307–10
Real Fact Comics 164–67, 165 (fig.), 181
Rex Morgan 304
Rode Ridder, De 257, 260
Rollerball 341
Rubrique-à-brac 356

Safe Area Goražde 394
Saga of the Swamp Thing, The 277, 326, 334
Sandman, The 9–10, 27–28, 30, 31 (fig.), 33–40, 35 (fig.), 37 (fig.), 74–76, 75 (fig.), 79, 80 (fig.), 81 (fig.), 82, 85–86, 90–91, 280, 326–30, 331 (fig.), 335, 396
Sandman Mystery Theatre 327
"Secret War of the Phantom General, The" 173, 175 (fig.)
Shade the Changing Man 327
Showcase 340
Signal to Noise 328–29, 329 (fig.)
Sinister House of Secret Love, The 276
"Smell of Exterior Street, The" 309
Sob Story 341
Special Exits 303
Spirit, The 208, 290, 304
Spirou 258–59
Spy vs. Spy 210
St. Peter Healing a Cripple and the Raising of Tabitha 224
"Strange Death of Batman, The" 174, 176 (fig.)
Superman 162, 249, 287, 290–91
Suske en Wiske 13, 255–57, 259–67

Tarzan 247
"Teen Plague" 309
Terry and the Pirates 245, 247–48, 250
Testament 280
"Those Behind Batman" 180
Tintin 109, 207, 258–60, 353–55
Tintin au pays des Soviets 353
Tom Poes 257
Traces en cases 71
Transmetropolitan 327
Trilby 51
"True Story of Batman and Robin: How a Big-Time Comic Is Born!, The" 164–67, 165 (fig.)

Unwritten, The 13, 208, 271–74, 276, 278–94, 288 (fig.), 291 (fig.)

"Unwritten, Miscellanea, The" 282

V for Vendetta (comic) 11, 198, 334–35
V for Vendetta (film) 11, 198, 342
"Valley of Giant Bees, The" 339

Walking with Samuel 10, 108, 109 (fig.), 113, 118, 119 (fig.)
Warrior Magazine 198, 335
Wash Tubbs 247
Watchmen (comic) 9, 27–30, 29 (fig.), 32–33, 43–45, 44 (fig.), 85, 118, 277, 281, 290, 334–35, 391
Watchmen (film) 342
"What Has the 'New Look' Done for Batman?" 180

Wild Party, The 304
Willowbank Wood 286
Wizard 170

XIII 265
X-Men 326

Yellow Kid, The 230, 314, 347
You Bet Your Life 341
You'll Never Know 303
Young Men 340

Zig et Puce 260

www.ingramcontent.com/pod-product-compliance
Lightning Source LLC
Chambersburg PA
CBHW021148230426
43667CB00006B/300